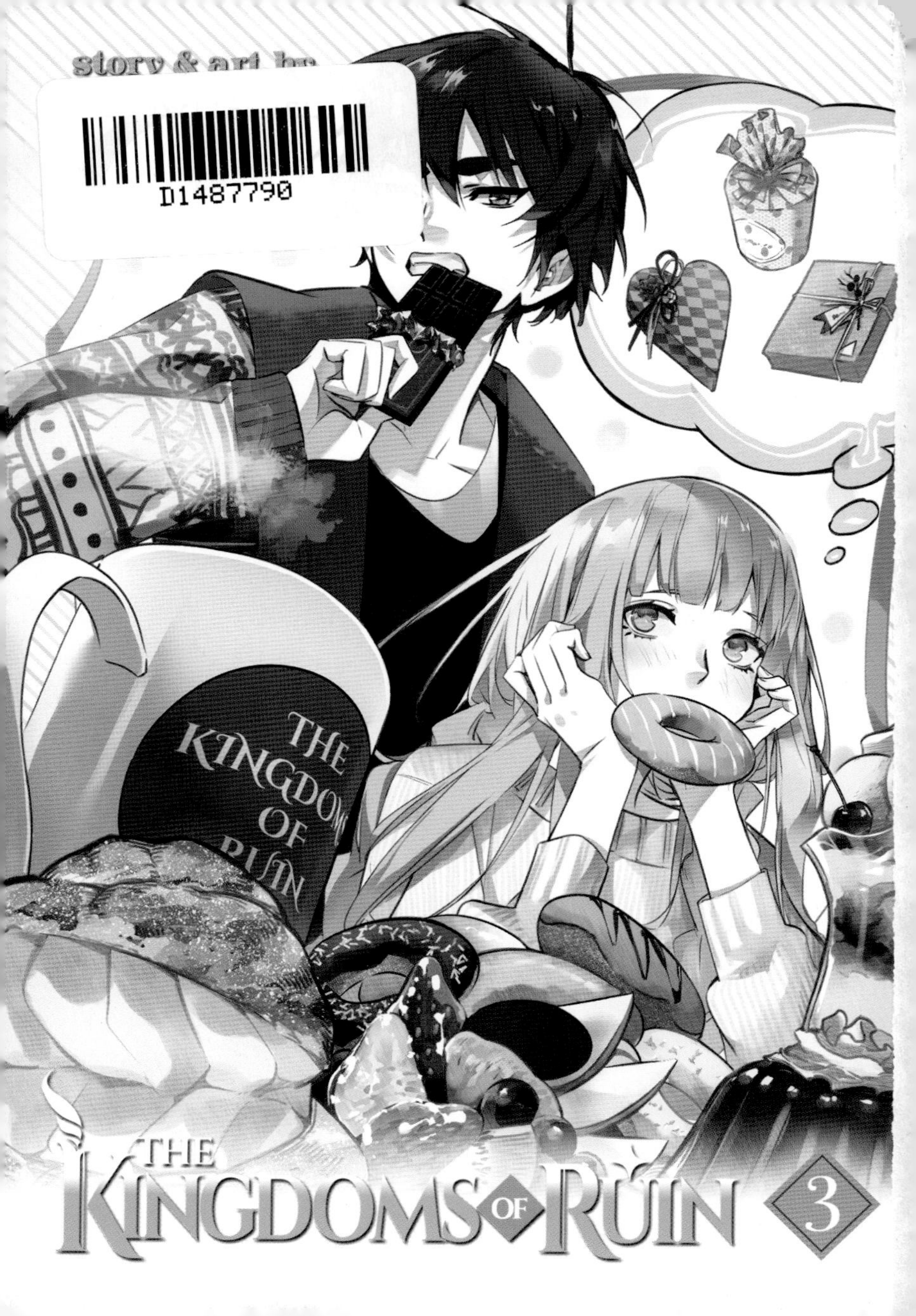
story & art by
THE KINGDOM OF RUIN
THE KINGDOMS OF RUIN
3

Contents

Chapter 11
Joy to the World
003

Chapter 12
The Witches Strike Back
041

Chapter 13
Evil Slaying
071

Chapter 14
Vs. Yamato
101

Chapter 15
The Witch Doroka
133

Chapter 16
Ensemble Verse
157

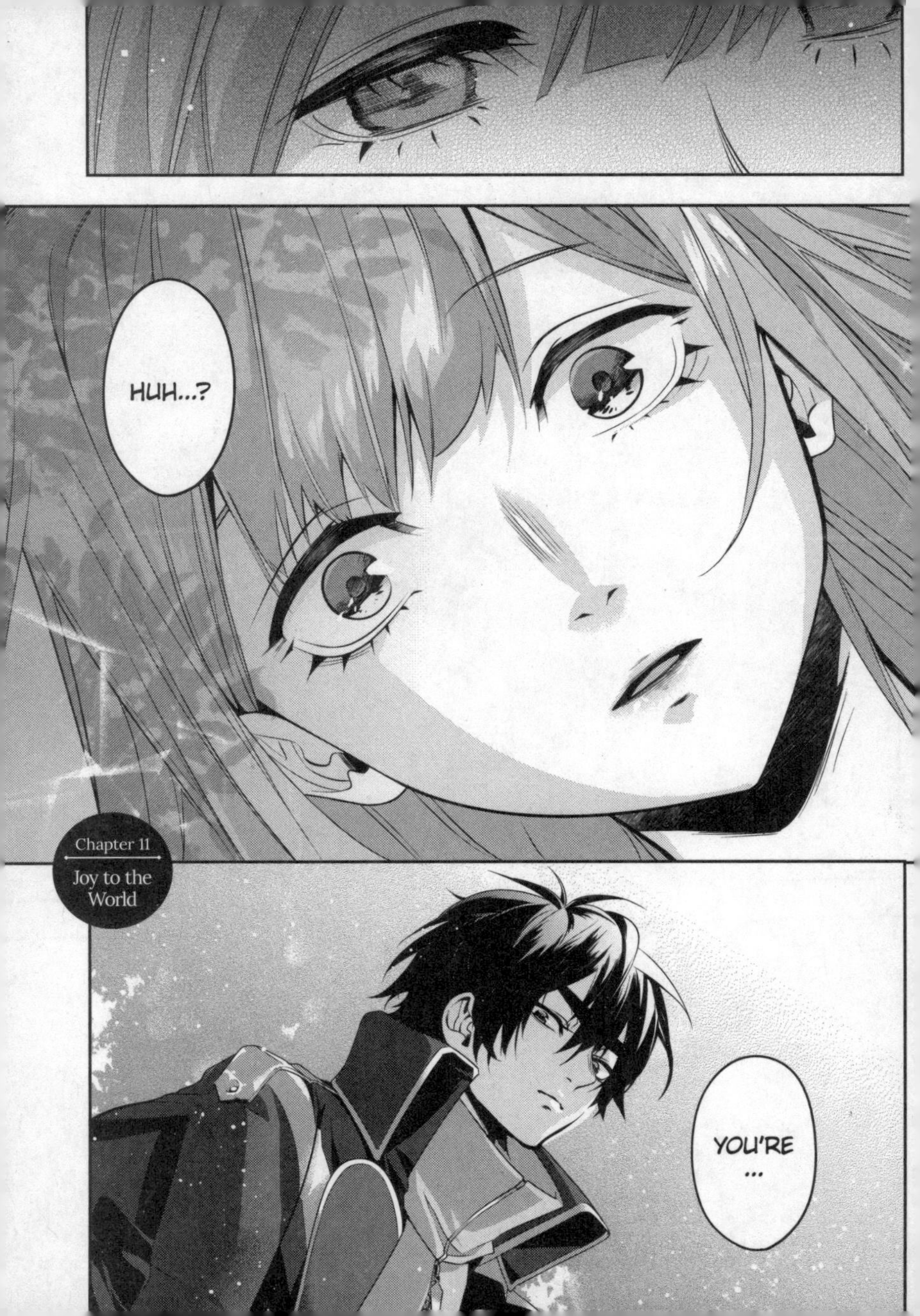
HUH...?
Chapter 11
Joy to the World
YOU'RE
...

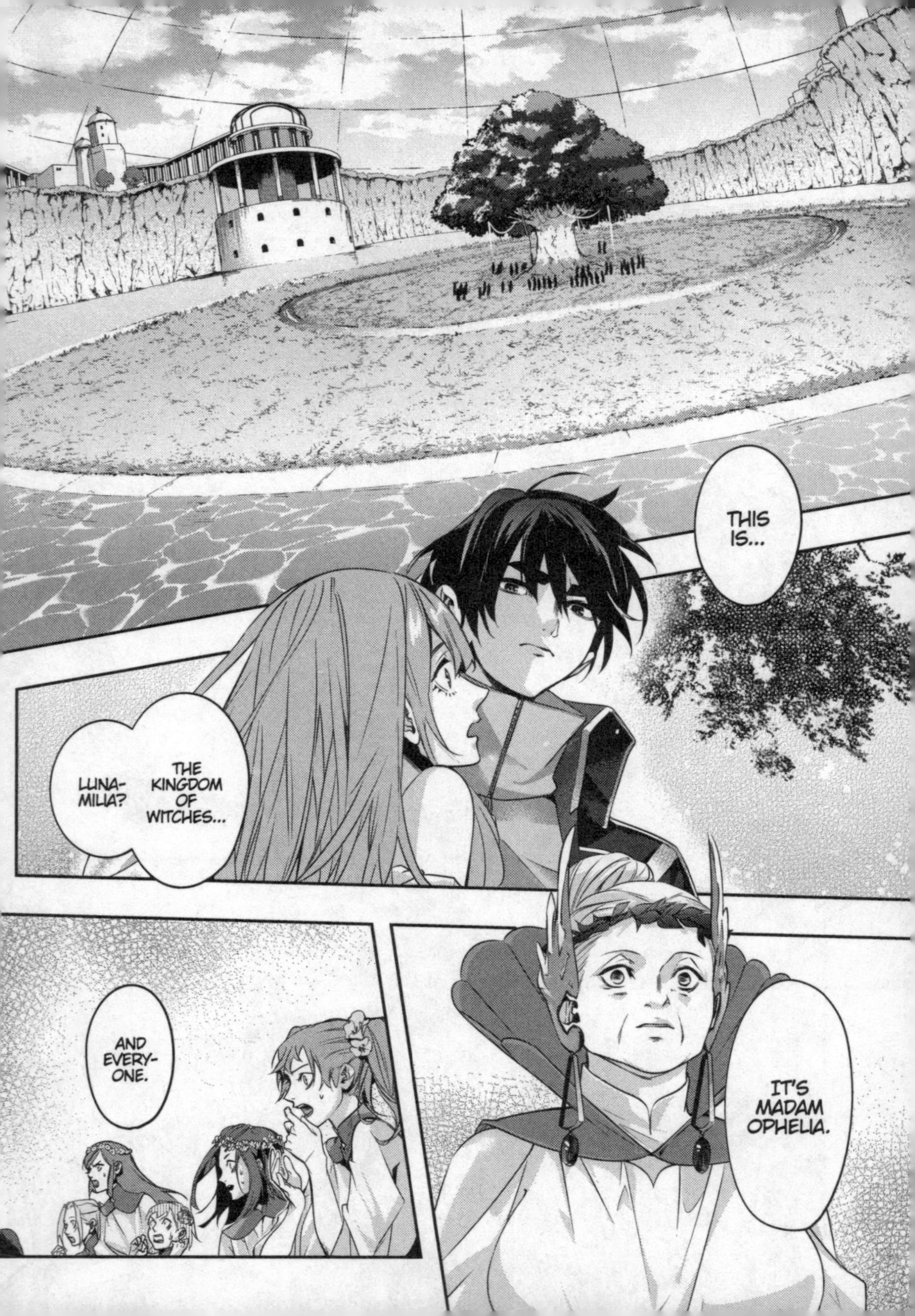
THIS IS...
THE KINGDOM OF WITCHES...
LUNA-MILIA?
IT'S MADAM OPHELIA.
AND EVERY-ONE.

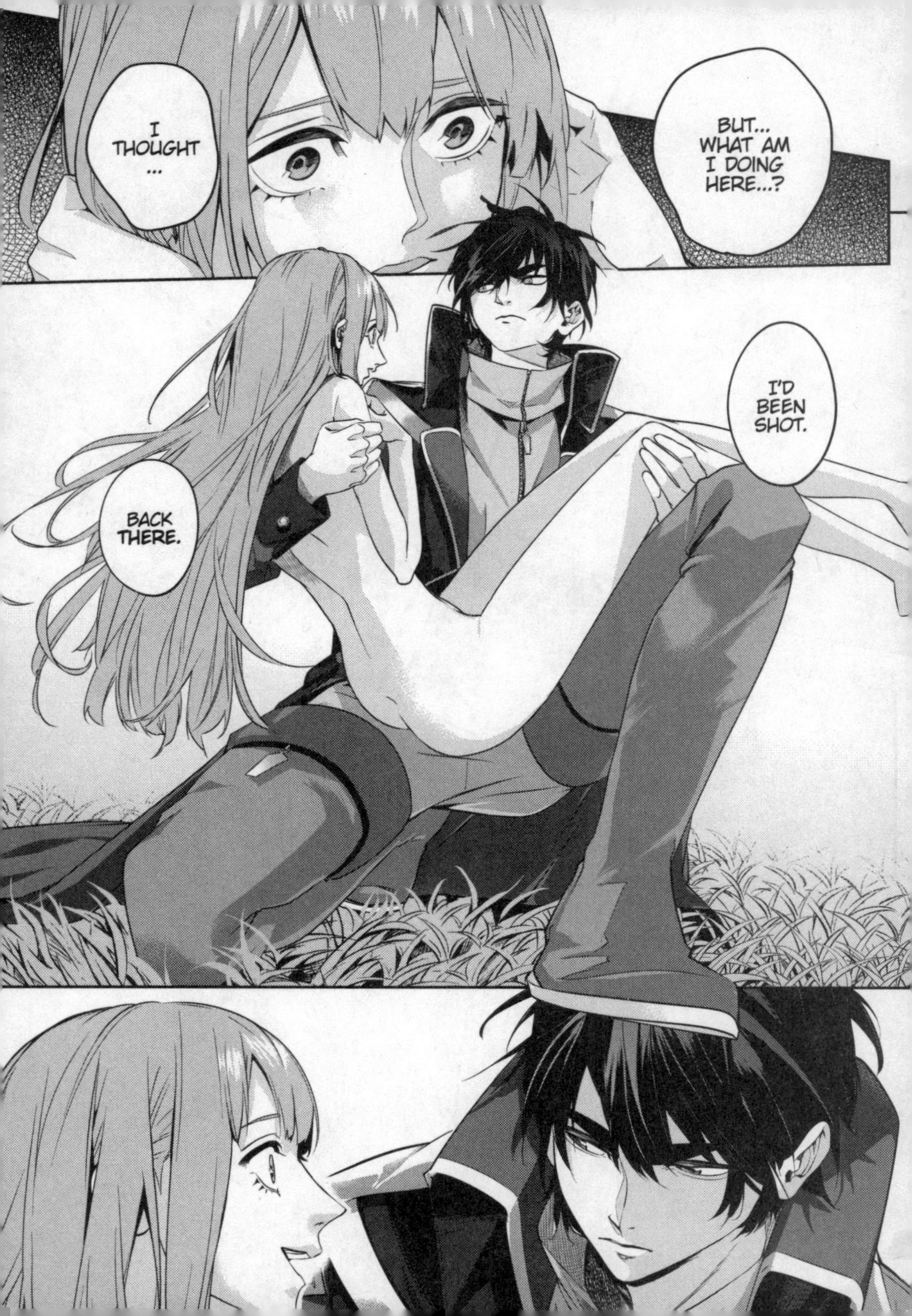
BUT... WHAT AM I DOING HERE...?
I THOUGHT ...
I'D BEEN SHOT.
BACK THERE.

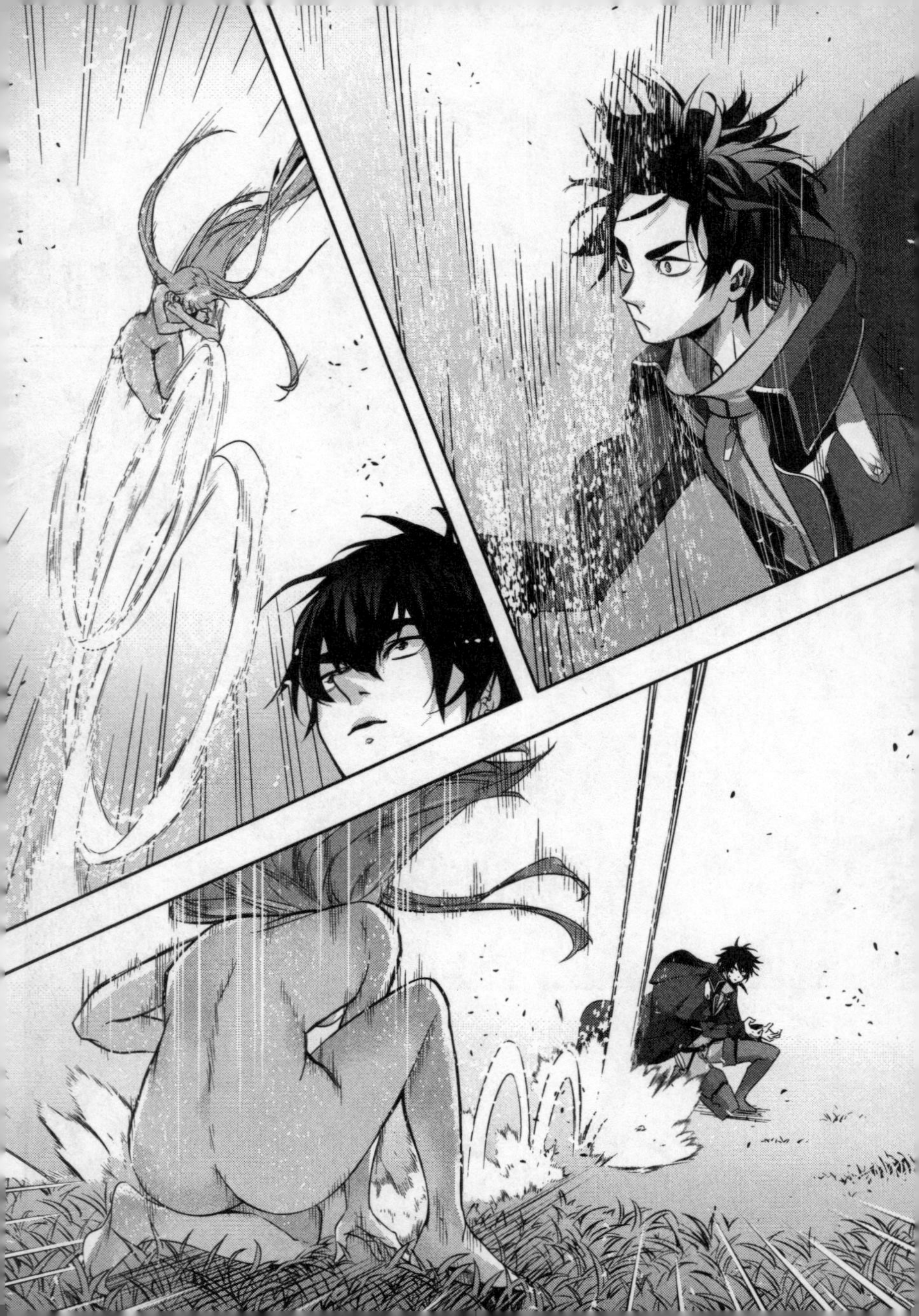

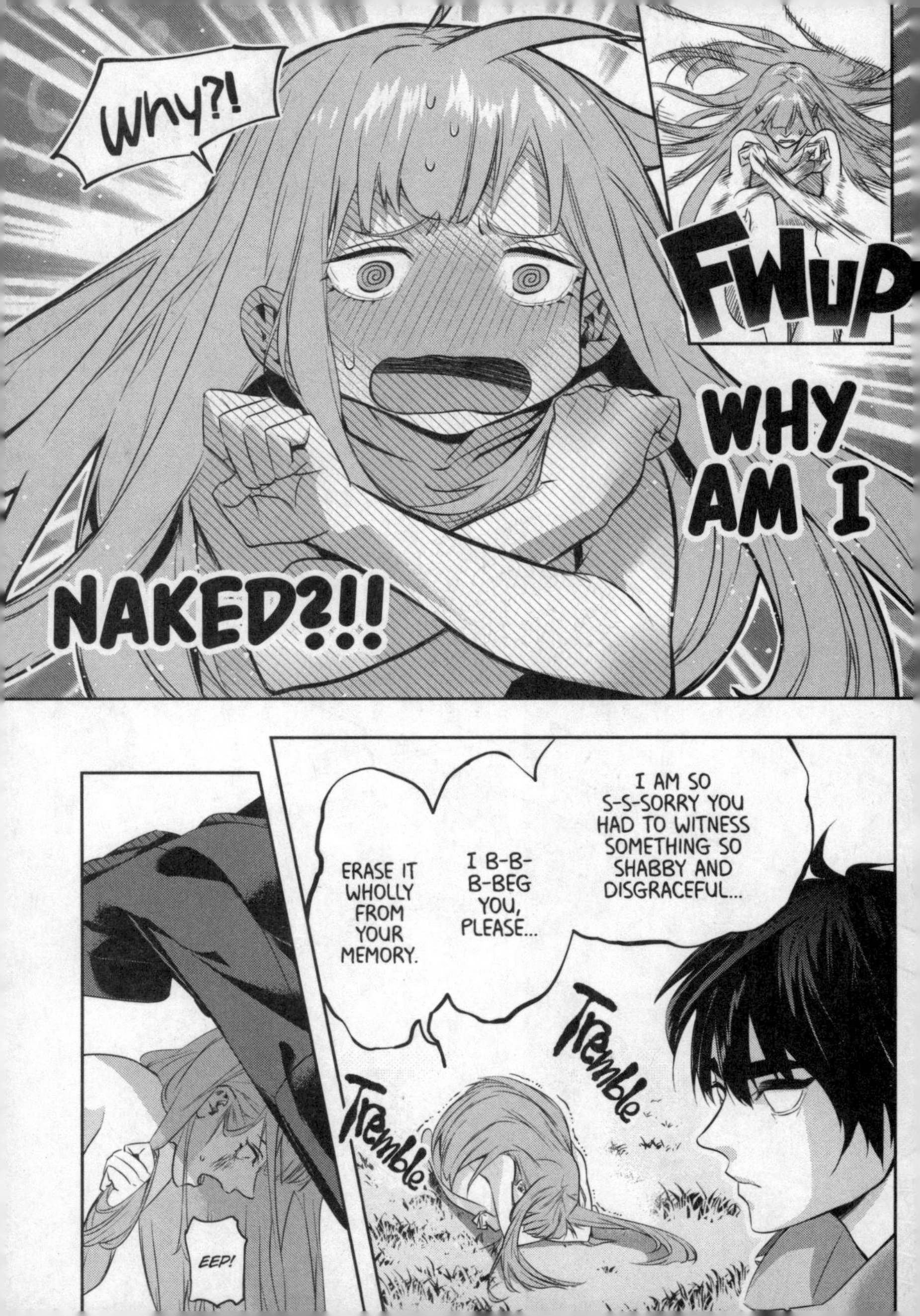
FWUP
Why?!
WHY AM I
NAKED?!!
I AM SO S-S-SORRY YOU HAD TO WITNESS SOMETHING SO SHABBY AND DISGRACEFUL...
I B-B-B-BEG YOU, PLEASE...
ERASE IT WHOLLY FROM YOUR MEMORY.
Tremble
Tremble
EEP!

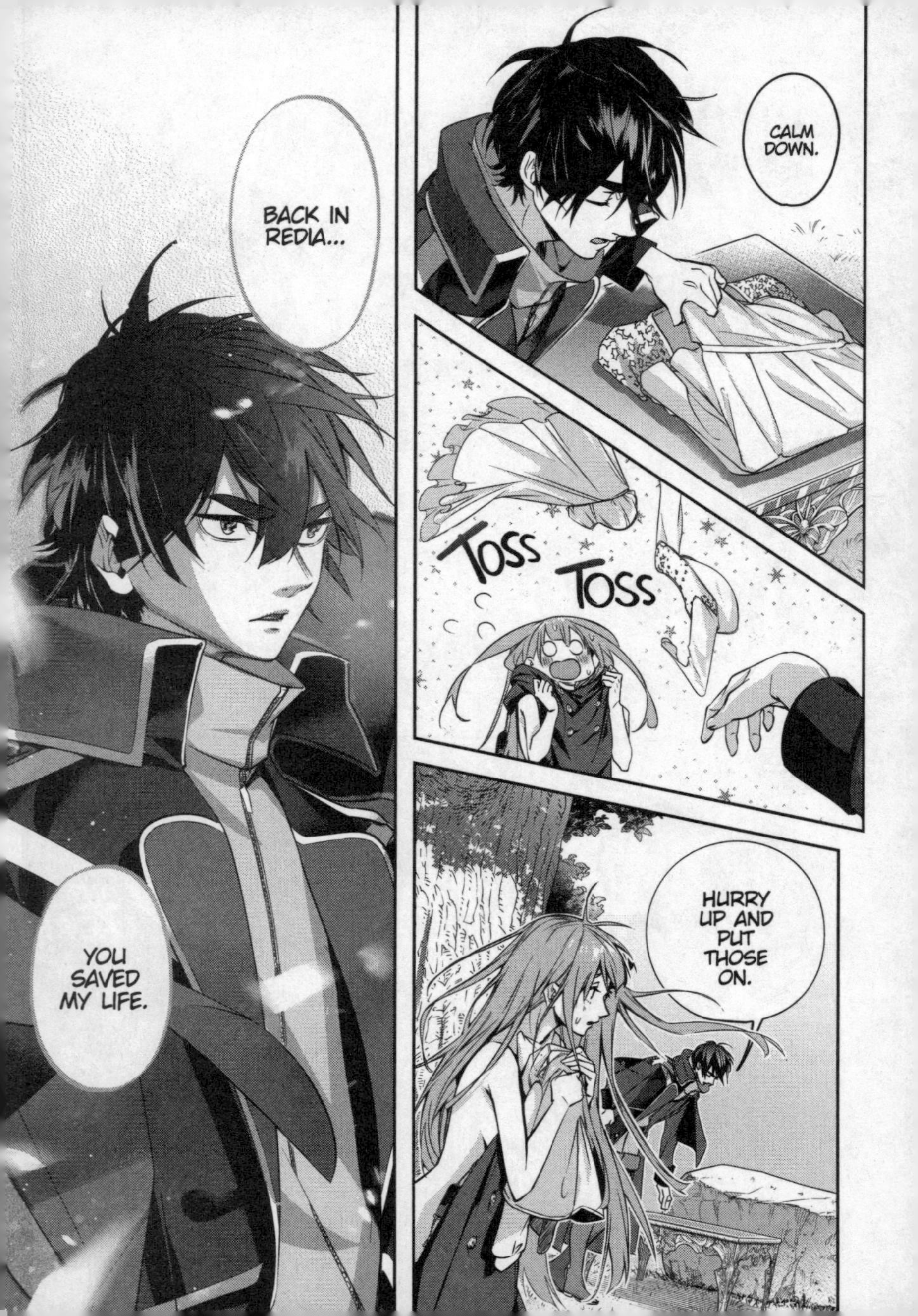
CALM DOWN.
TOSS TOSS
HURRY UP AND PUT THOSE ON.
BACK IN REDIA...
YOU SAVED MY LIFE.

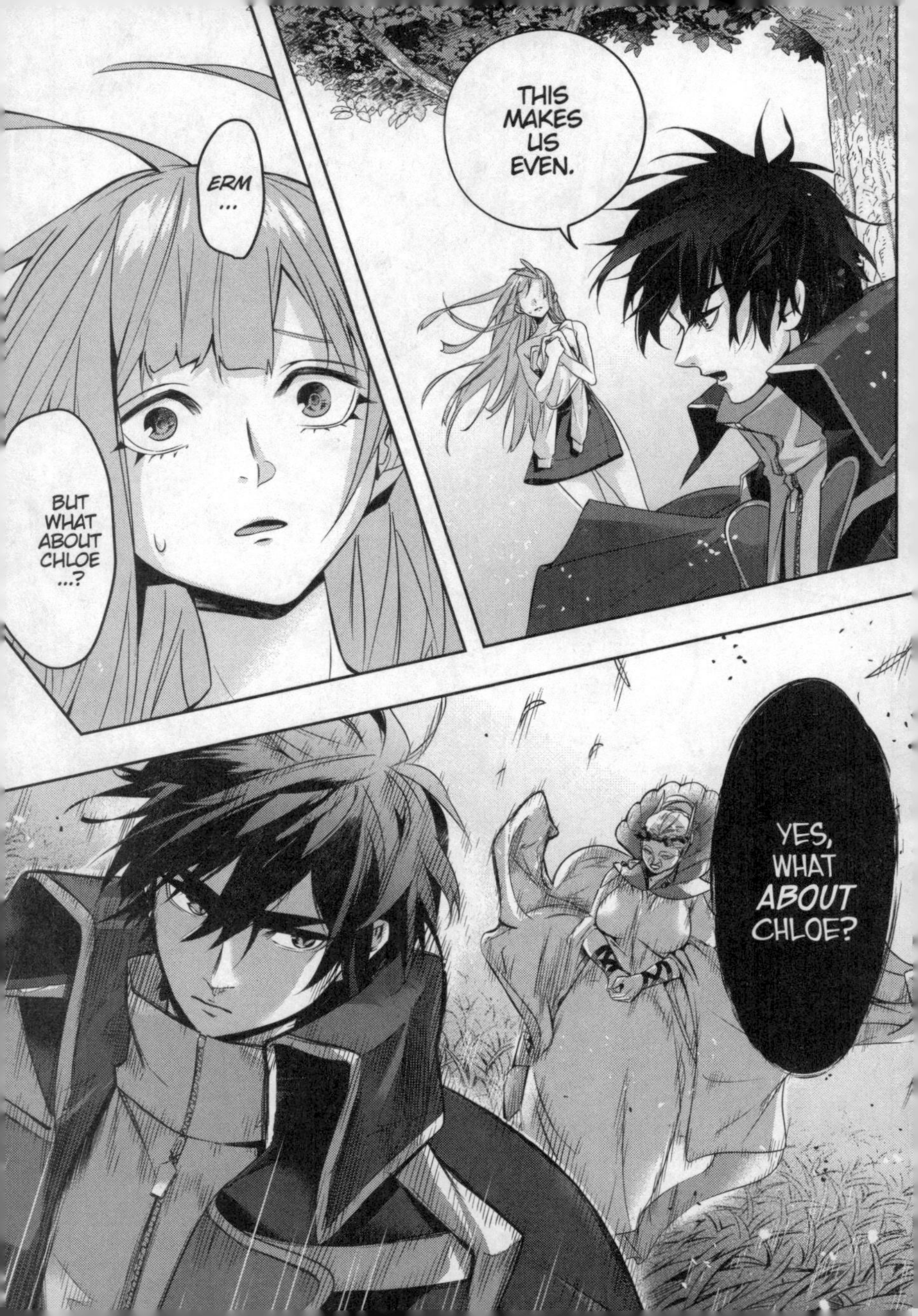
THIS MAKES US EVEN.
ERM ...
BUT WHAT ABOUT CHLOE ...?
YES, WHAT *ABOUT* CHLOE?

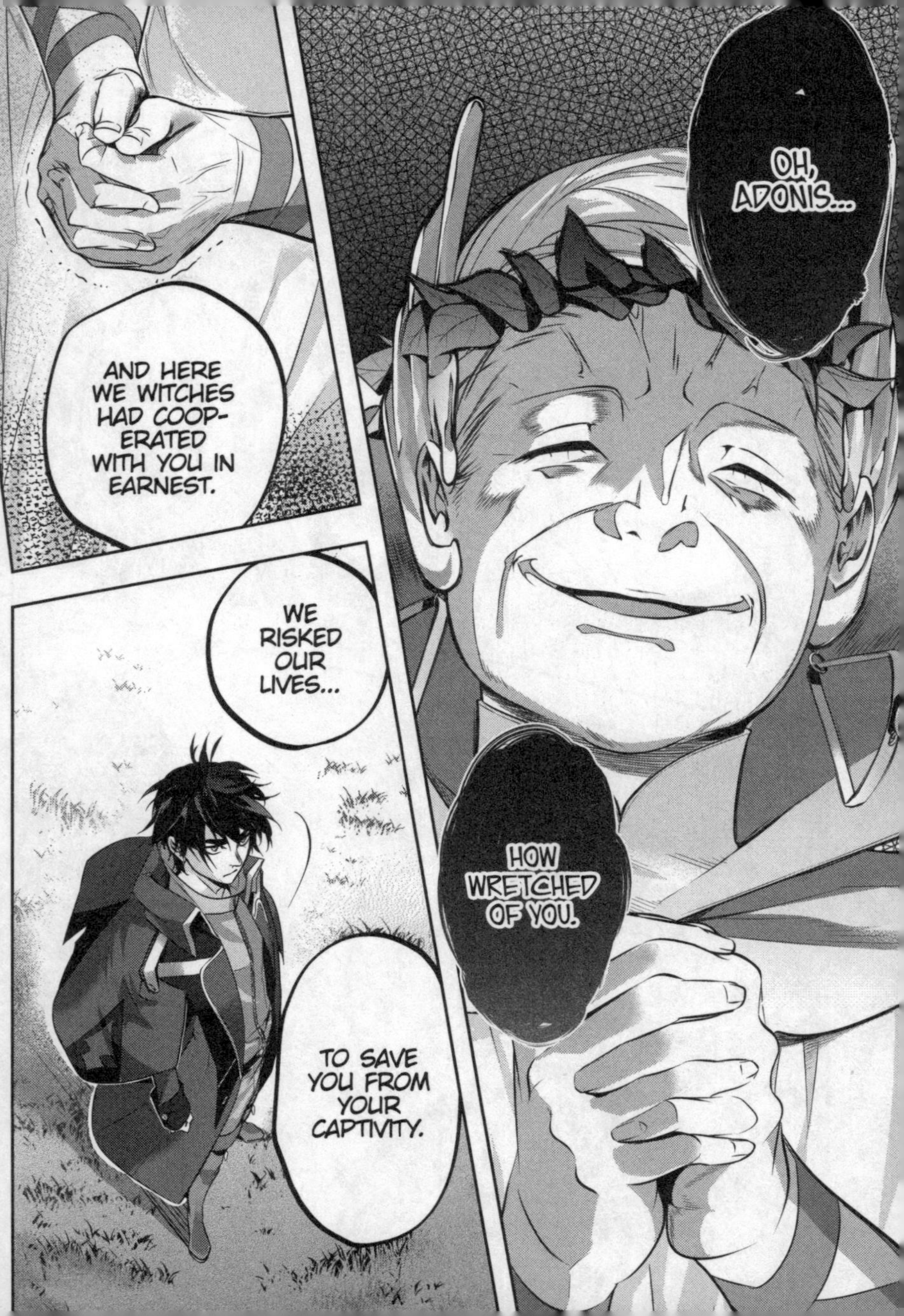
OH, ADONIS...
HOW WRETCHED OF YOU.
AND HERE WE WITCHES HAD COOPERATED WITH YOU IN EARNEST.
WE RISKED OUR LIVES...
TO SAVE YOU FROM YOUR CAPTIVITY.

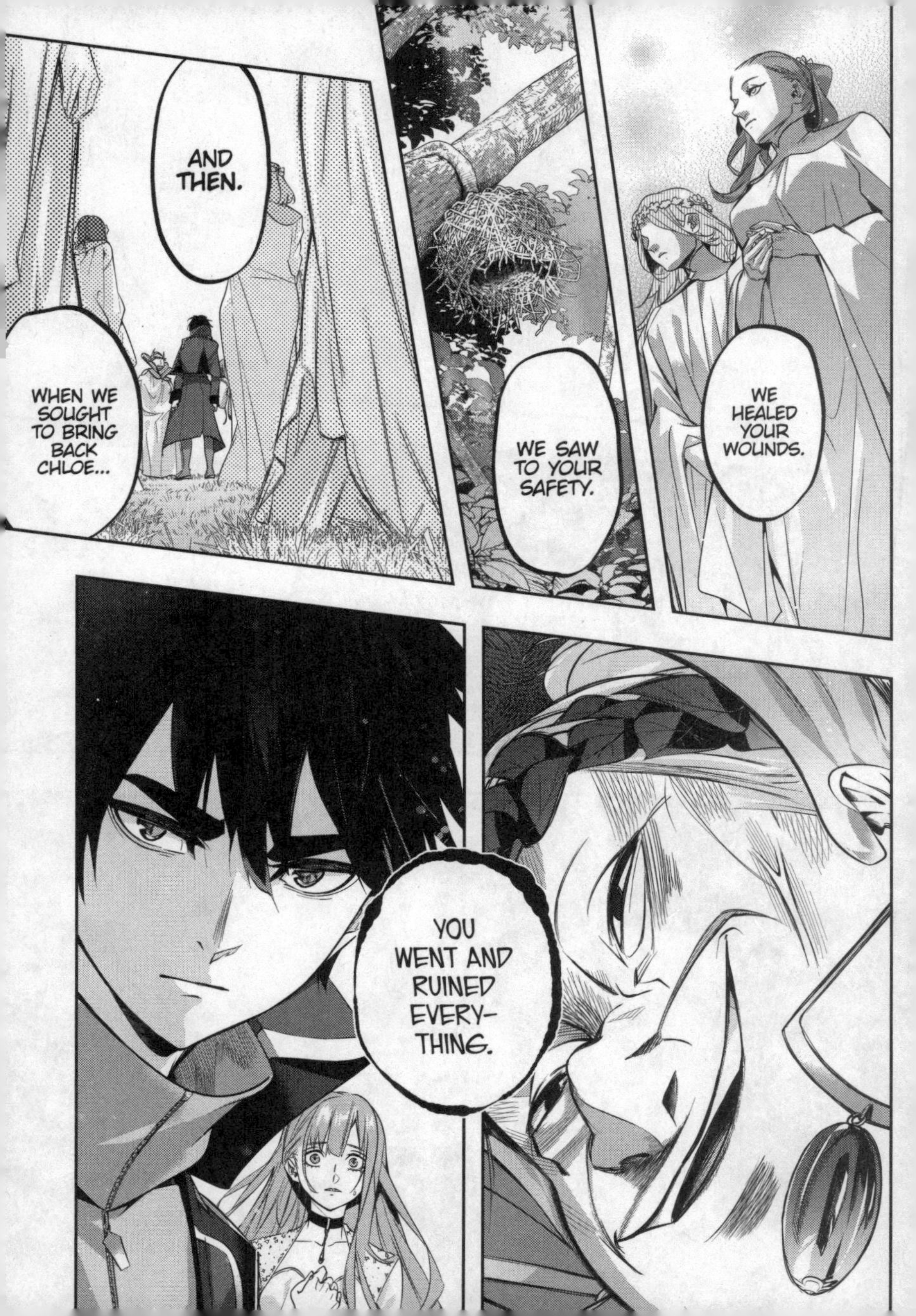
WE HEALED YOUR WOUNDS.
WE SAW TO YOUR SAFETY.
AND THEN.
WHEN WE SOUGHT TO BRING BACK CHLOE...
YOU WENT AND RUINED EVERY-THING.

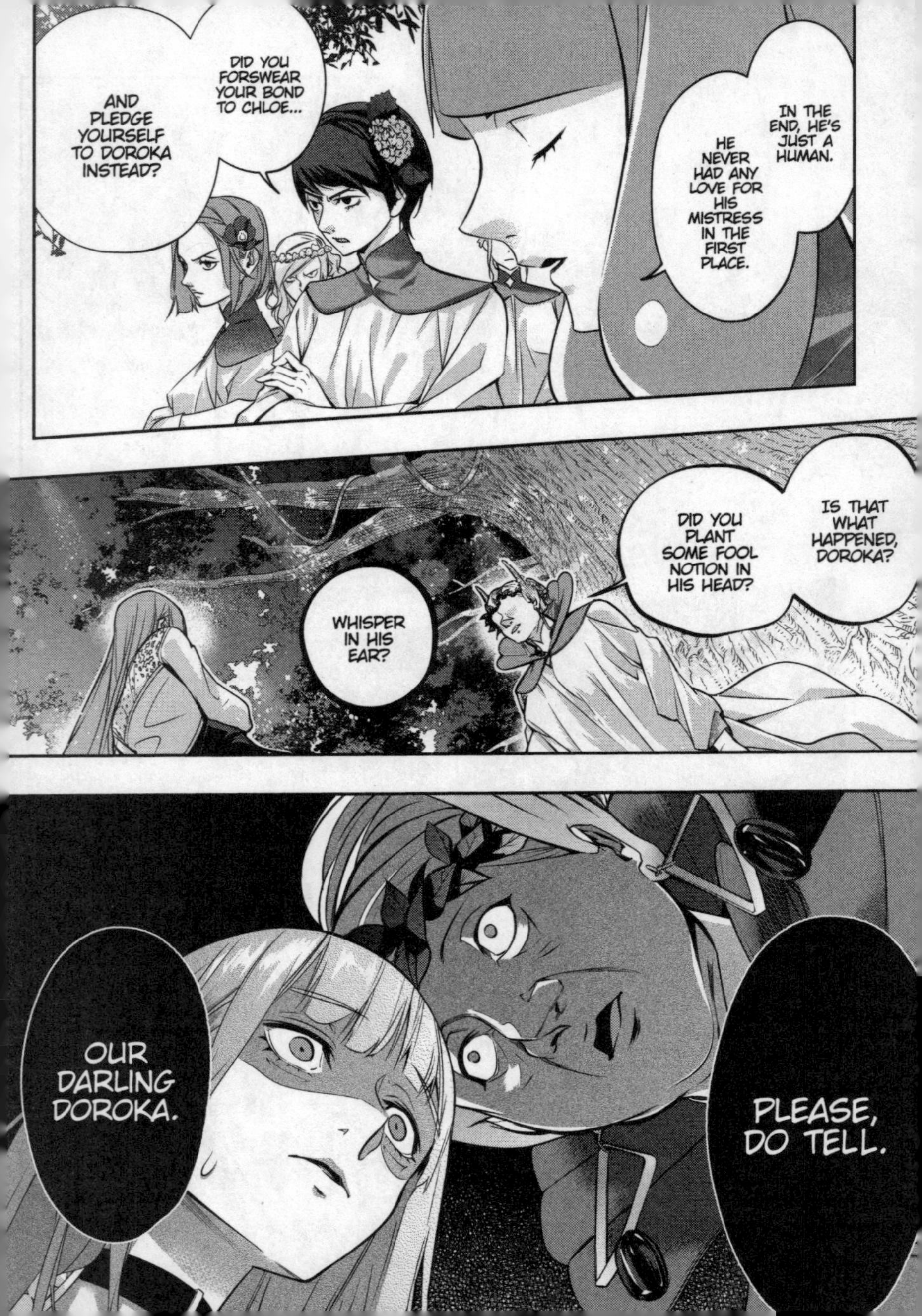
IN THE END, HE'S JUST A HUMAN.
HE NEVER HAD ANY LOVE FOR HIS MISTRESS IN THE FIRST PLACE.
DID YOU FORSWEAR YOUR BOND TO CHLOE...
AND PLEDGE YOURSELF TO DOROKA INSTEAD?
IS THAT WHAT HAPPENED, DOROKA?
DID YOU PLANT SOME FOOL NOTION IN HIS HEAD?
WHISPER IN HIS EAR?
PLEASE, DO TELL.
OUR DARLING DOROKA.

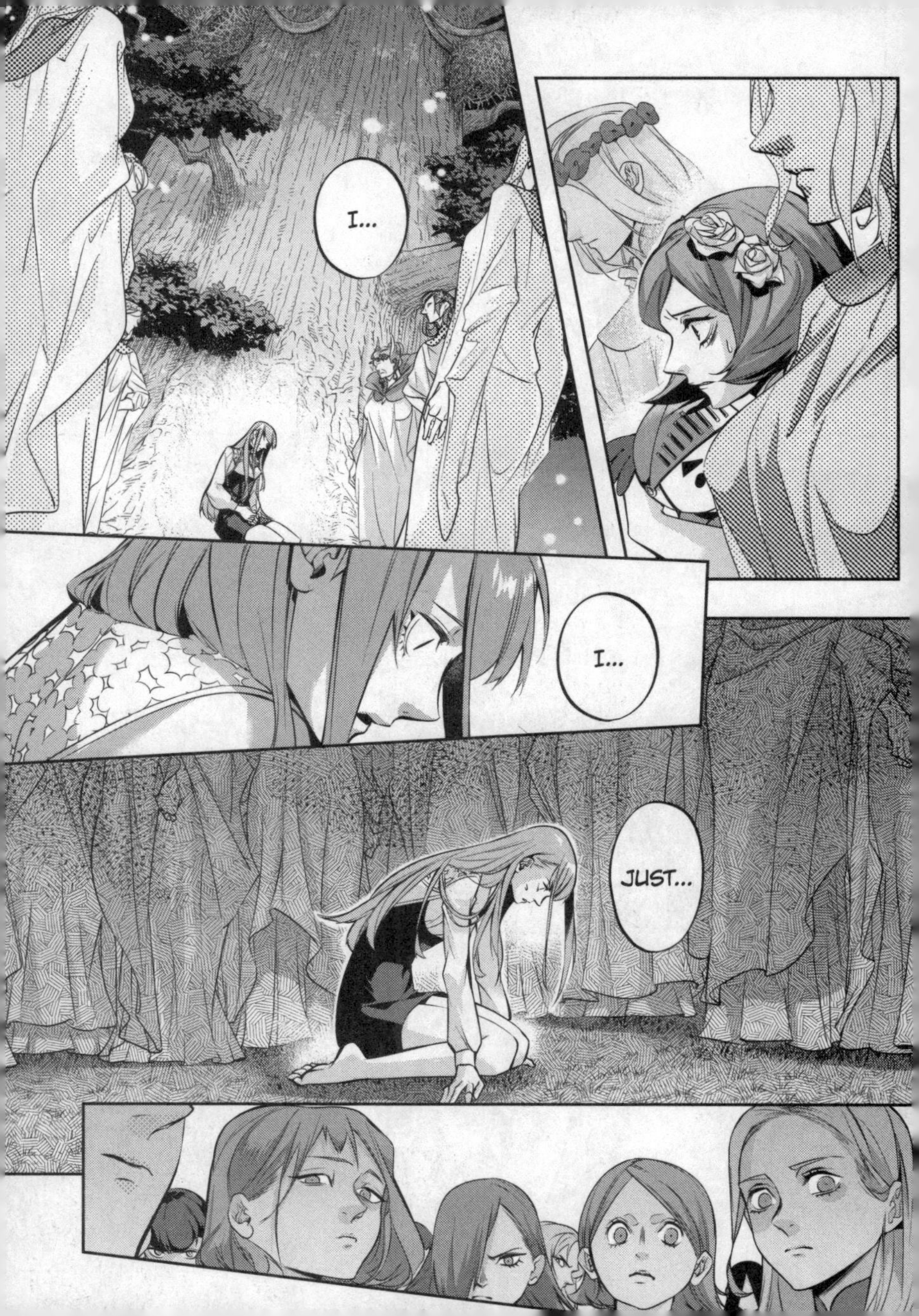
I...
I...
JUST...

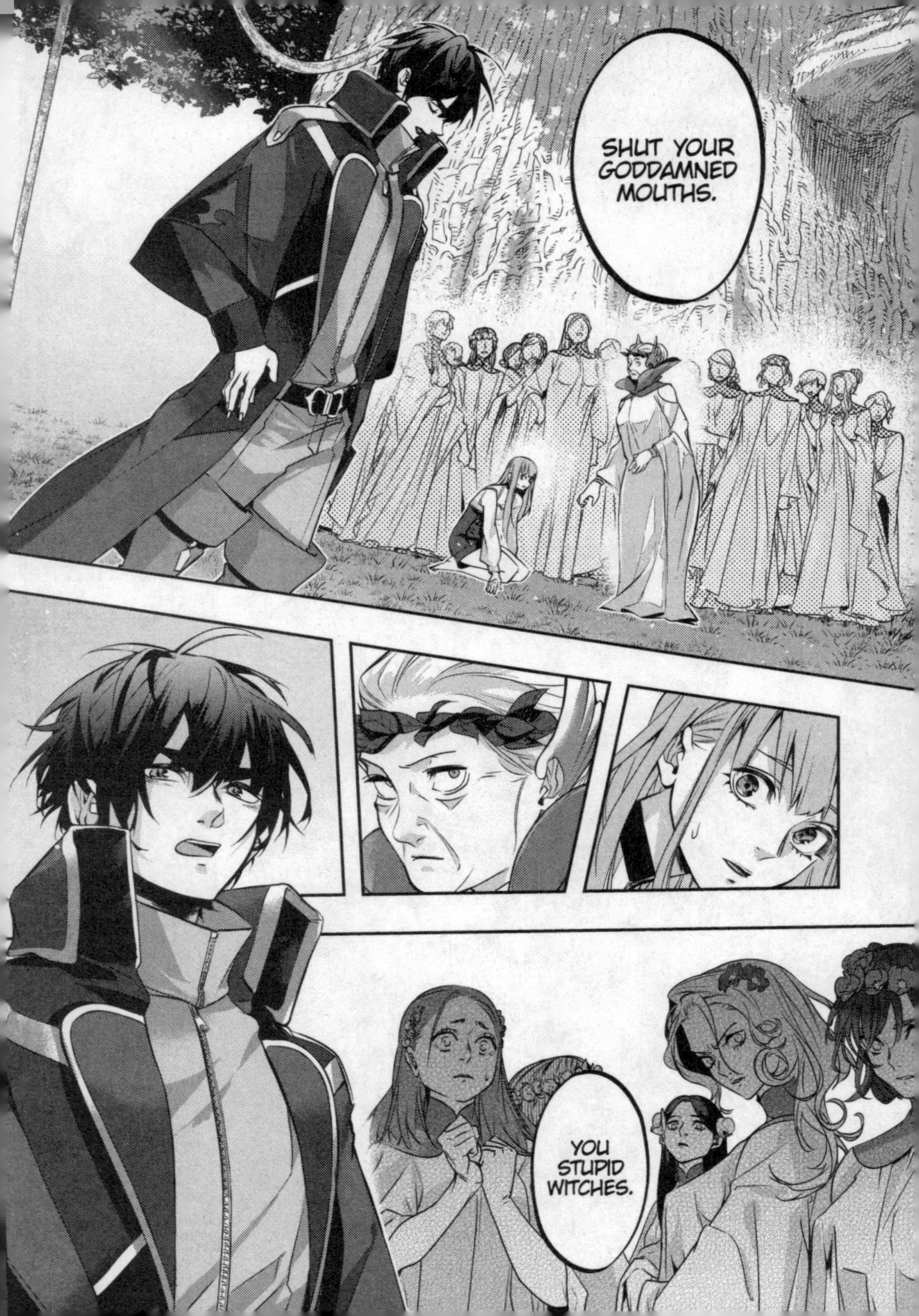
SHUT YOUR GODDAMNED MOUTHS.
YOU STUPID WITCHES.

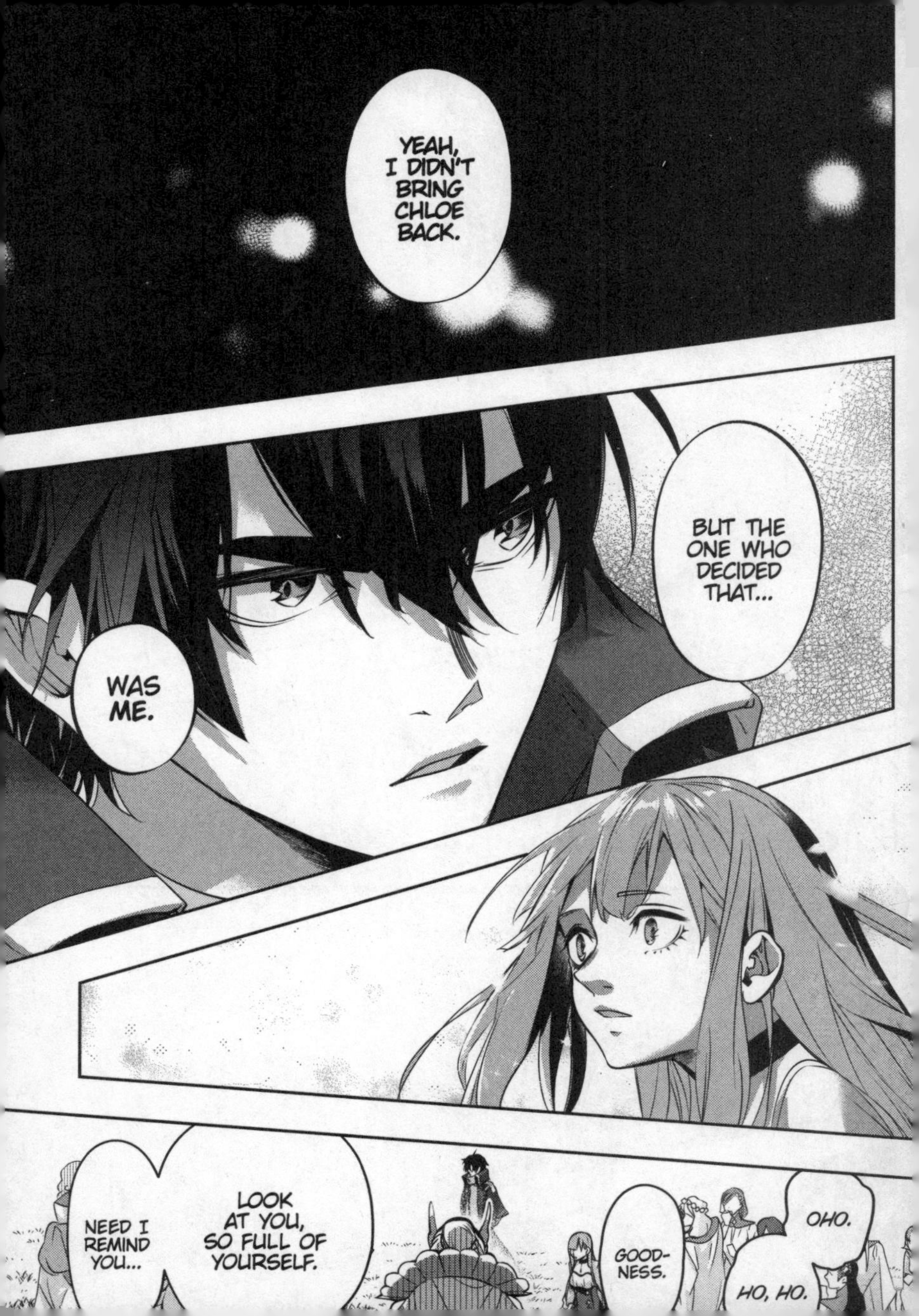
YEAH, I DIDN'T BRING CHLOE BACK.
BUT THE ONE WHO DECIDED THAT...
WAS ME.
OHO.
HO, HO.
GOOD-NESS.
LOOK AT YOU, SO FULL OF YOURSELF.
NEED I REMIND YOU...

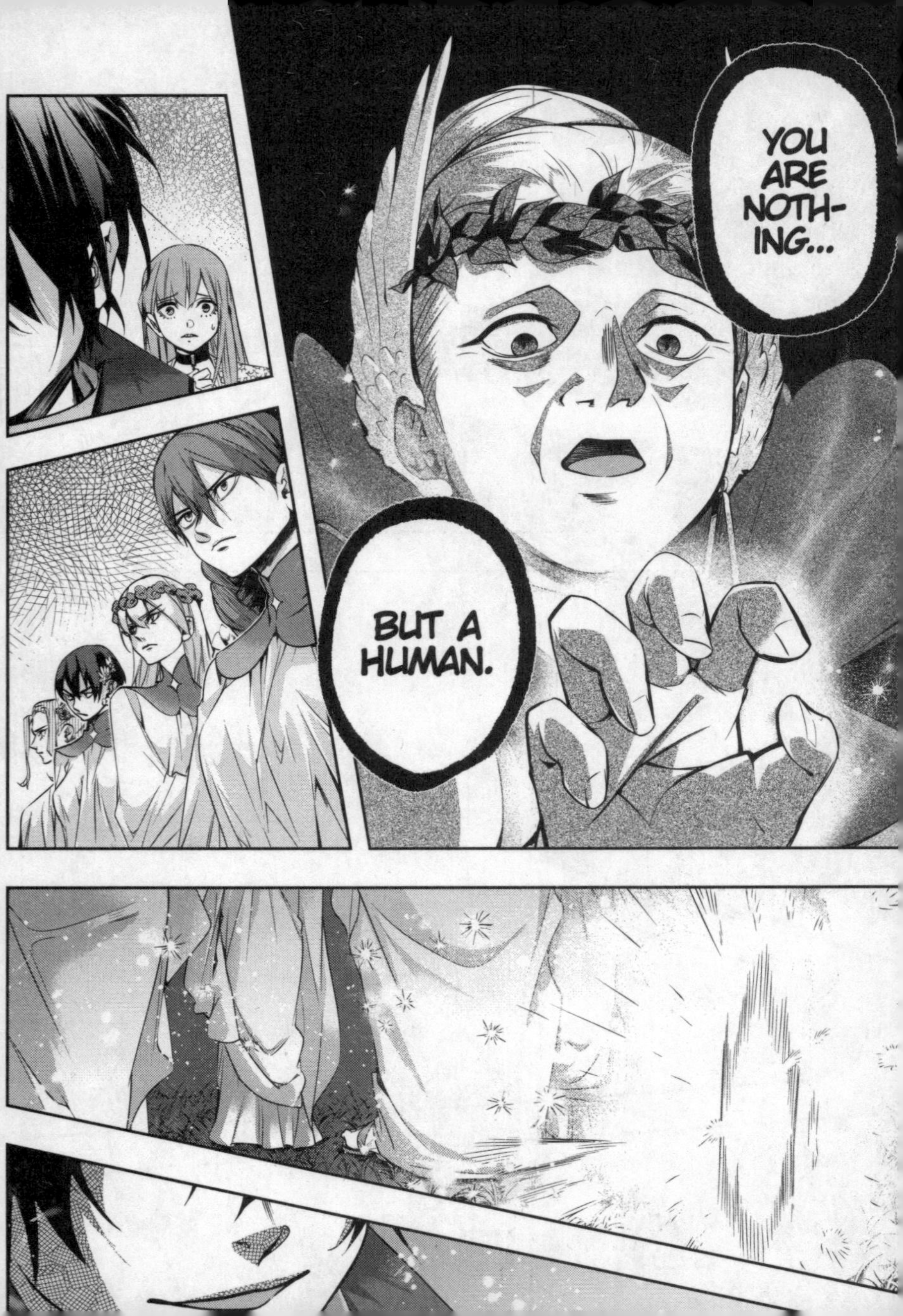
YOU ARE NOTH-ING...
BUT A HUMAN.

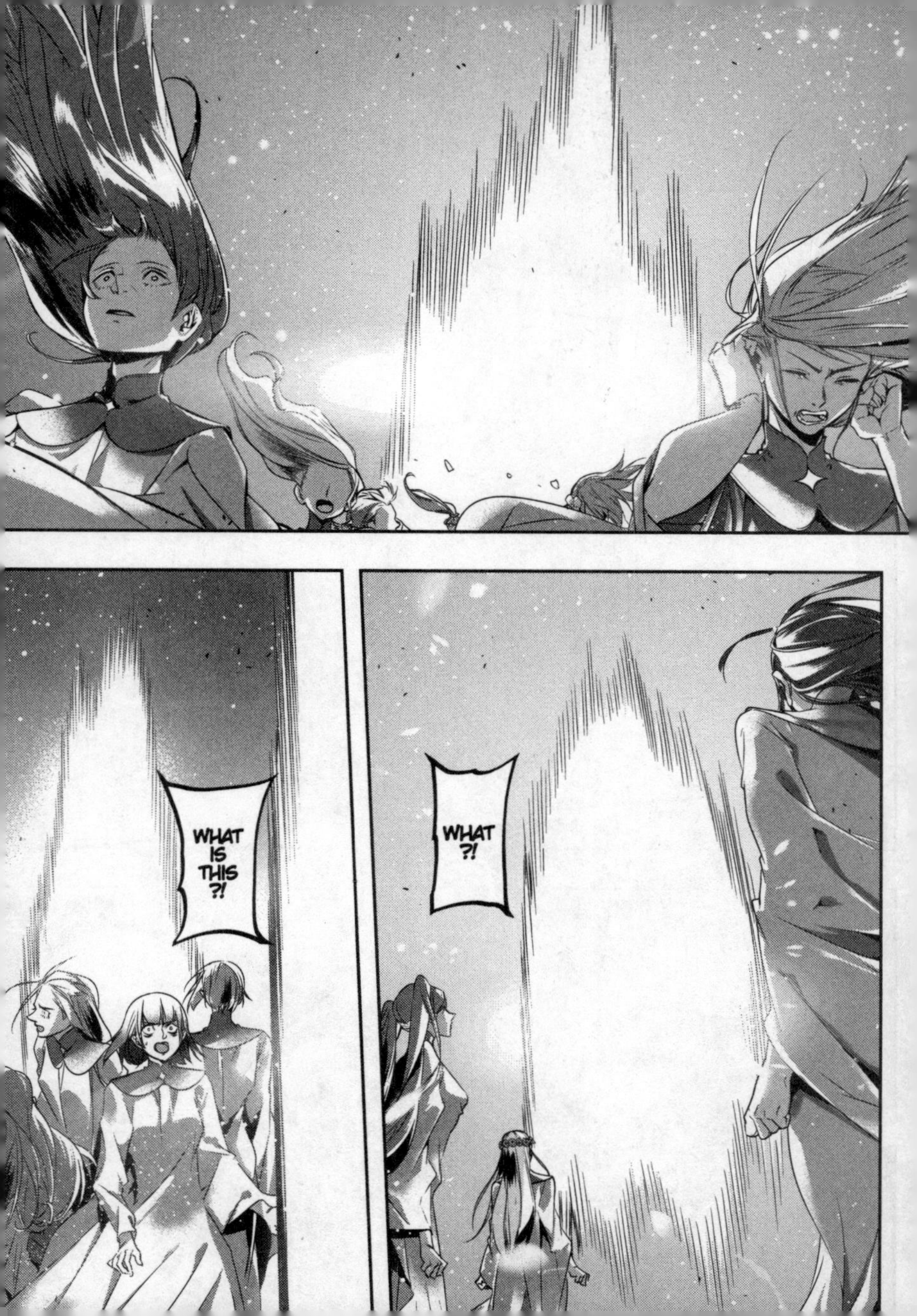
WHAT ?!
WHAT IS THIS ?!

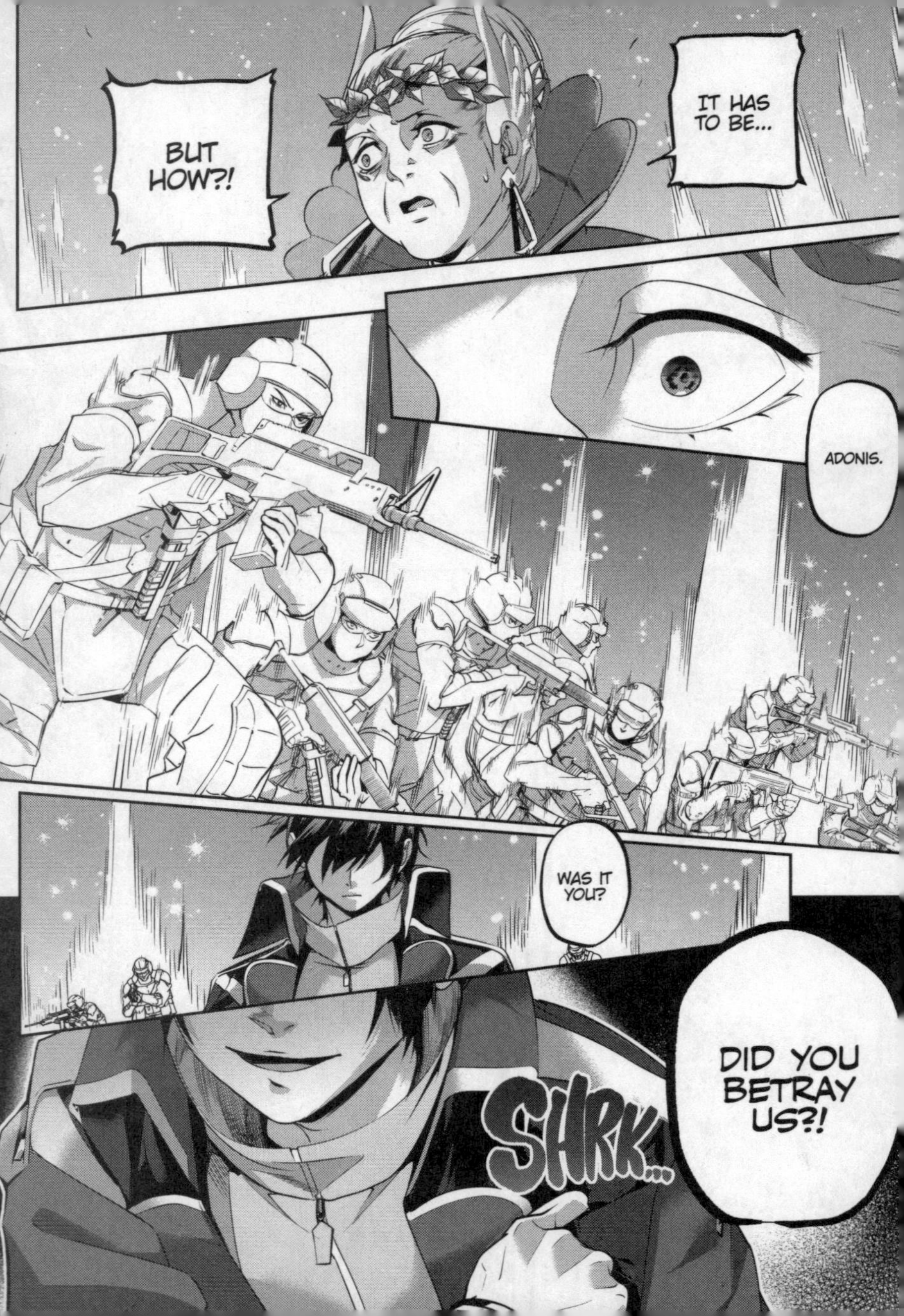
IT HAS TO BE...
BUT HOW?!
ADONIS.
WAS IT YOU?
DID YOU BETRAY US?!
SHRK...

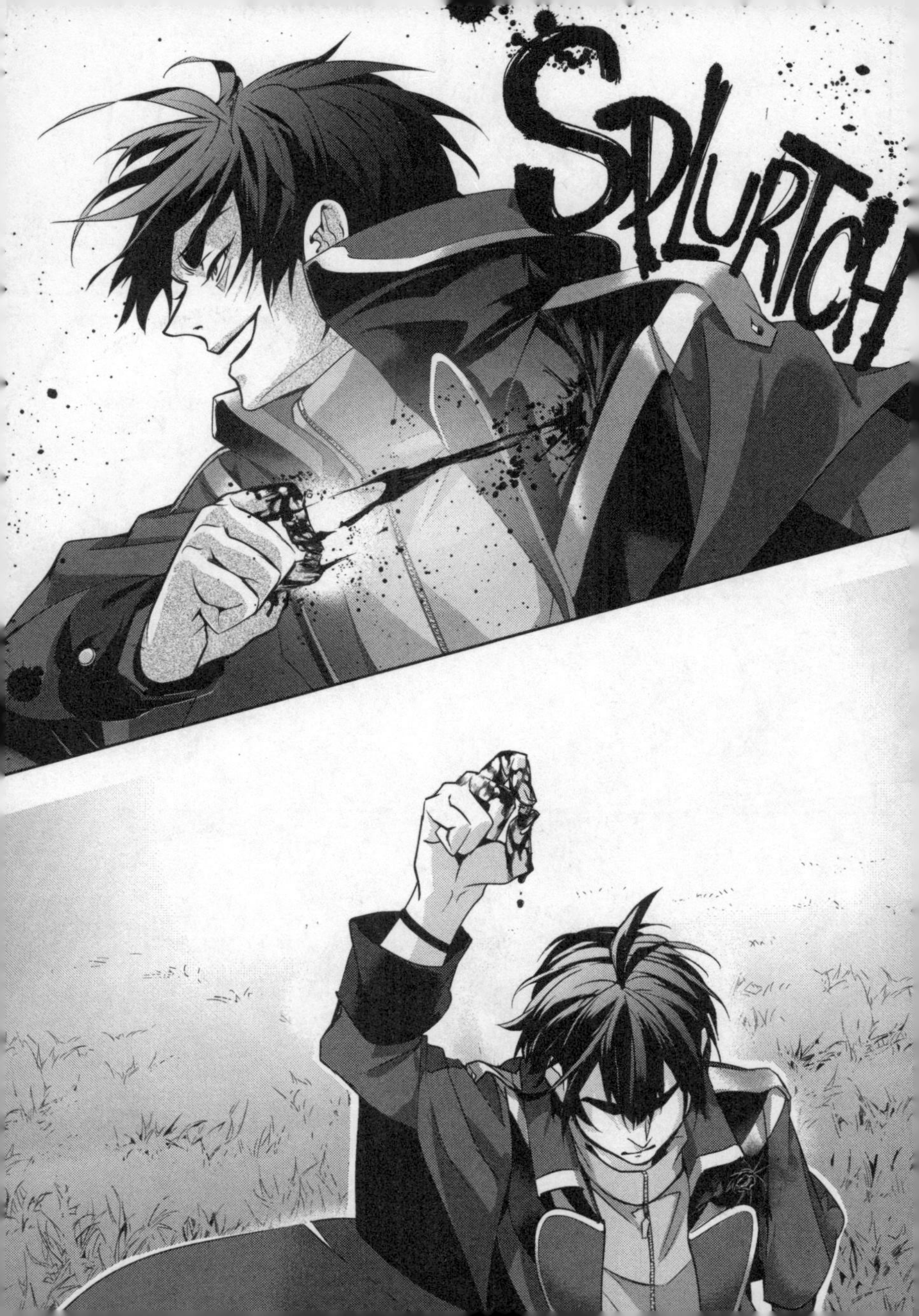
SPLURTCH

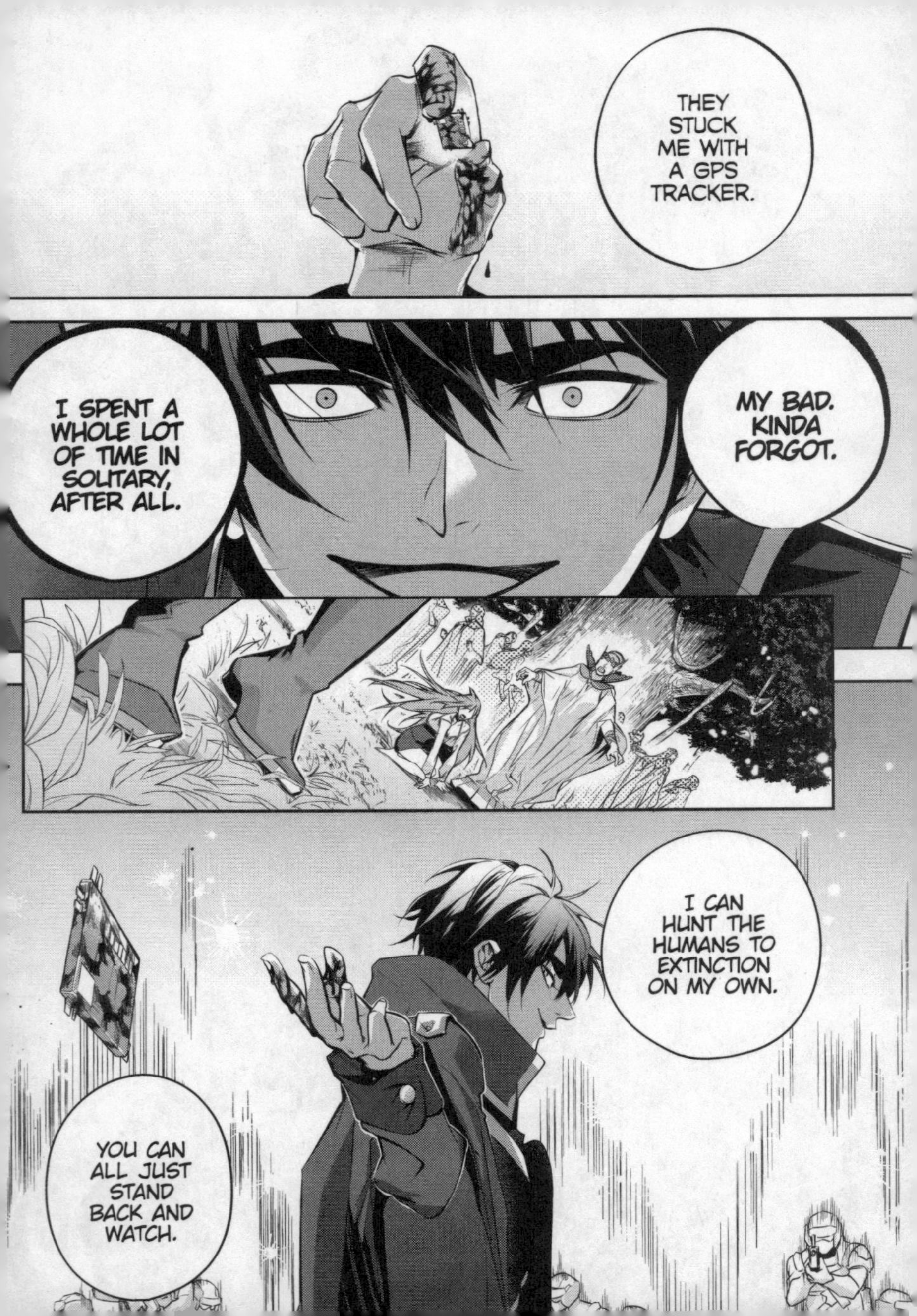
THEY STUCK ME WITH A GPS TRACKER.
MY BAD. KINDA FORGOT.
I SPENT A WHOLE LOT OF TIME IN SOLITARY, AFTER ALL.
I CAN HUNT THE HUMANS TO EXTINCTION ON MY OWN.
YOU CAN ALL JUST STAND BACK AND WATCH.

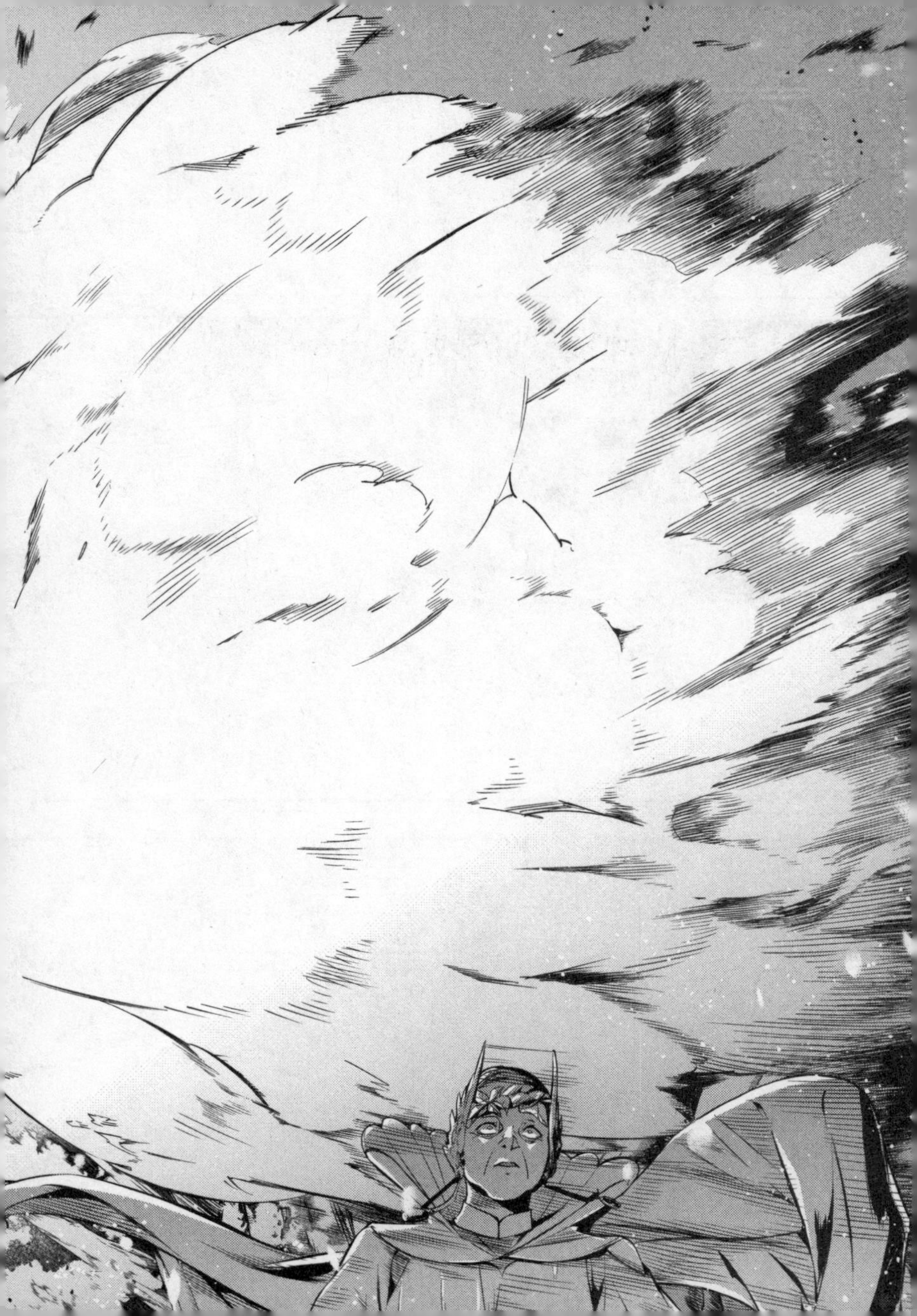

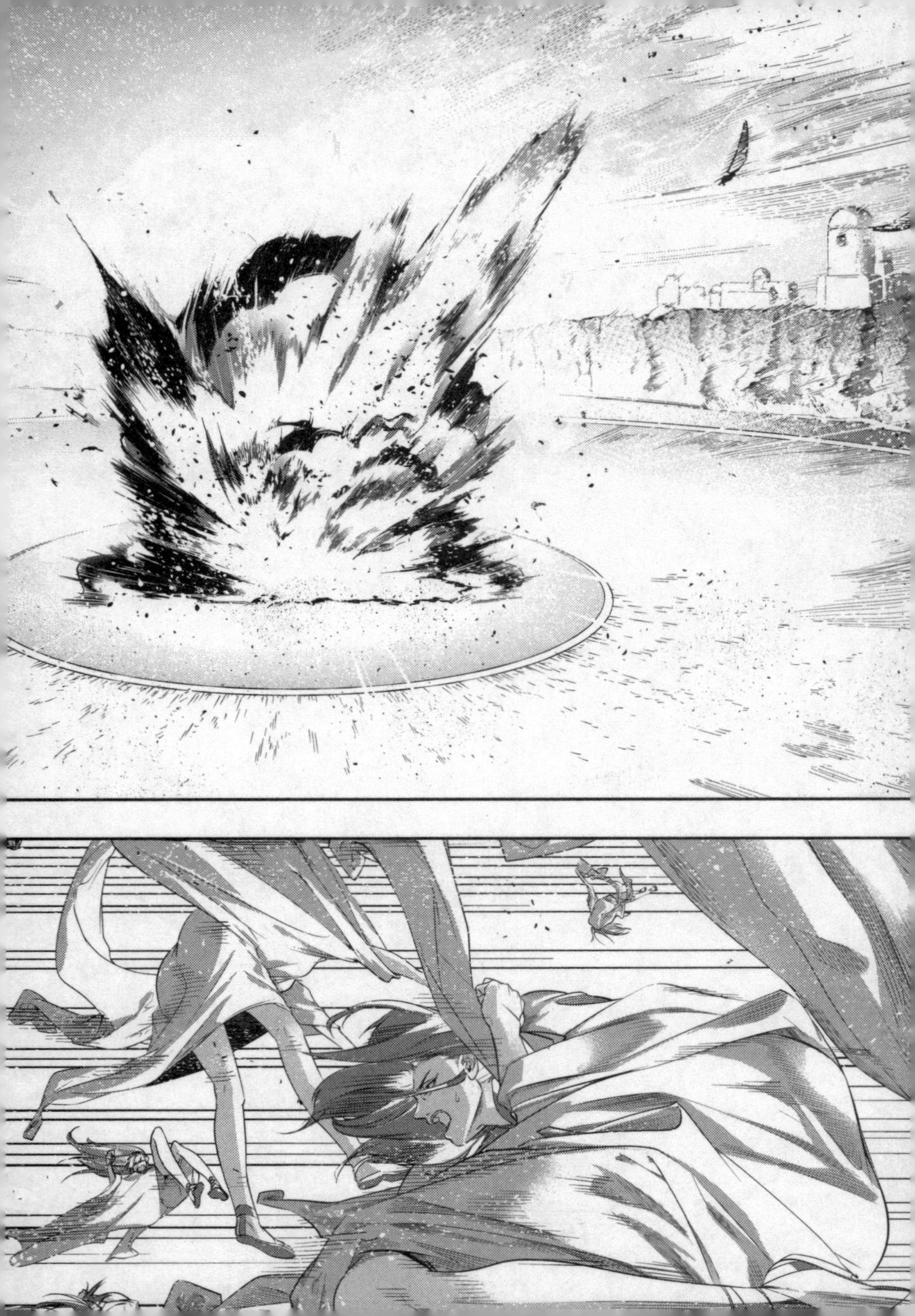

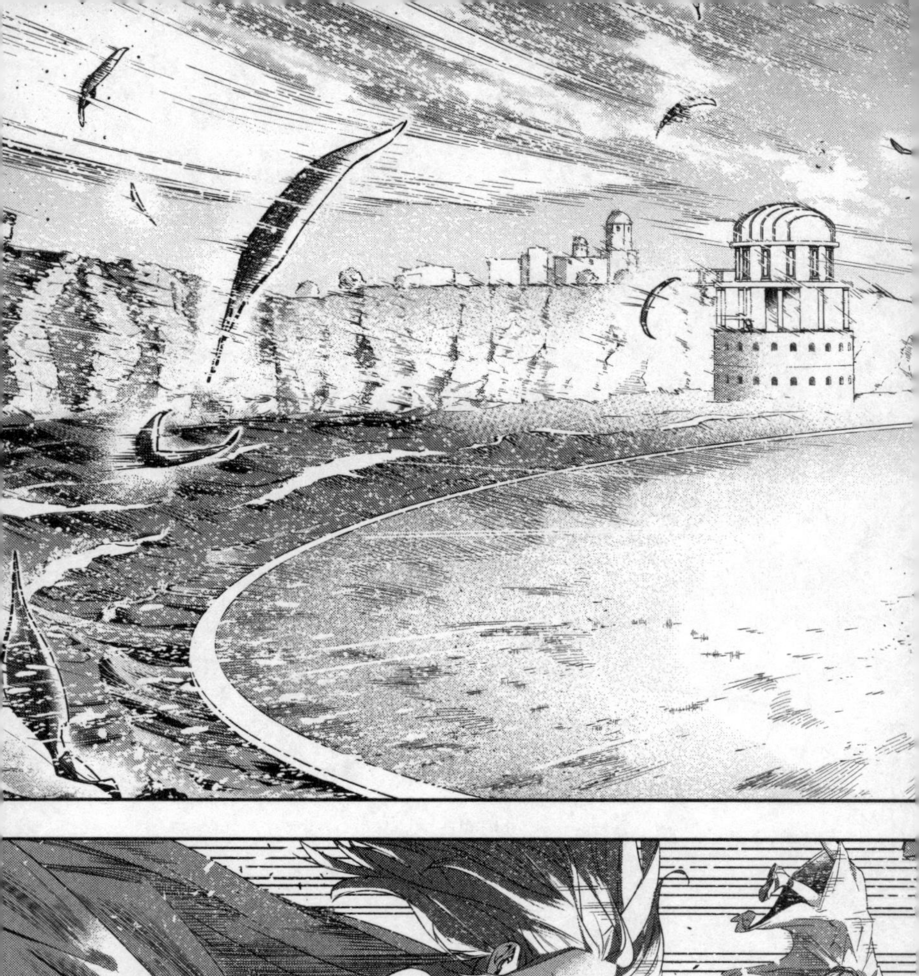
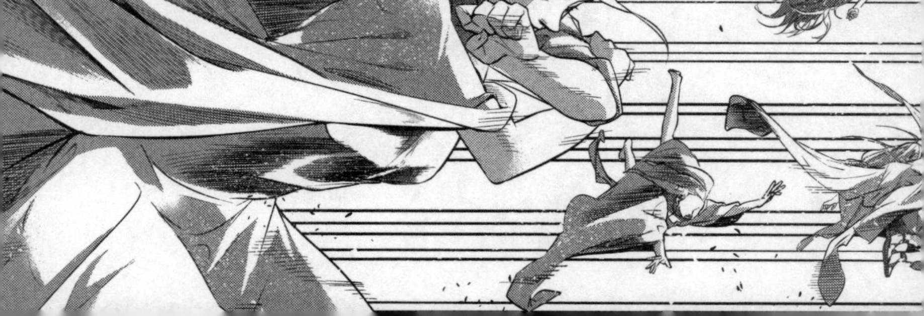

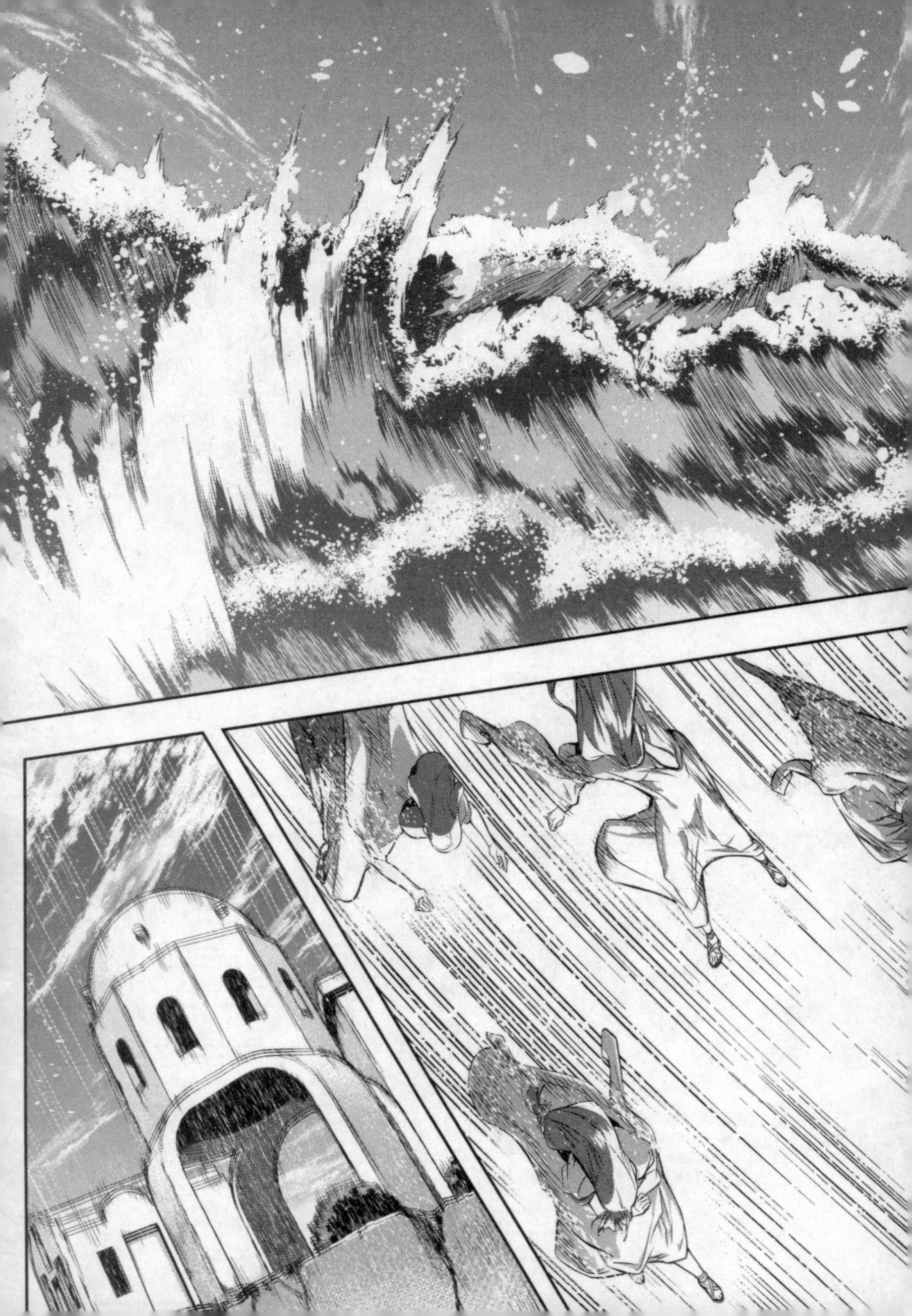

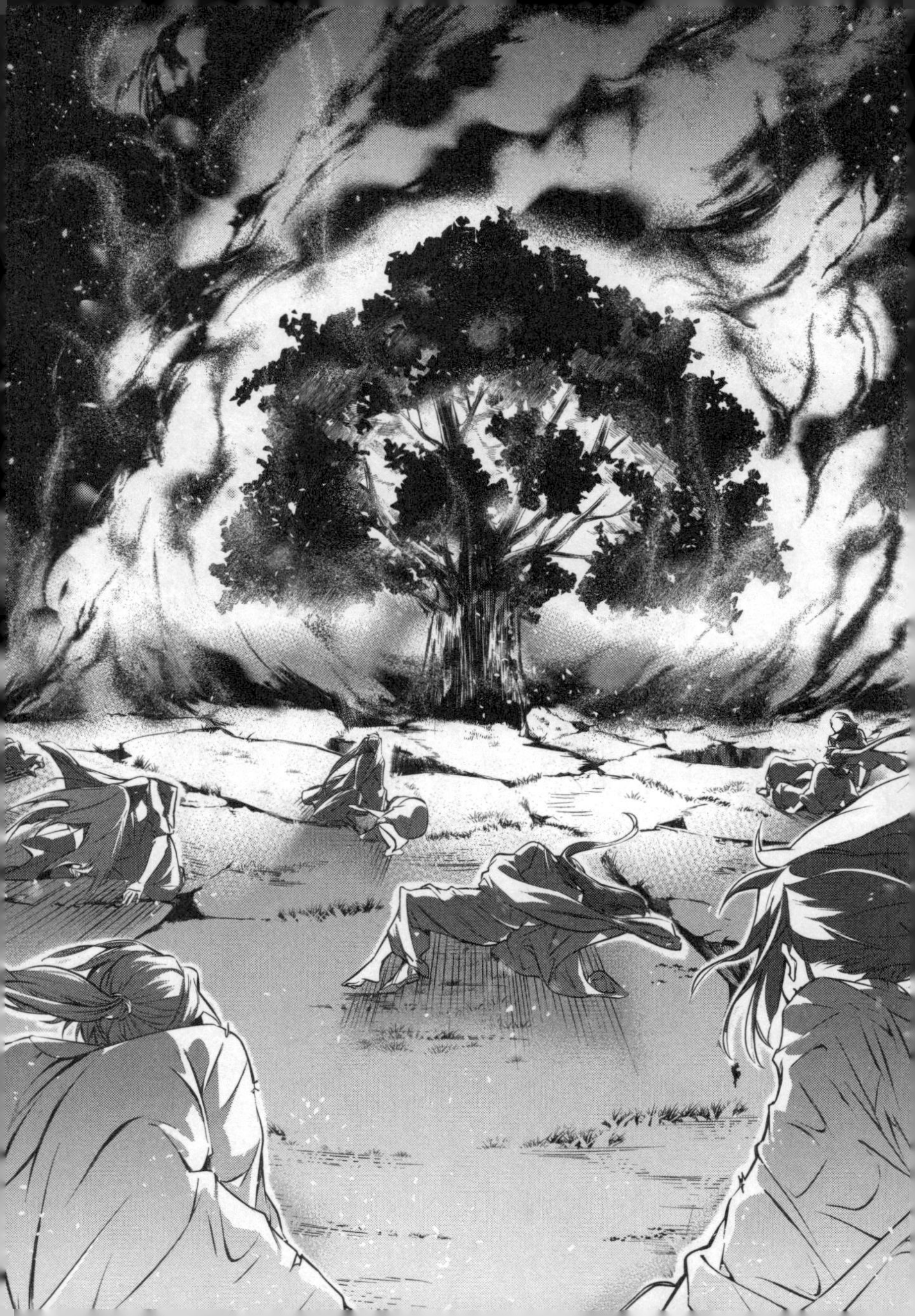

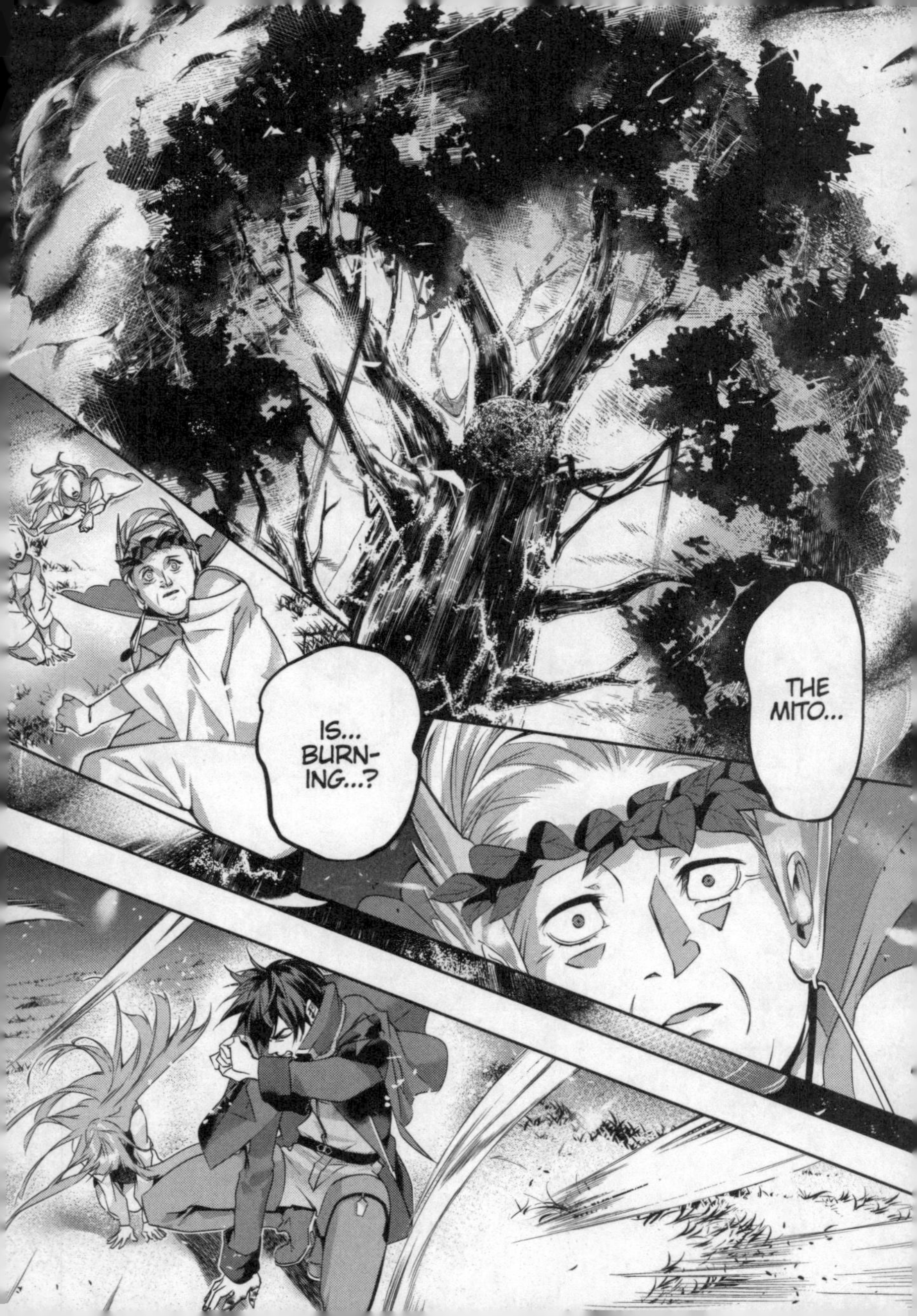
THE MITO...
IS... BURN-ING...?

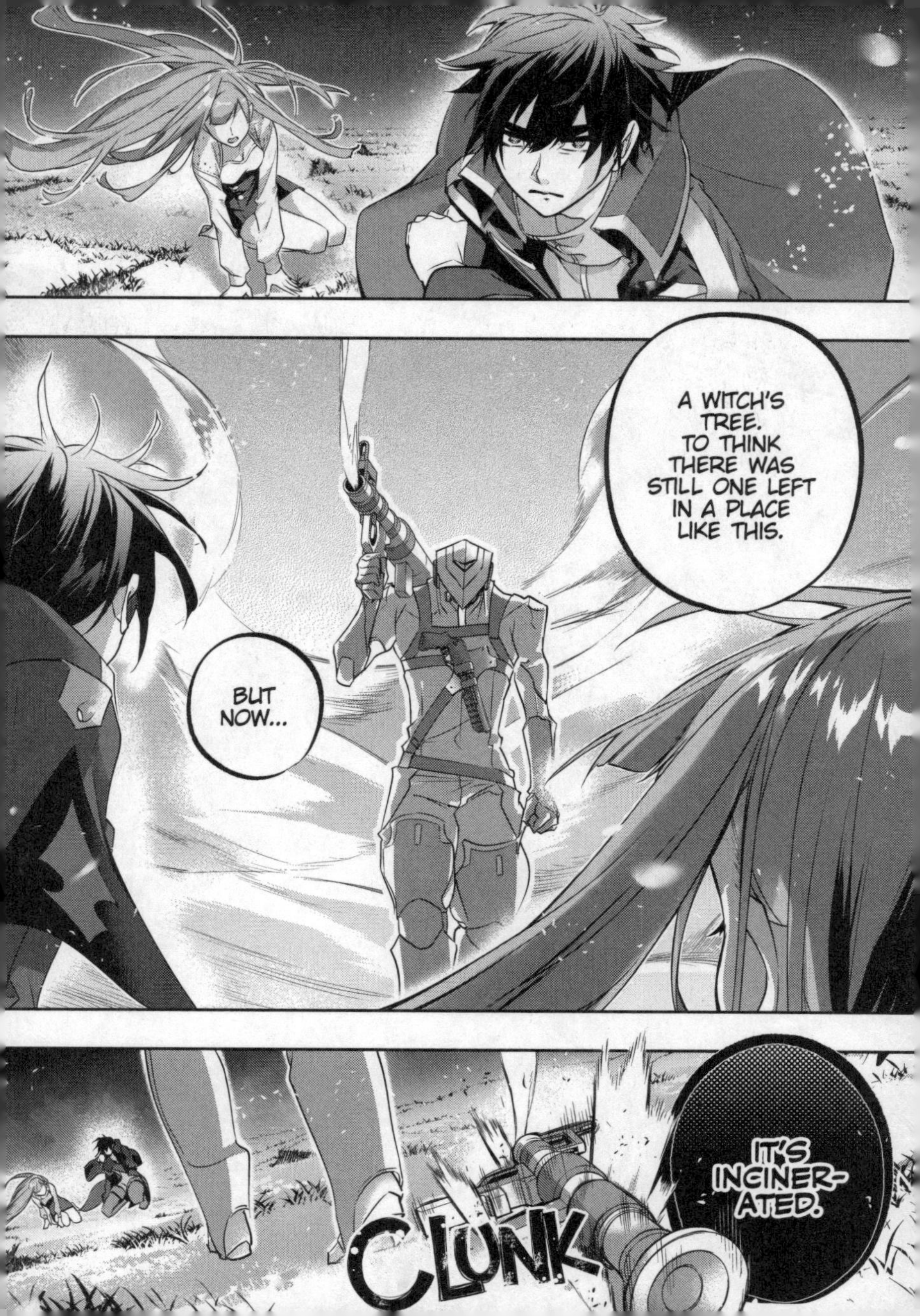
A WITCH'S TREE. TO THINK THERE WAS STILL ONE LEFT IN A PLACE LIKE THIS.
BUT NOW...
IT'S INCINER-ATED.
CLUNK

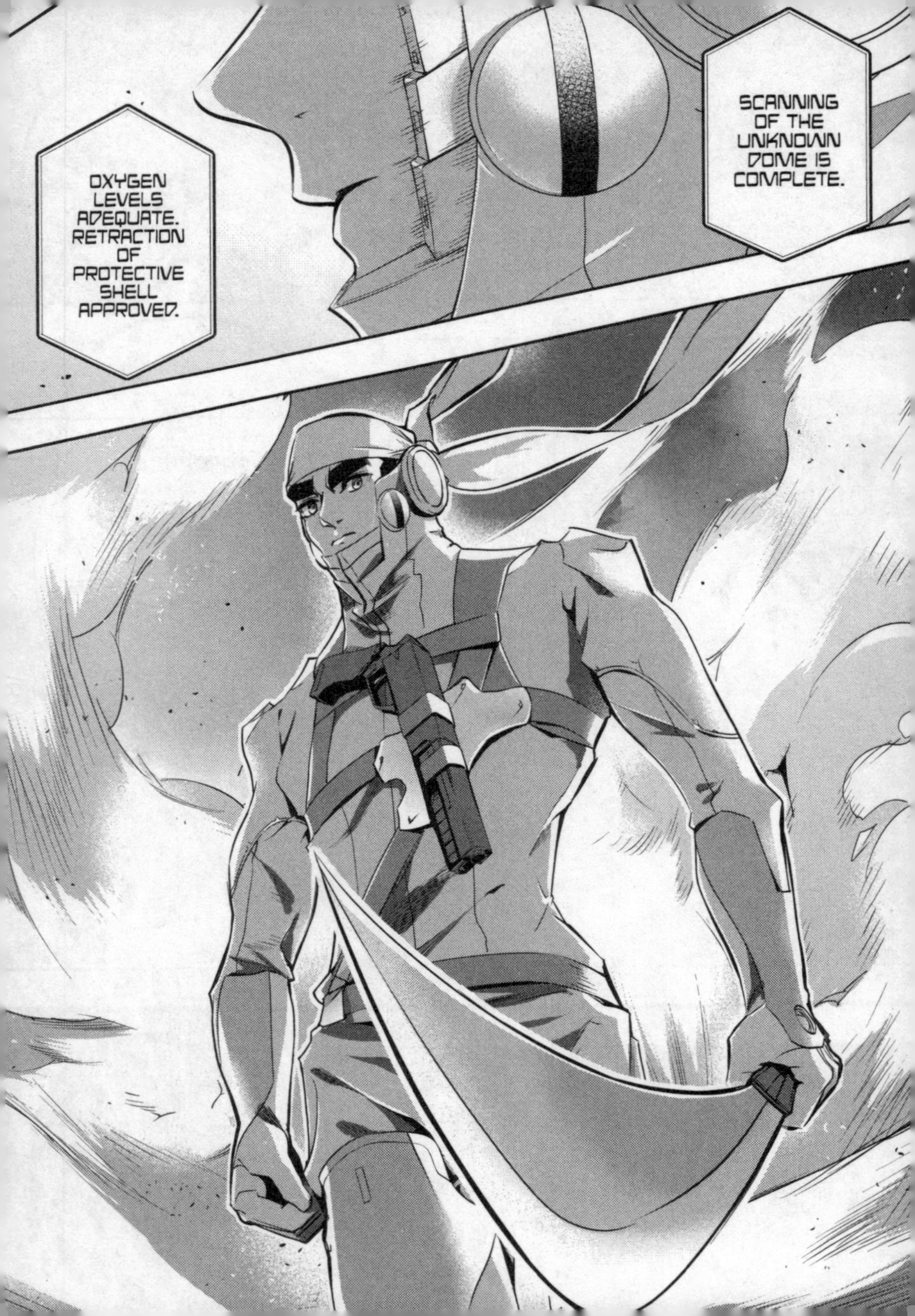
SCANNING OF THE UNKNOWN DOME IS COMPLETE.
OXYGEN LEVELS ADEQUATE. RETRACTION OF PROTECTIVE SHELL APPROVED.

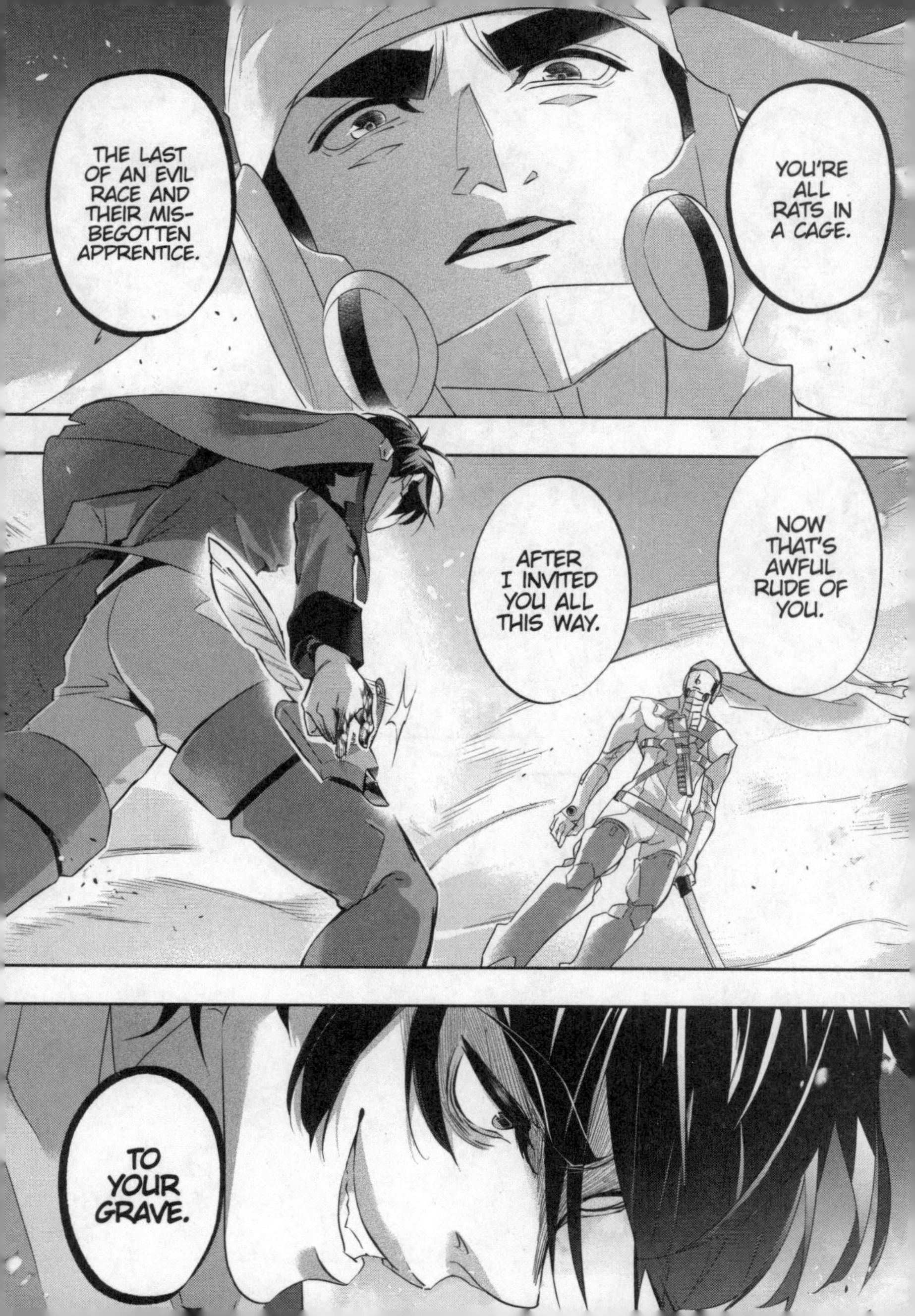
YOU'RE ALL RATS IN A CAGE.
THE LAST OF AN EVIL RACE AND THEIR MIS-BEGOTTEN APPRENTICE.
NOW THAT'S AWFUL RUDE OF YOU.
AFTER I INVITED YOU ALL THIS WAY.
TO YOUR GRAVE.

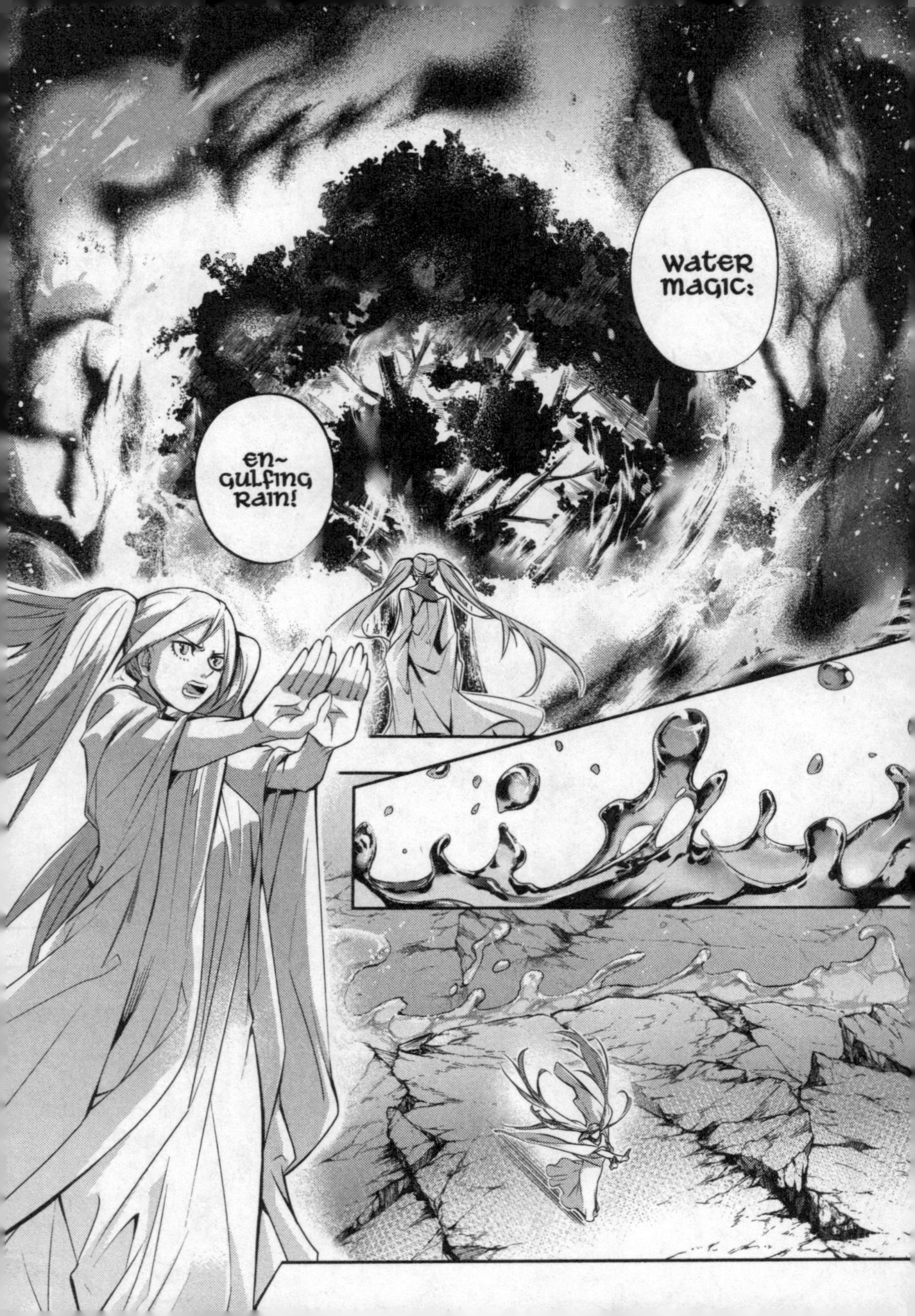
WATER MAGIC:
EN-GULFING RAIN!

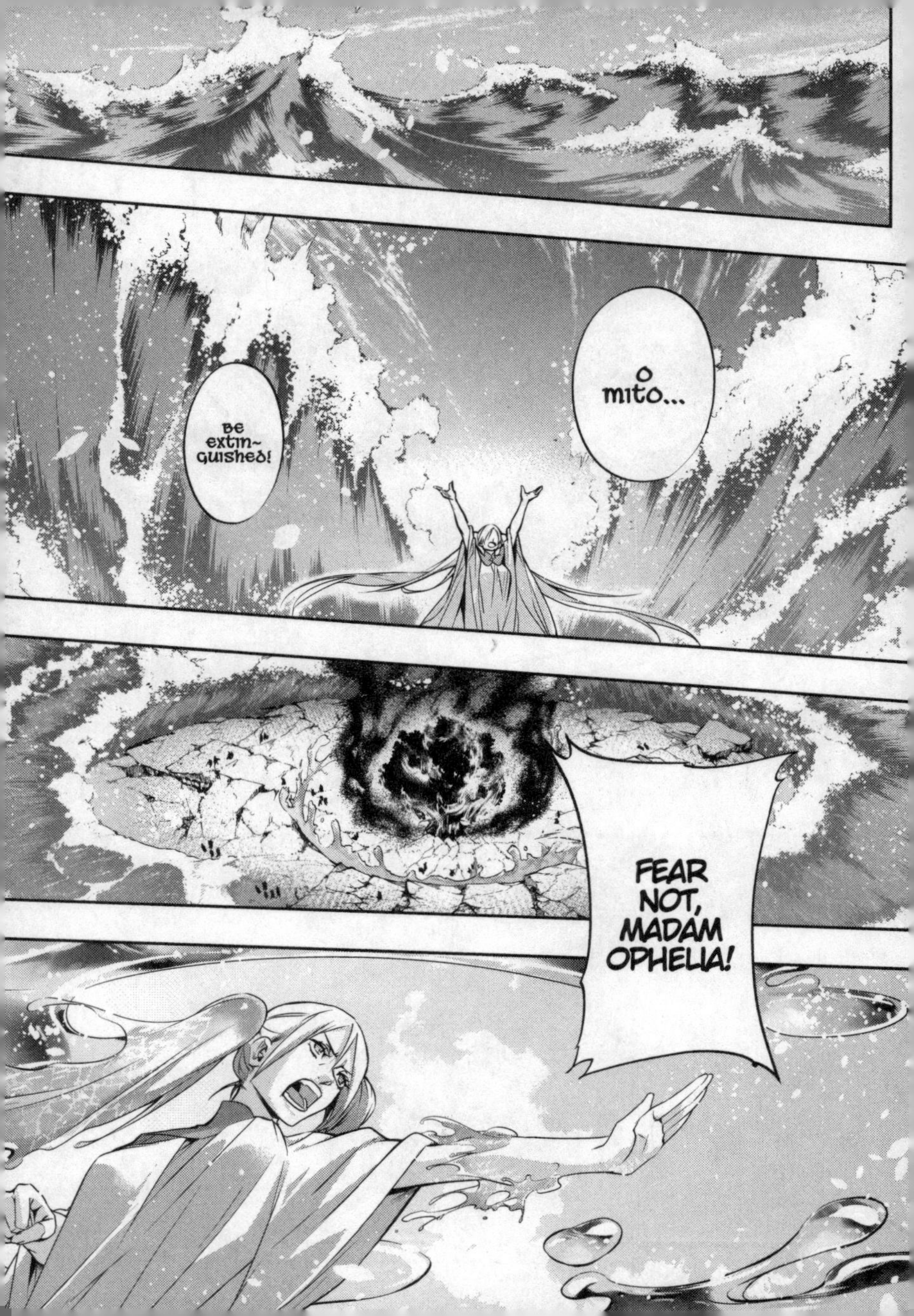
O mito...
Be extin-guished!
FEAR NOT, MADAM OPHELIA!

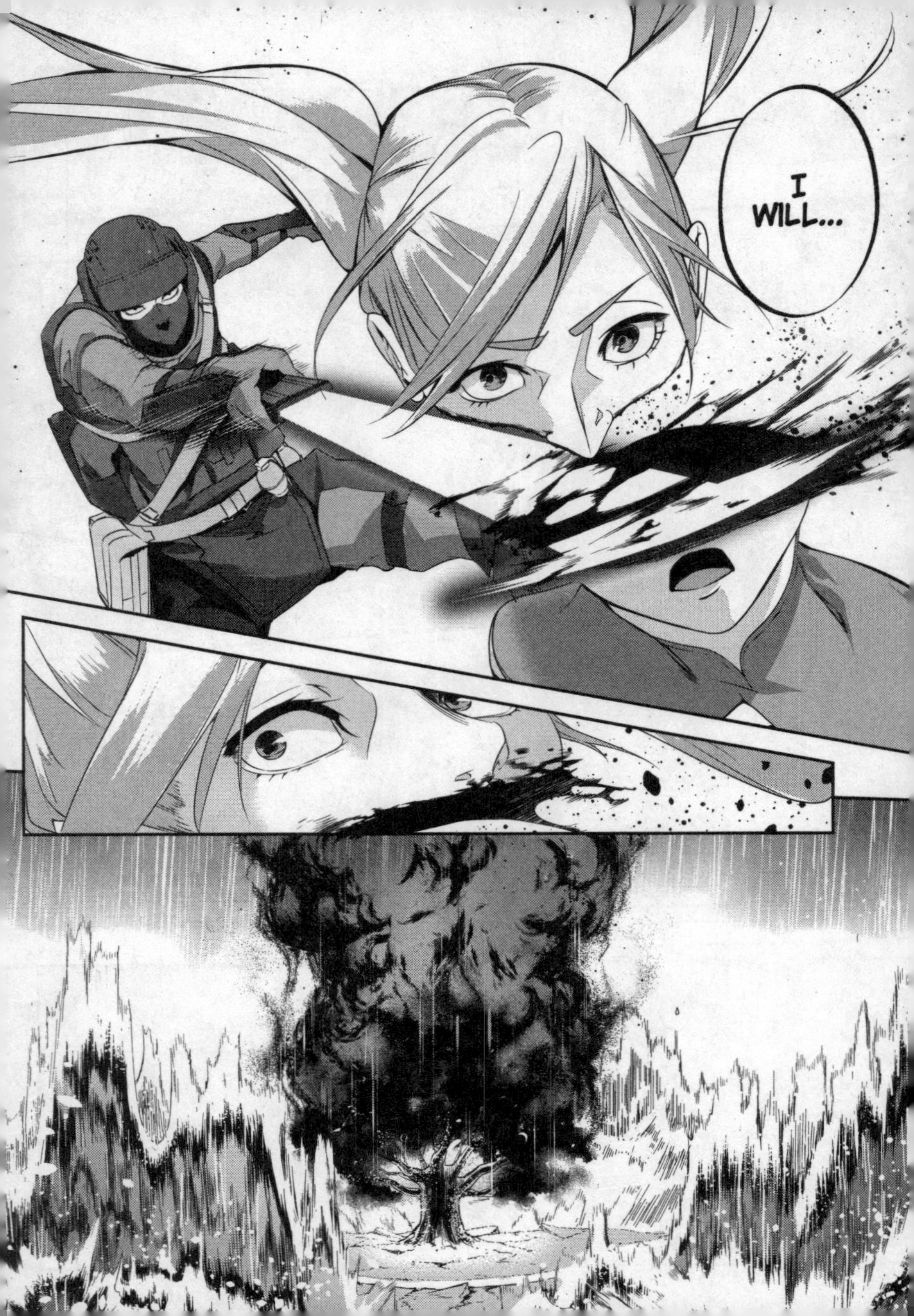
I WILL...

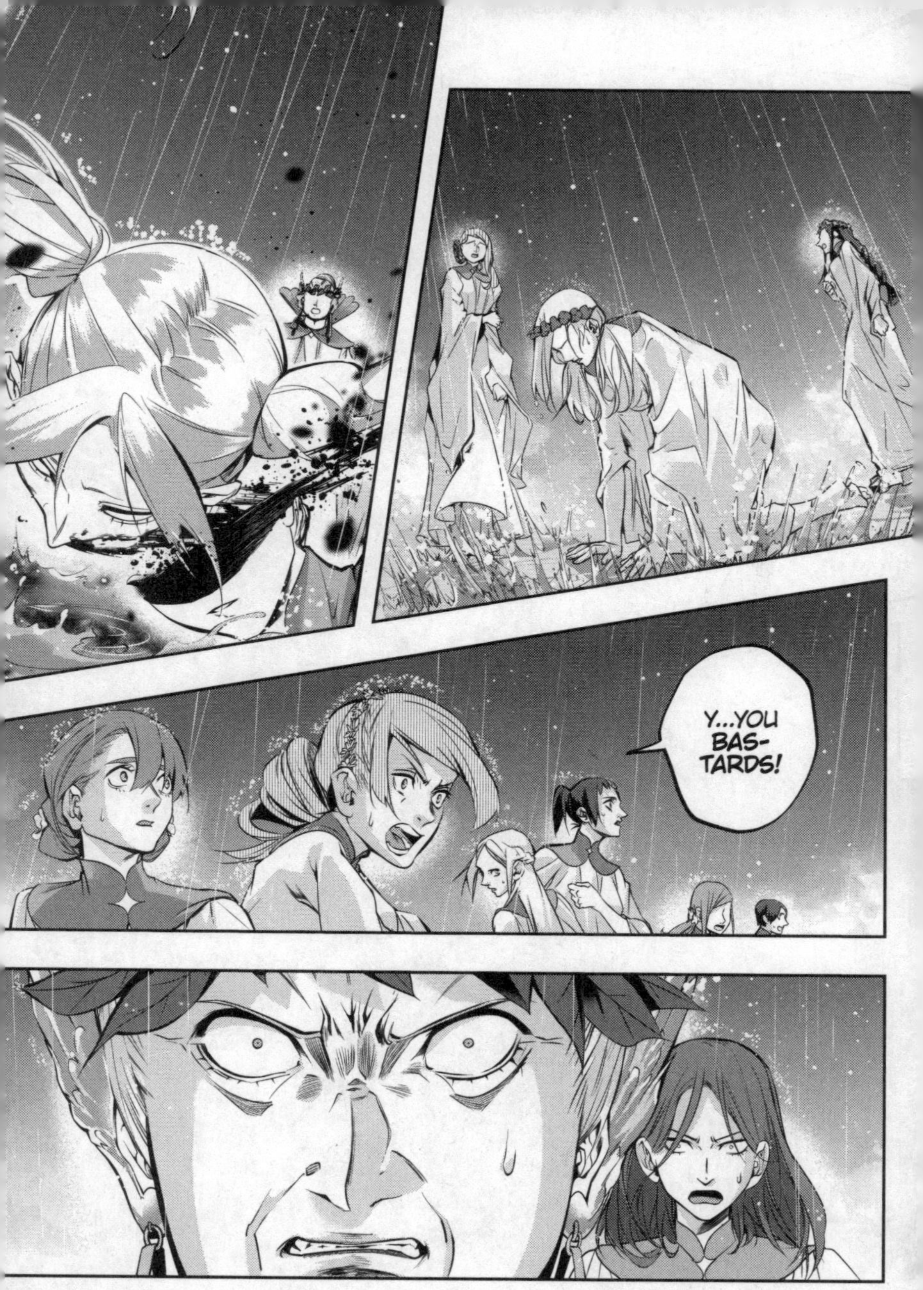
Y...YOU BAS-TARDS!

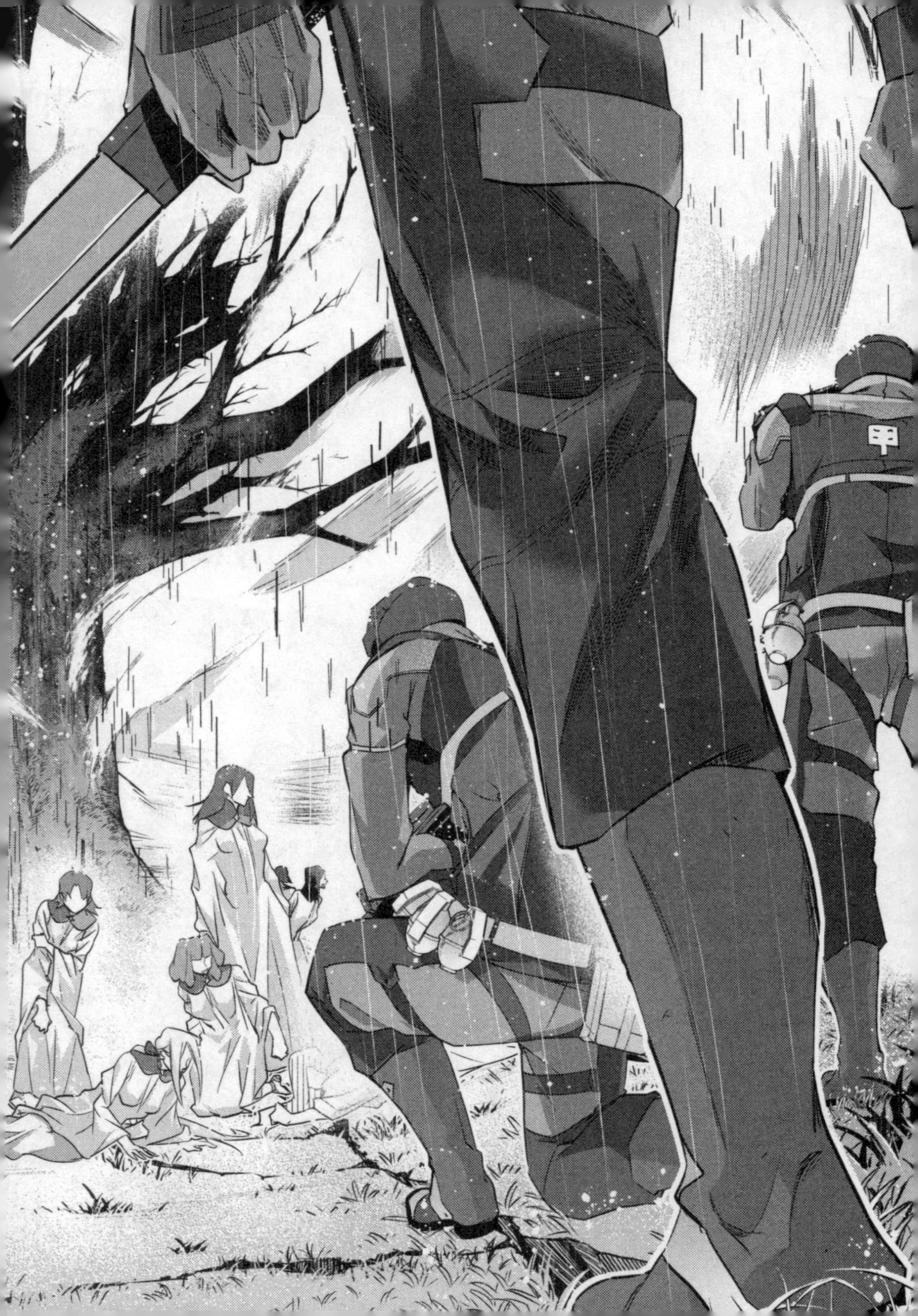
甲

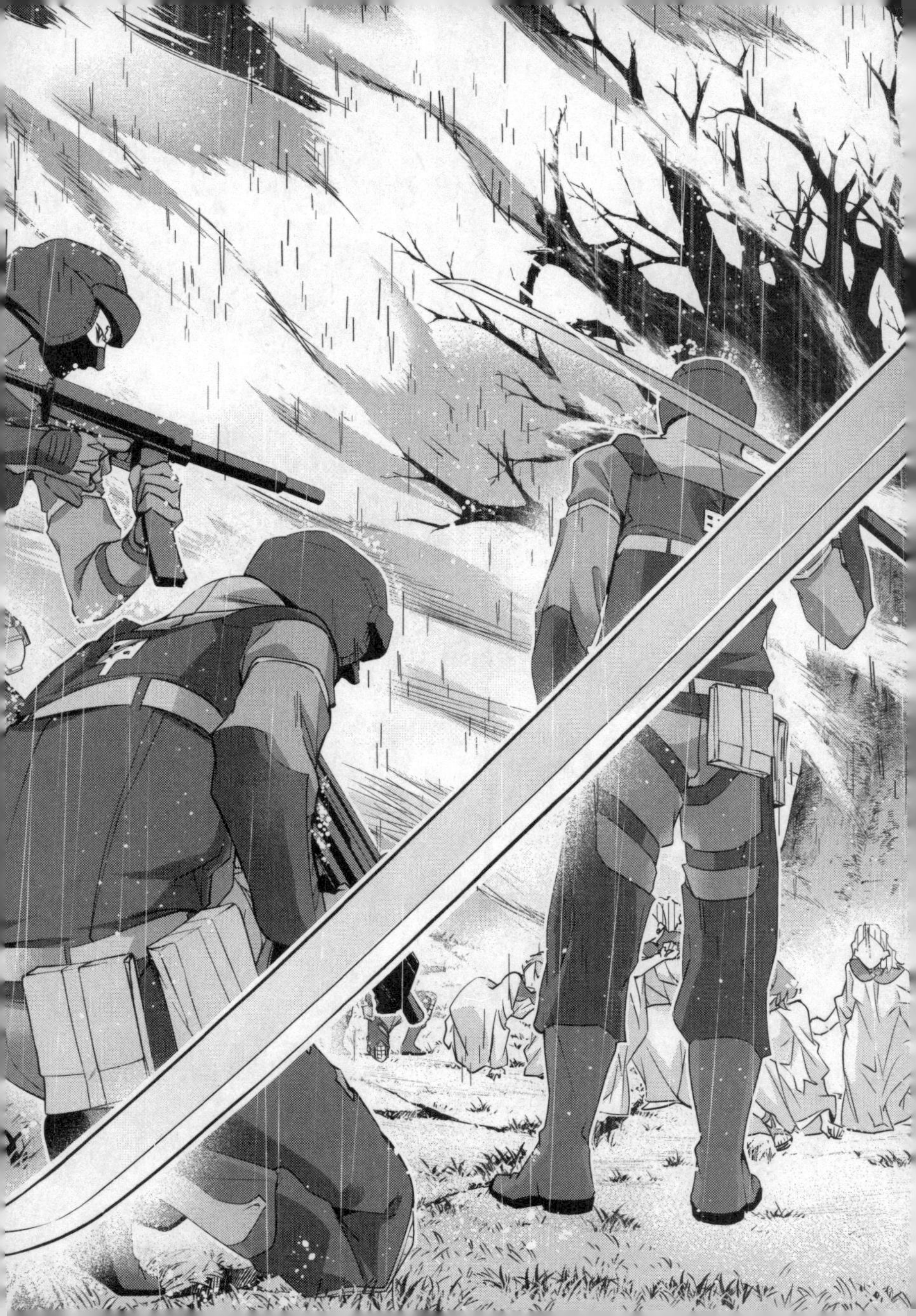

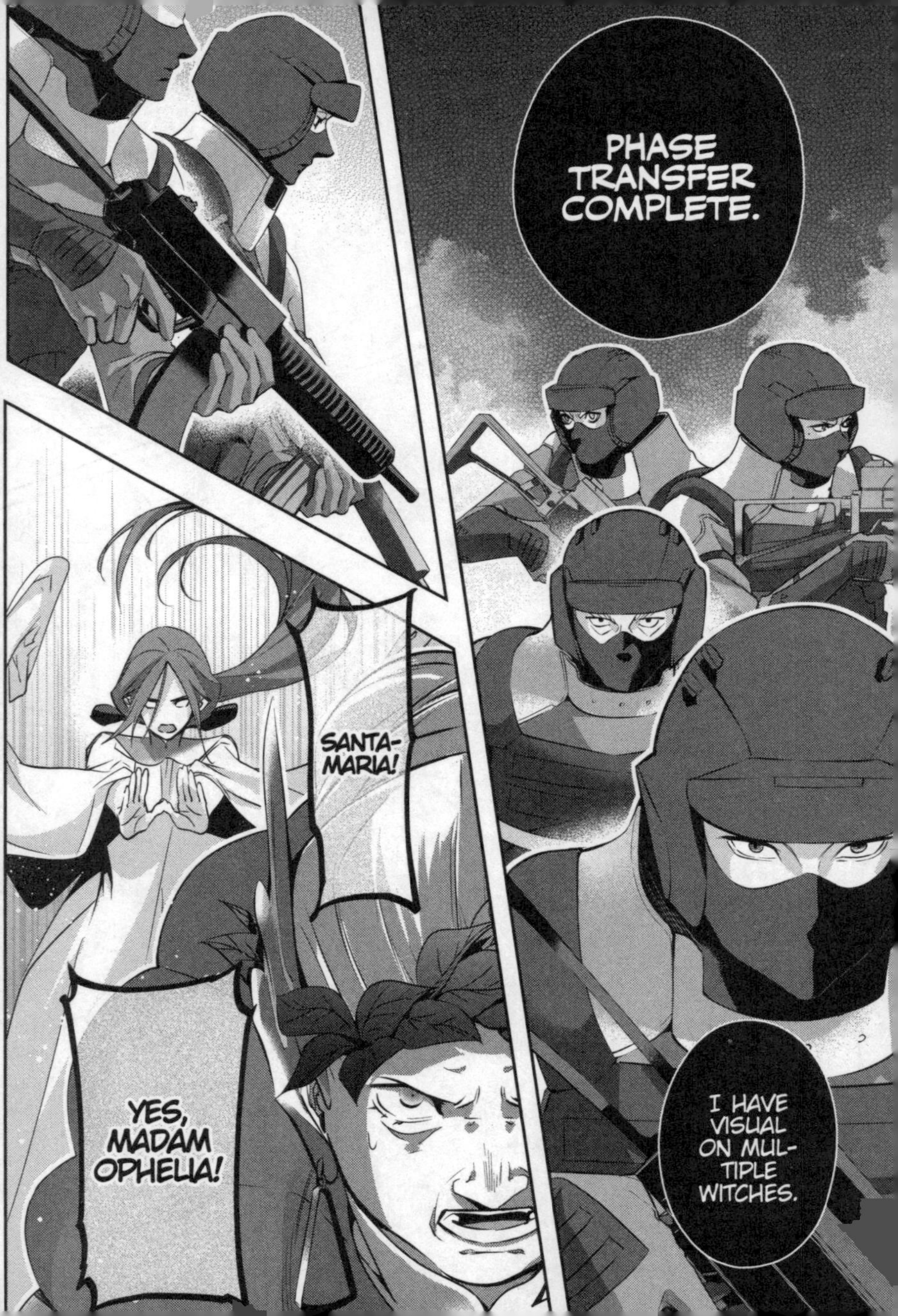
PHASE TRANSFER COMPLETE.
I HAVE VISUAL ON MUL-TIPLE WITCHES.
SANTA-MARIA!
YES, MADAM OPHELIA!

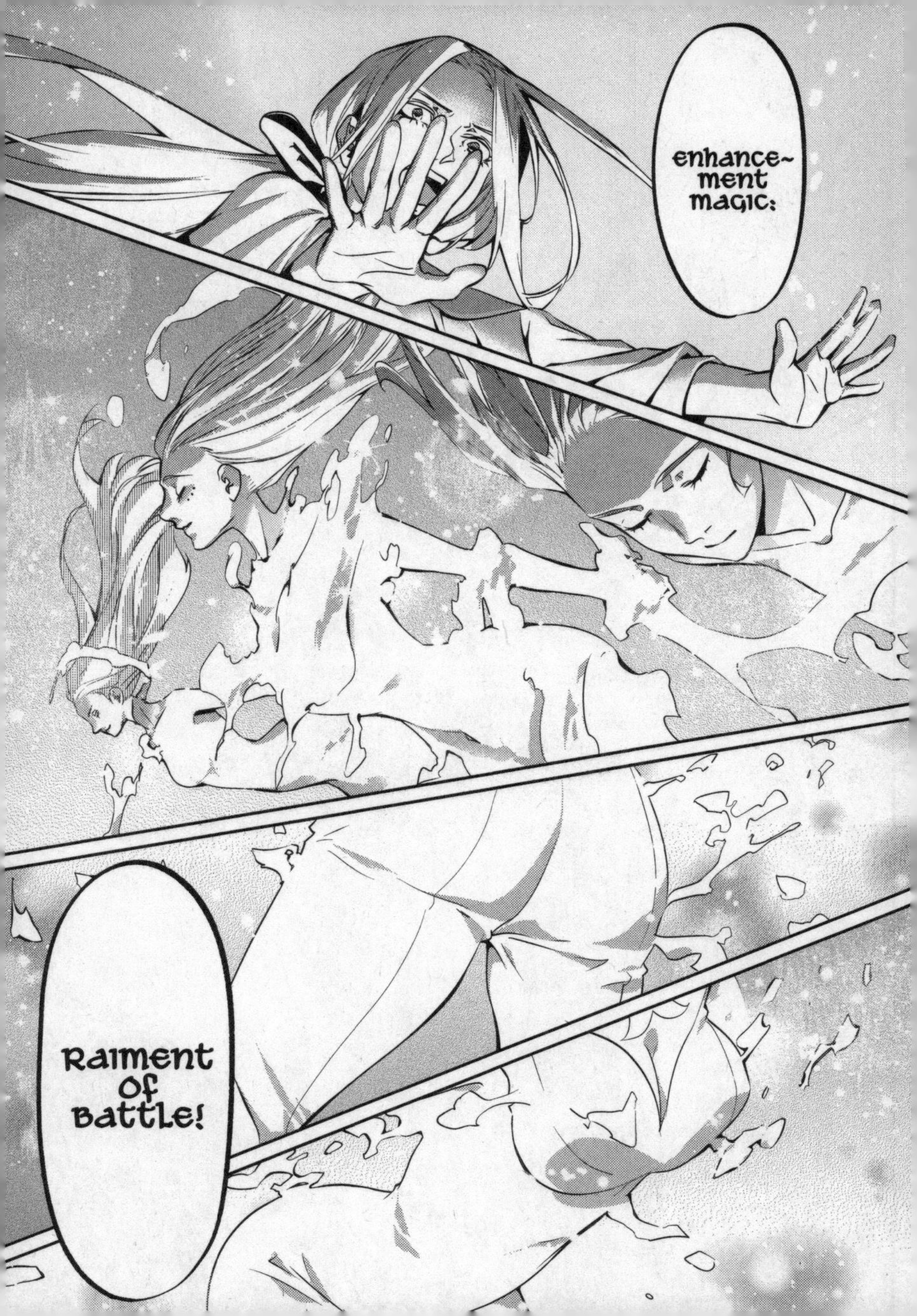
enhancement magic:
Raiment of Battle!

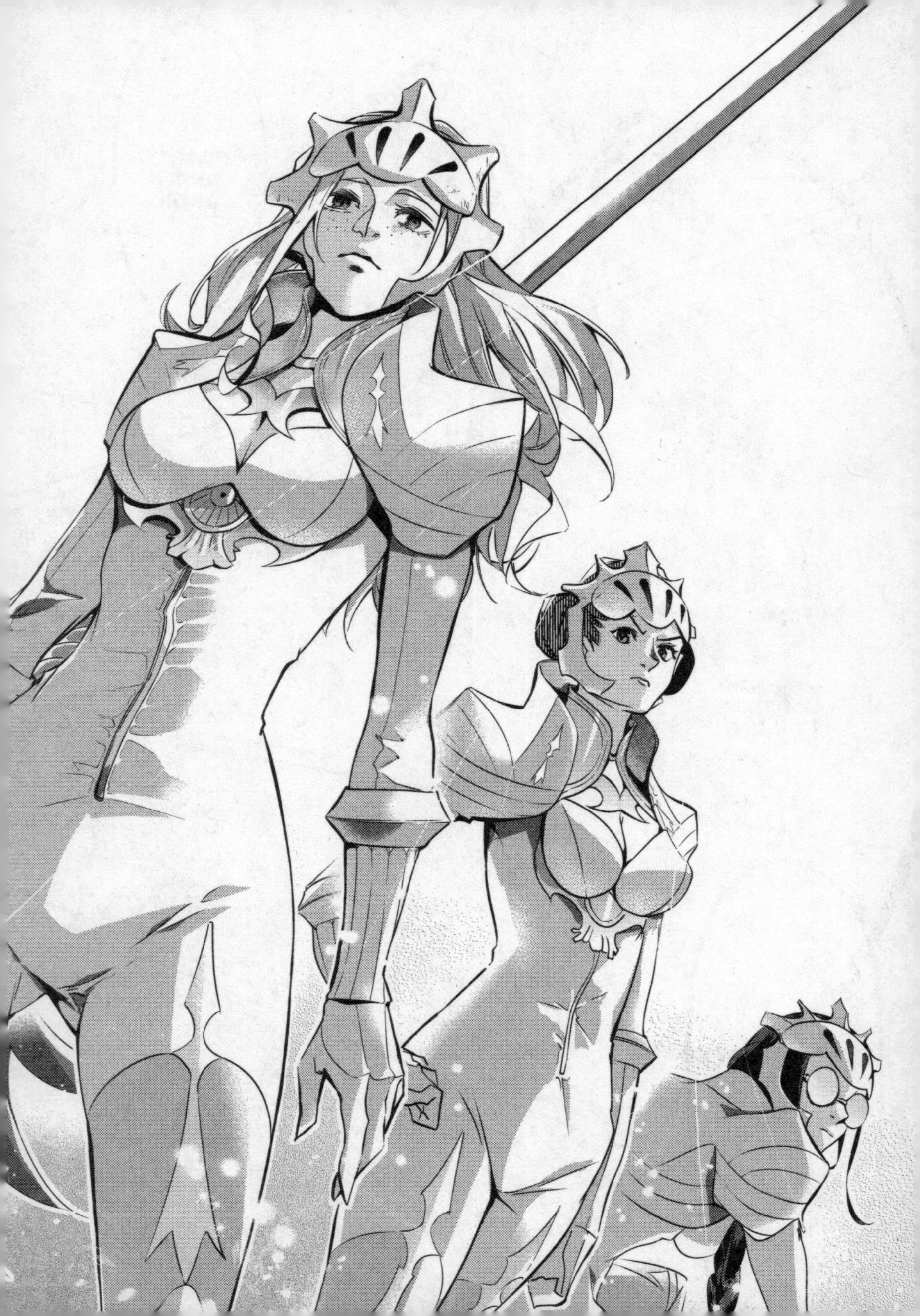

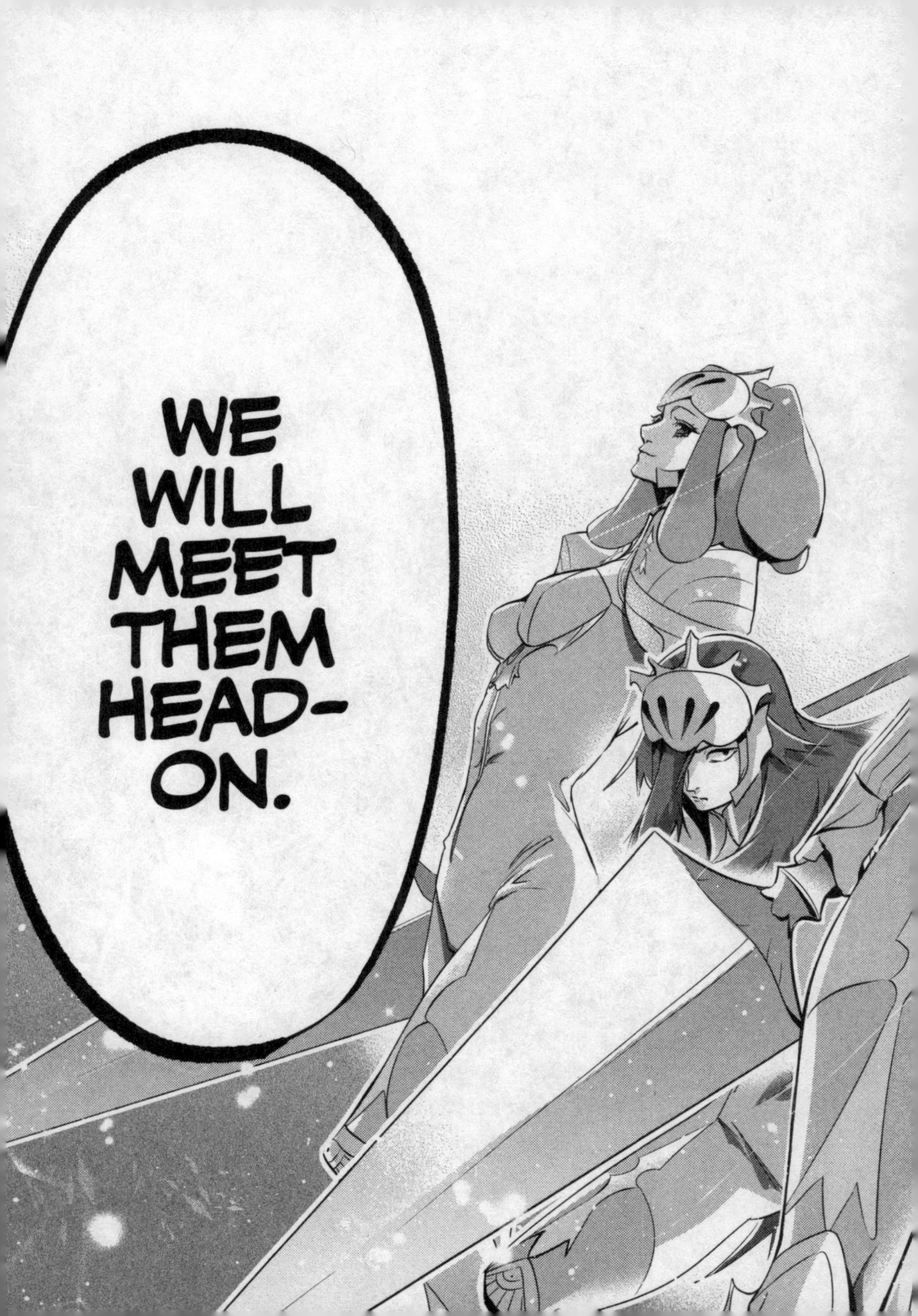
WE WILL MEET THEM HEAD-ON.

THE
KINGDOMS
OF RUIN

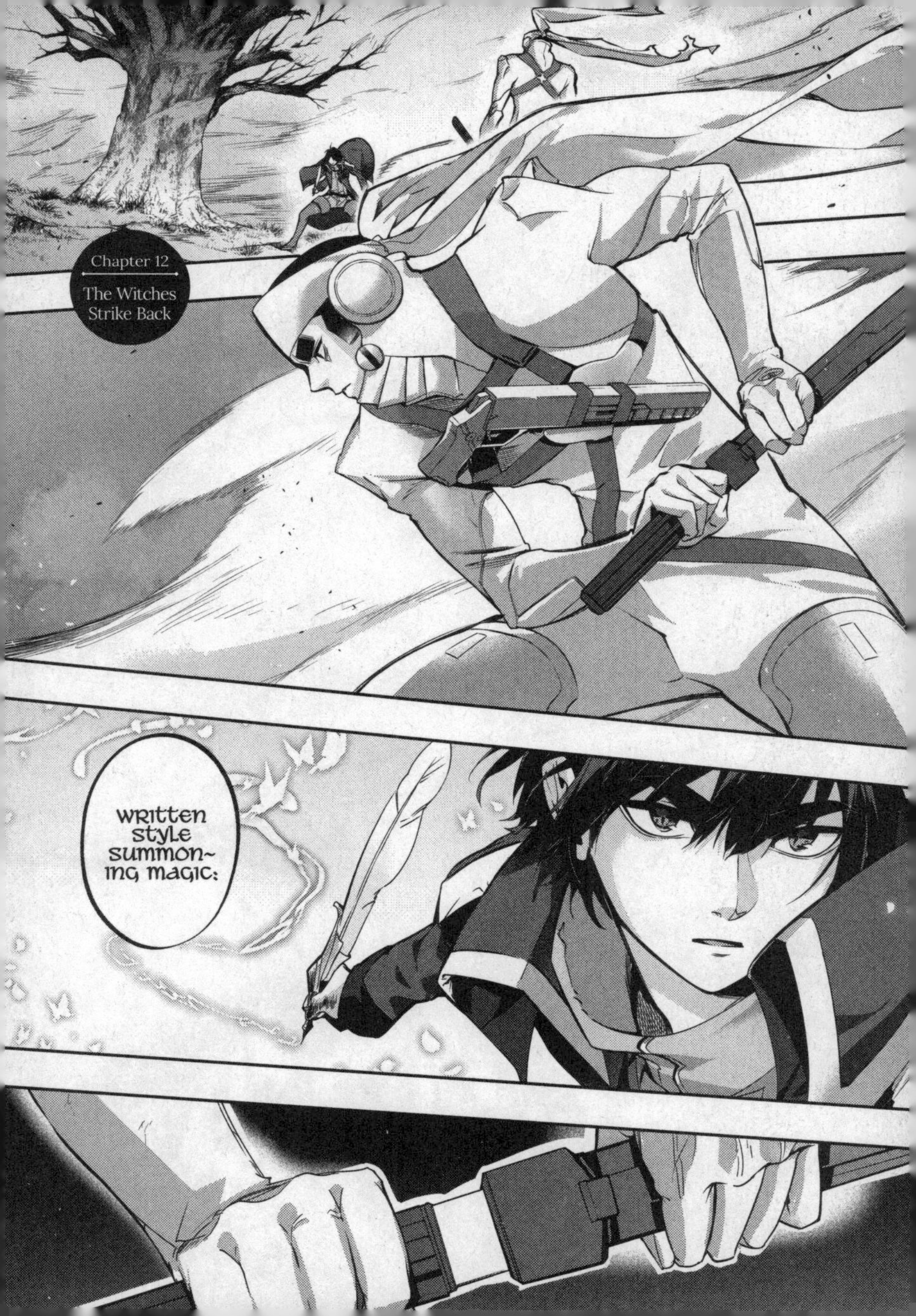
Chapter 12
The Witches Strike Back
Written style summon-ing magic:

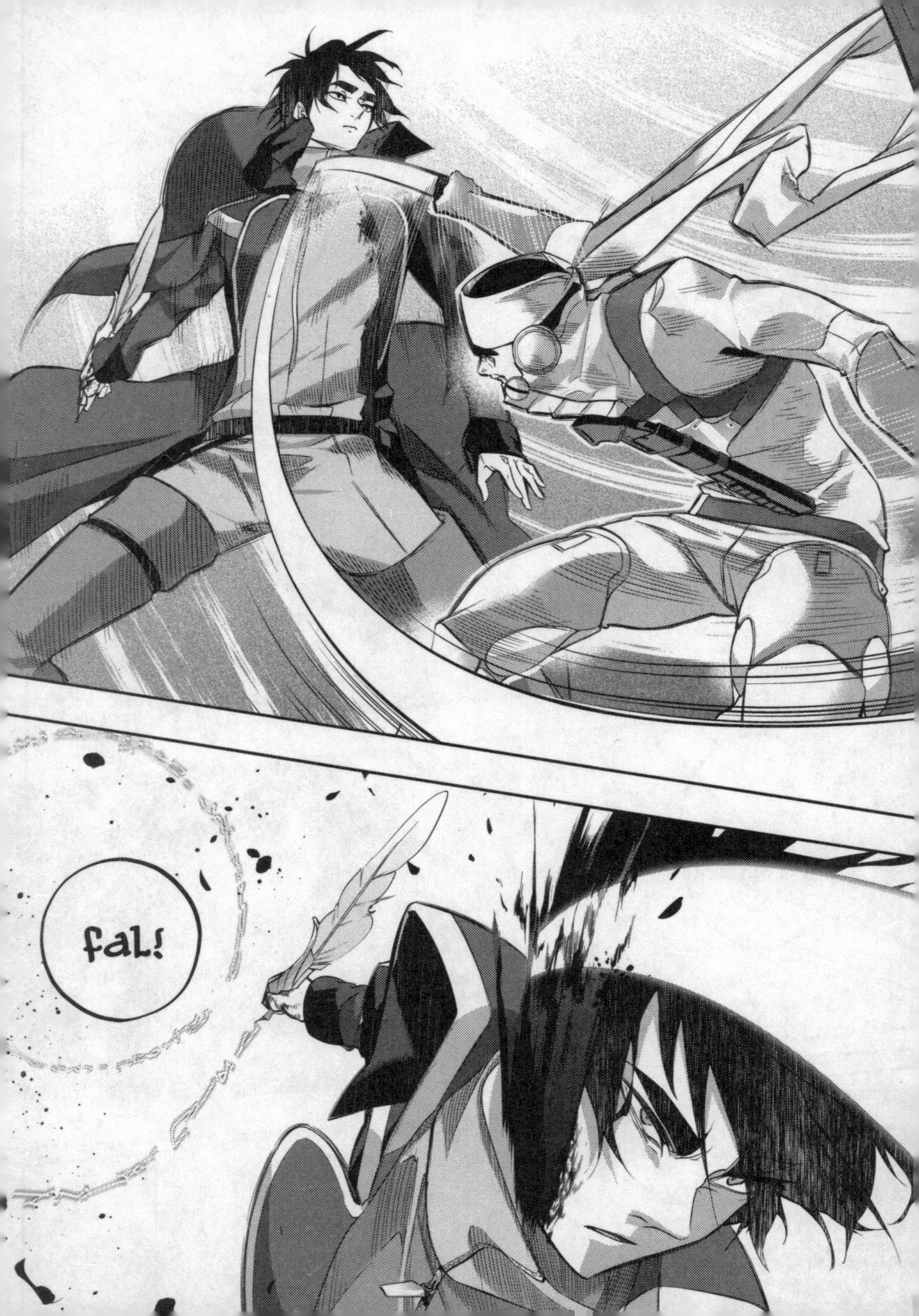
fal!

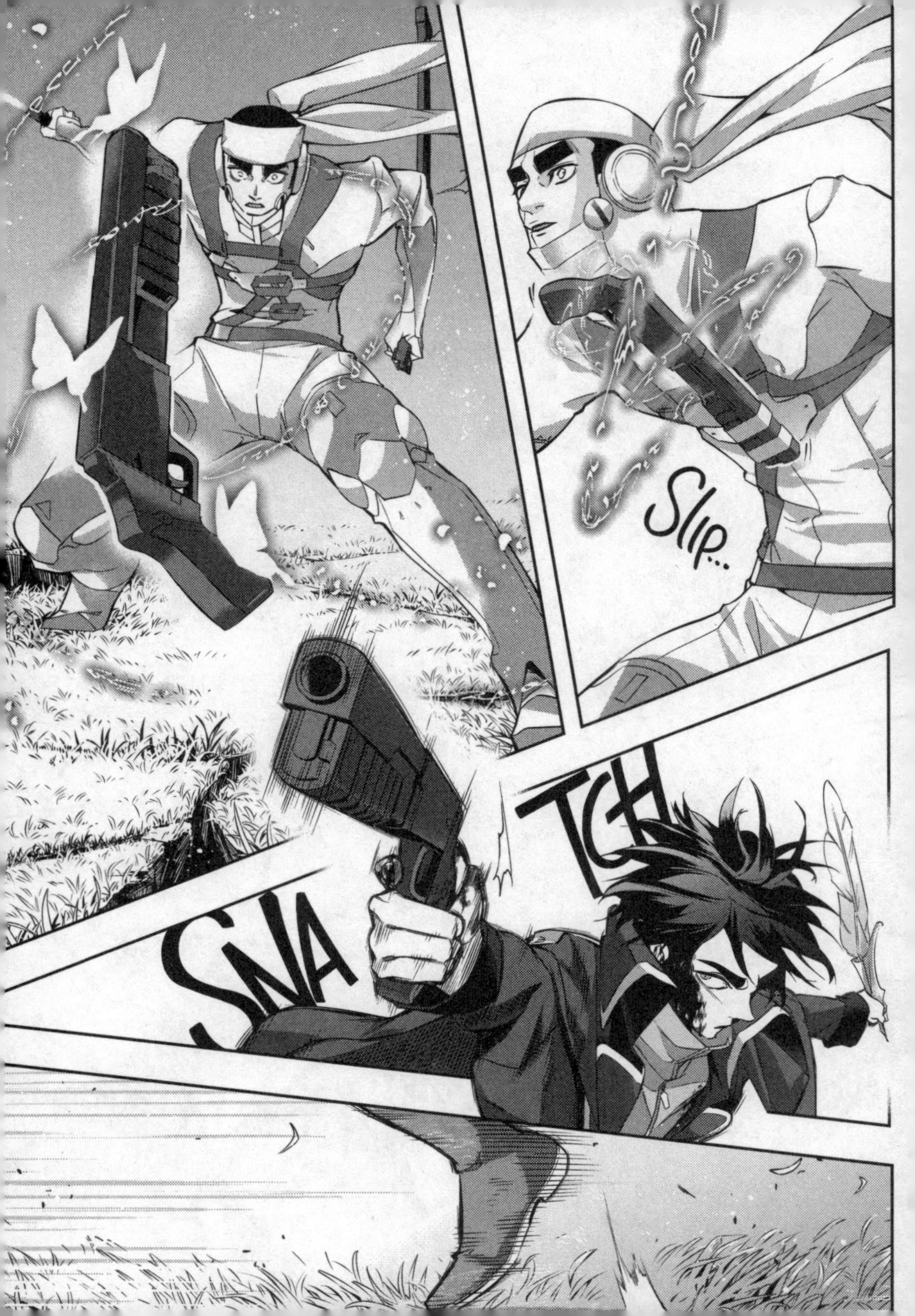
SLIP...
SNATCH

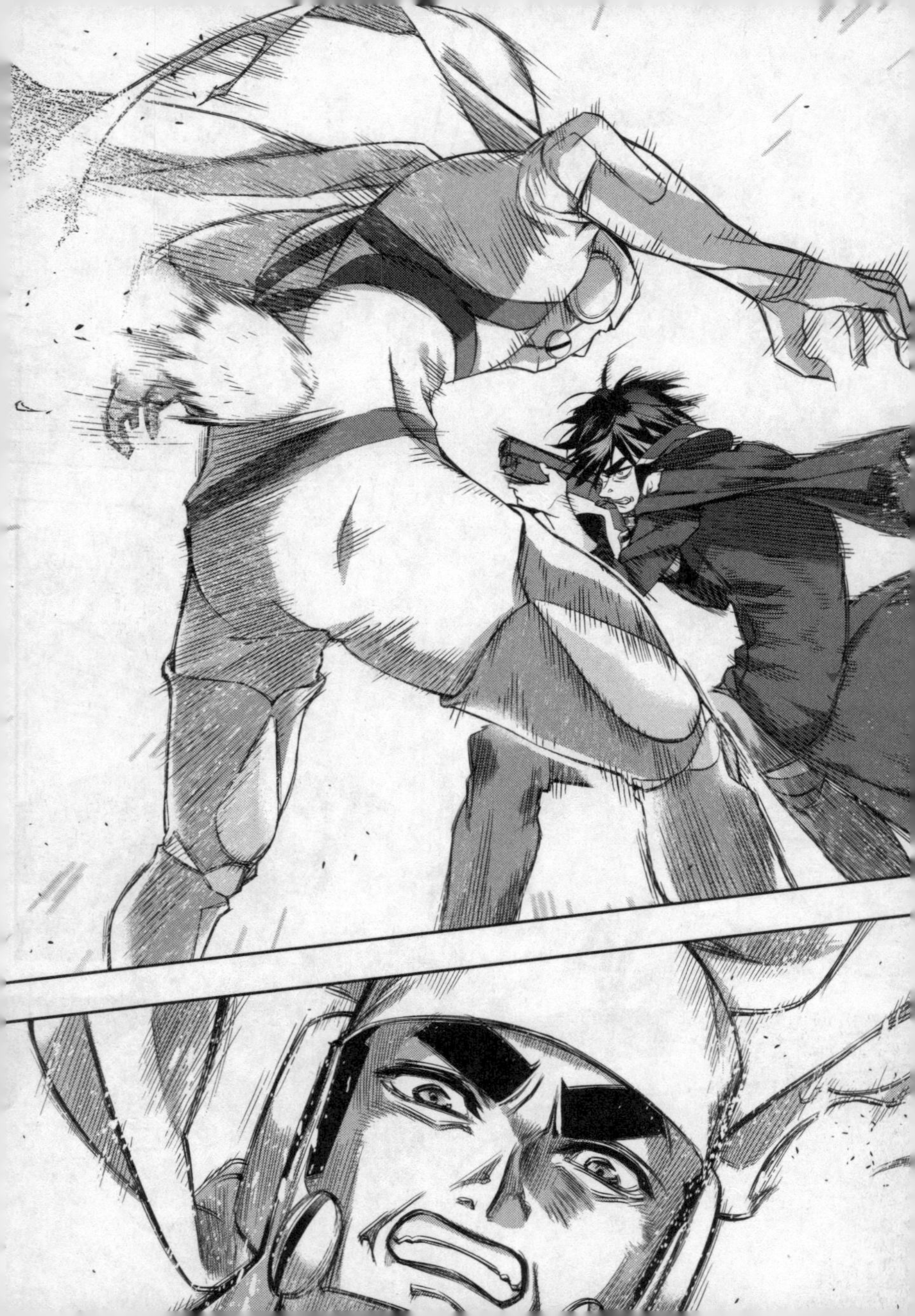

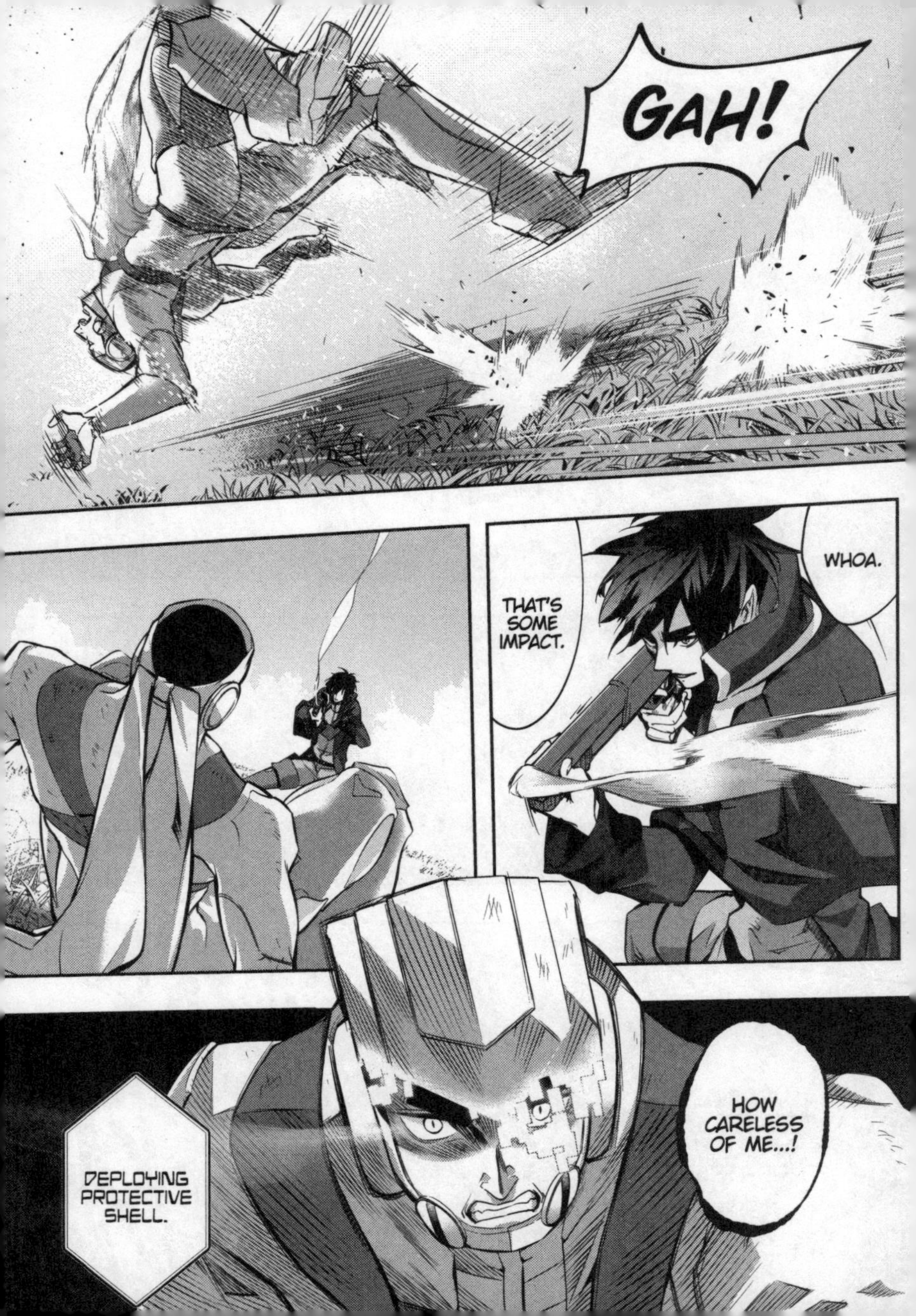
GAH!
WHOA.
THAT'S SOME IMPACT.
HOW CARELESS OF ME...!
DEPLOYING PROTECTIVE SHELL.

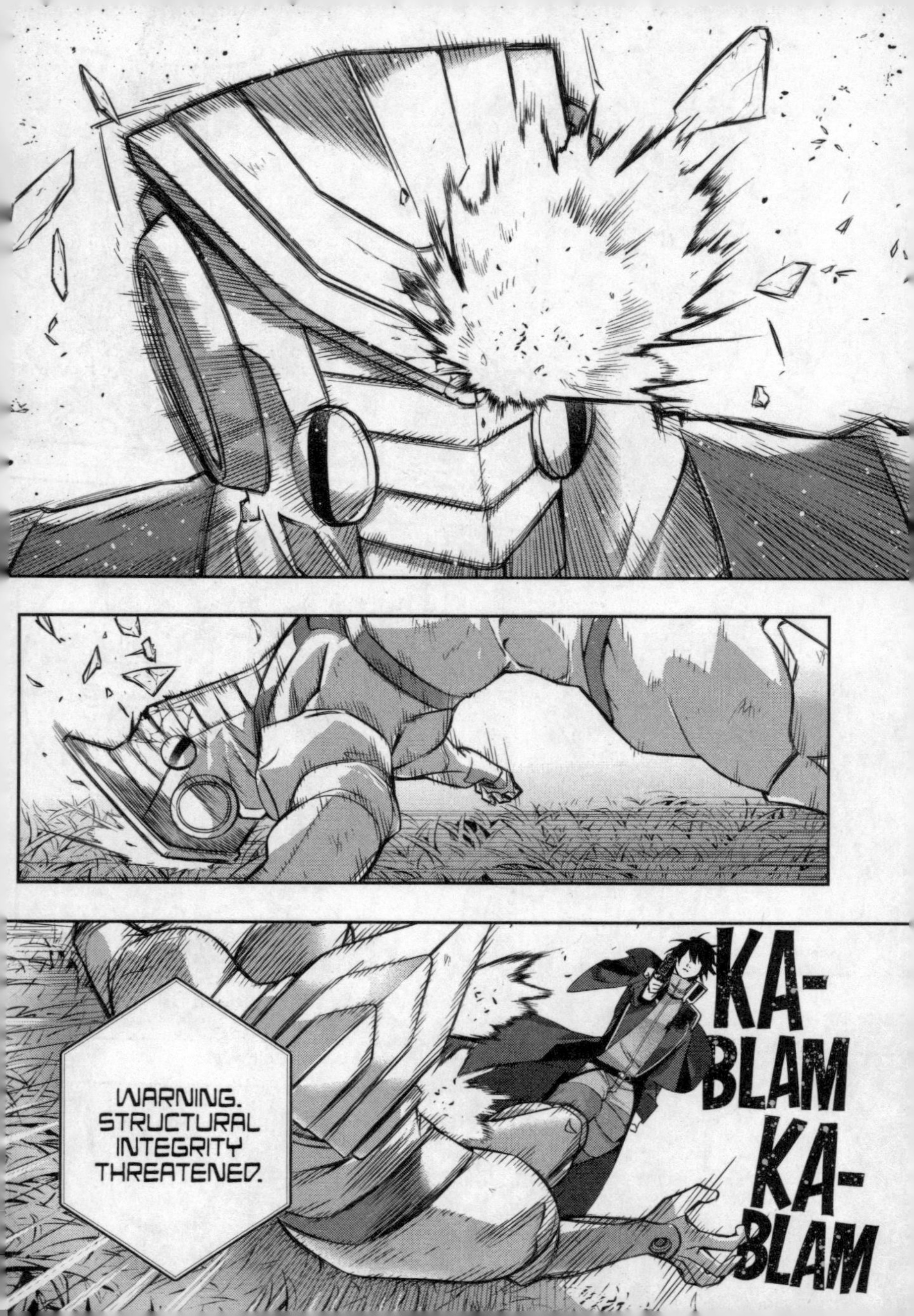
KA-BLAM KA-BLAM
WARNING. STRUCTURAL INTEGRITY THREATENED.

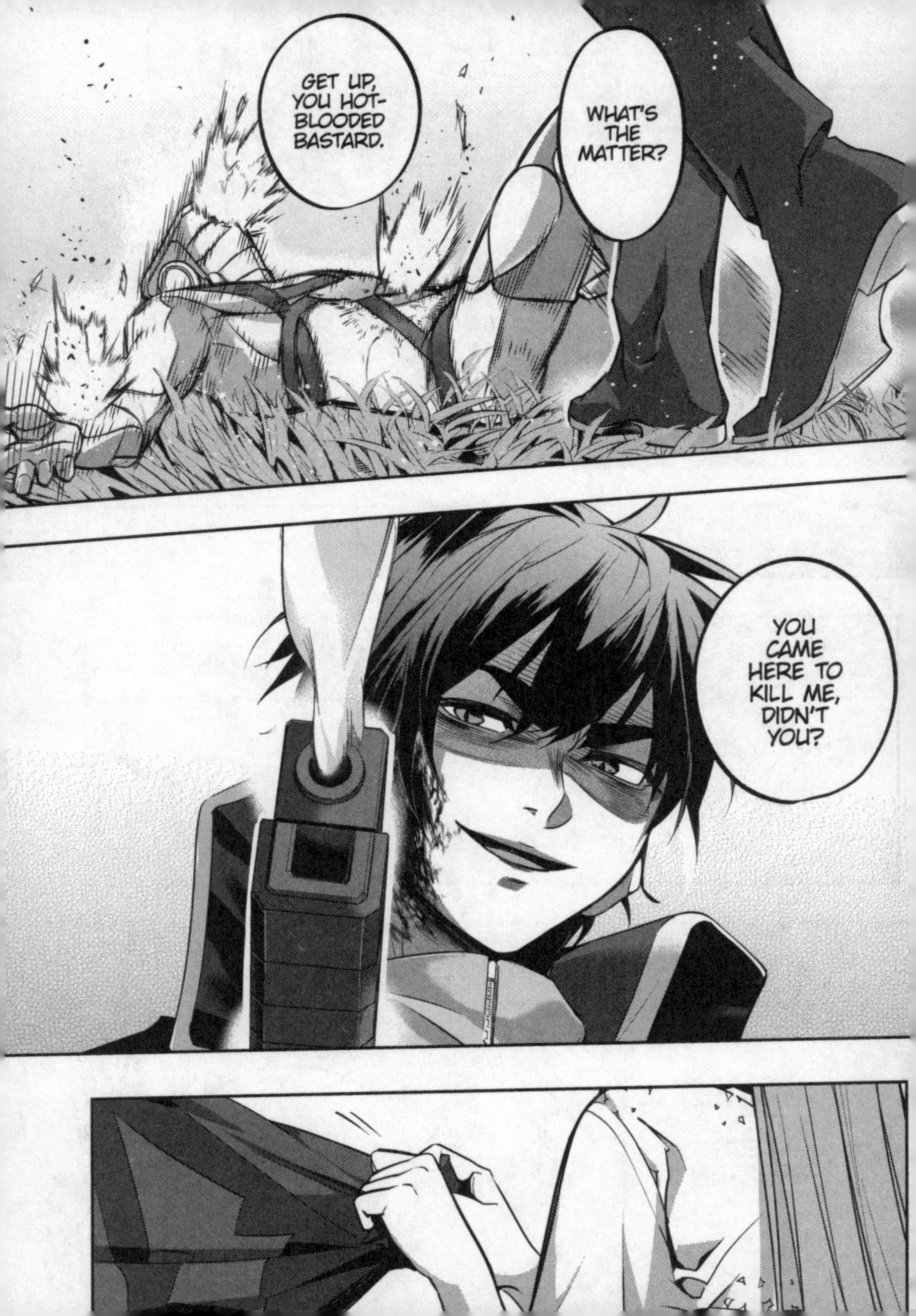
WHAT'S THE MATTER?
GET UP, YOU HOT-BLOODED BASTARD.
YOU CAME HERE TO KILL ME, DIDN'T YOU?

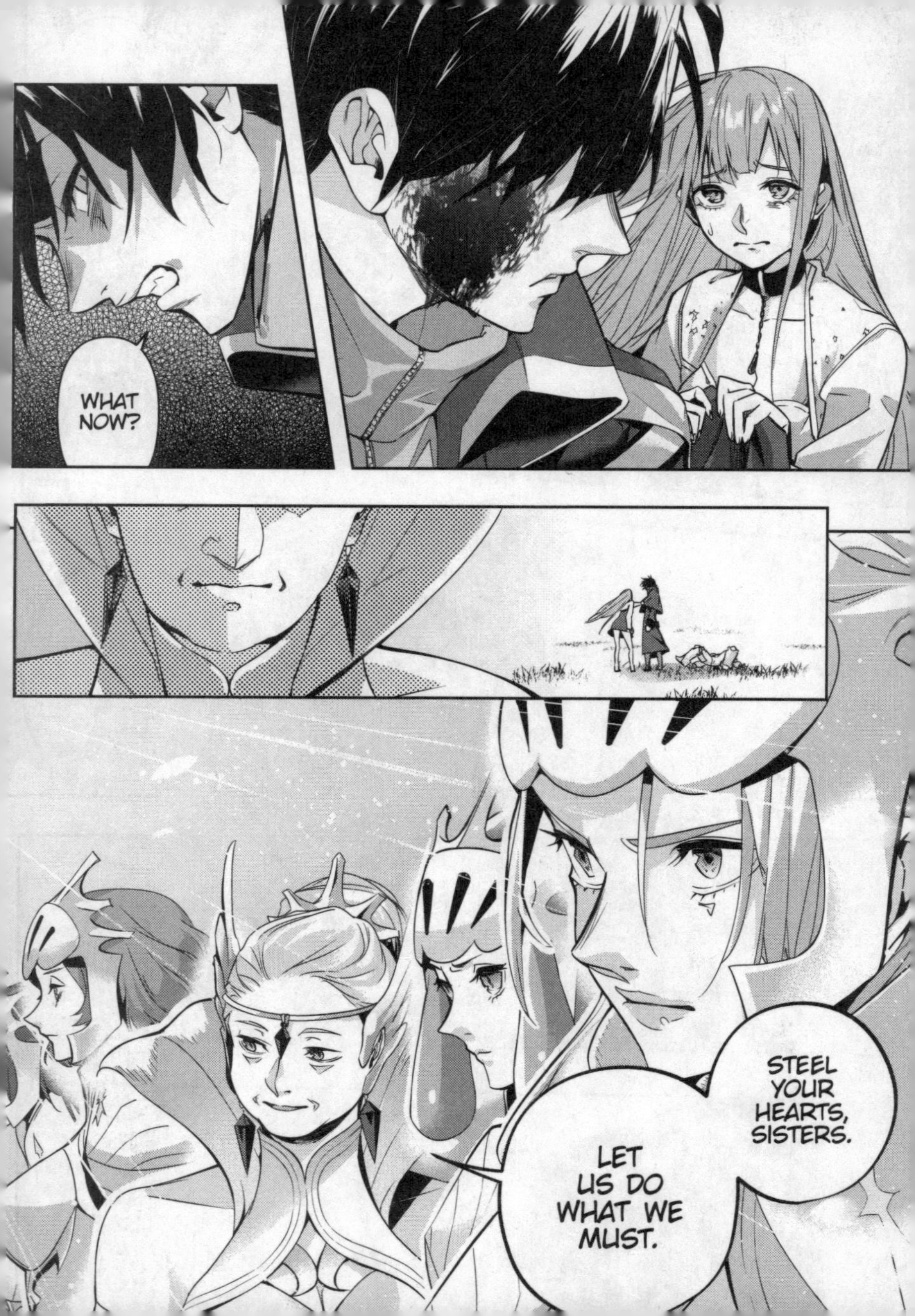
WHAT NOW?
STEEL YOUR HEARTS, SISTERS.
LET US DO WHAT WE MUST.

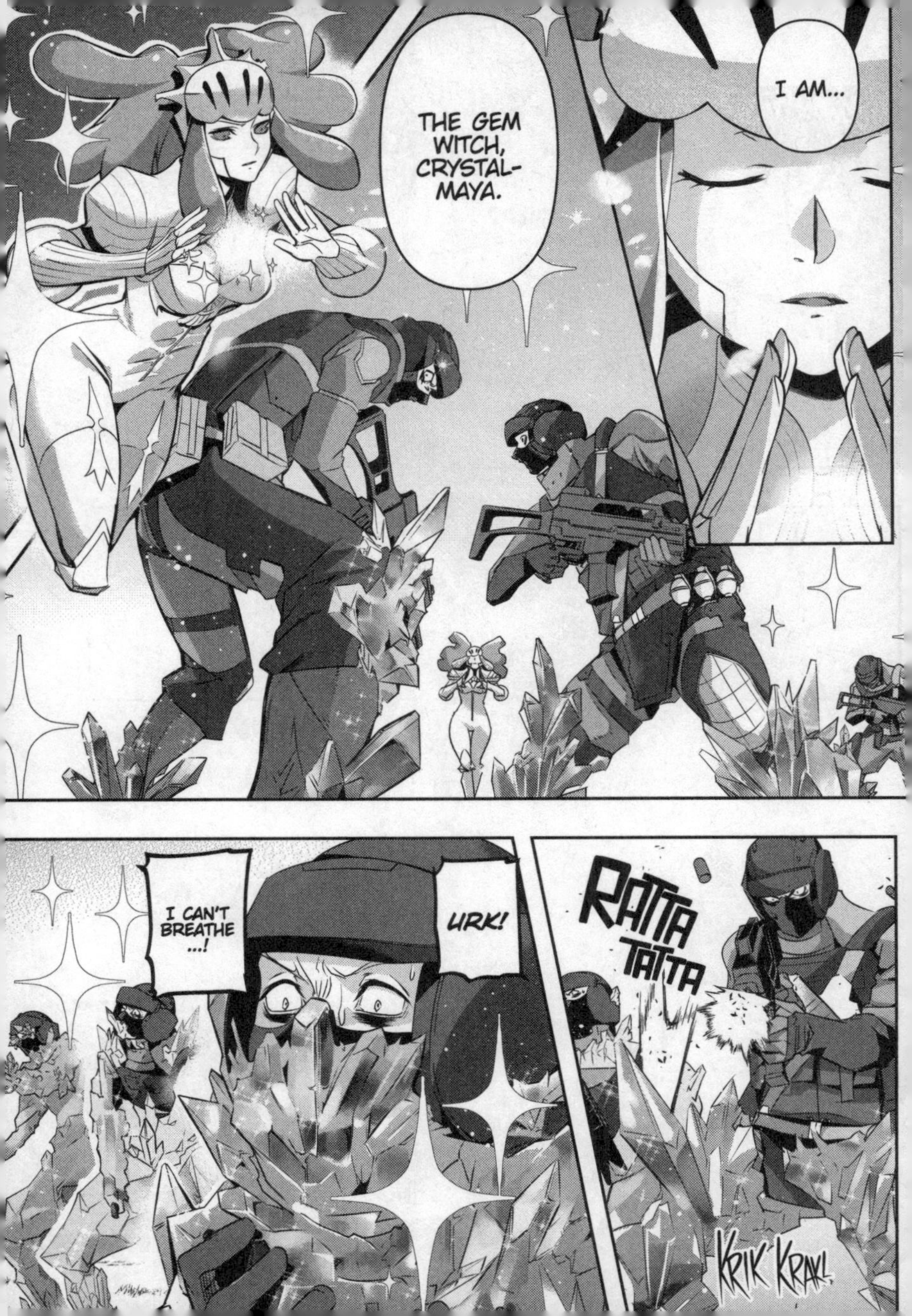
I AM...
THE GEM WITCH, CRYSTAL-MAYA.
RATTA TATTA
KRIK KRAKL
URK!
I CAN'T BREATHE ...!

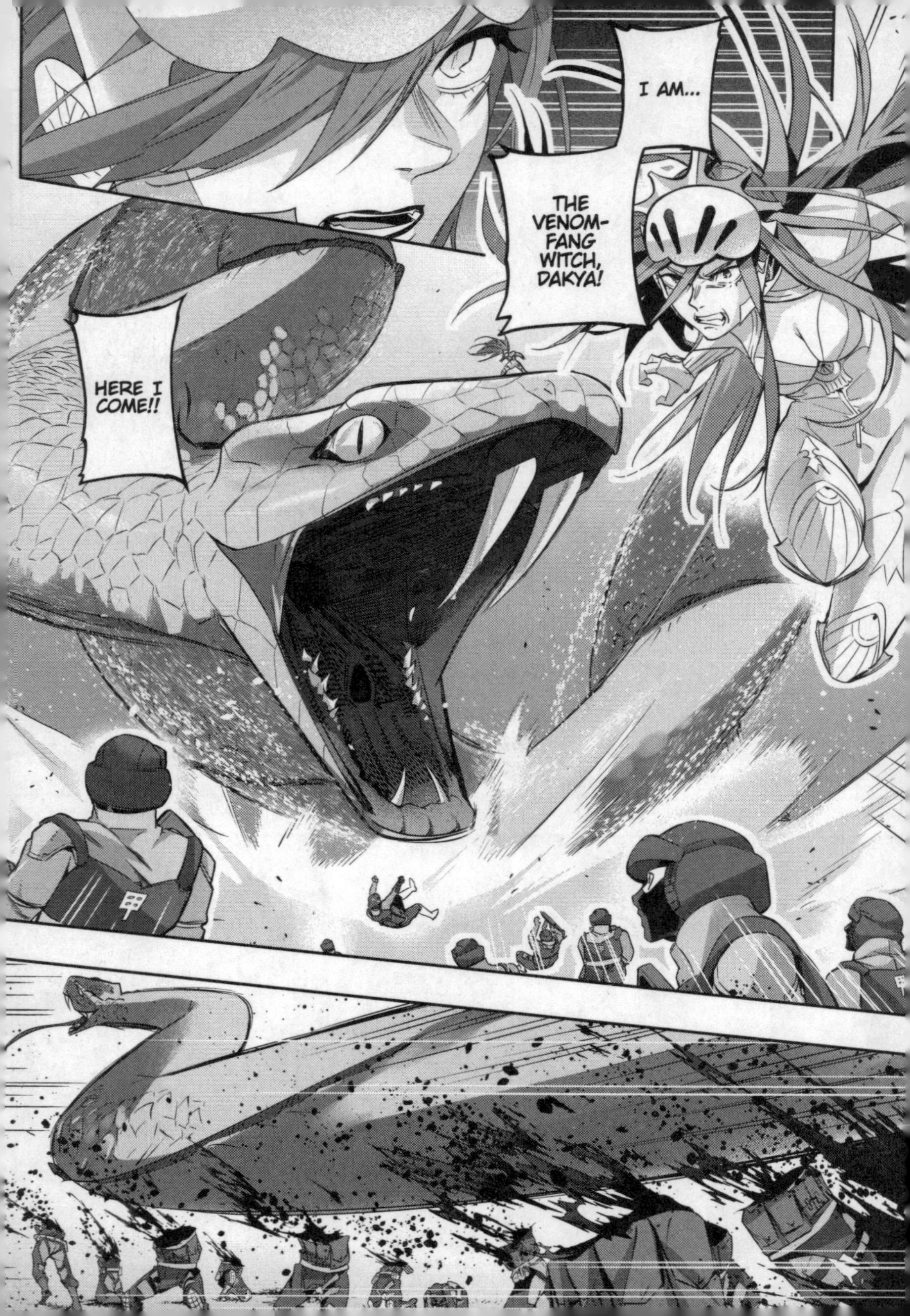
I AM...
THE VENOM-FANG WITCH, DAKYA!
HERE I COME!!

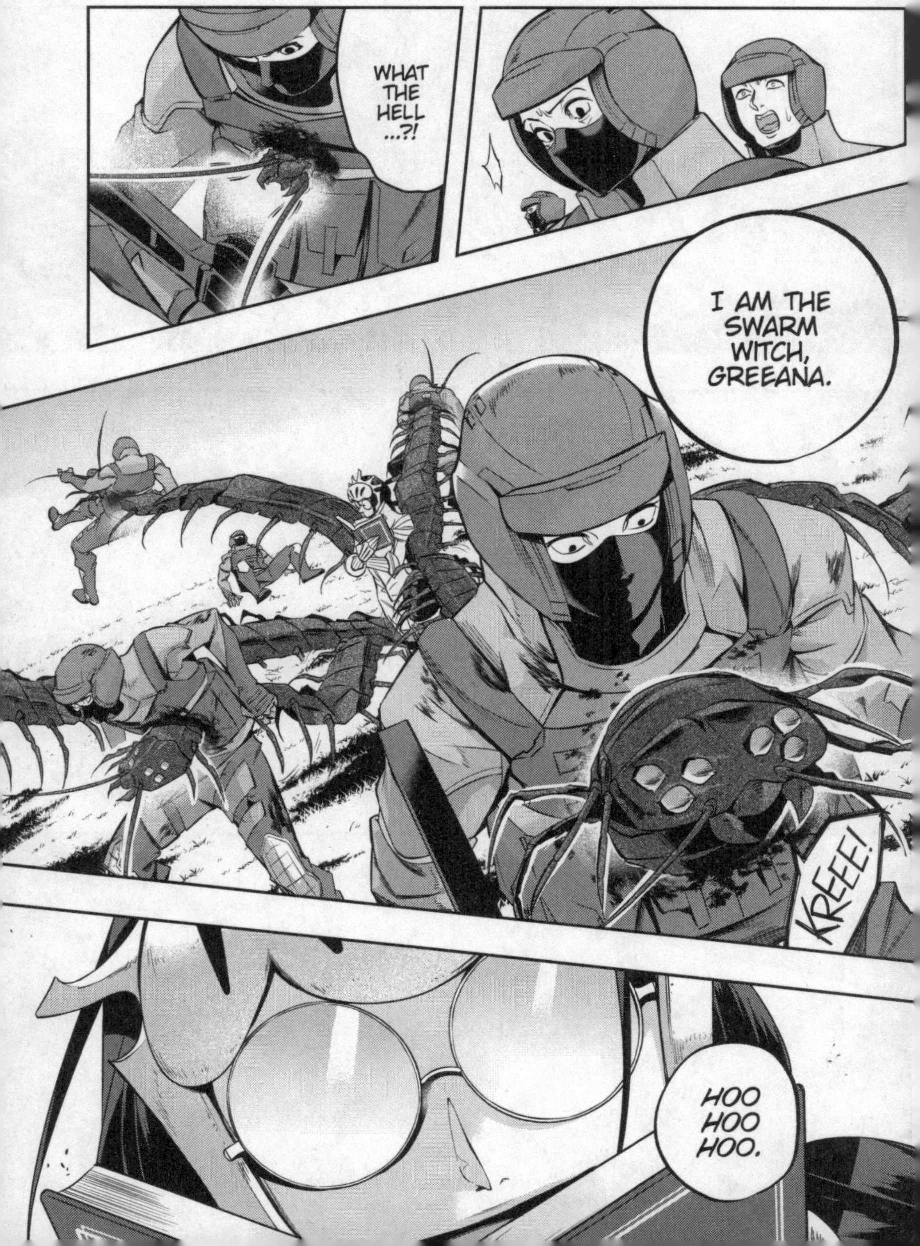
WHAT THE HELL ...?!
I AM THE SWARM WITCH, GREEANA.
KREEE!
HOO HOO HOO.

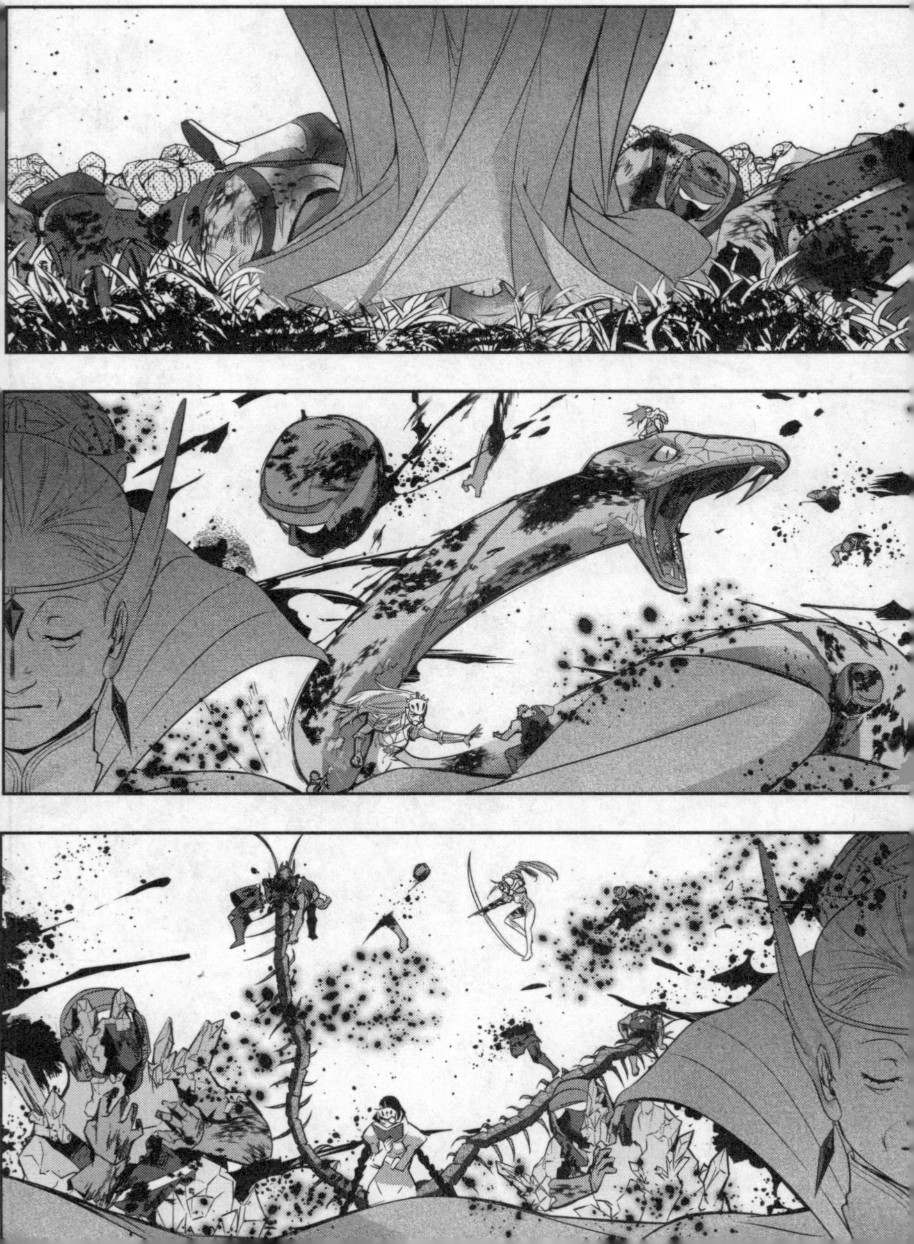

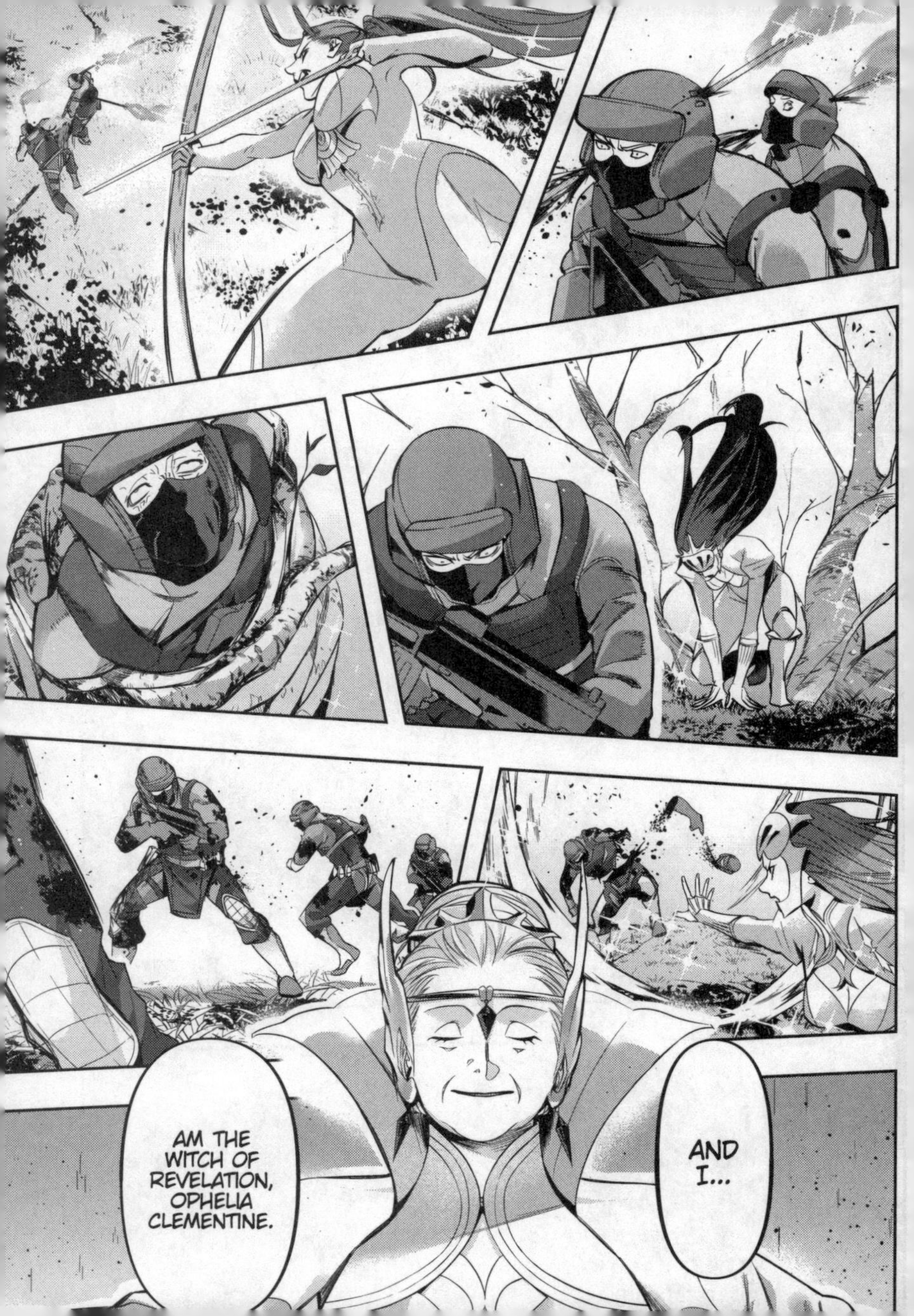
AND I...
AM THE WITCH OF REVELATION, OPHELIA CLEMENTINE.

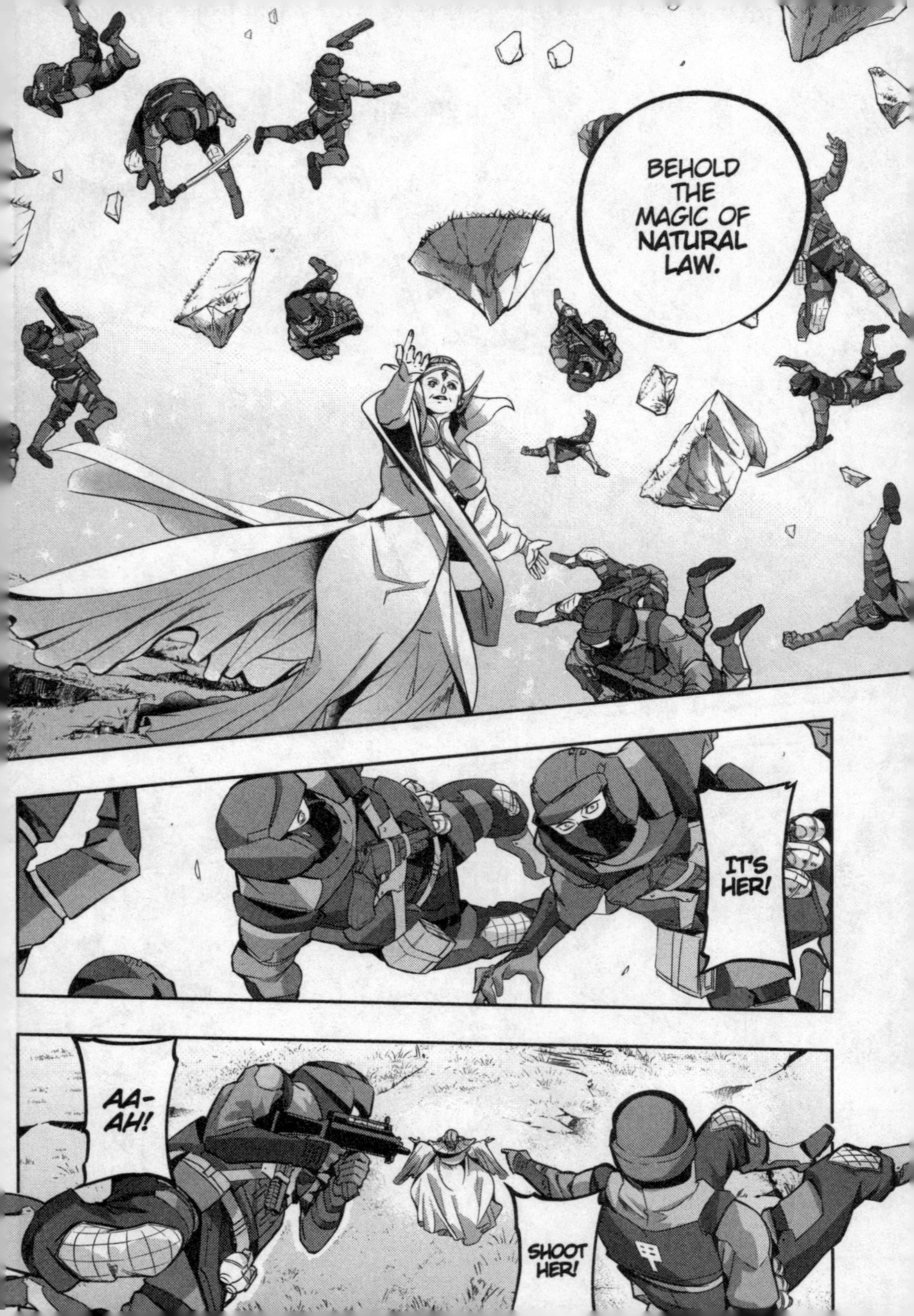
BEHOLD THE MAGIC OF NATURAL LAW.
IT'S HER!
SHOOT HER!
AA-AH!

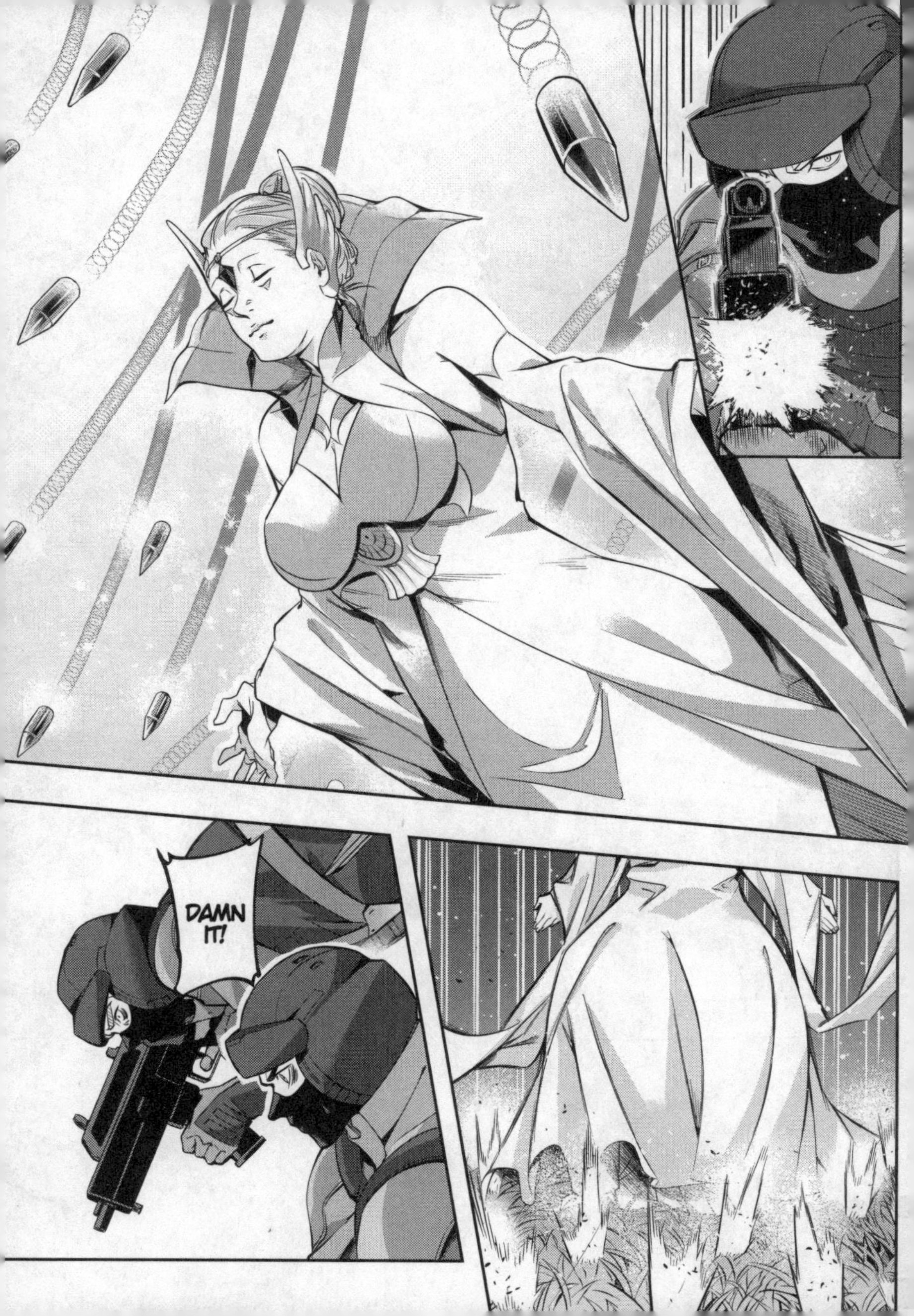
DAMN IT!

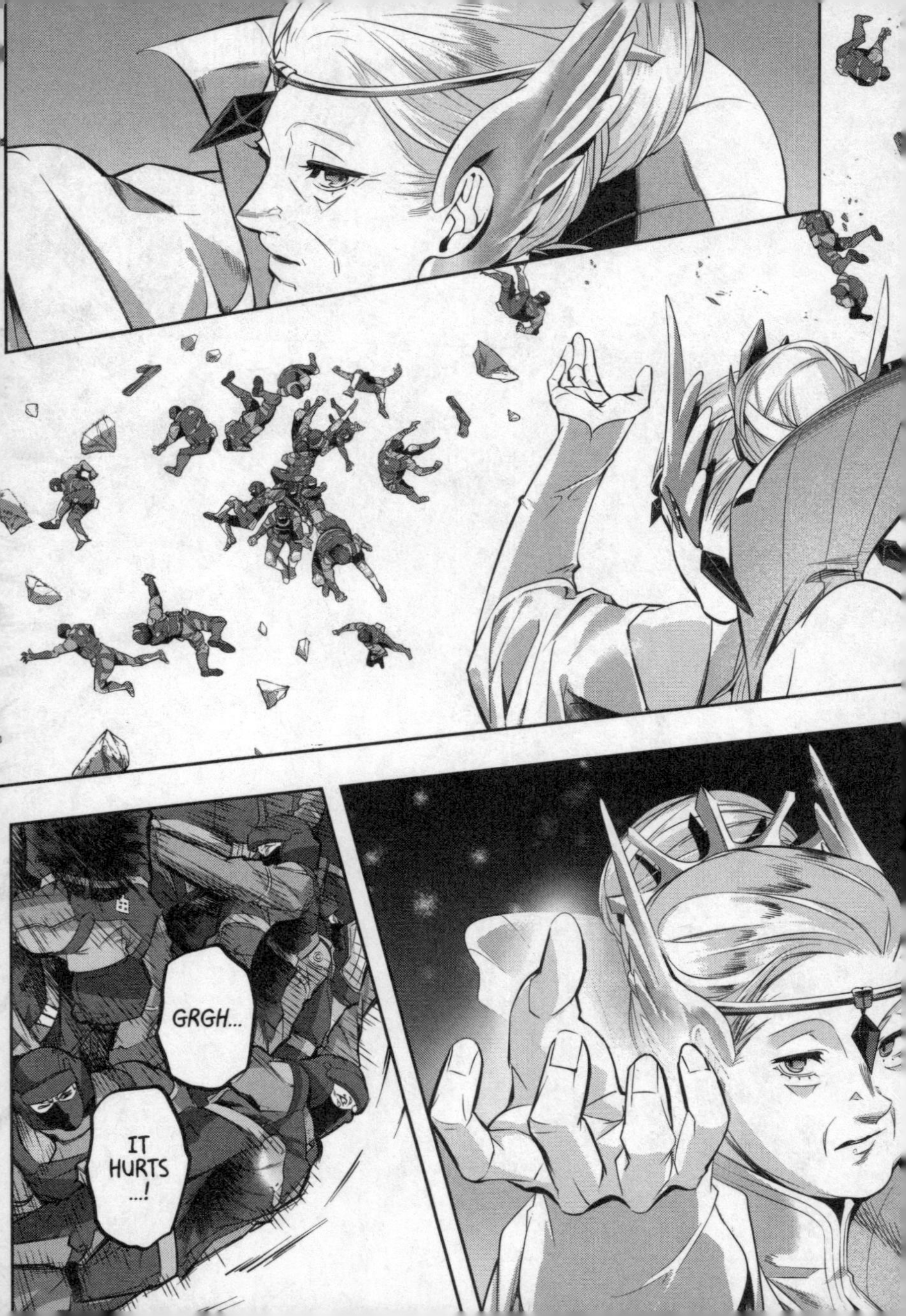
GRGH...
IT HURTS ...!

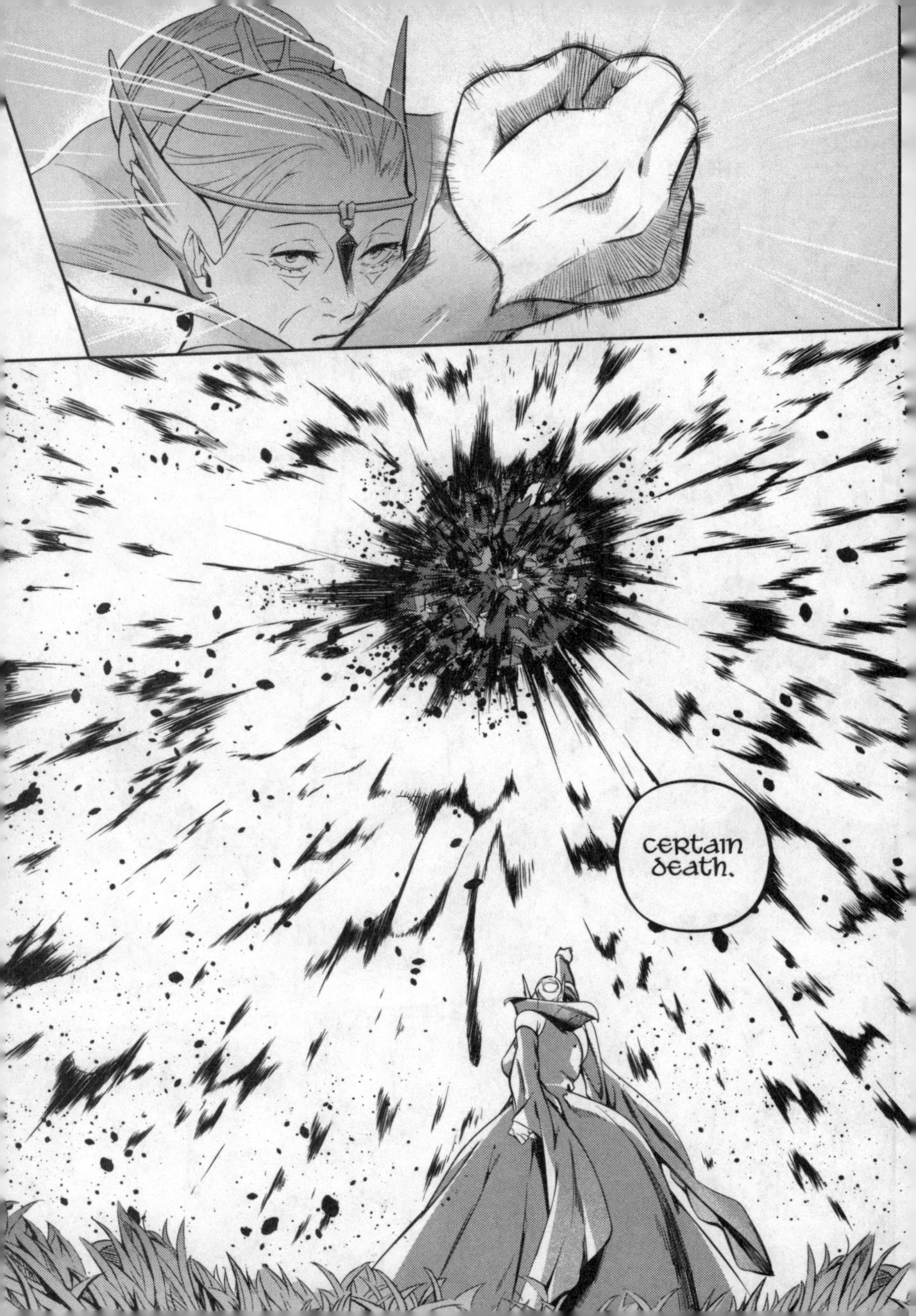
Certain death.

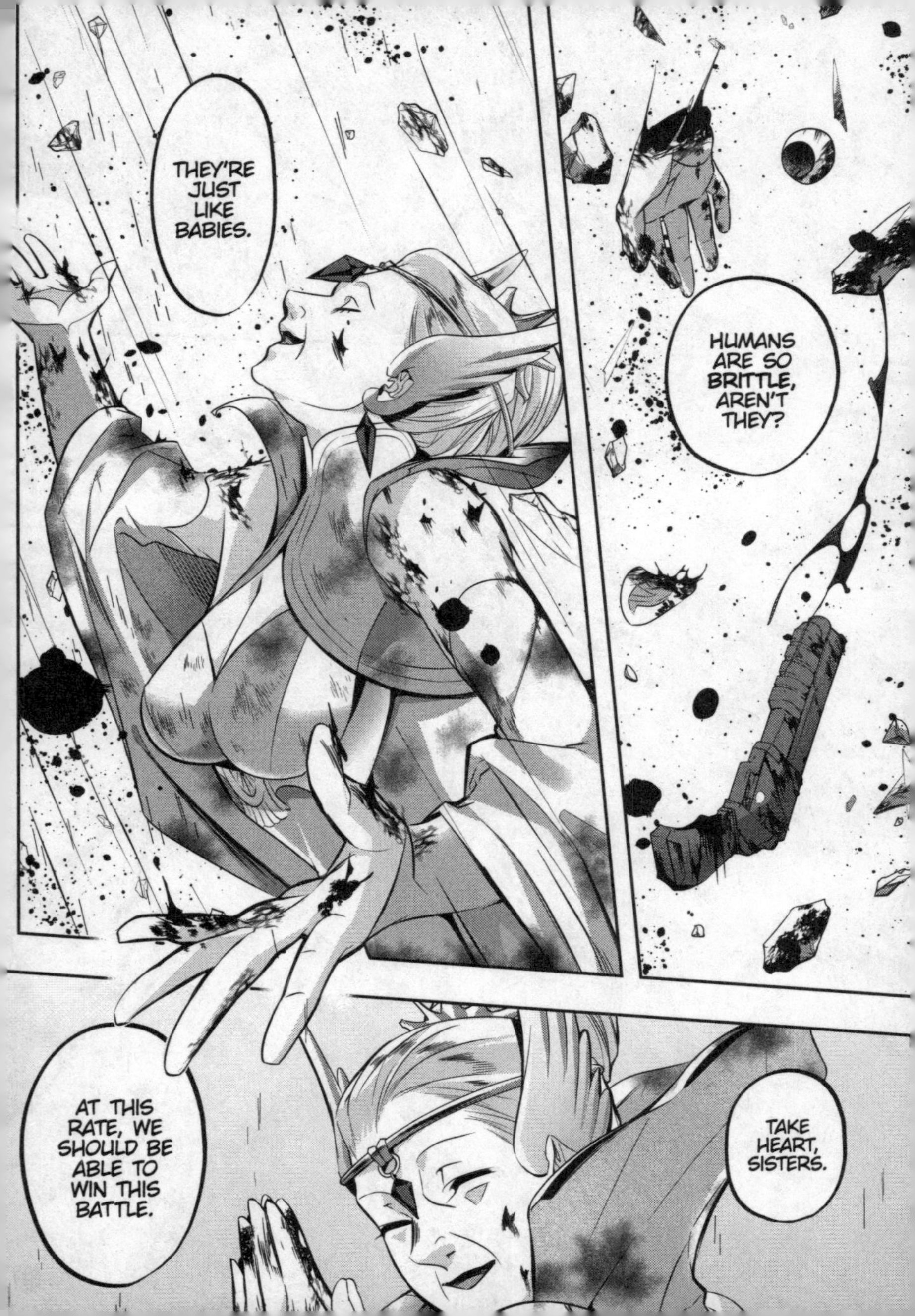
HUMANS ARE SO BRITTLE, AREN'T THEY?
THEY'RE JUST LIKE BABIES.
TAKE HEART, SISTERS.
AT THIS RATE, WE SHOULD BE ABLE TO WIN THIS BATTLE.

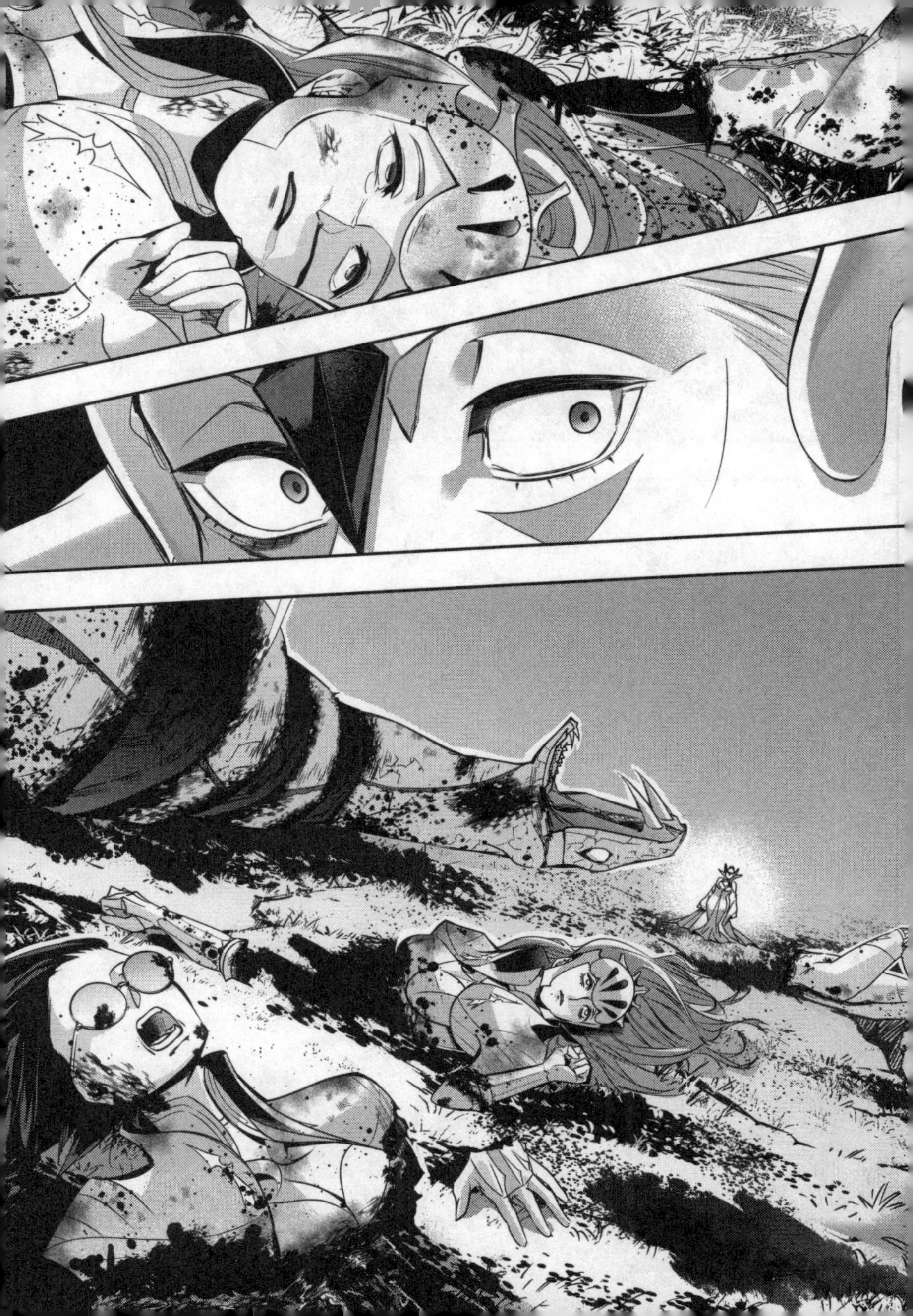

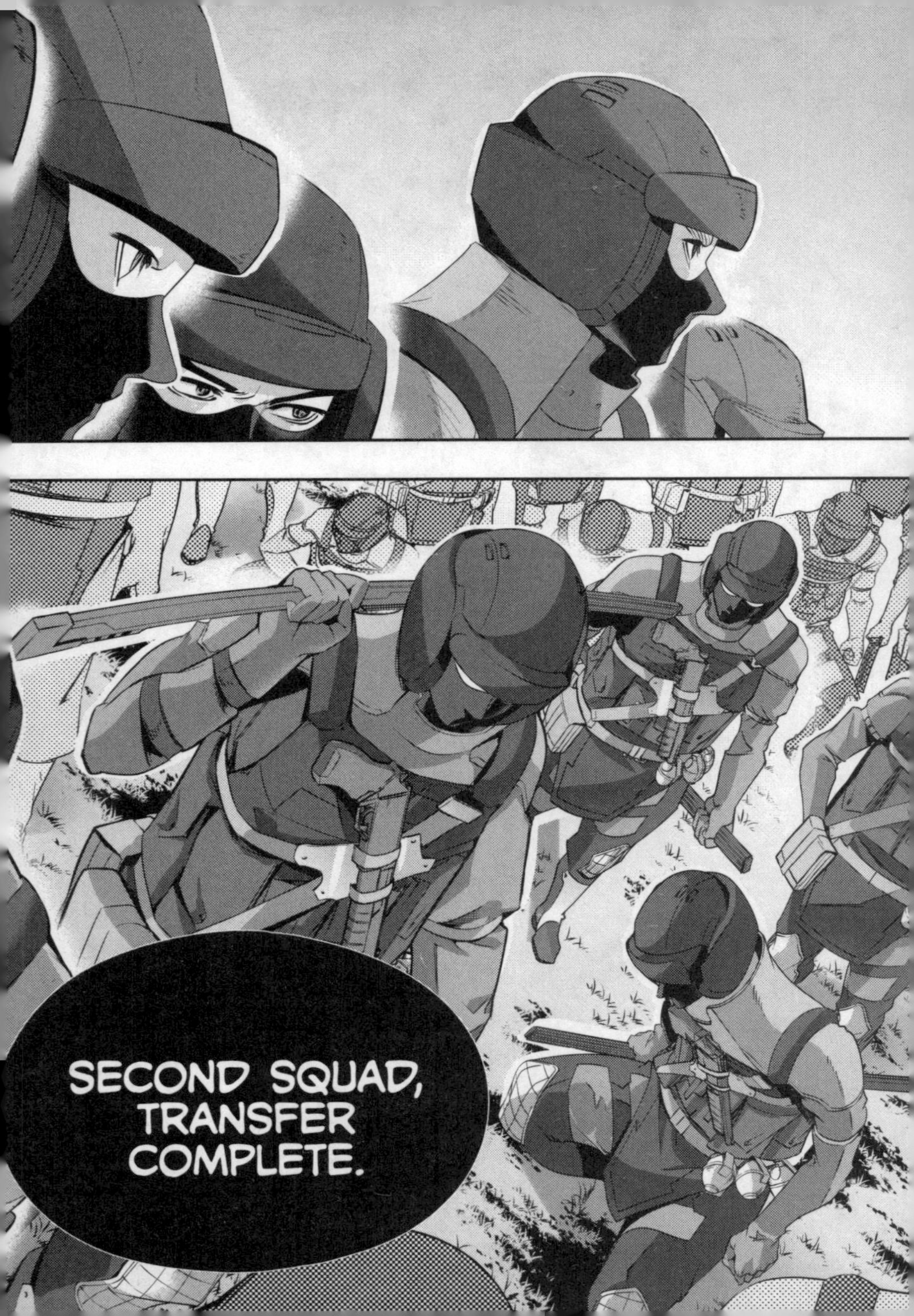
SECOND SQUAD, TRANSFER COMPLETE.

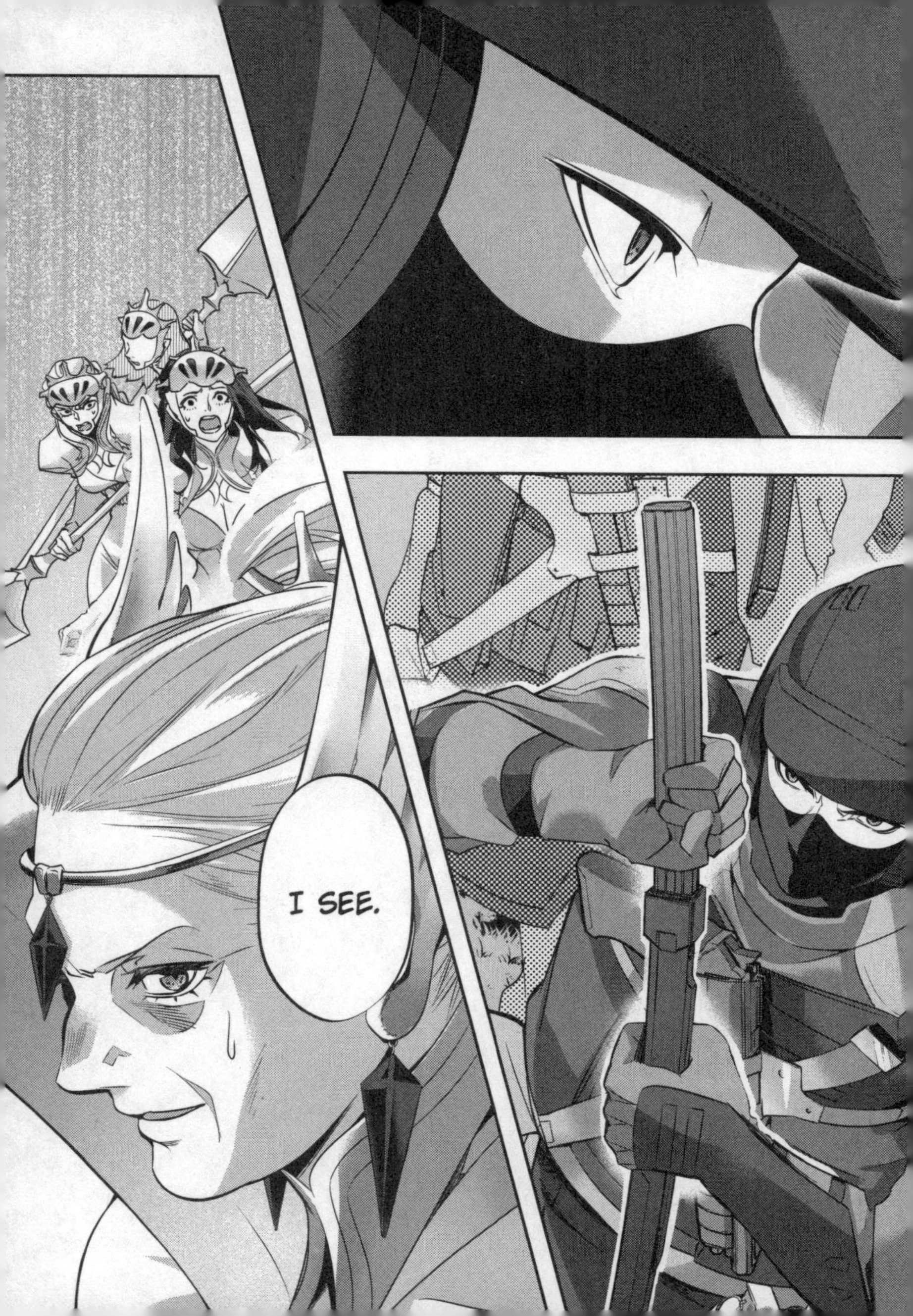
I SEE.

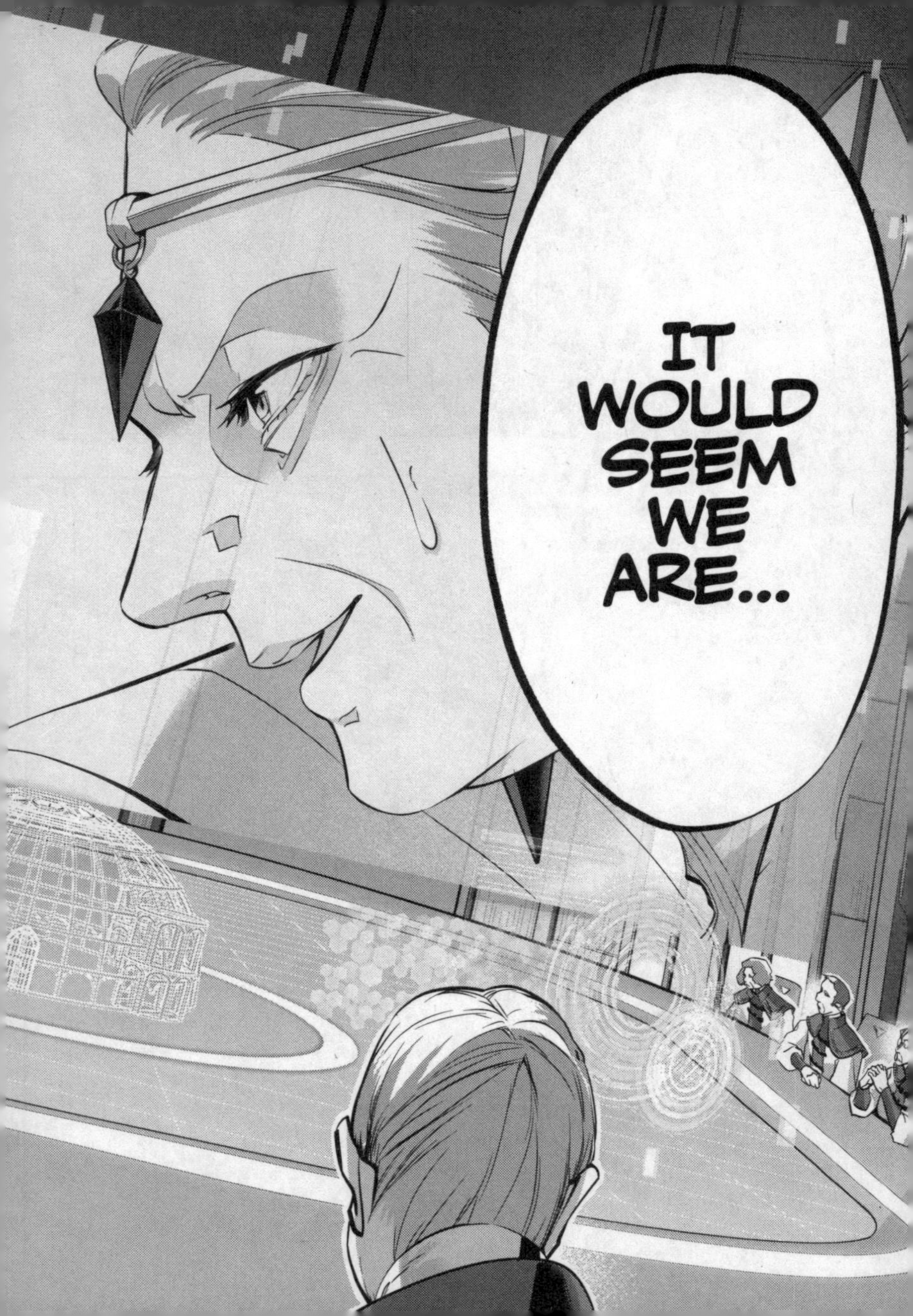
IT WOULD SEEM WE ARE...

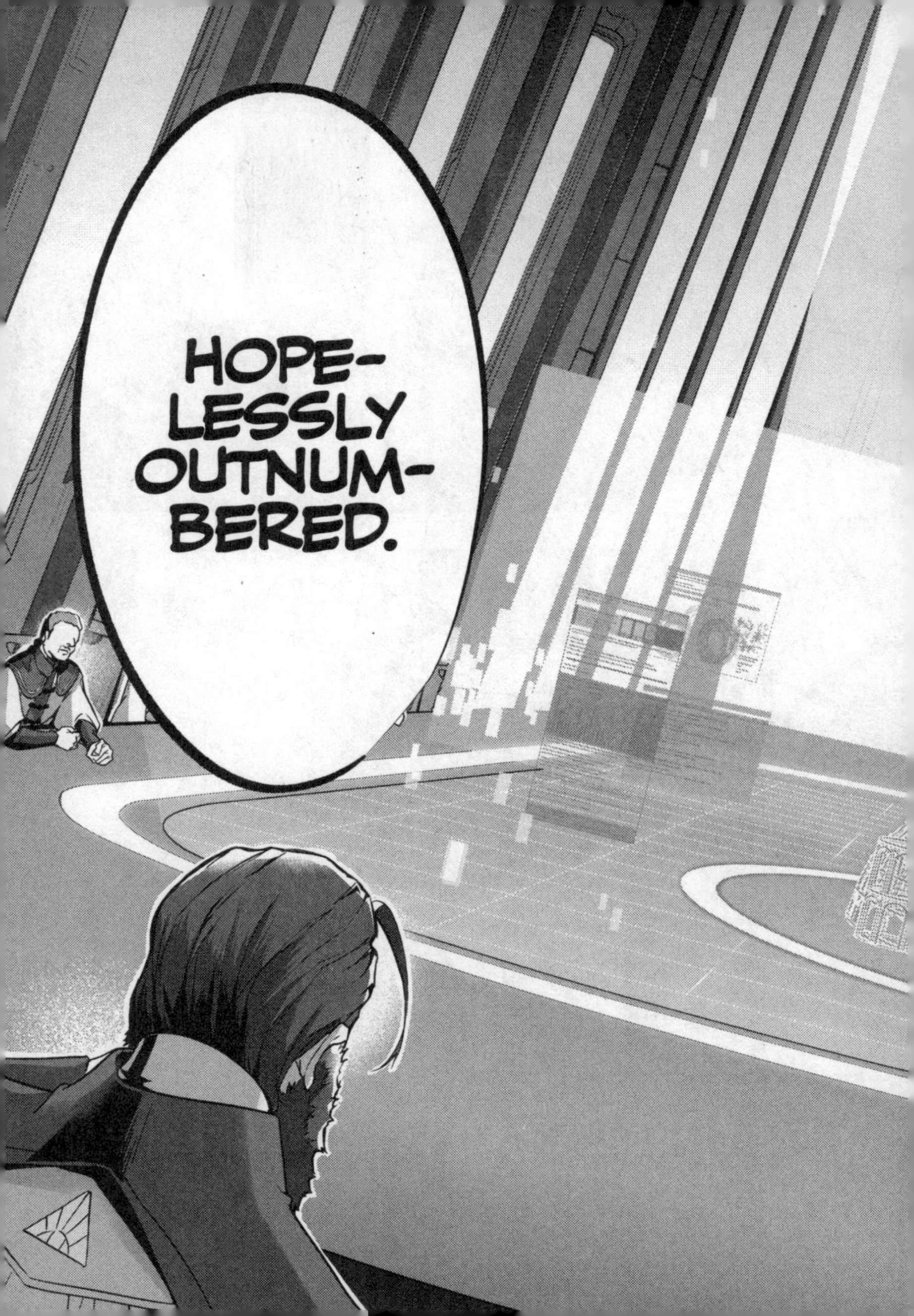
HOPE-LESSLY OUTNUM-BERED.

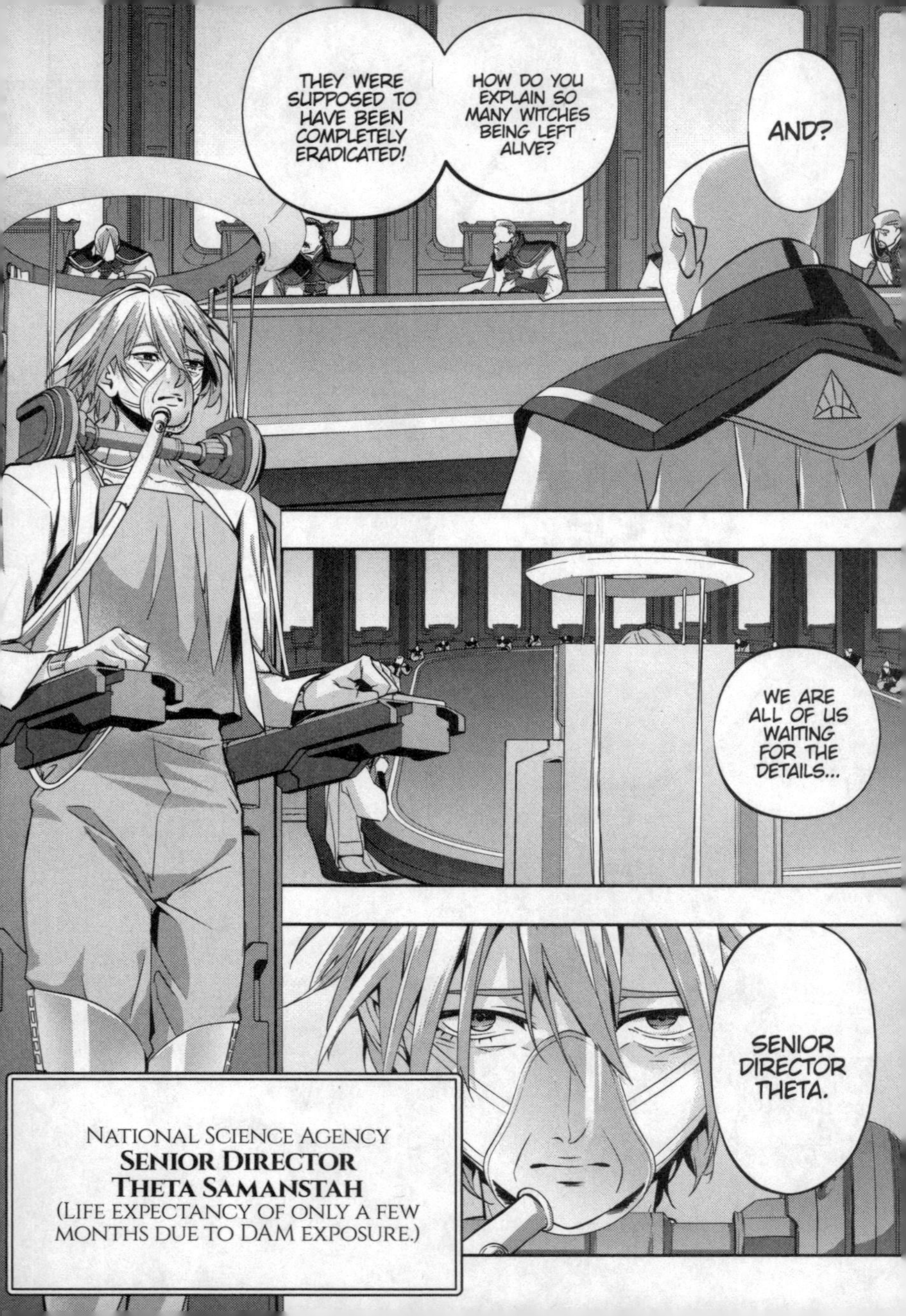
AND?
HOW DO YOU EXPLAIN SO MANY WITCHES BEING LEFT ALIVE?
THEY WERE SUPPOSED TO HAVE BEEN COMPLETELY ERADICATED!
WE ARE ALL OF US WAITING FOR THE DETAILS...
SENIOR DIRECTOR THETA.
NATIONAL SCIENCE AGENCY
SENIOR DIRECTOR
THETA SAMANSTAH
(LIFE EXPECTANCY OF ONLY A FEW MONTHS DUE TO DAM EXPOSURE.)

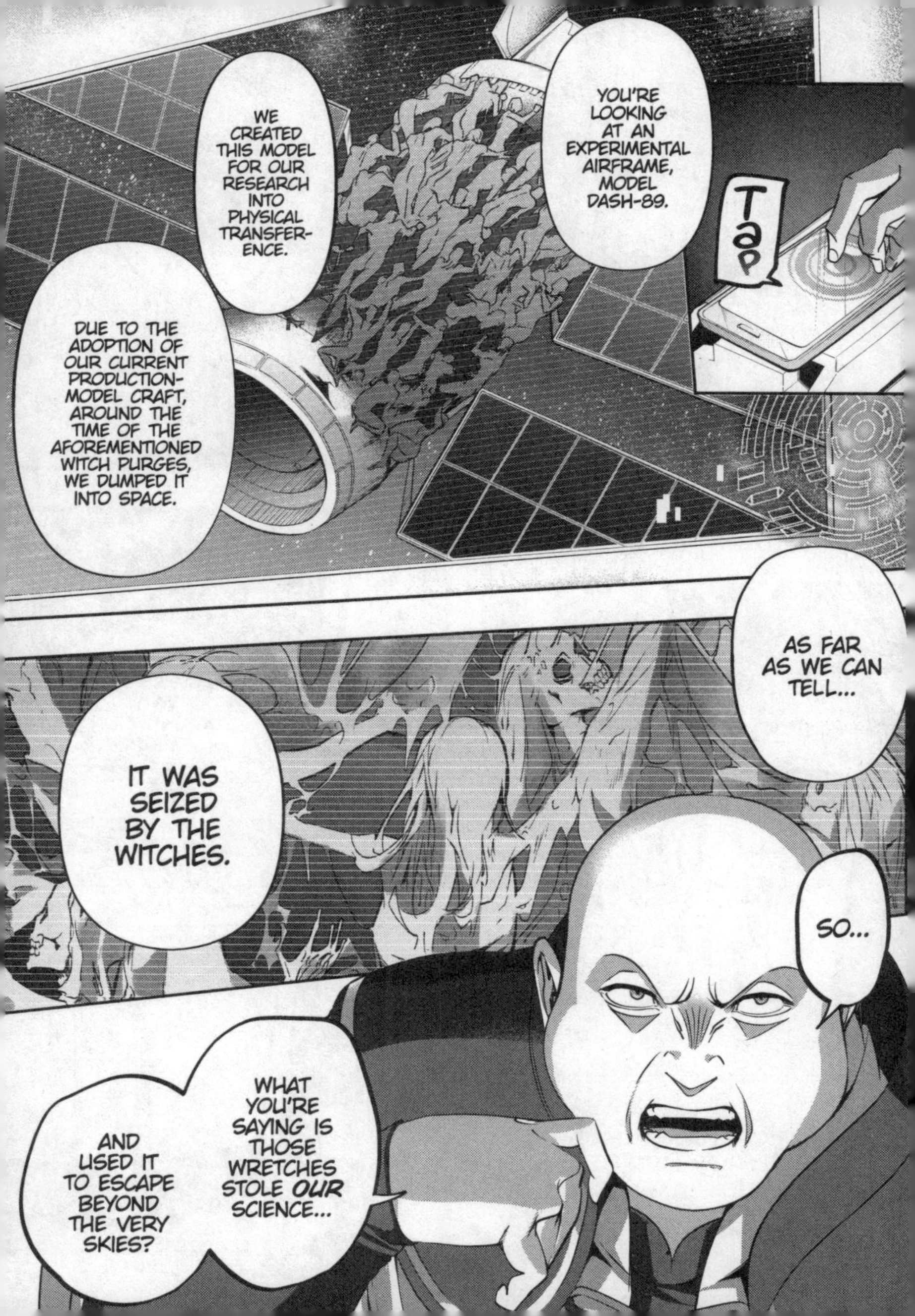
Tap
YOU'RE LOOKING AT AN EXPERIMENTAL AIRFRAME, MODEL DASH-89.
WE CREATED THIS MODEL FOR OUR RESEARCH INTO PHYSICAL TRANSFERENCE.
DUE TO THE ADOPTION OF OUR CURRENT PRODUCTION-MODEL CRAFT, AROUND THE TIME OF THE AFOREMENTIONED WITCH PURGES, WE DUMPED IT INTO SPACE.
AS FAR AS WE CAN TELL...
IT WAS SEIZED BY THE WITCHES.
SO...
WHAT YOU'RE SAYING IS THOSE WRETCHES STOLE *OUR* SCIENCE...
AND USED IT TO ESCAPE BEYOND THE VERY SKIES?

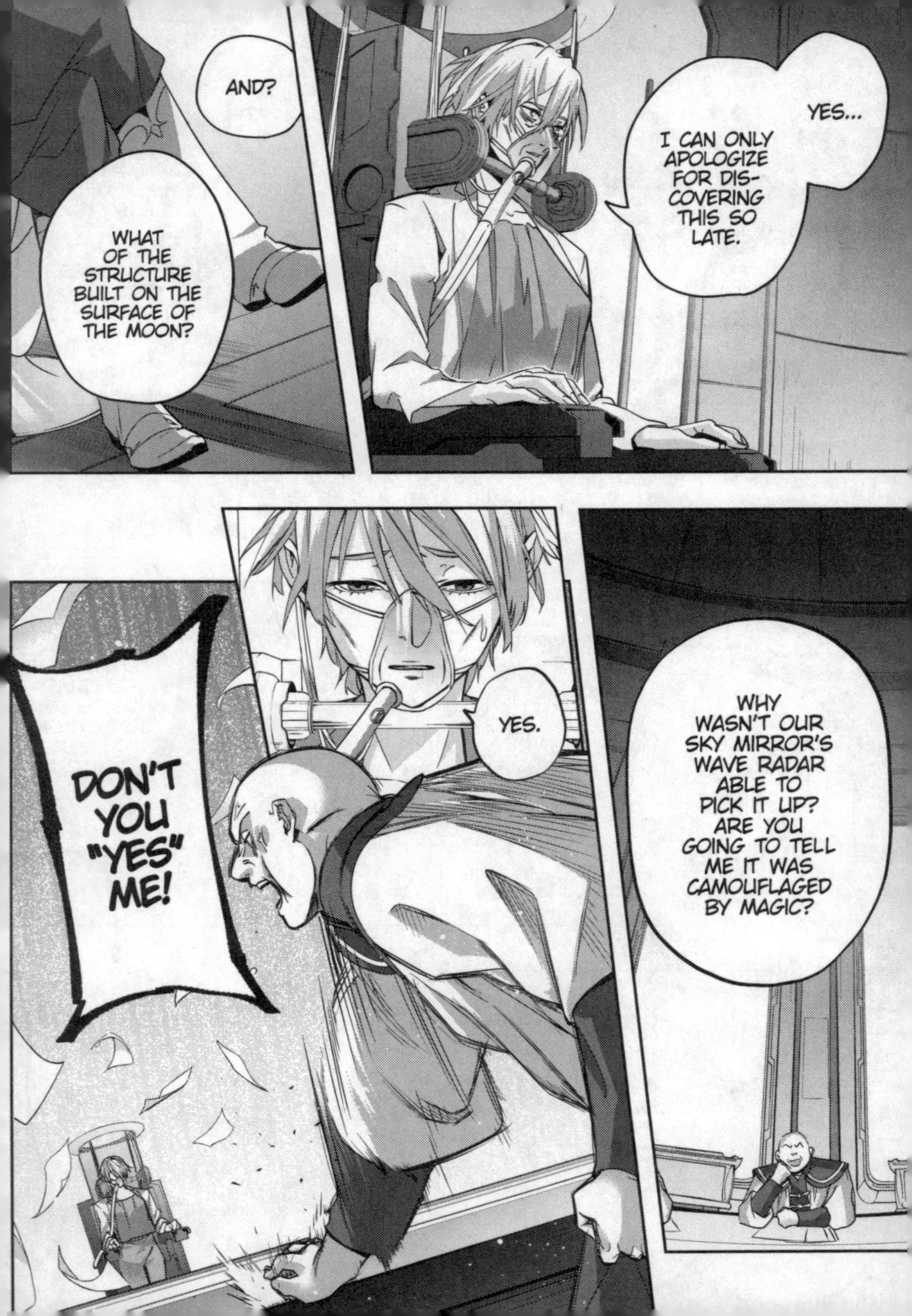
YES...
I CAN ONLY APOLOGIZE FOR DIS-COVERING THIS SO LATE.
AND?
WHAT OF THE STRUCTURE BUILT ON THE SURFACE OF THE MOON?
WHY WASN'T OUR SKY MIRROR'S WAVE RADAR ABLE TO PICK IT UP? ARE YOU GOING TO TELL ME IT WAS CAMOUFLAGED BY MAGIC?
YES.
DON'T YOU "YES" ME!

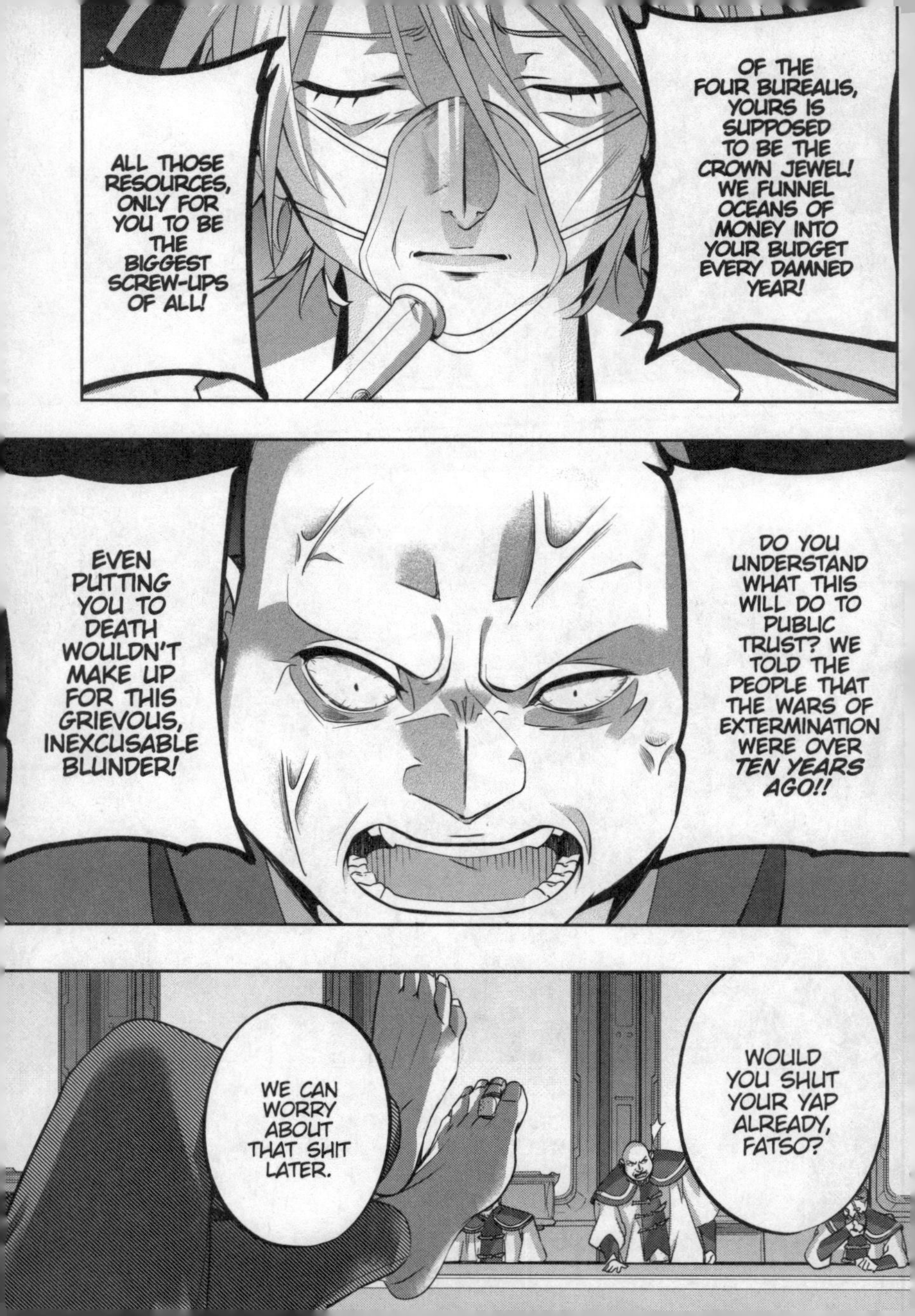
OF THE FOUR BUREAUS, YOURS IS SUPPOSED TO BE THE CROWN JEWEL! WE FUNNEL OCEANS OF MONEY INTO YOUR BUDGET EVERY DAMNED YEAR!
ALL THOSE RESOURCES, ONLY FOR YOU TO BE THE BIGGEST SCREW-UPS OF ALL!
DO YOU UNDERSTAND WHAT THIS WILL DO TO PUBLIC TRUST? WE TOLD THE PEOPLE THAT THE WARS OF EXTERMINATION WERE OVER *TEN YEARS AGO!!*
EVEN PUTTING YOU TO DEATH WOULDN'T MAKE UP FOR THIS GRIEVOUS, INEXCUSABLE BLUNDER!
WOULD YOU SHUT YOUR YAP ALREADY, FATSO?
WE CAN WORRY ABOUT THAT SHIT LATER.

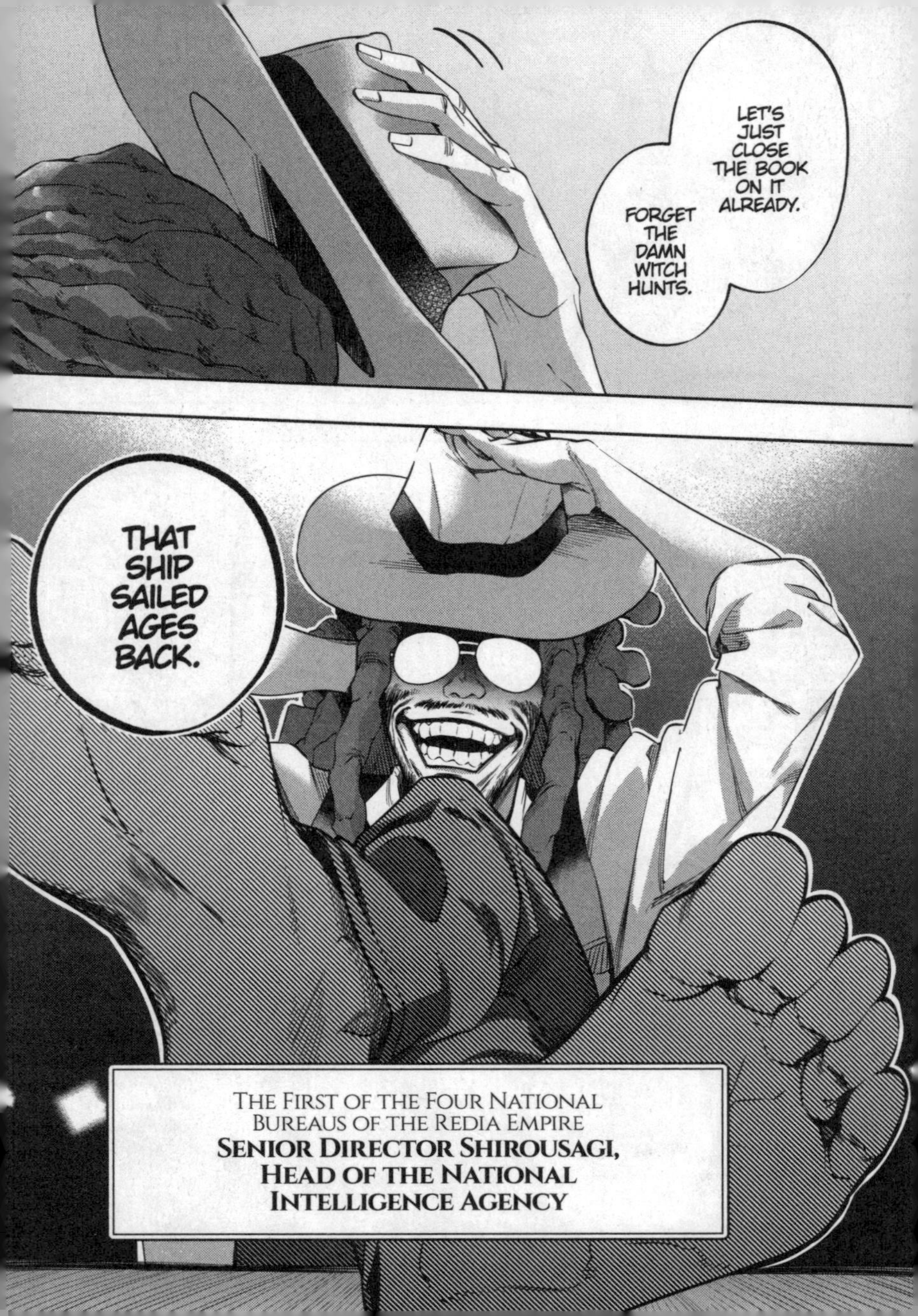
LET'S JUST CLOSE THE BOOK ON IT ALREADY.
FORGET THE DAMN WITCH HUNTS.
THAT SHIP SAILED AGES BACK.
THE FIRST OF THE FOUR NATIONAL BUREAUS OF THE REDIA EMPIRE
SENIOR DIRECTOR SHIROUSAGI, HEAD OF THE NATIONAL INTELLIGENCE AGENCY

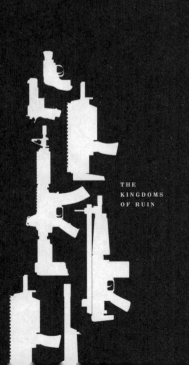

THE
KINGDOMS
OF RUIN

THE
KINGDOMS
OF RUIN

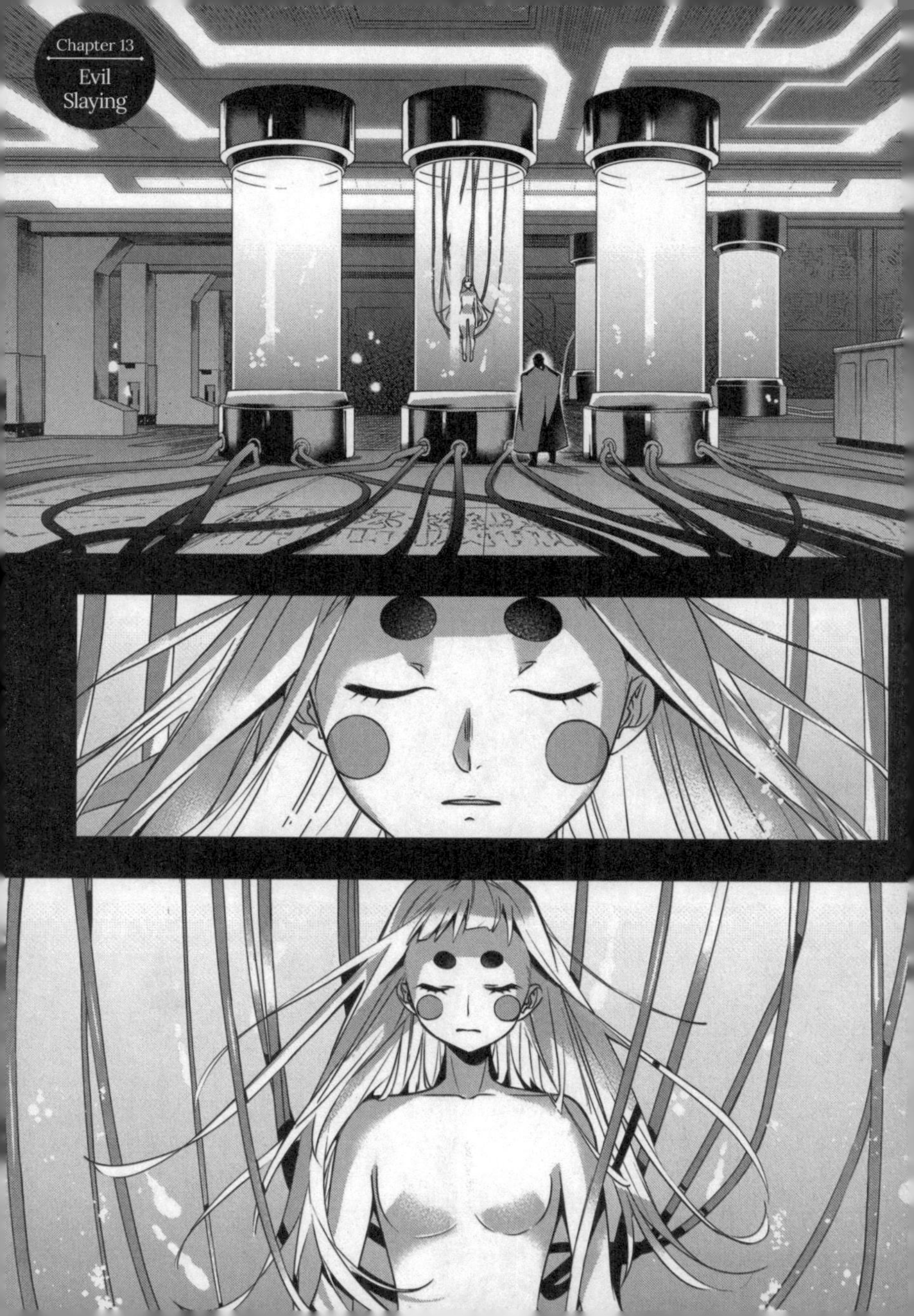
Chapter 13
Evil Slaying

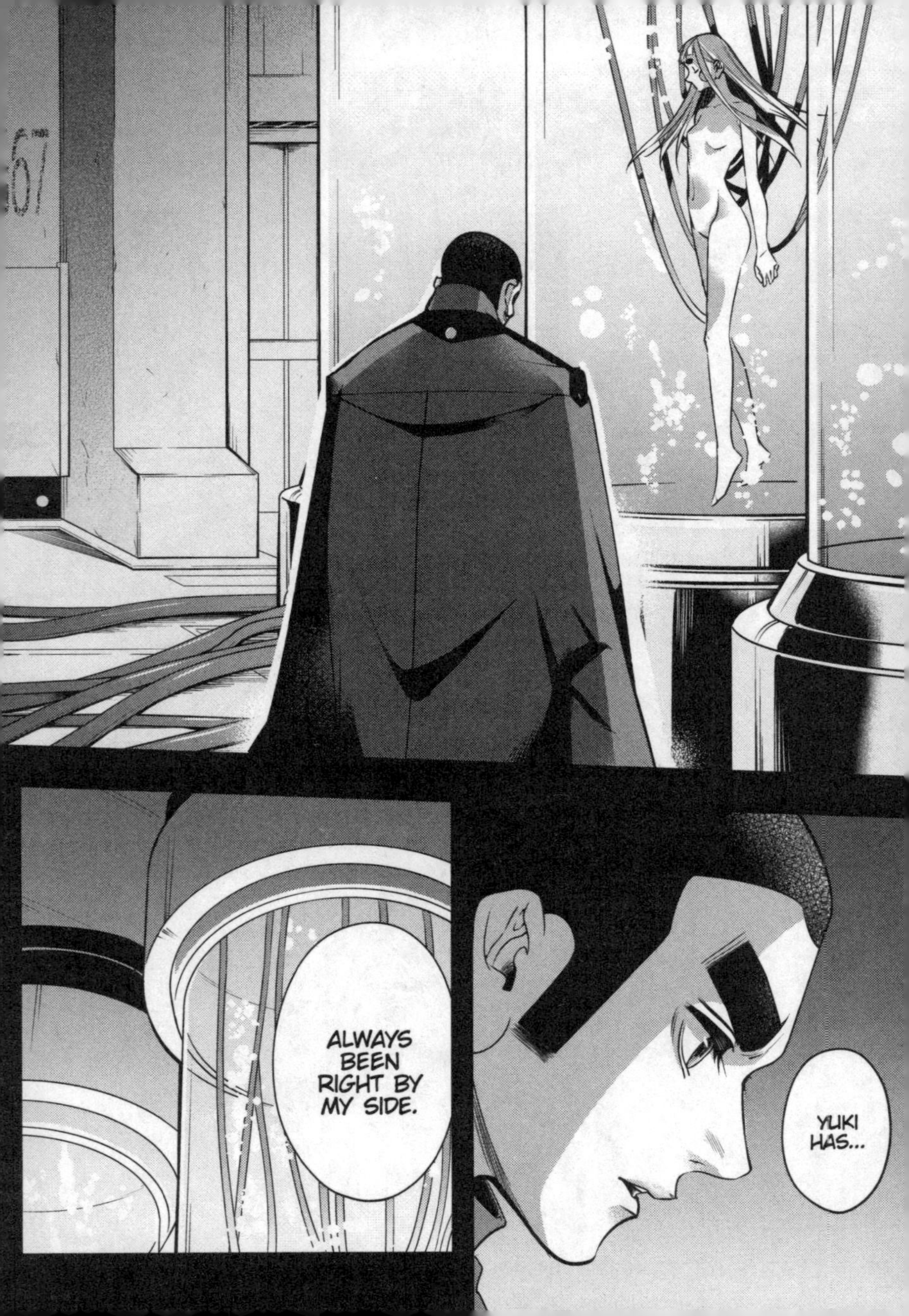
YUKI HAS...
ALWAYS BEEN RIGHT BY MY SIDE.

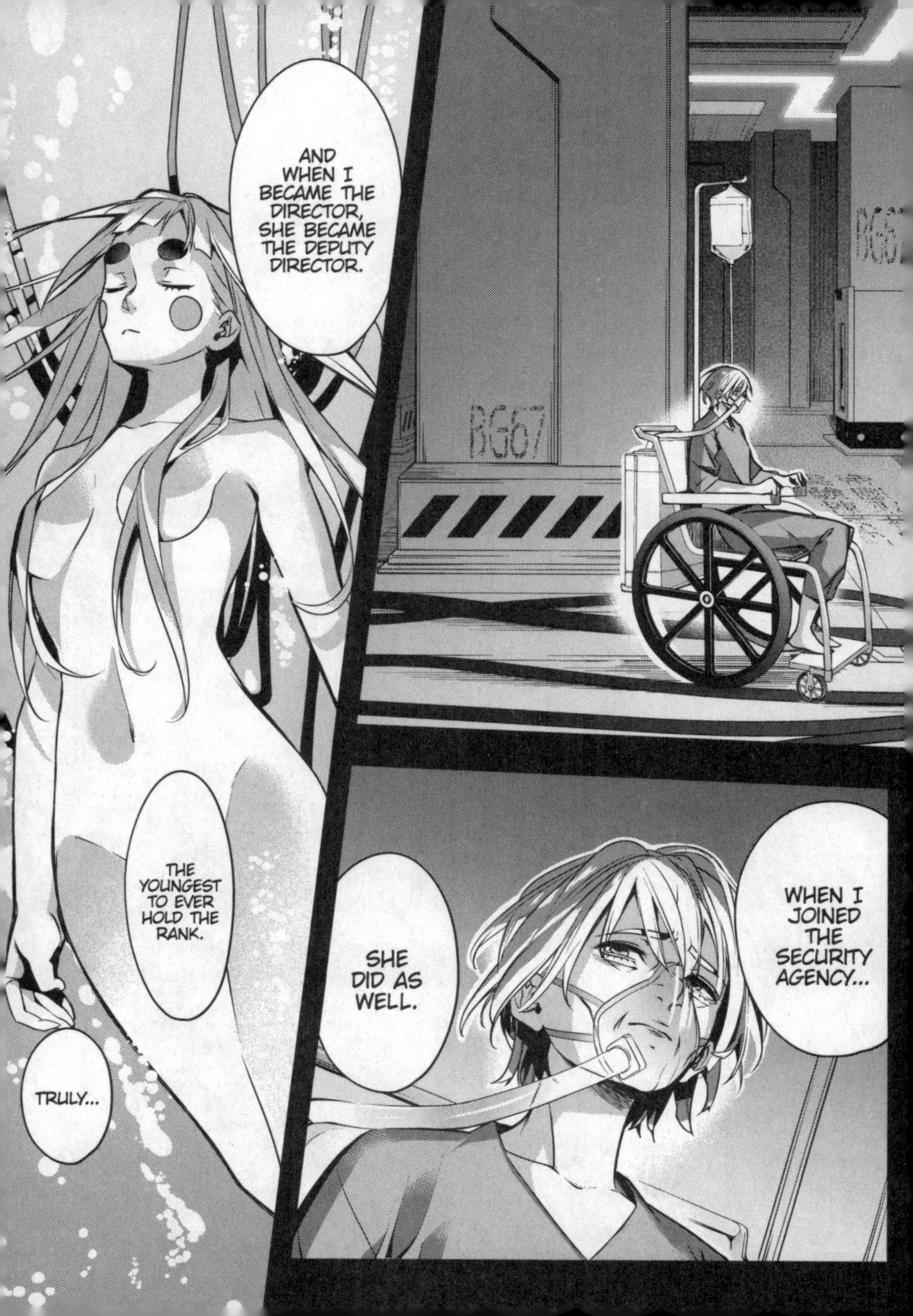
BG67
WHEN I JOINED THE SECURITY AGENCY...
SHE DID AS WELL.
AND WHEN I BECAME THE DIRECTOR, SHE BECAME THE DEPUTY DIRECTOR.
THE YOUNGEST TO EVER HOLD THE RANK.
TRULY...

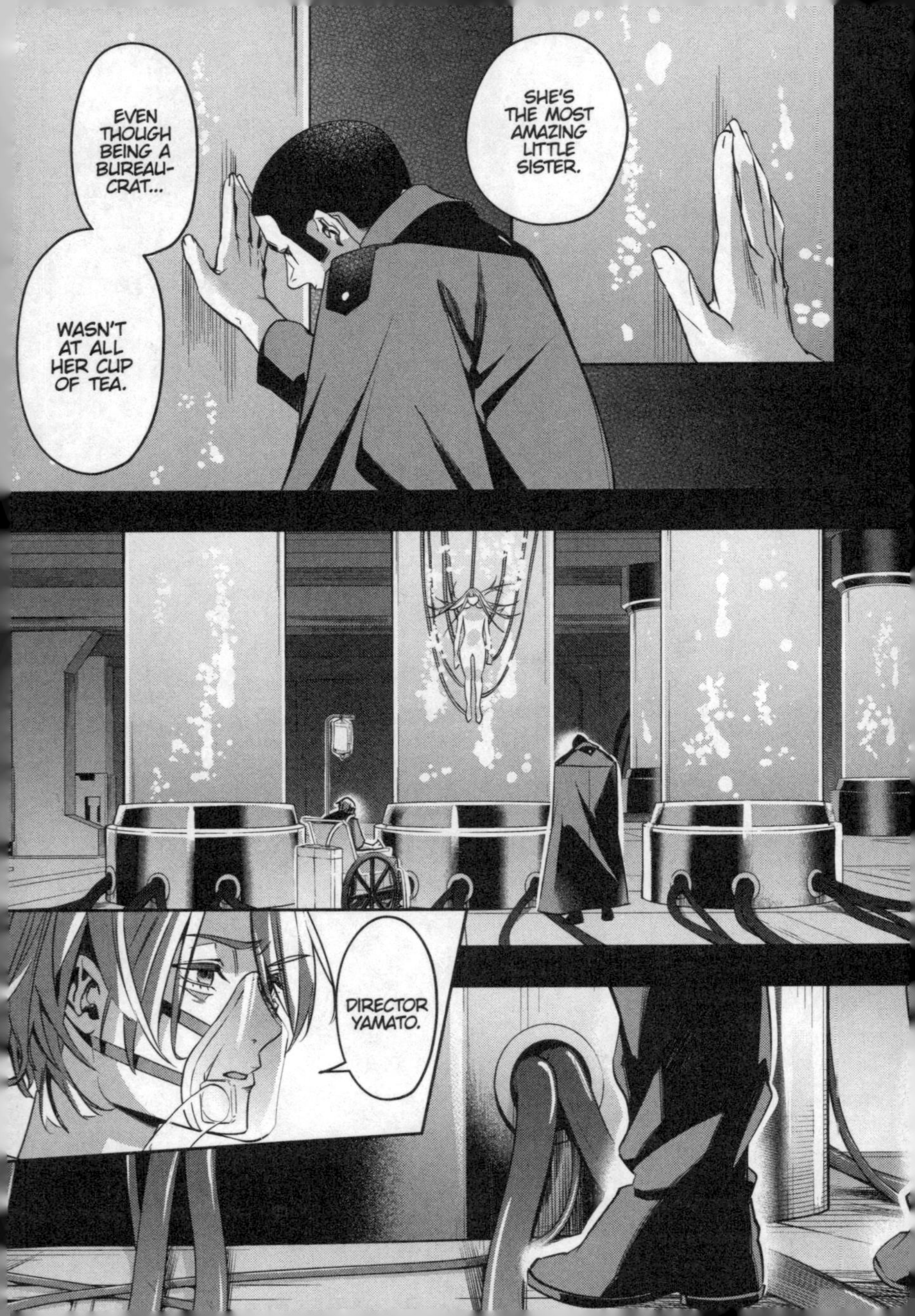
SHE'S THE MOST AMAZING LITTLE SISTER.
EVEN THOUGH BEING A BUREAU-CRAT...
WASN'T AT ALL HER CUP OF TEA.
DIRECTOR YAMATO.

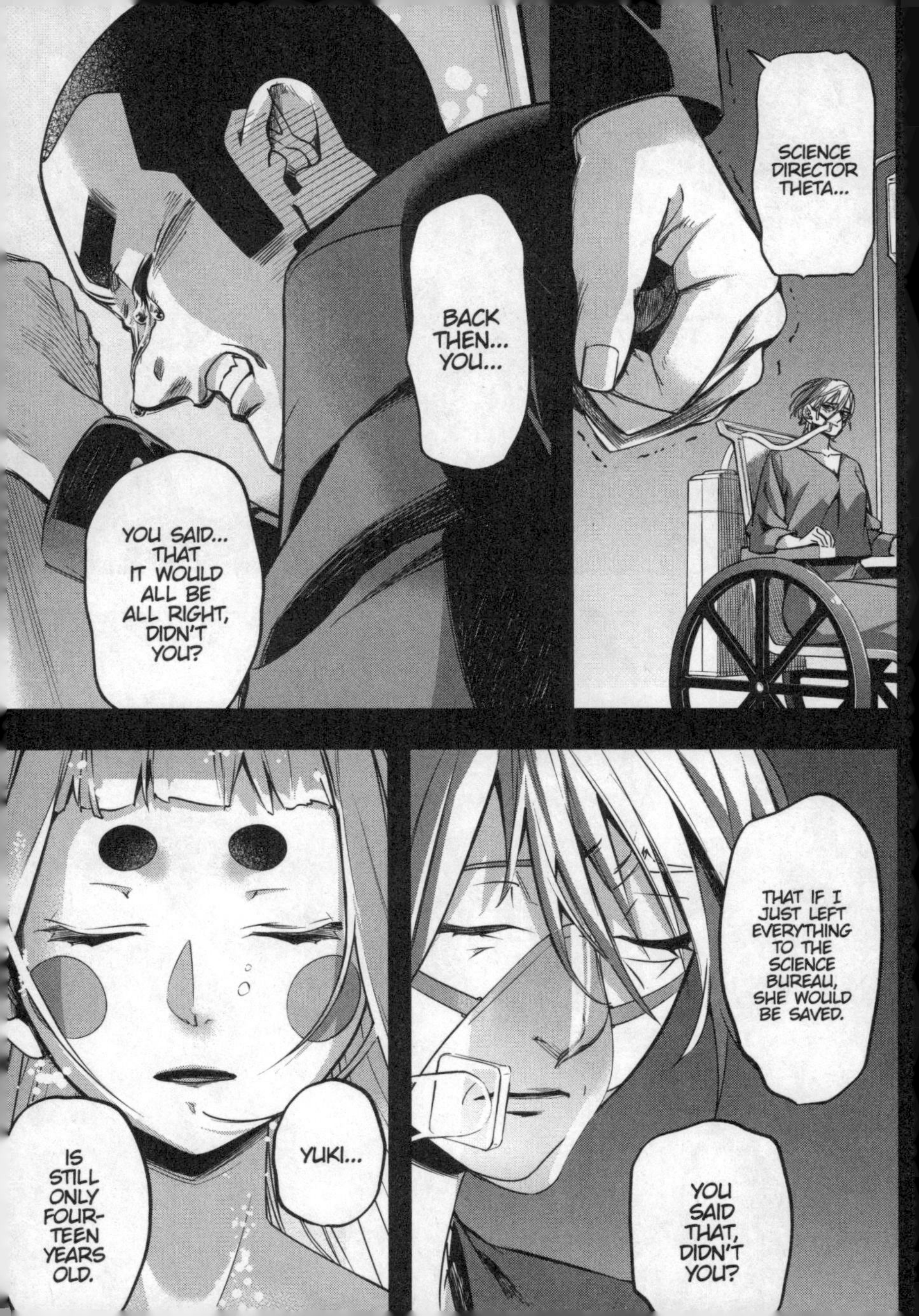
SCIENCE DIRECTOR THETA...
BACK THEN... YOU...
YOU SAID... THAT IT WOULD ALL BE ALL RIGHT, DIDN'T YOU?
THAT IF I JUST LEFT EVERYTHING TO THE SCIENCE BUREAU, SHE WOULD BE SAVED.
YOU SAID THAT, DIDN'T YOU?
YUKI...
IS STILL ONLY FOUR-TEEN YEARS OLD.

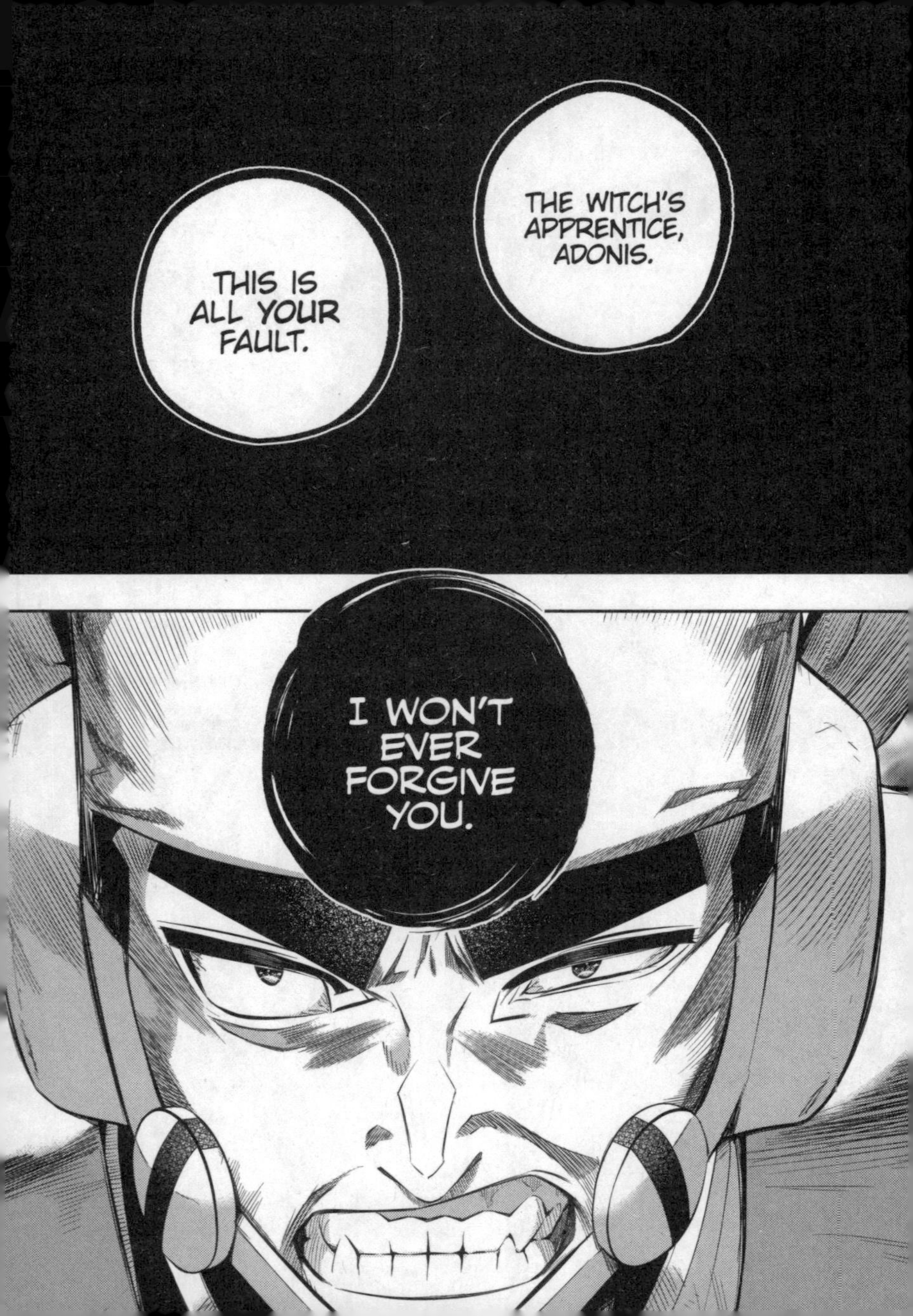
THE WITCH'S APPRENTICE, ADONIS.
THIS IS ALL YOUR FAULT.
I WON'T EVER FORGIVE YOU.

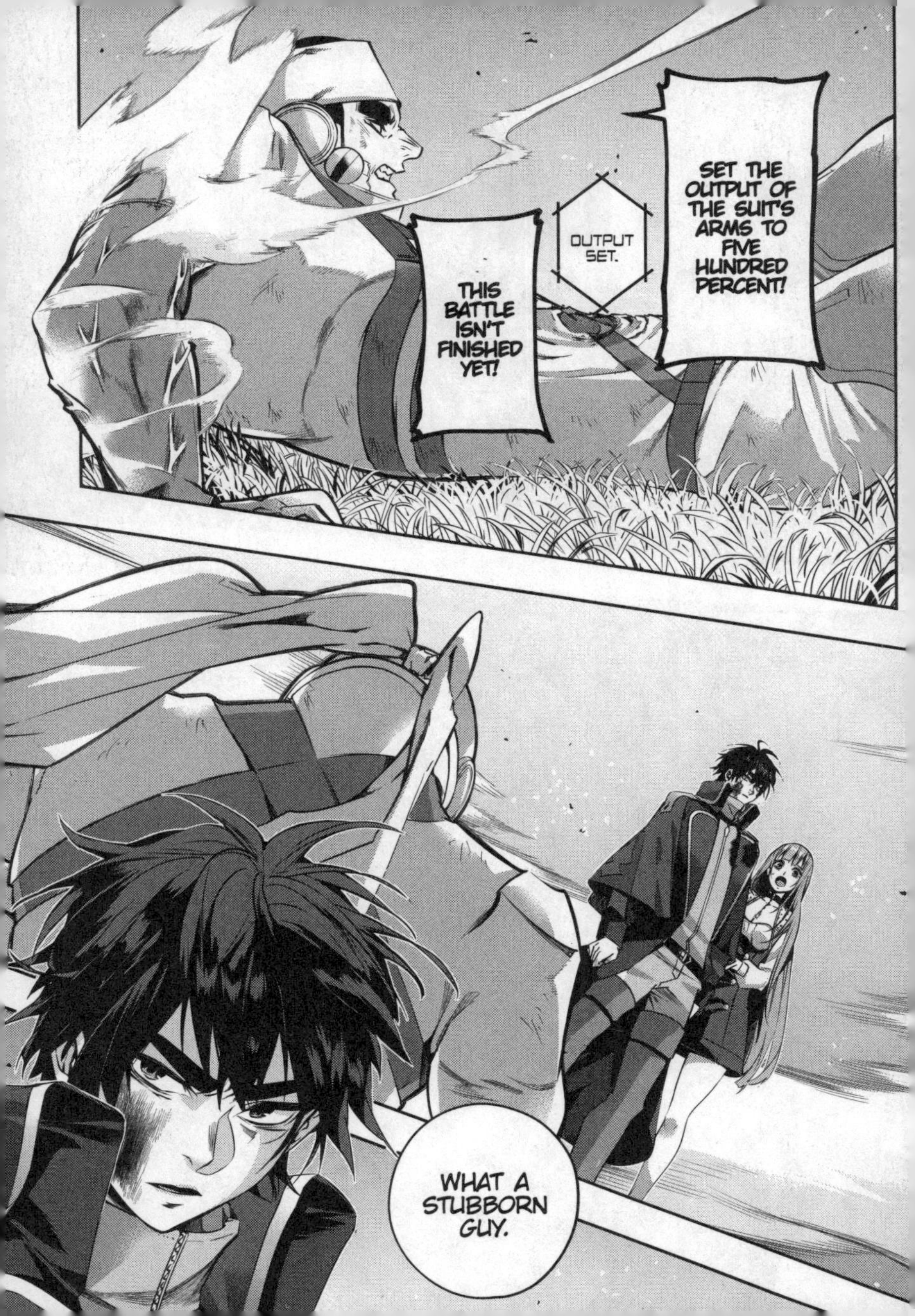
SET THE OUTPUT OF THE SUIT'S ARMS TO FIVE HUNDRED PERCENT!
OUTPUT SET.
THIS BATTLE ISN'T FINISHED YET!
WHAT A STUBBORN GUY.

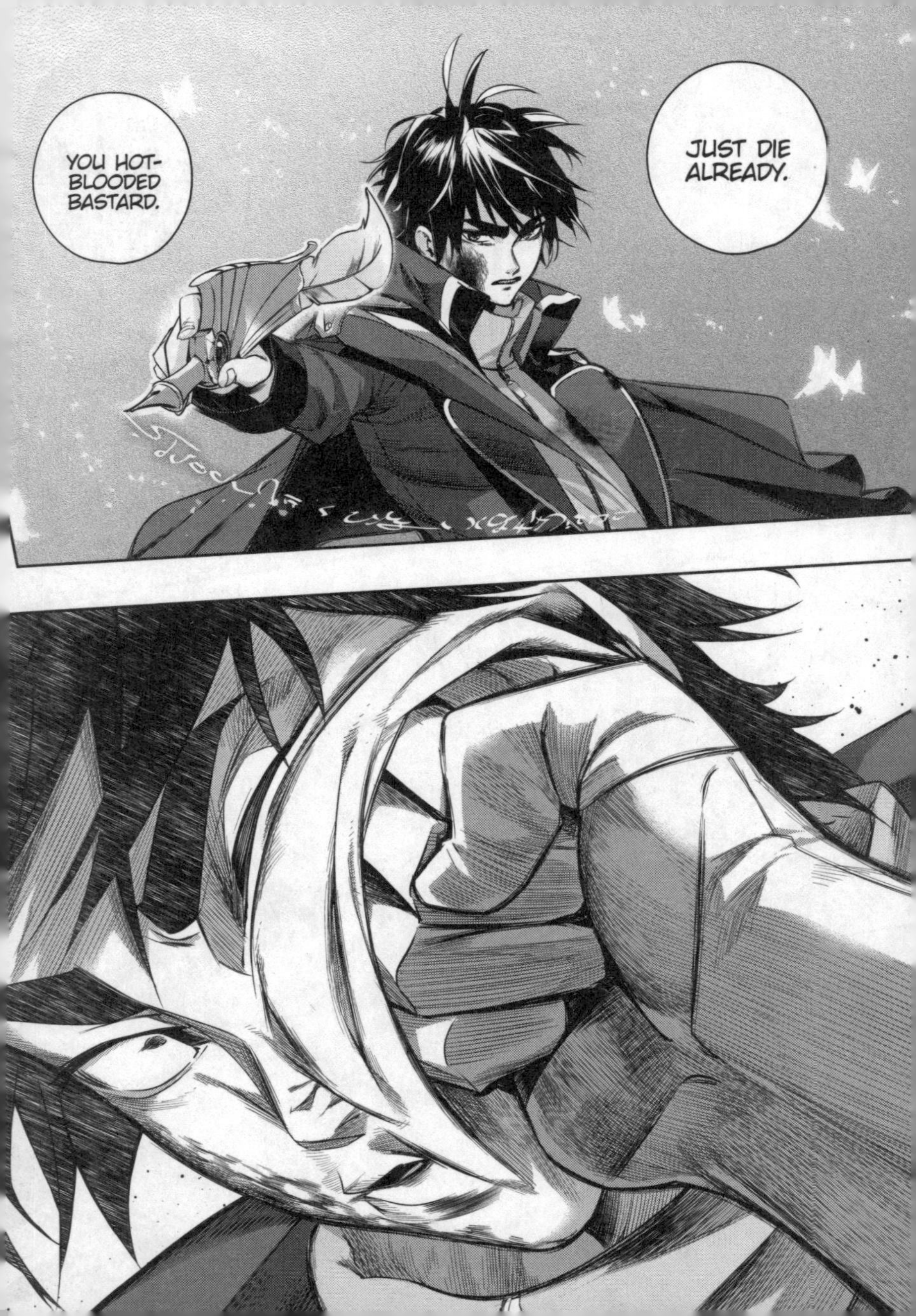
JUST DIE ALREADY.
YOU HOT-BLOODED BASTARD.

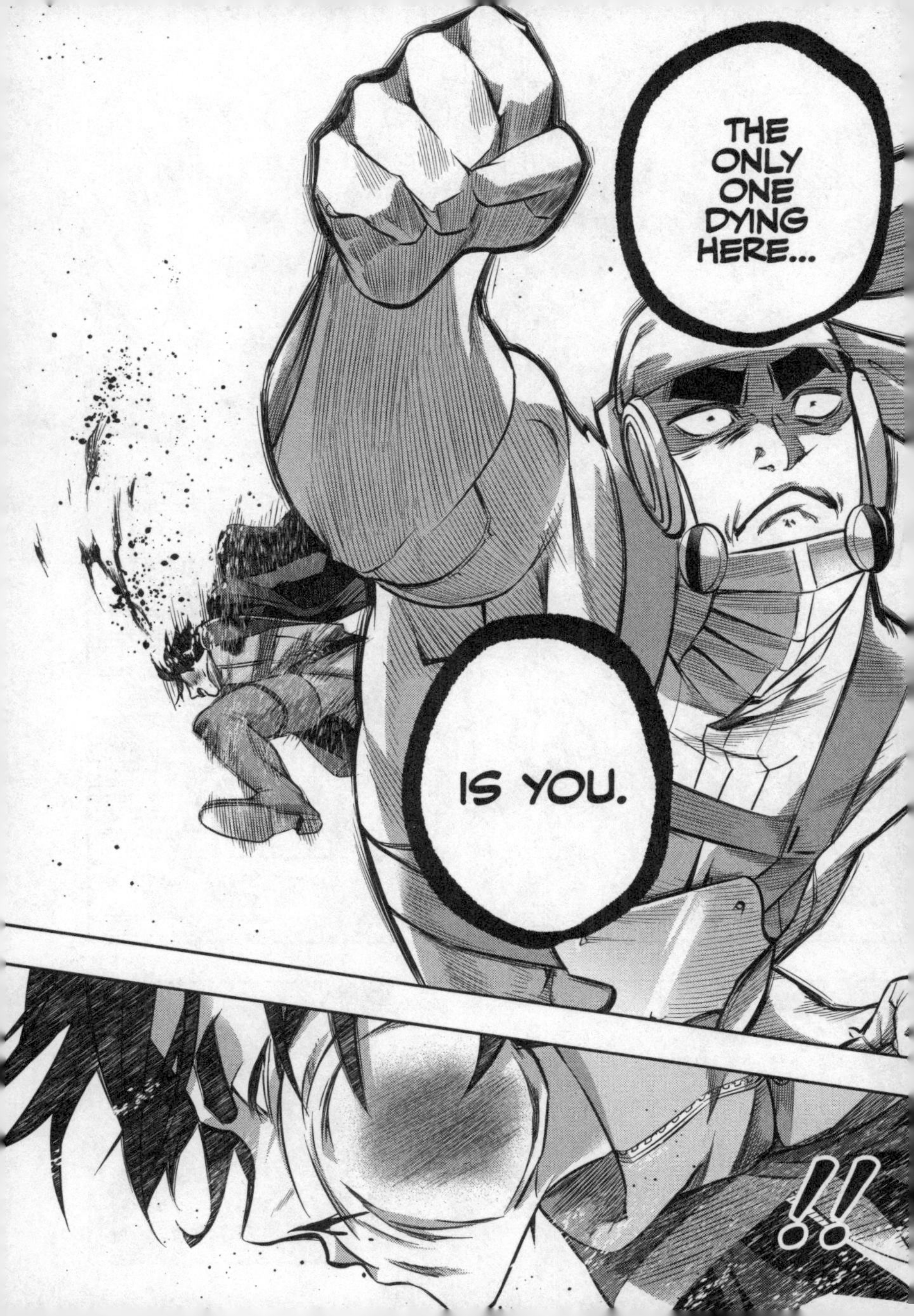
THE ONLY ONE DYING HERE...
IS YOU.
!!

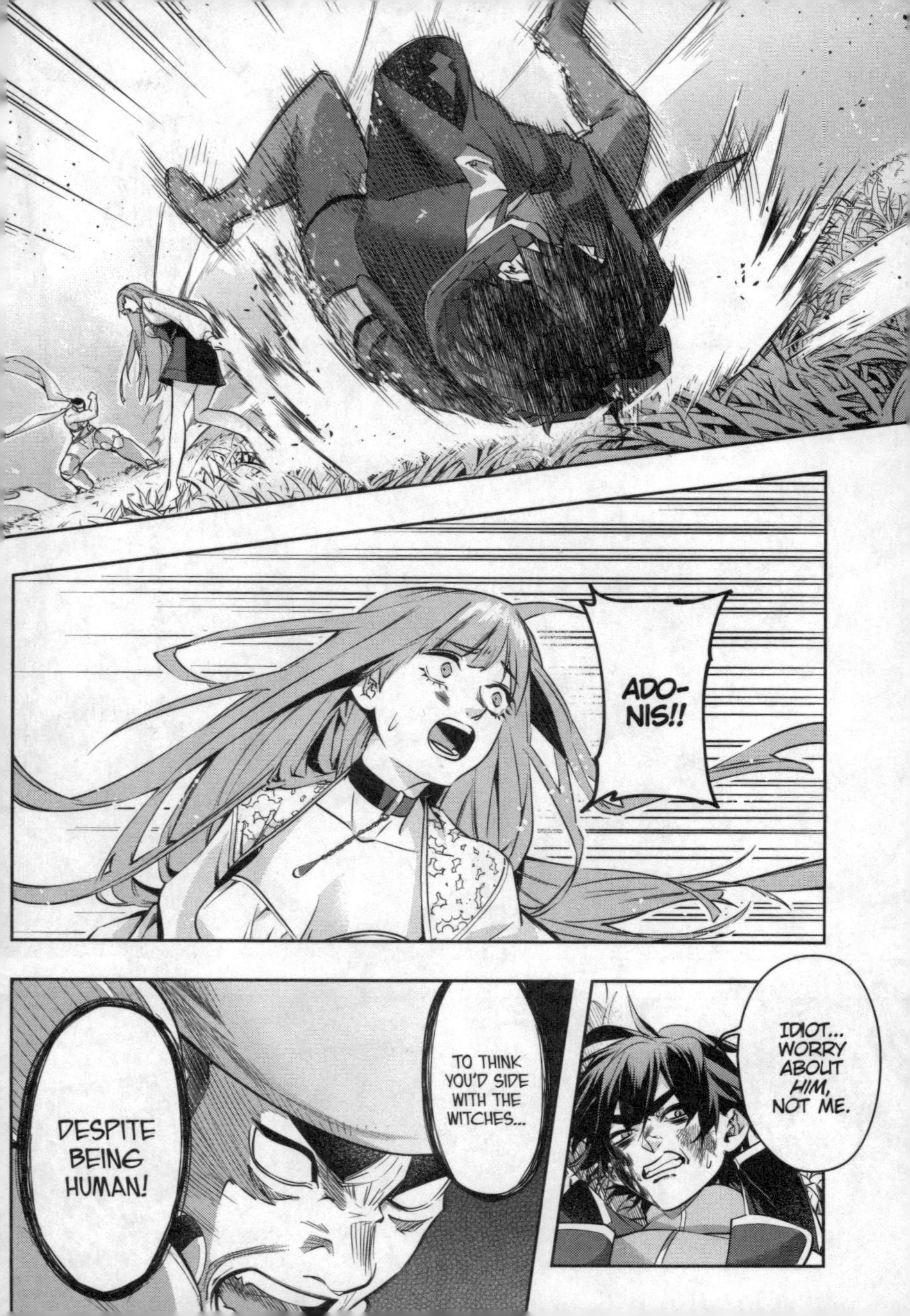
ADO-NIS!!
IDIOT... WORRY ABOUT HIM, NOT ME.
TO THINK YOU'D SIDE WITH THE WITCHES...
DESPITE BEING HUMAN!

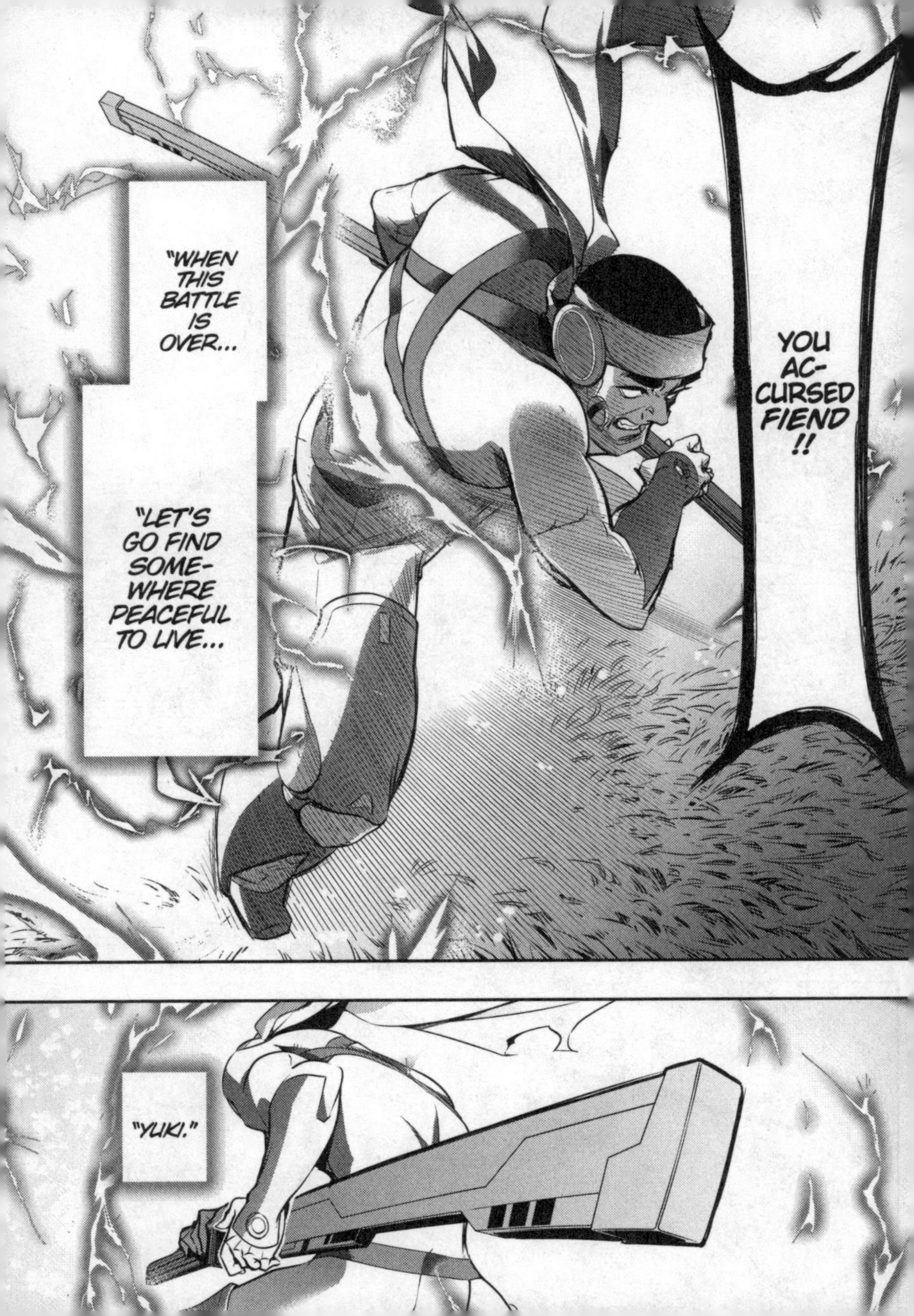
YOU AC-CURSED FIEND!!
"WHEN THIS BATTLE IS OVER...
"LET'S GO FIND SOME-WHERE PEACEFUL TO LIVE...
"YUKI."

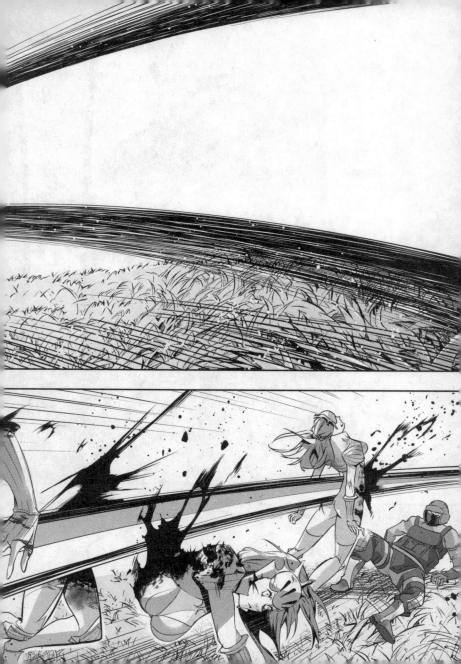

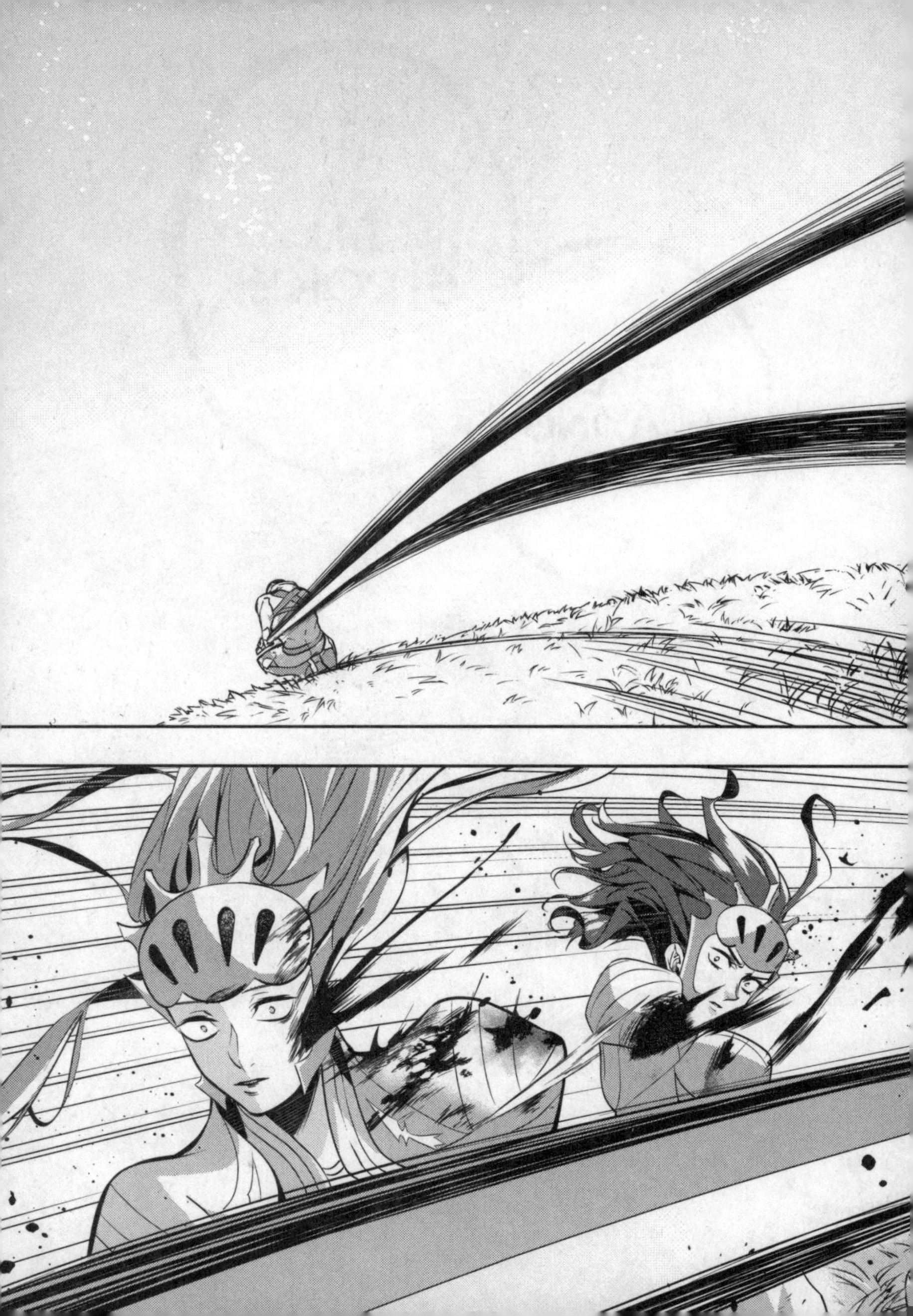

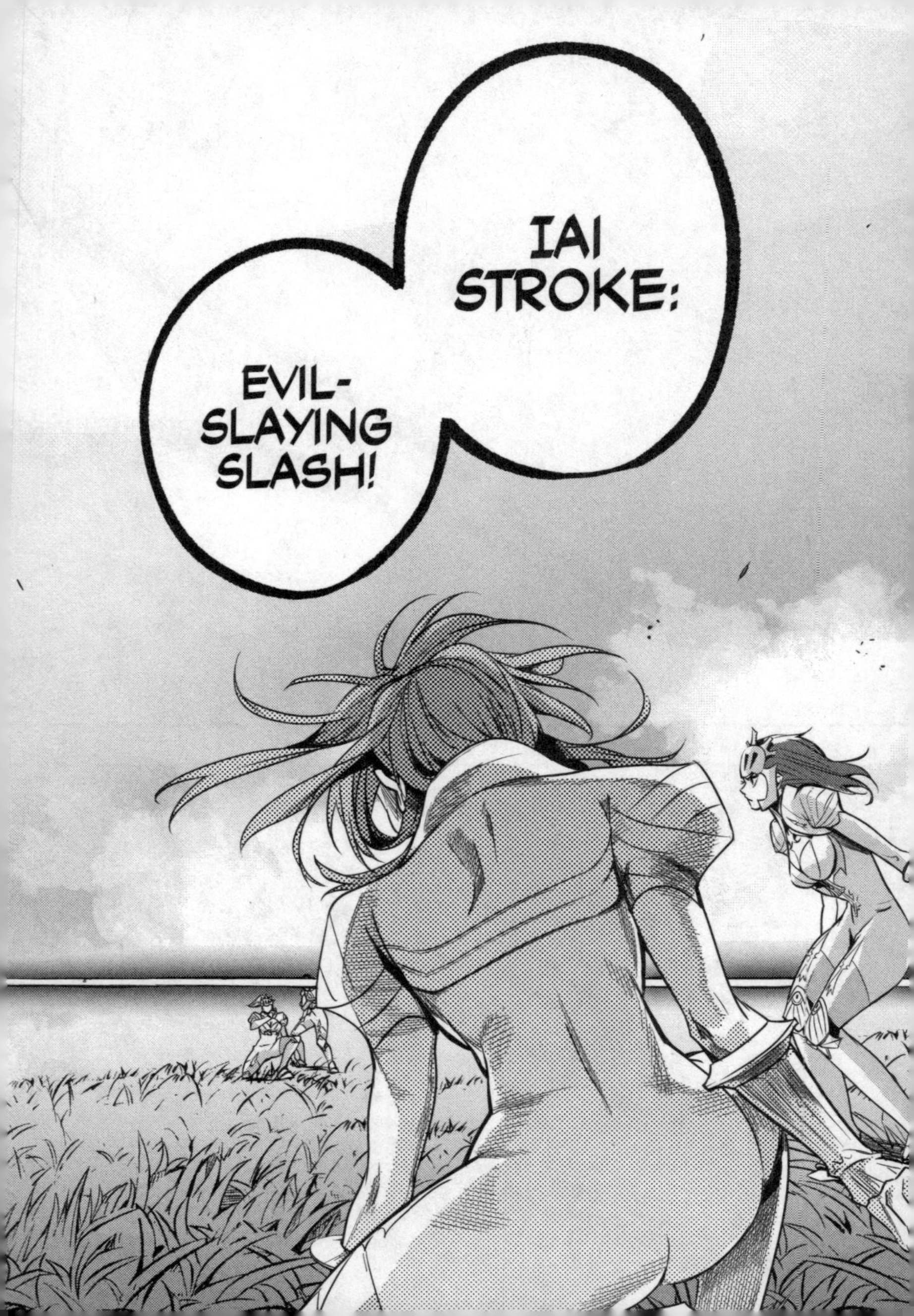
IAI STROKE:
EVIL-SLAYING SLASH!

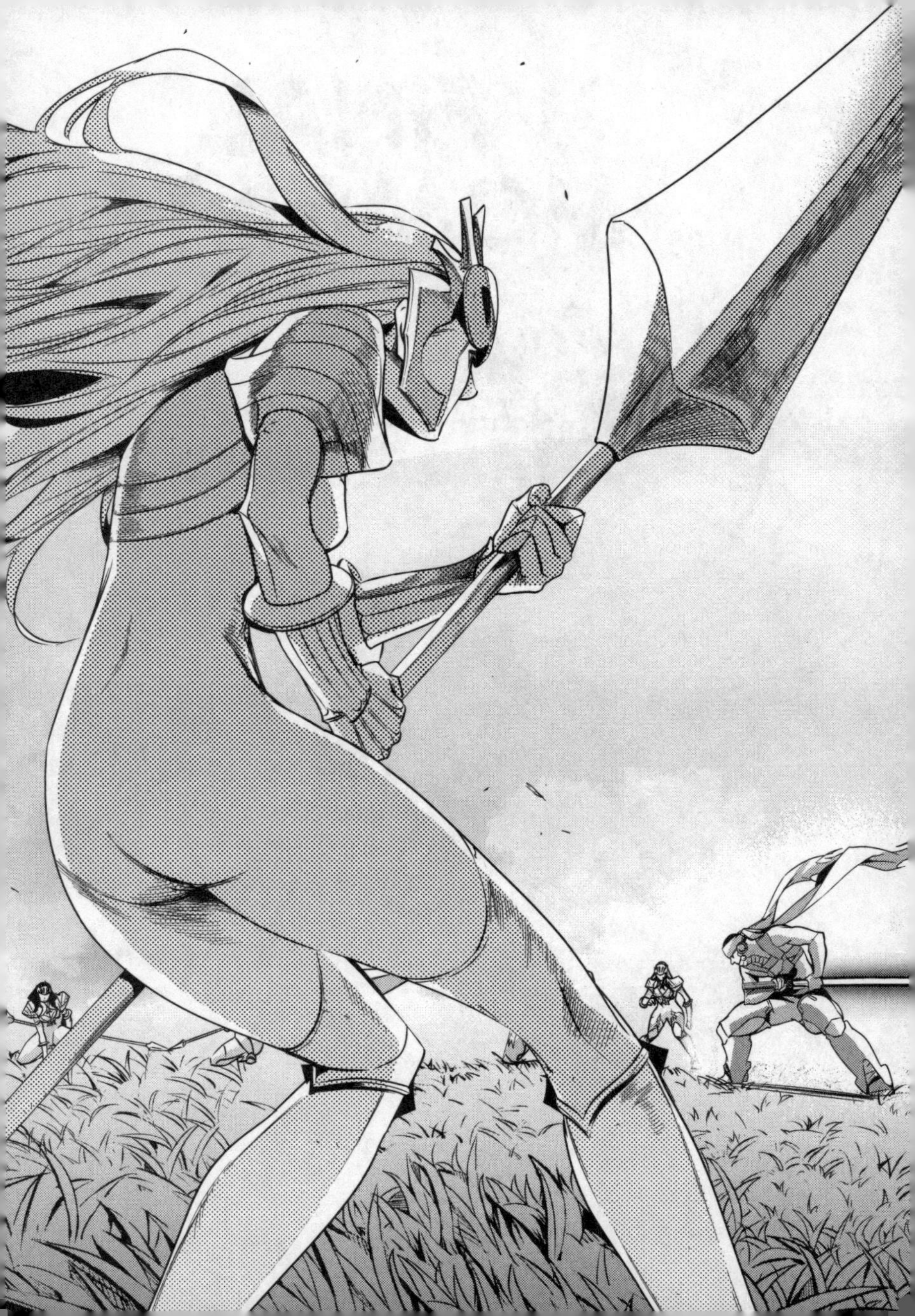

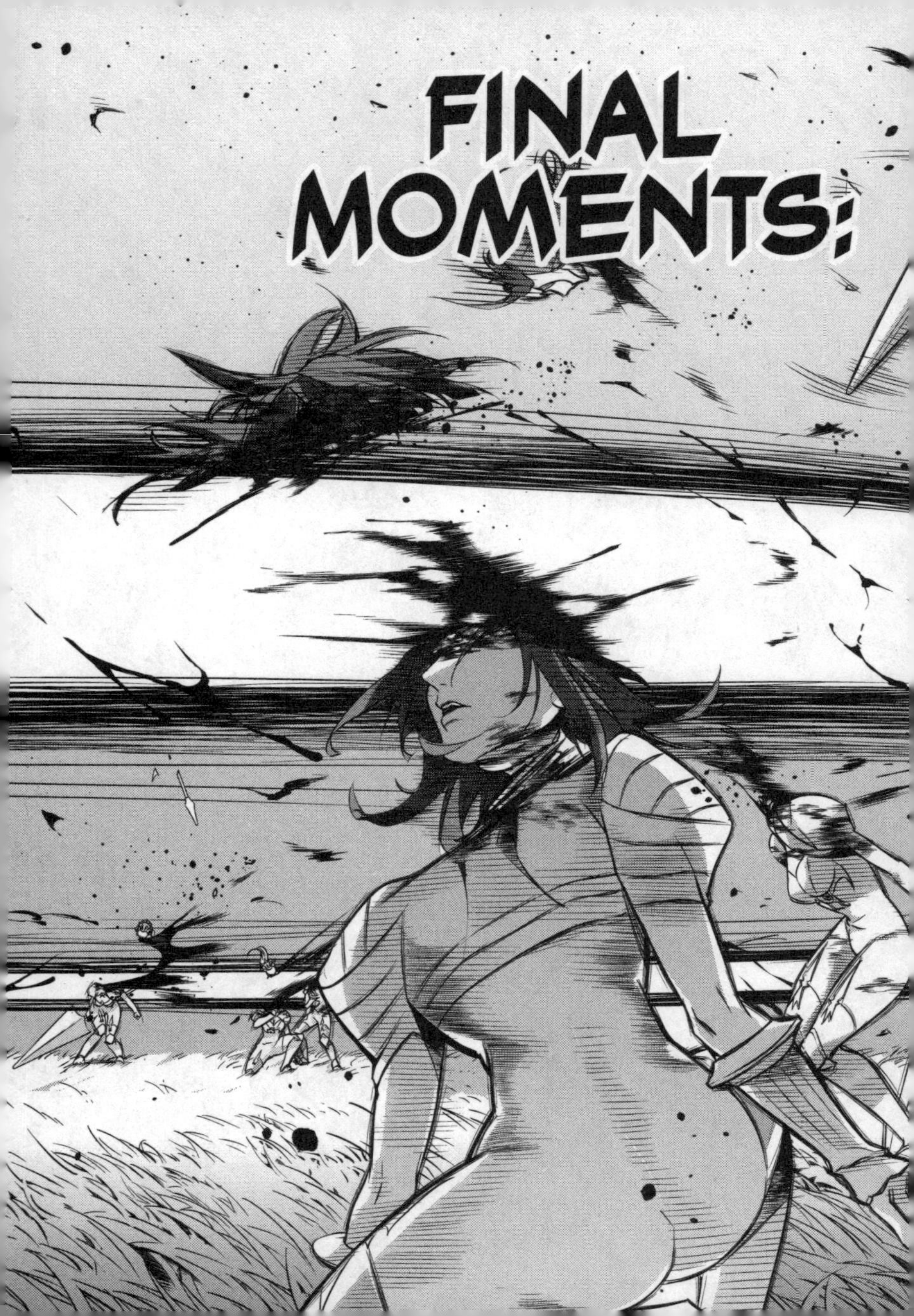
FINAL MOMENTS:

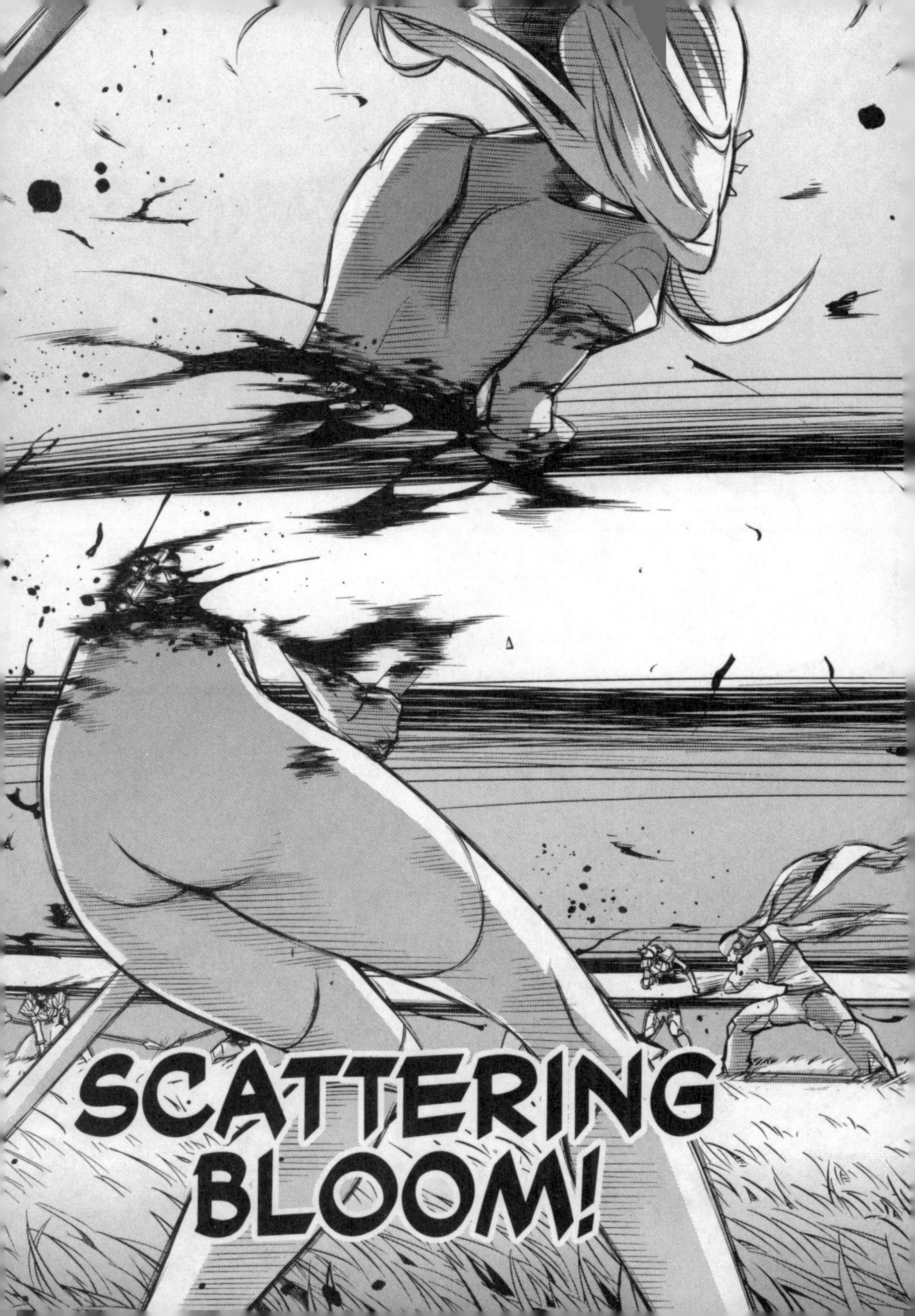
SCATTERING BLOOM!

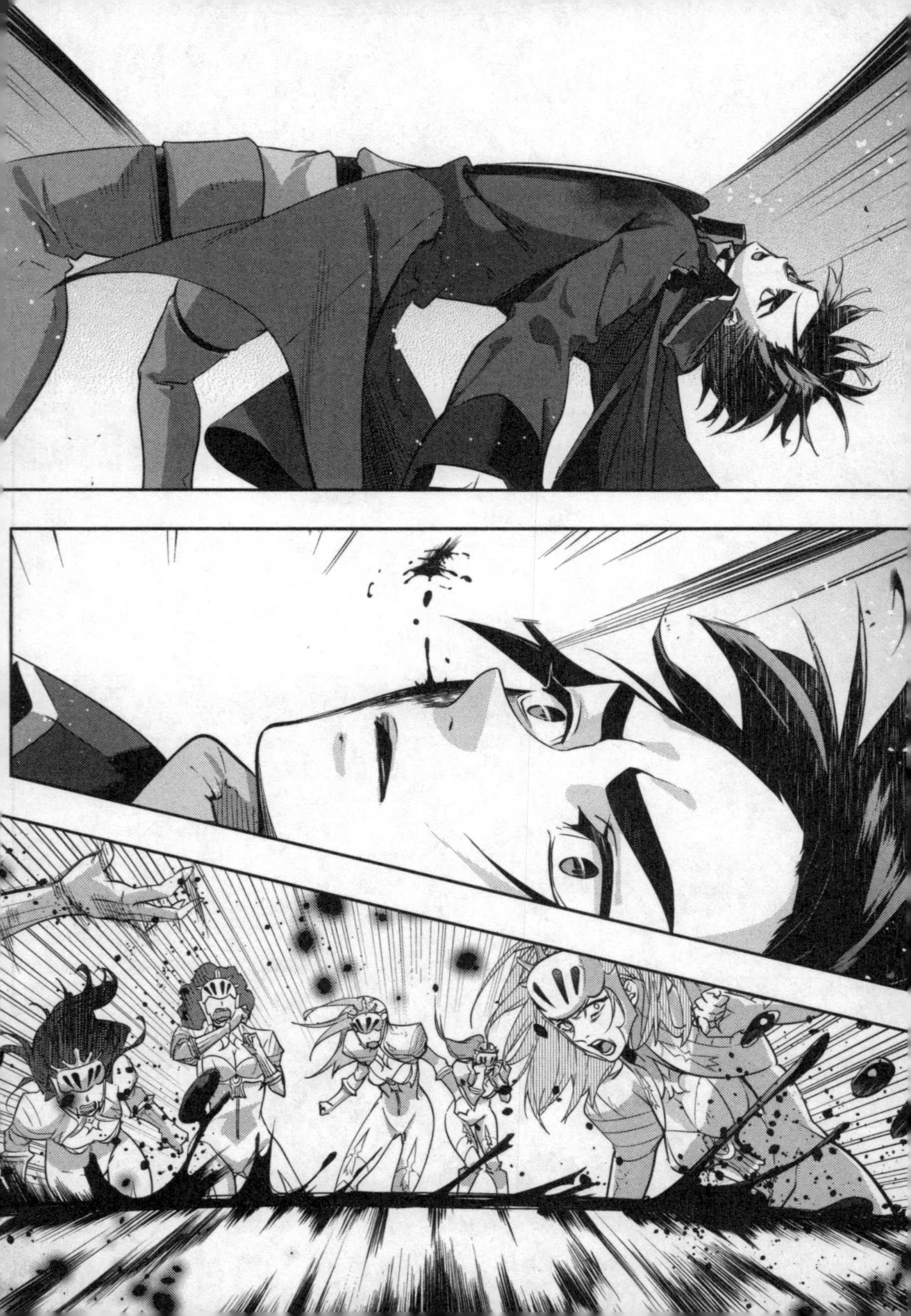

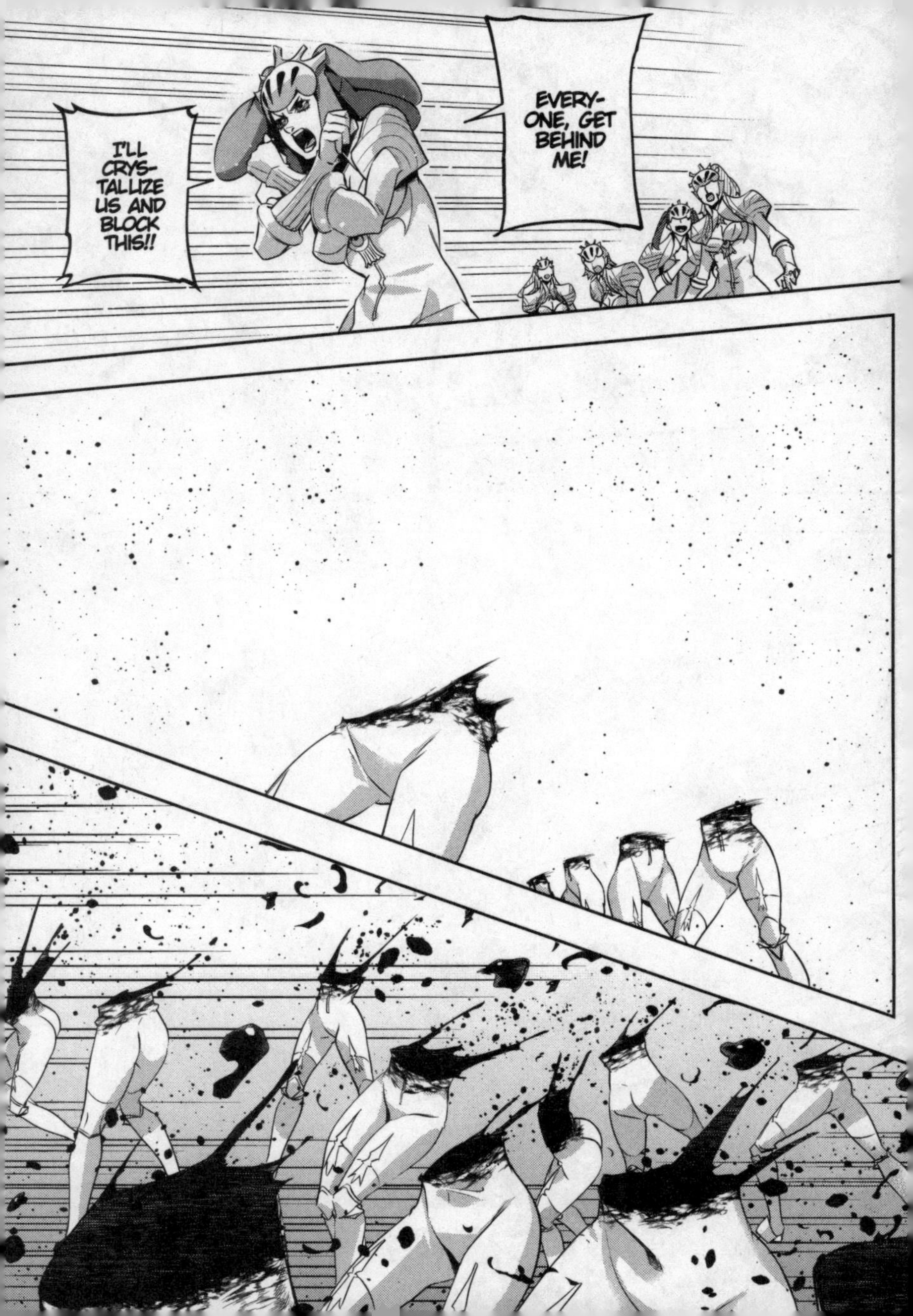
EVERY-ONE, GET BEHIND ME!
I'LL CRYS-TALLIZE US AND BLOCK THIS!!

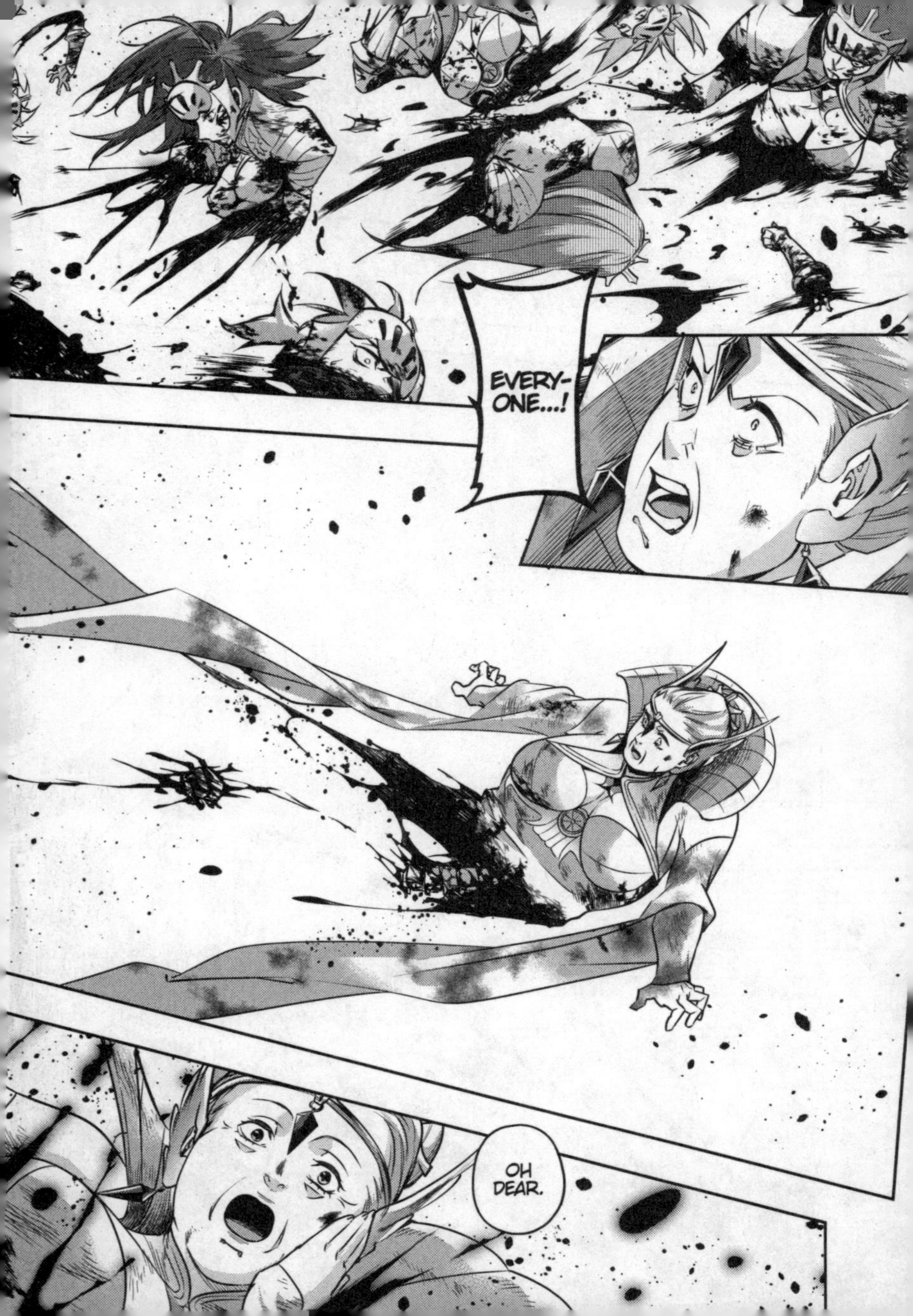
EVERY-ONE...!
OH DEAR.

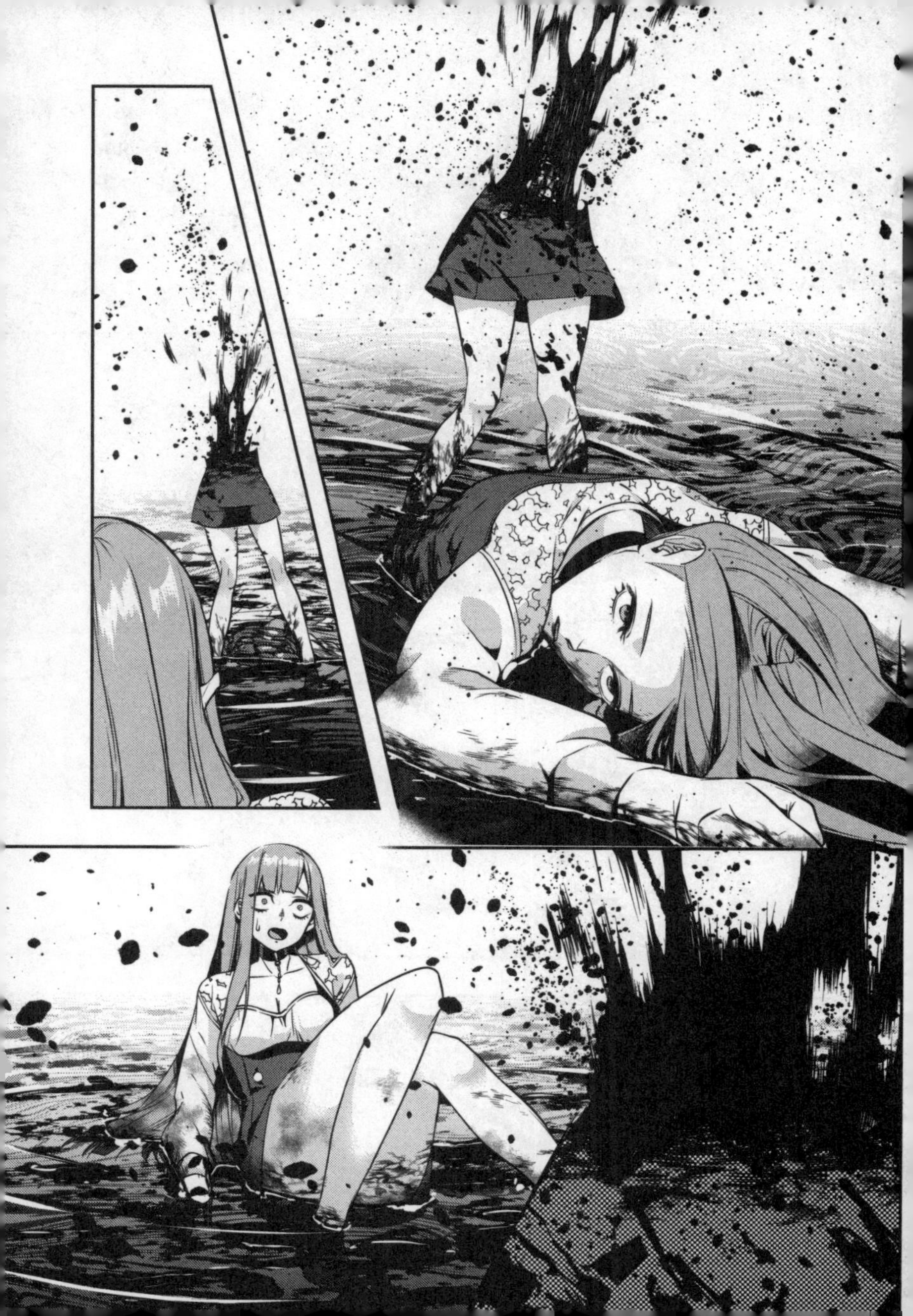

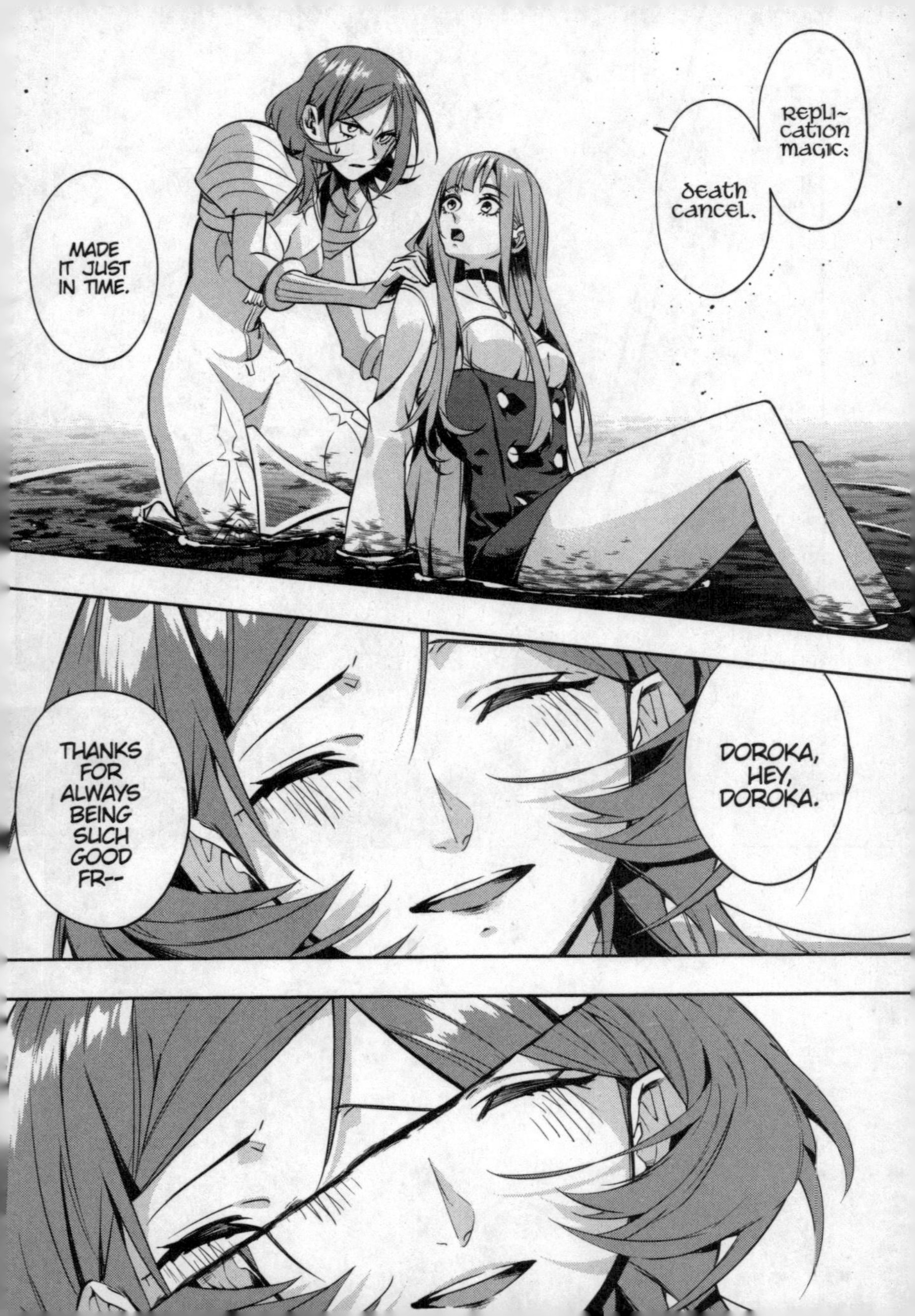
REPLI-CATION MAGIC:
DEATH CANCEL.
MADE IT JUST IN TIME.
DOROKA, HEY, DOROKA.
THANKS FOR ALWAYS BEING SUCH GOOD FR--

I LOVE YOU.

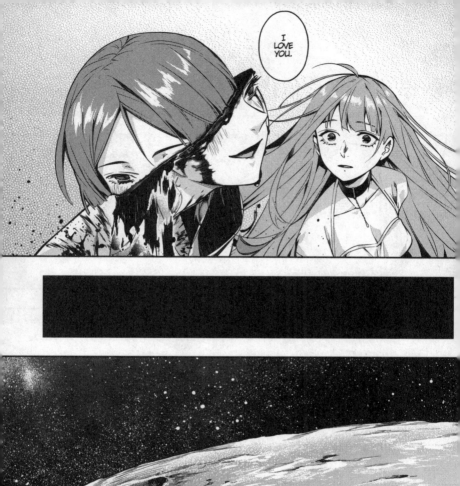

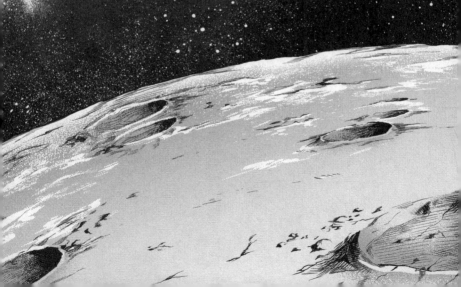

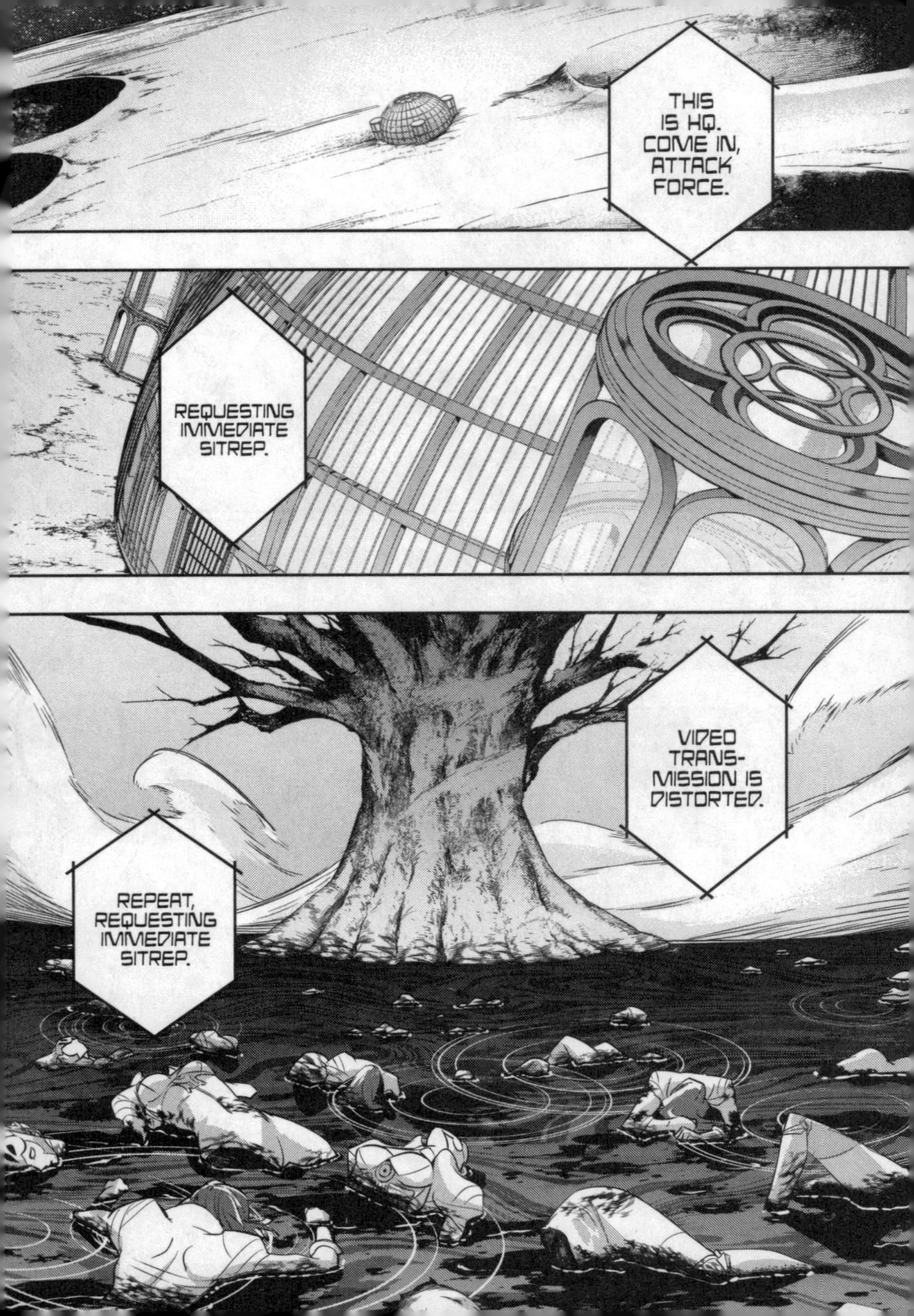
THIS IS HQ. COME IN, ATTACK FORCE.
REQUESTING IMMEDIATE SITREP.
VIDEO TRANS-MISSION IS DISTORTED.
REPEAT, REQUESTING IMMEDIATE SITREP.

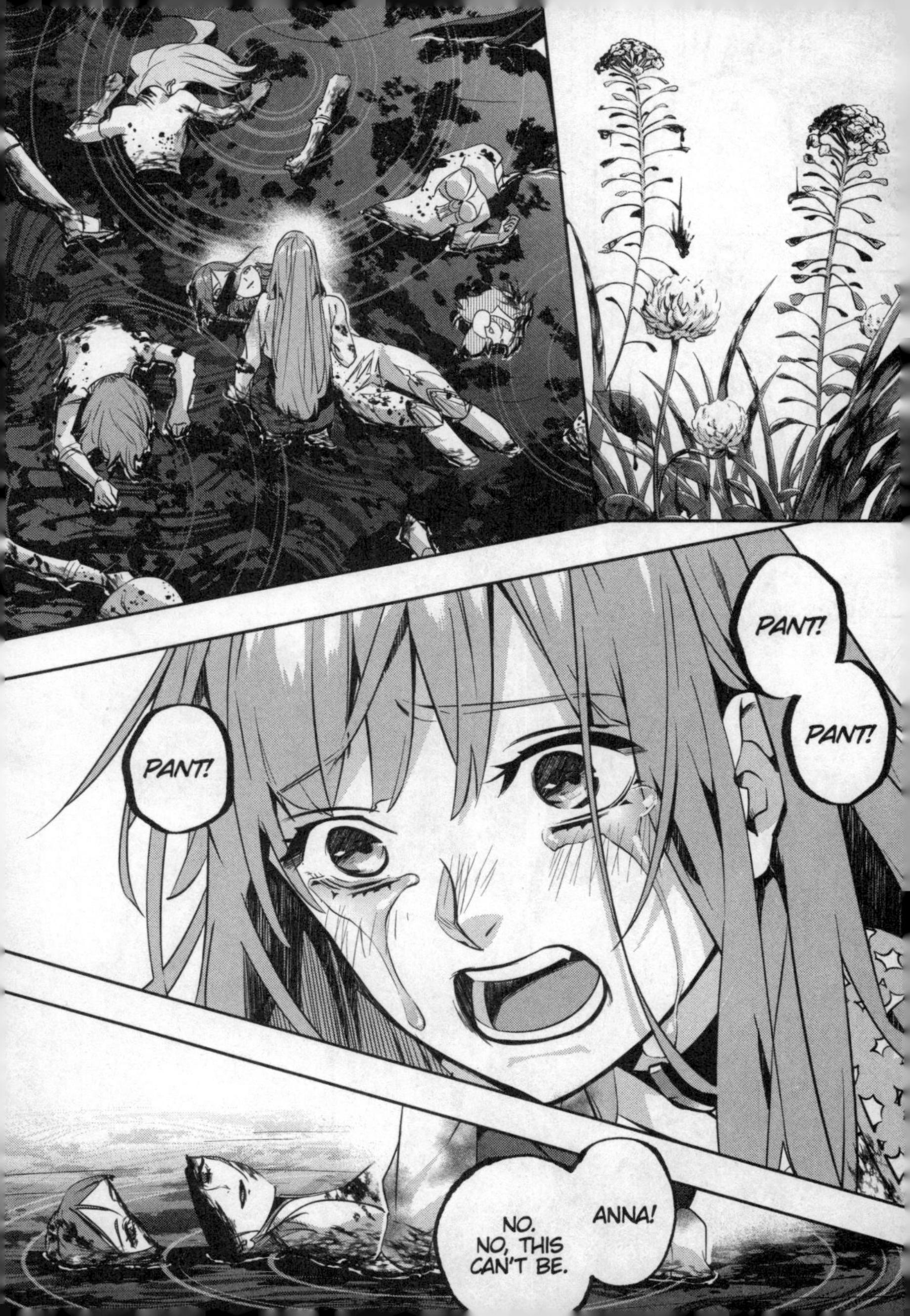
PANT!
PANT!
PANT!
ANNA!
NO. NO, THIS CAN'T BE.

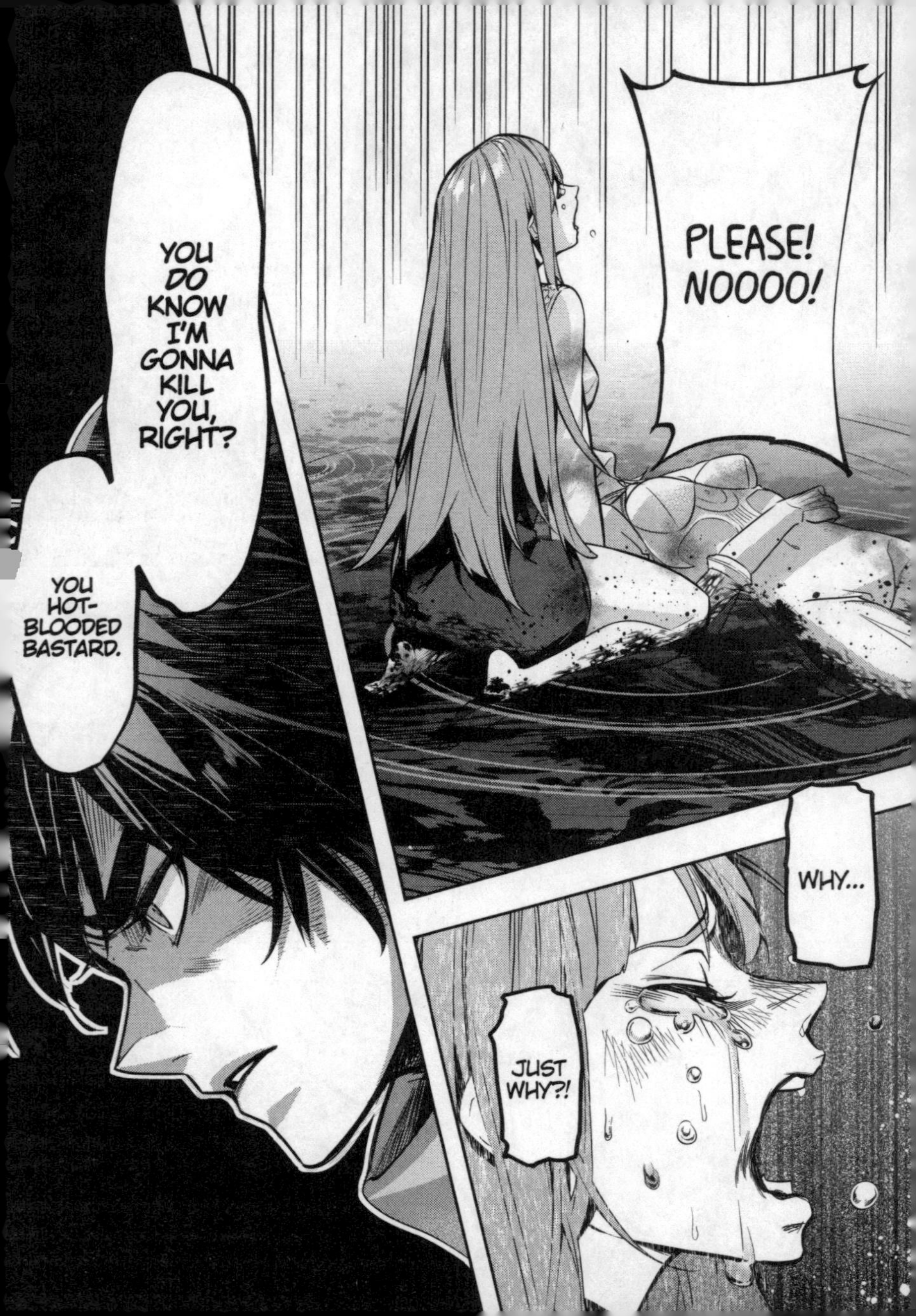
PLEASE! NOOOO!
WHY...
JUST WHY?!
YOU DO KNOW I'M GONNA KILL YOU, RIGHT?
YOU HOT-BLOODED BASTARD.

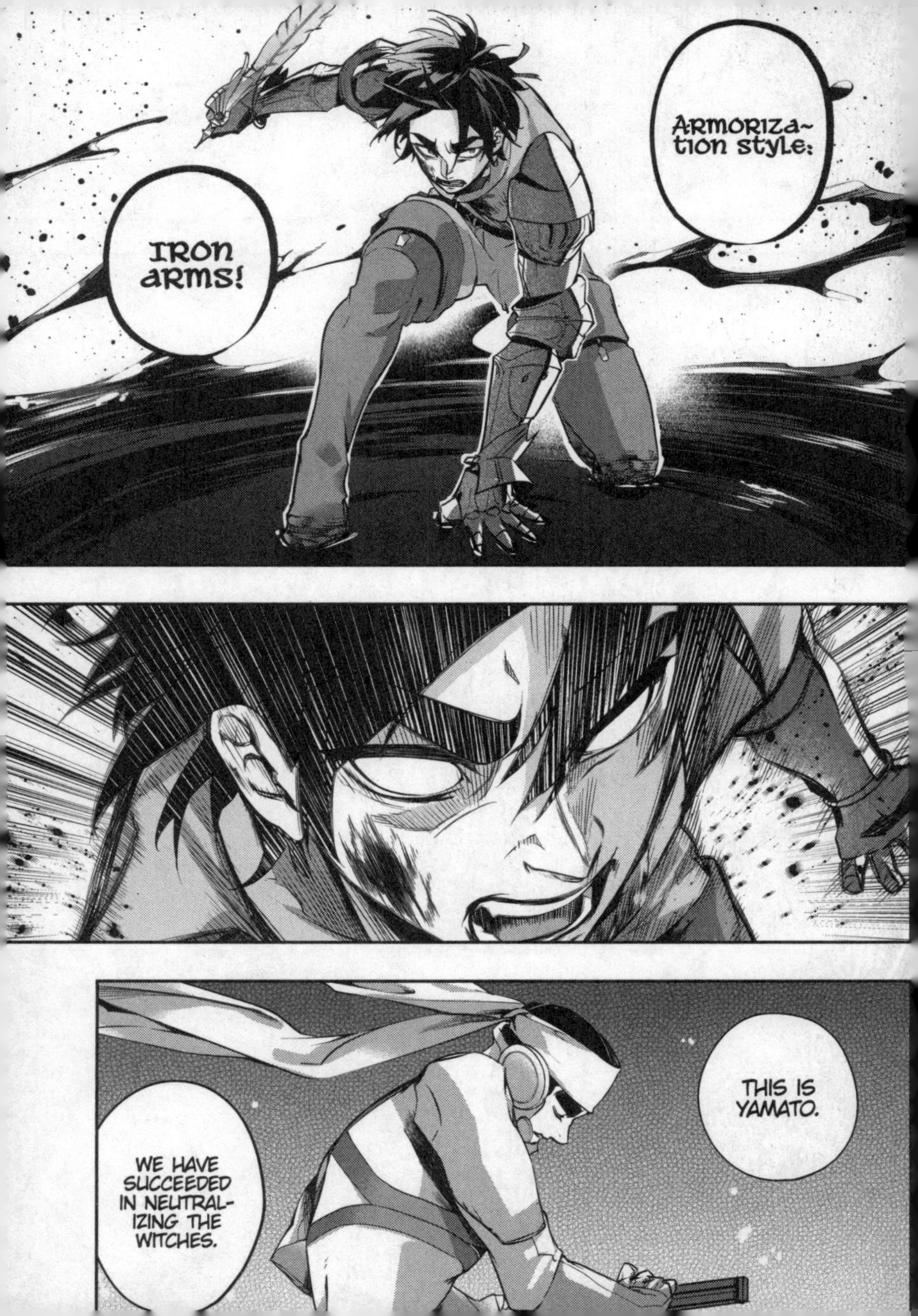
ARMORIZA-TION STYLE:
IRON ARMS!
THIS IS YAMATO.
WE HAVE SUCCEEDED IN NEUTRAL-IZING THE WITCHES.

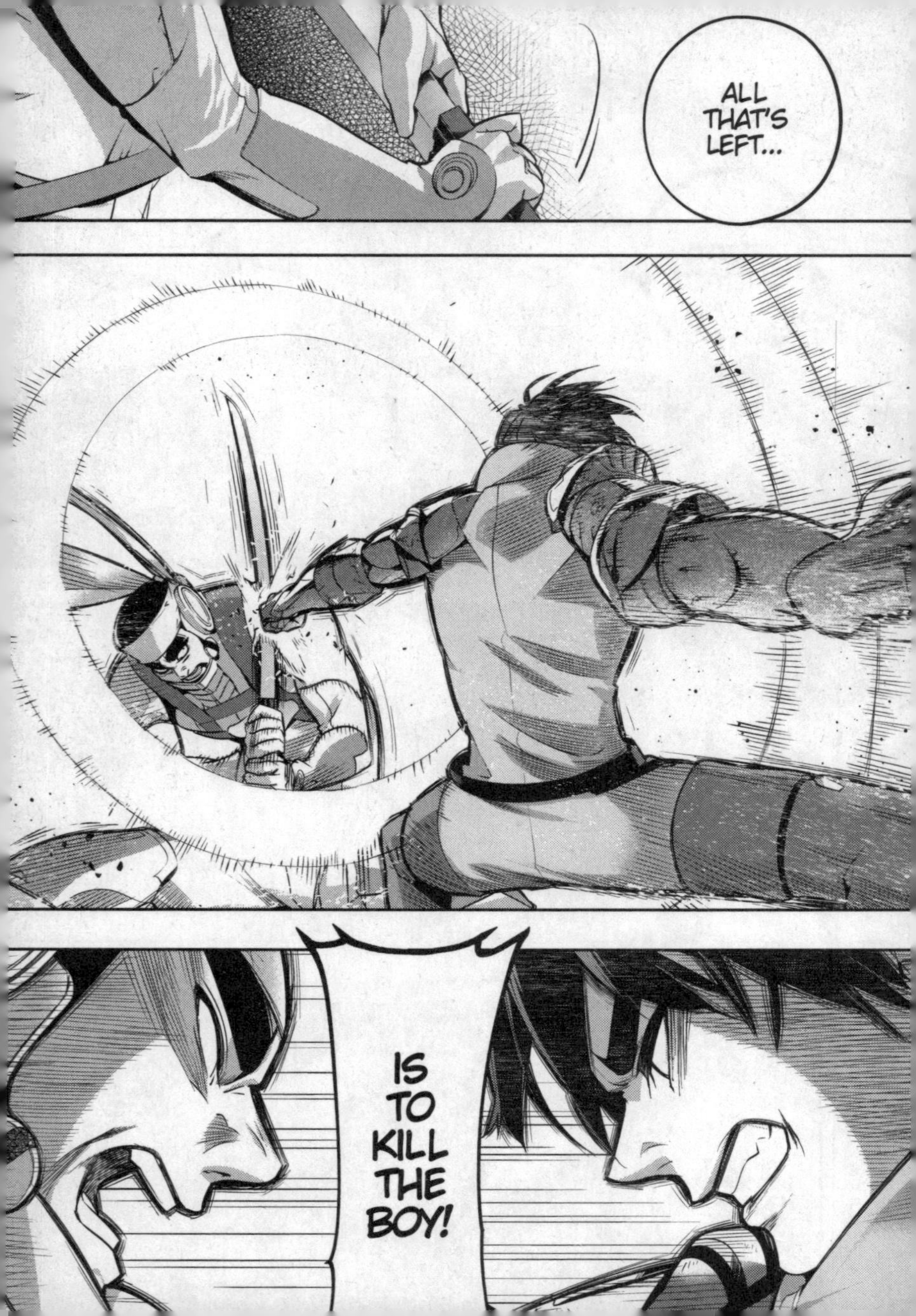
ALL THAT'S LEFT...
IS TO KILL THE BOY!

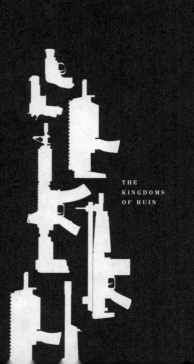

THE
KINGDOMS
OF RUIN

THE
KINGDOMS
OF RUIN

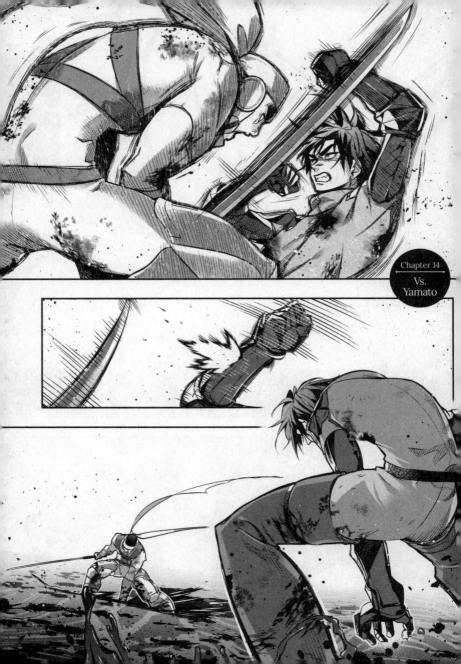

Chapter 14
Vs.
Yamato

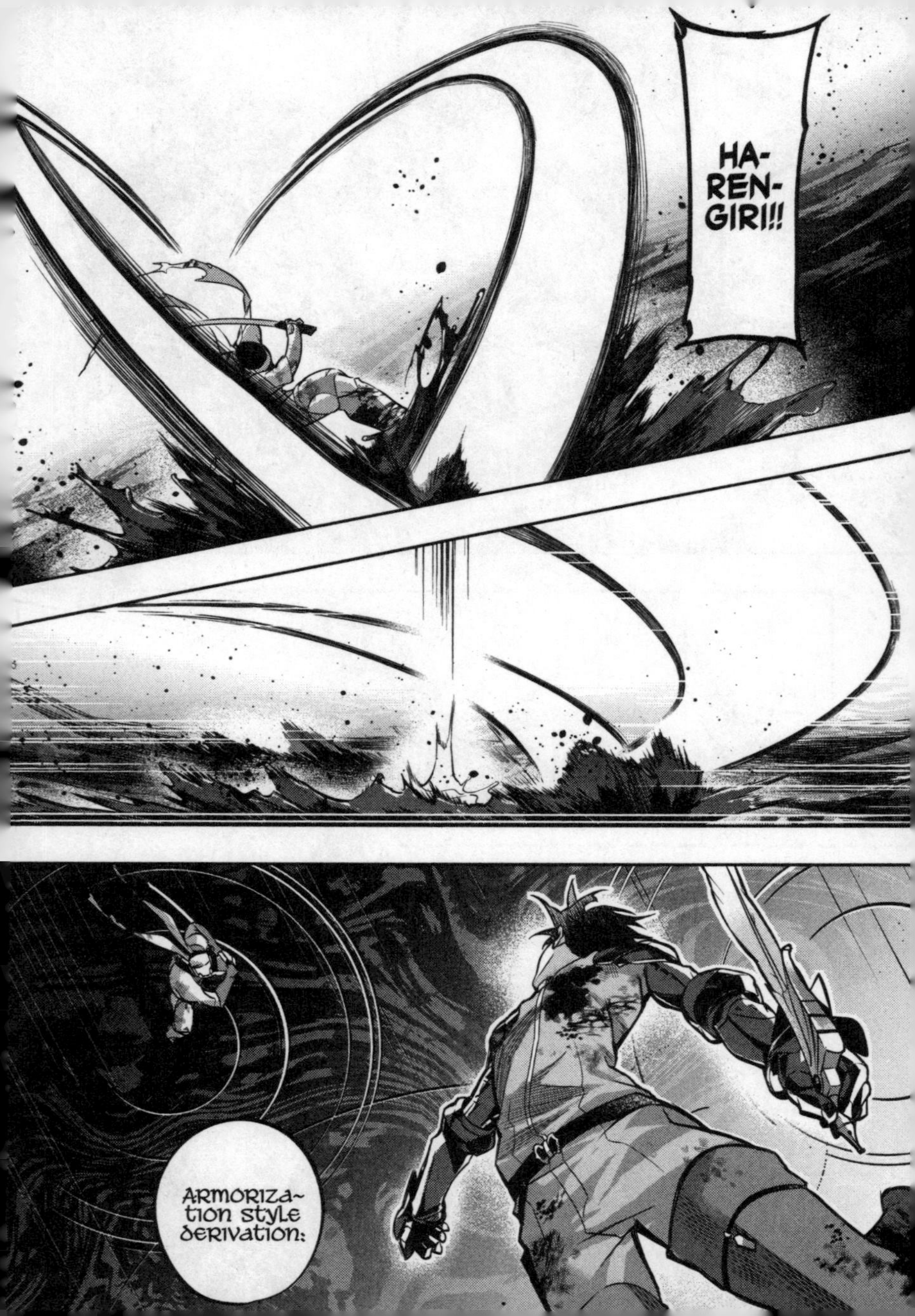
HA-
REN-
GIRI!!
ARMORIZA-
TION STYLE
DERIVATION:

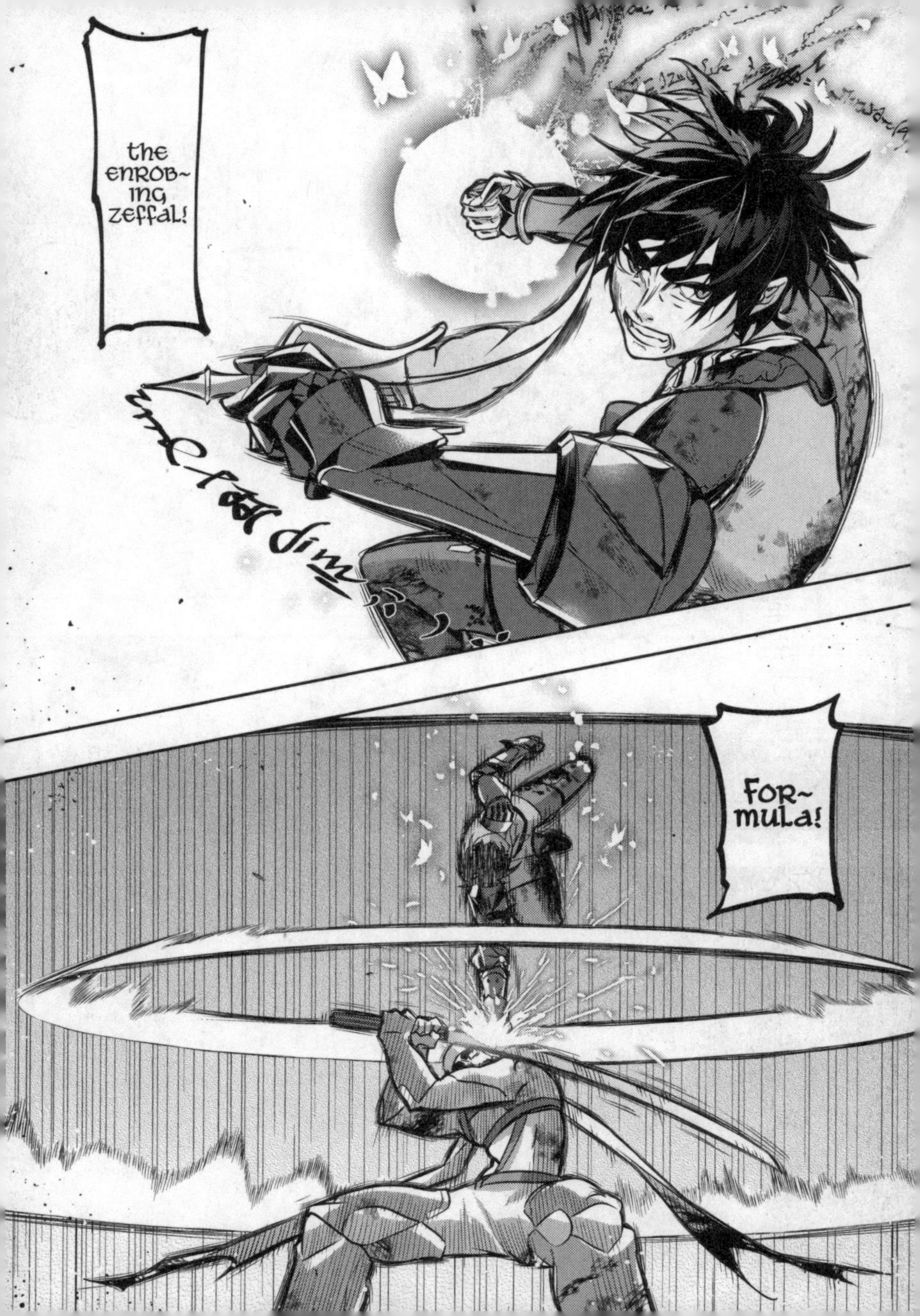
the ENROB~
ING
ZEFFAL!
FOR~
MULA!

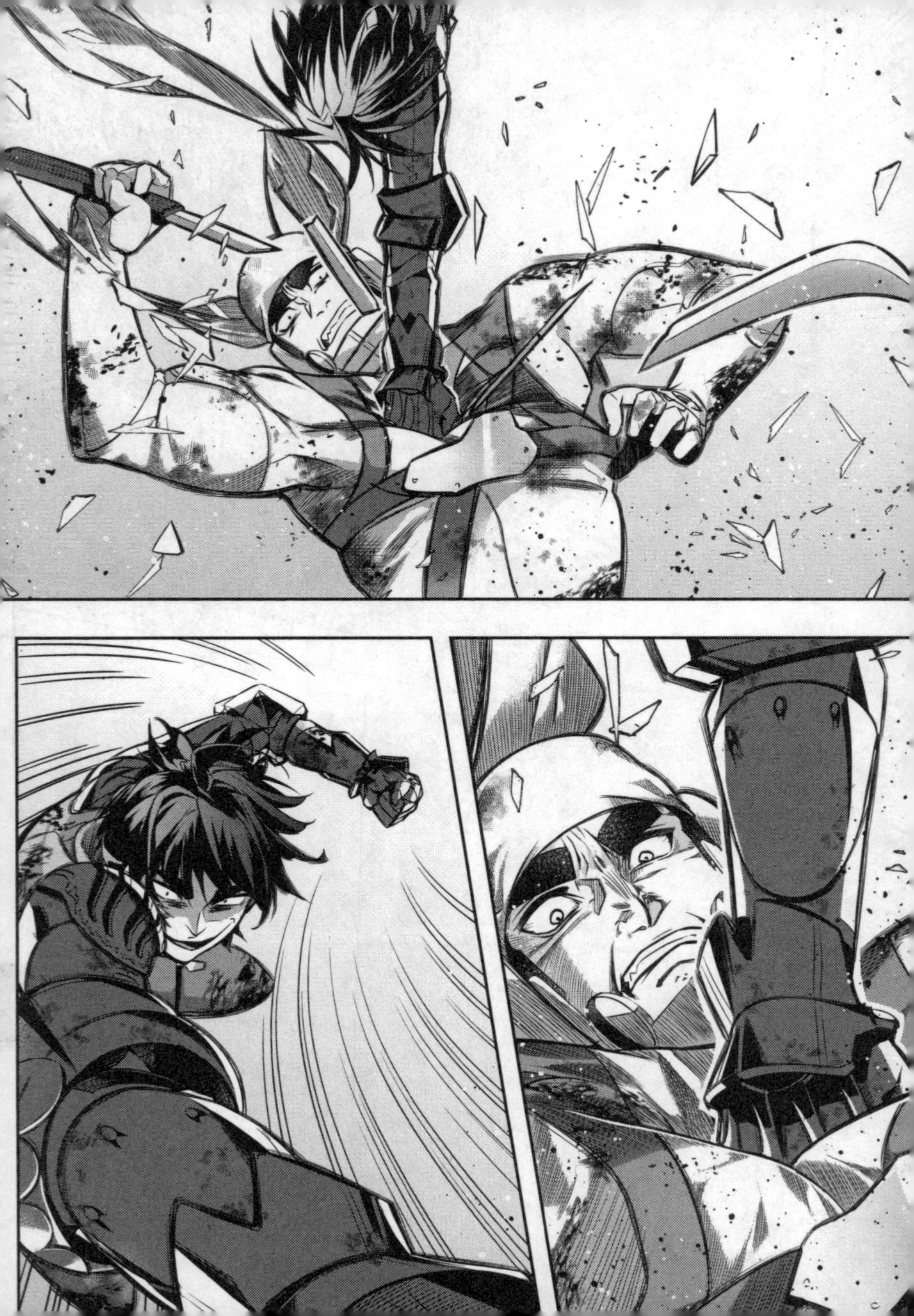

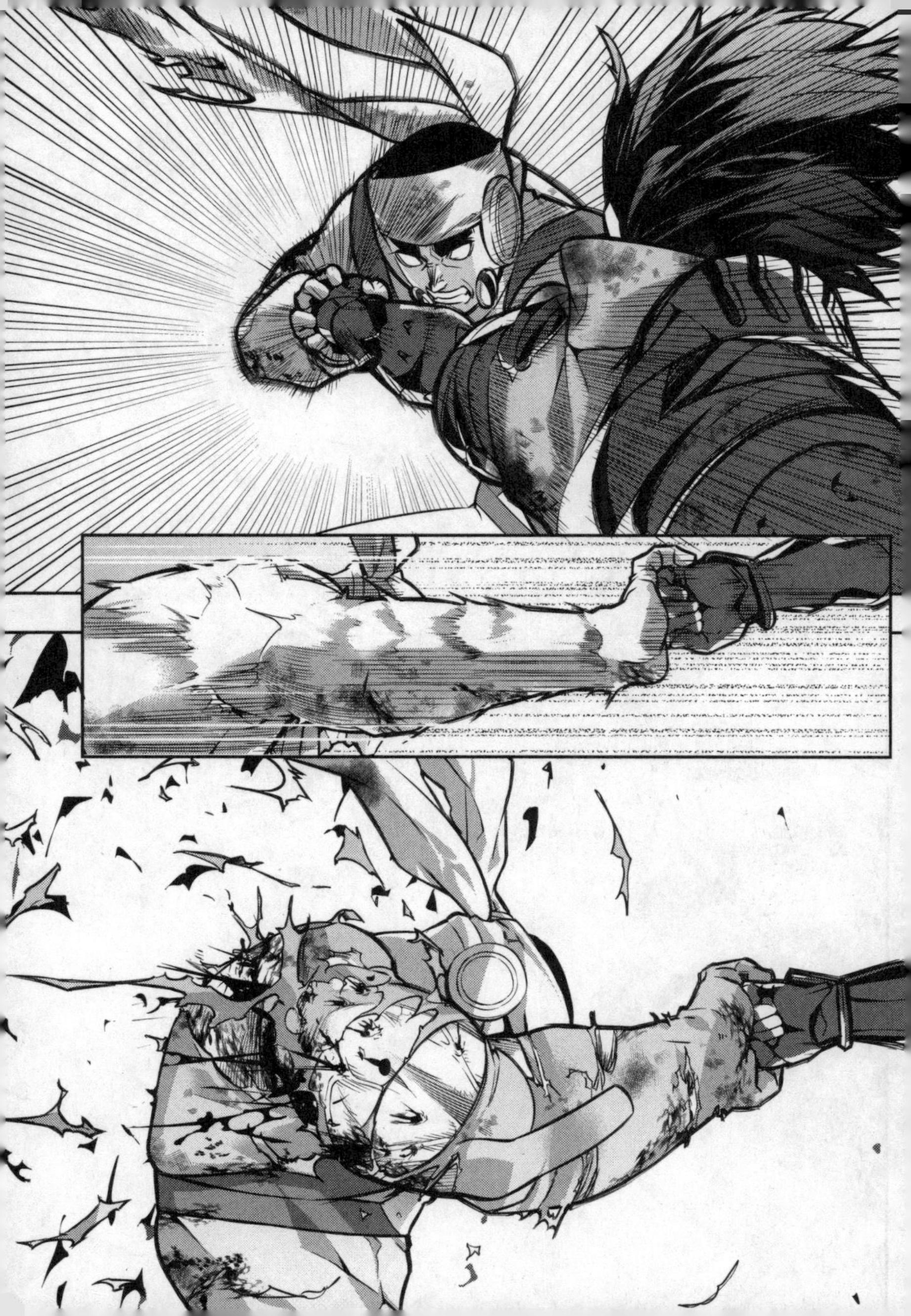

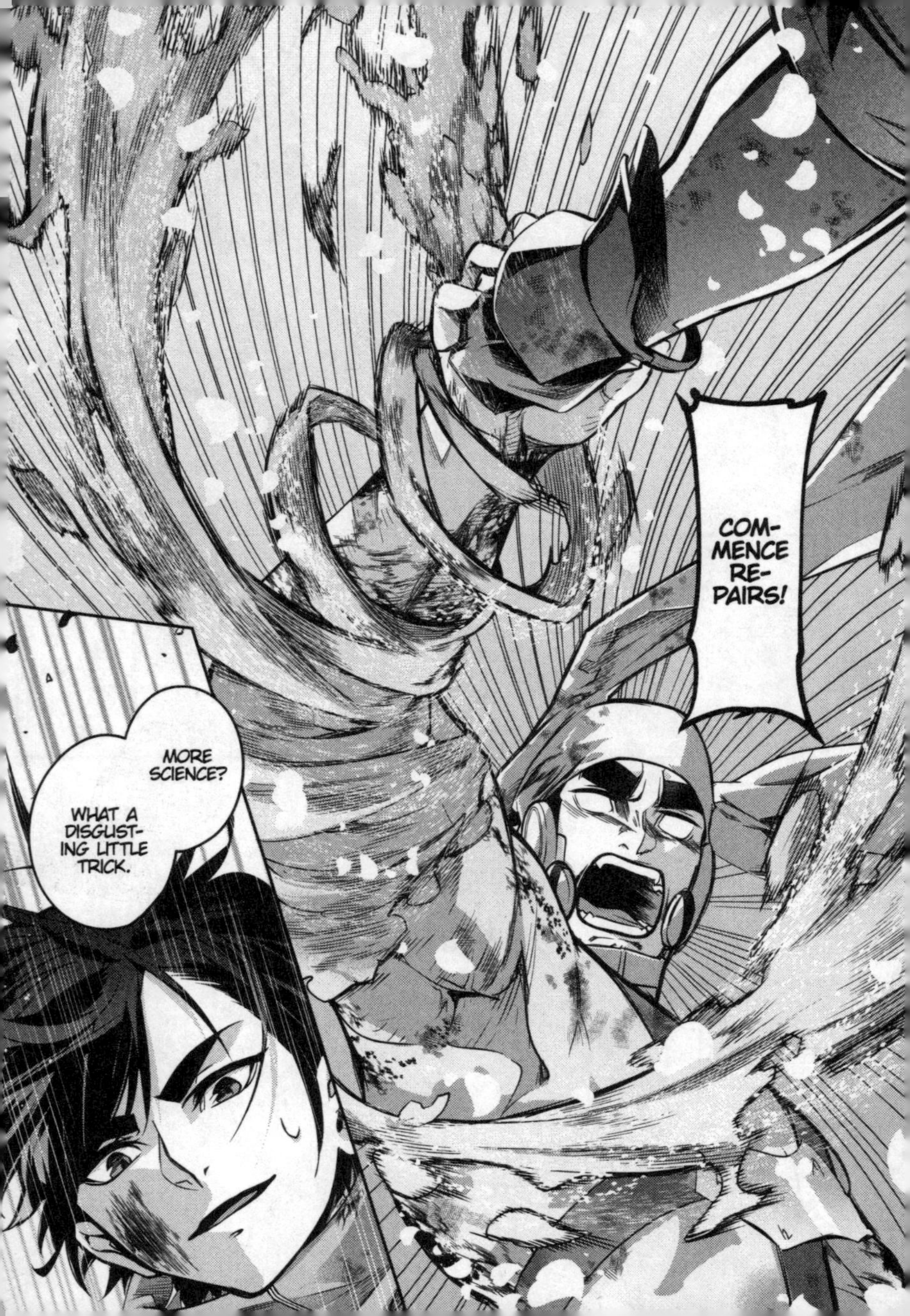
COM-MENCE RE-PAIRS!
MORE SCIENCE?
WHAT A DISGUST-ING LITTLE TRICK.

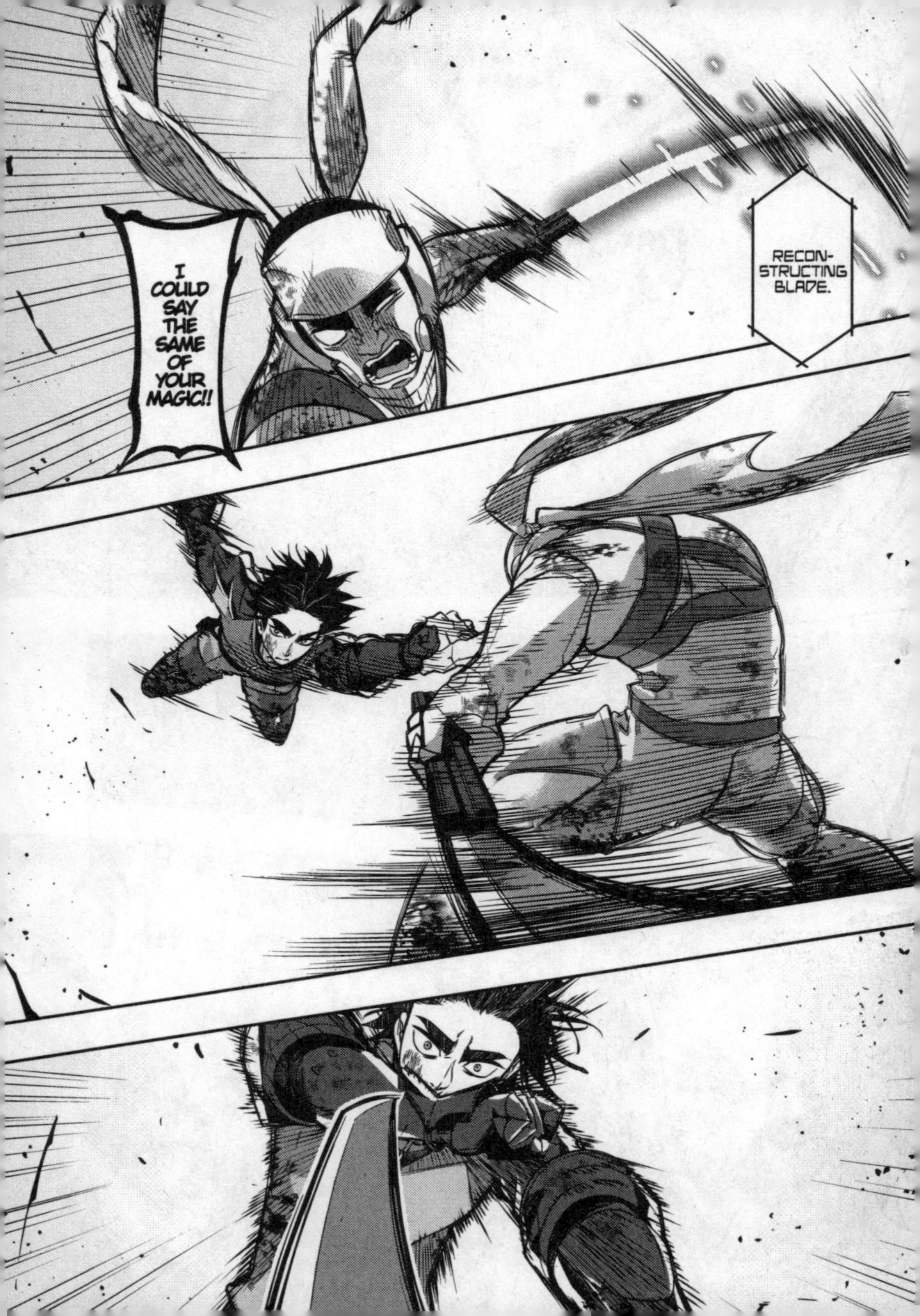
RECON-
STRUCTING
BLADE.
I COULD SAY THE SAME OF YOUR MAGIC!!

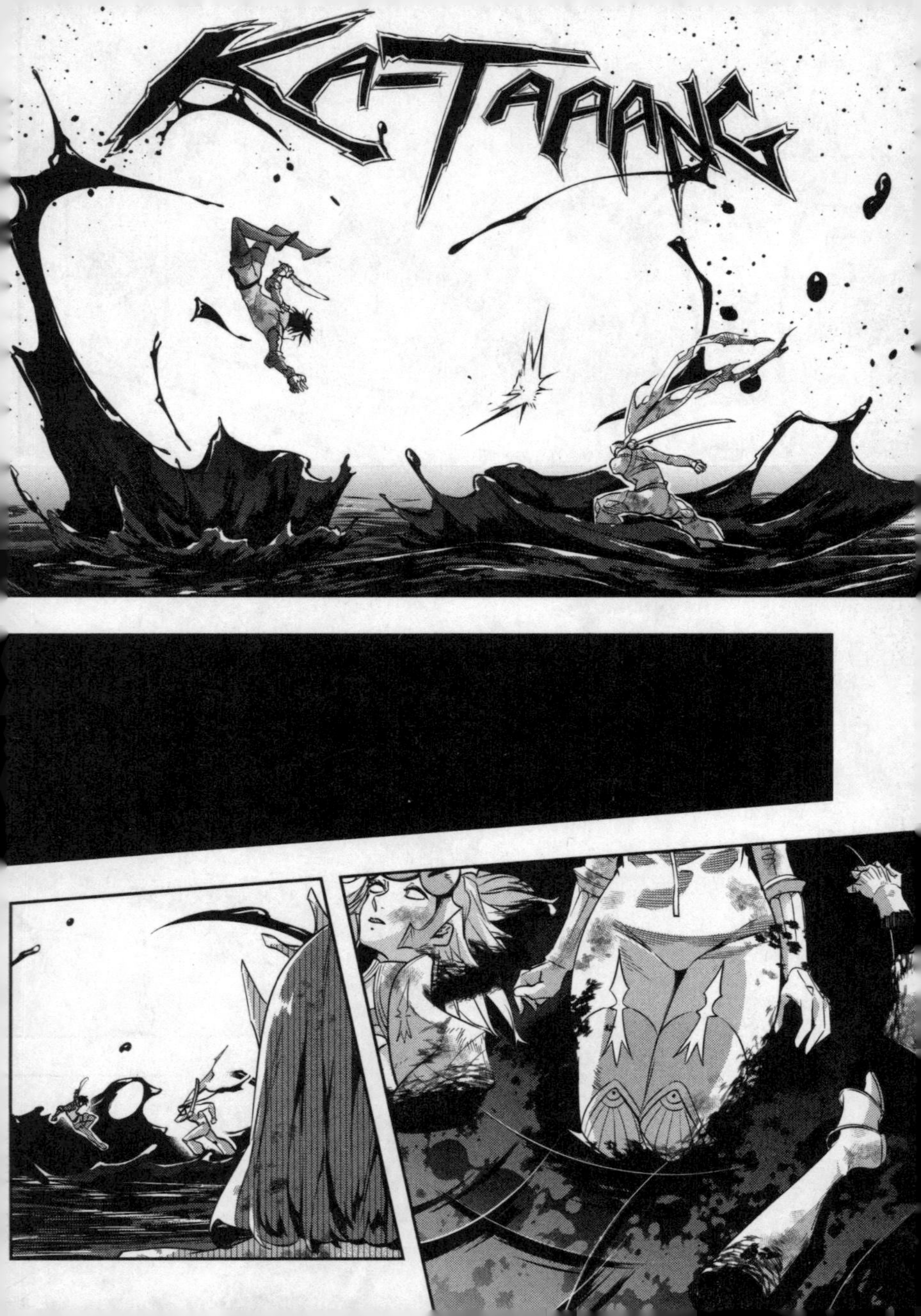
KA-TAAANG

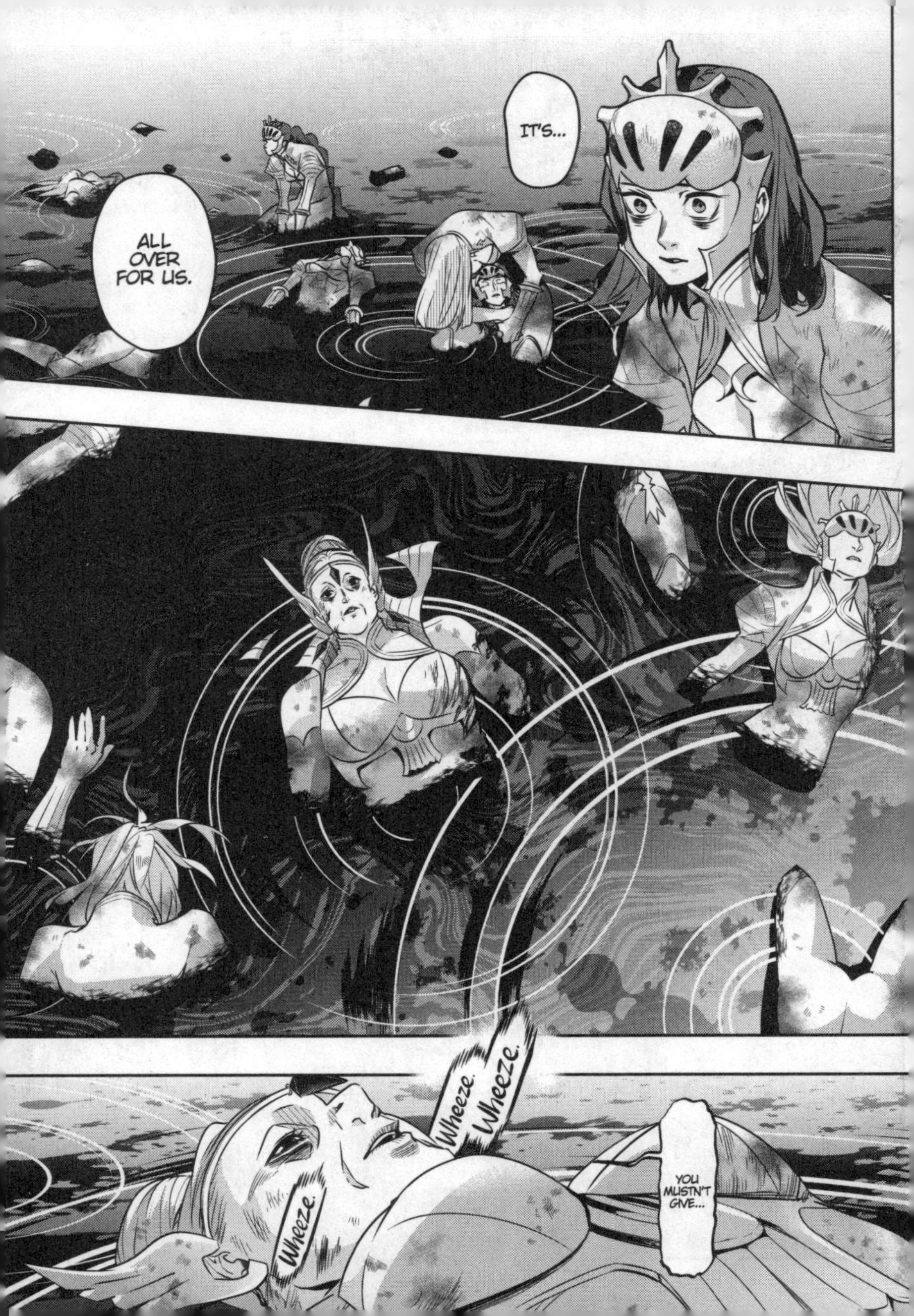
IT'S...
ALL OVER FOR US.
Wheeze.
Wheeze.
YOU MUSTN'T GIVE...
Wheeze.

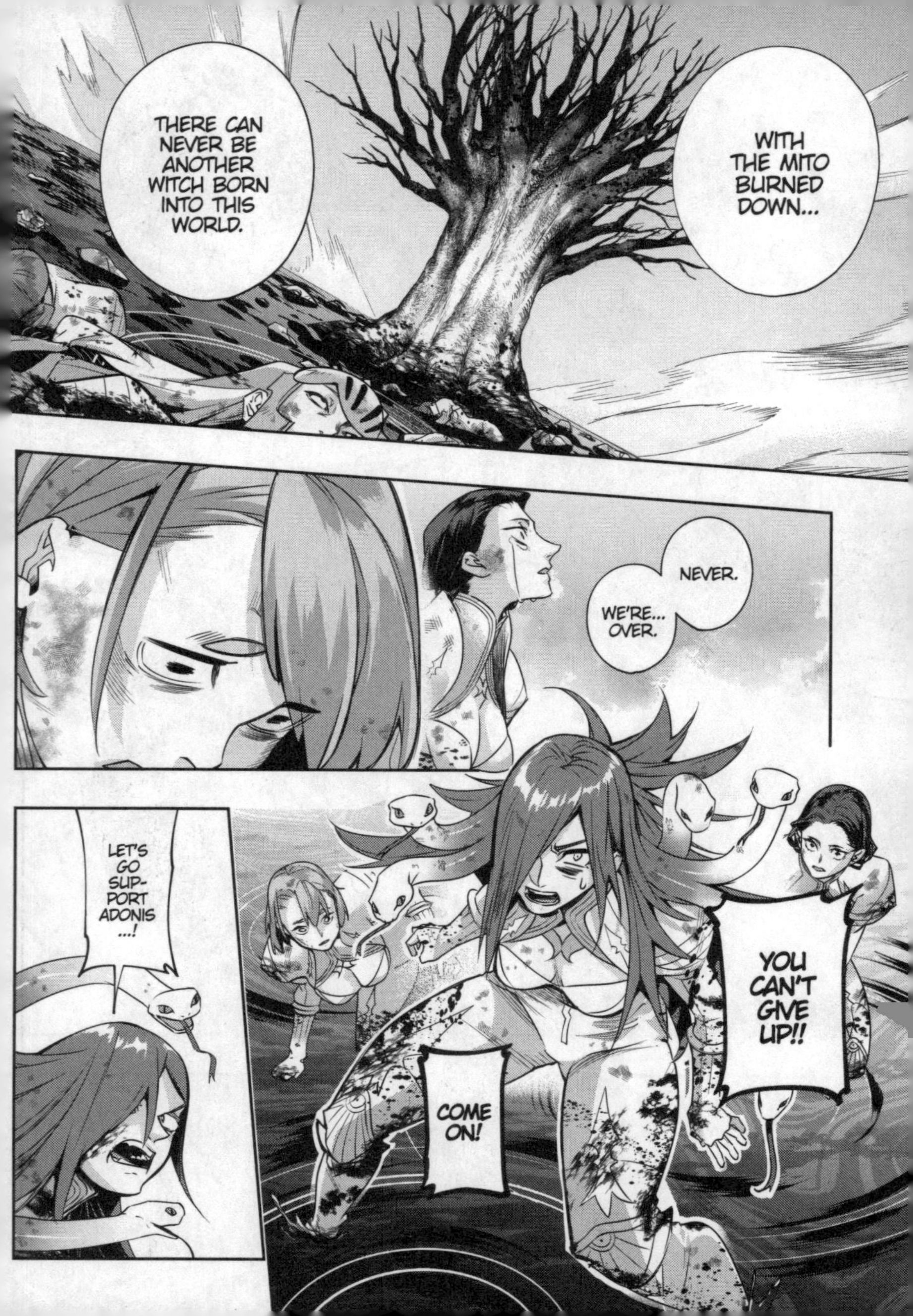
WITH THE MITO BURNED DOWN...
THERE CAN NEVER BE ANOTHER WITCH BORN INTO THIS WORLD.
NEVER.
WE'RE... OVER.
YOU CAN'T GIVE UP!!
COME ON!
LET'S GO SUPPORT ADONIS ...!

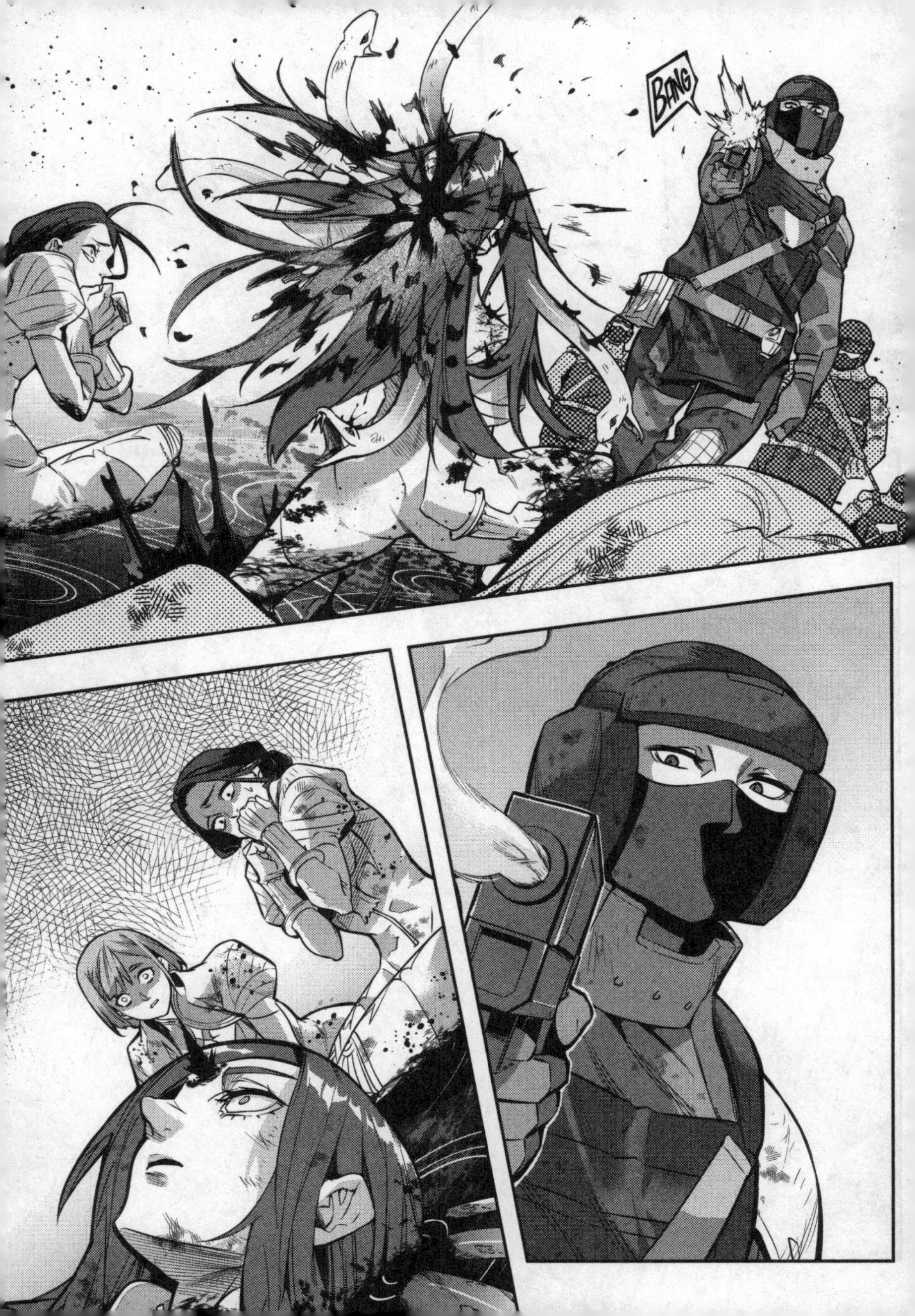
BANG

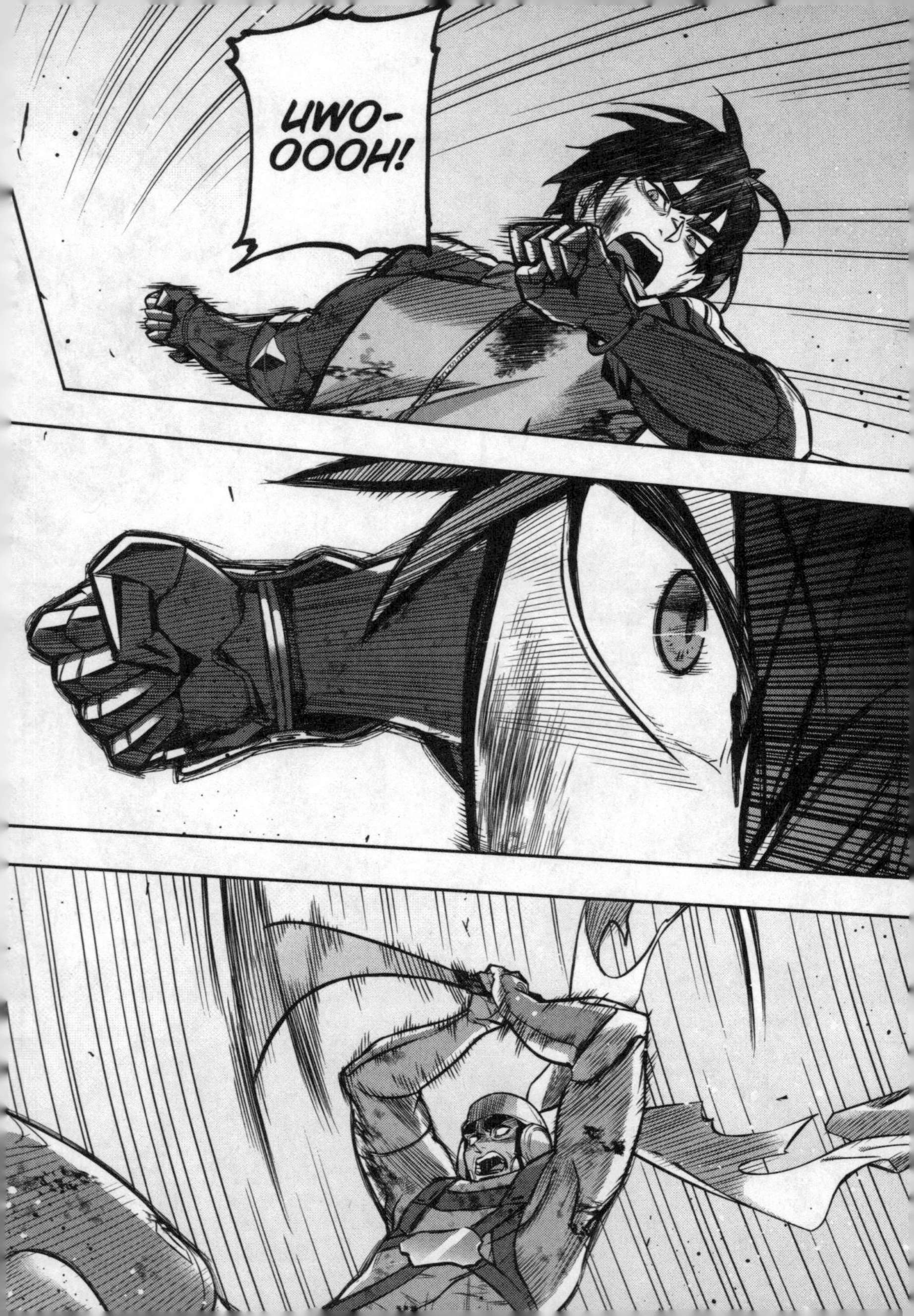
UWO-OOOH!

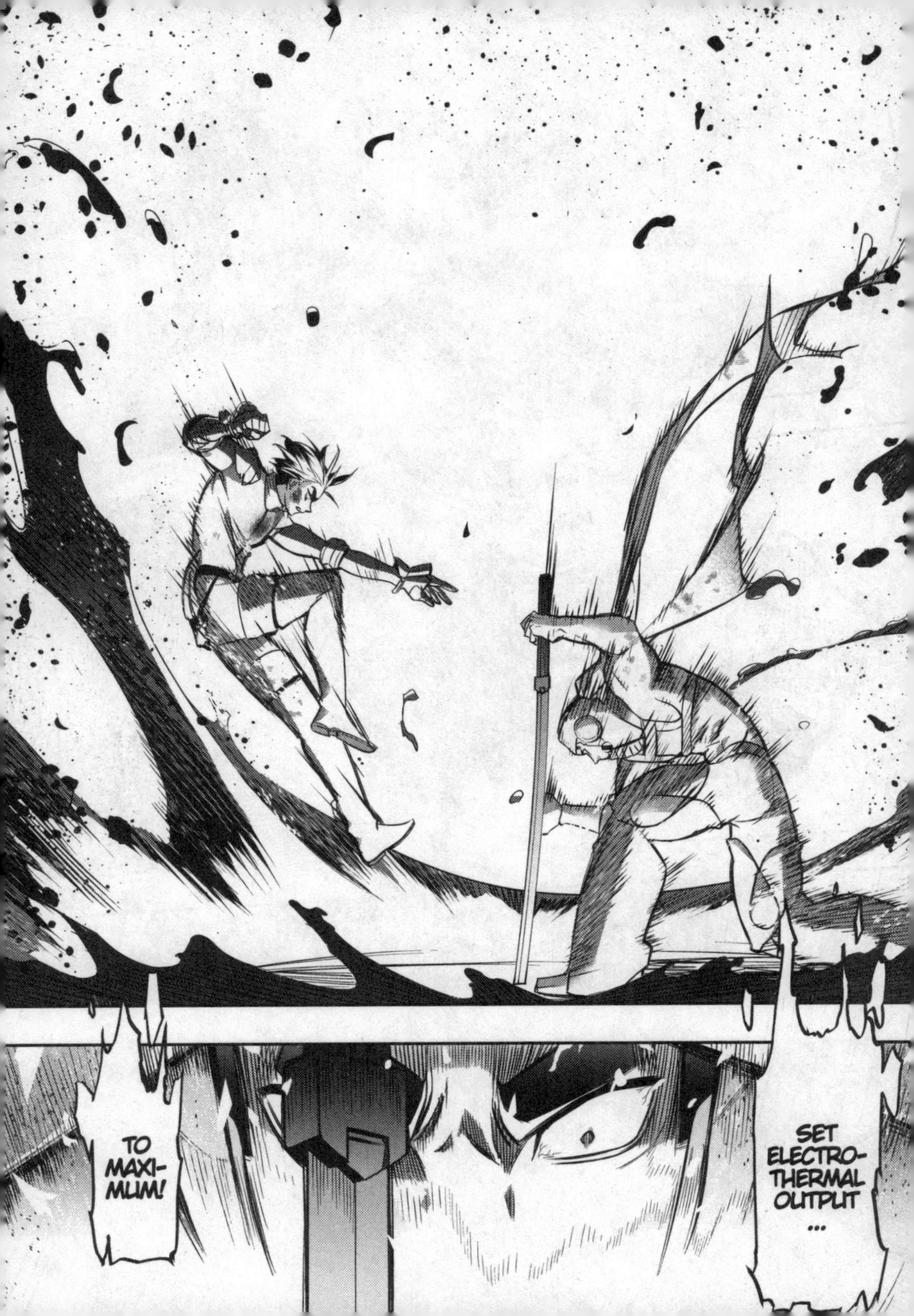
SET ELECTRO-THERMAL OUTPUT ...
TO MAXI-MUM!

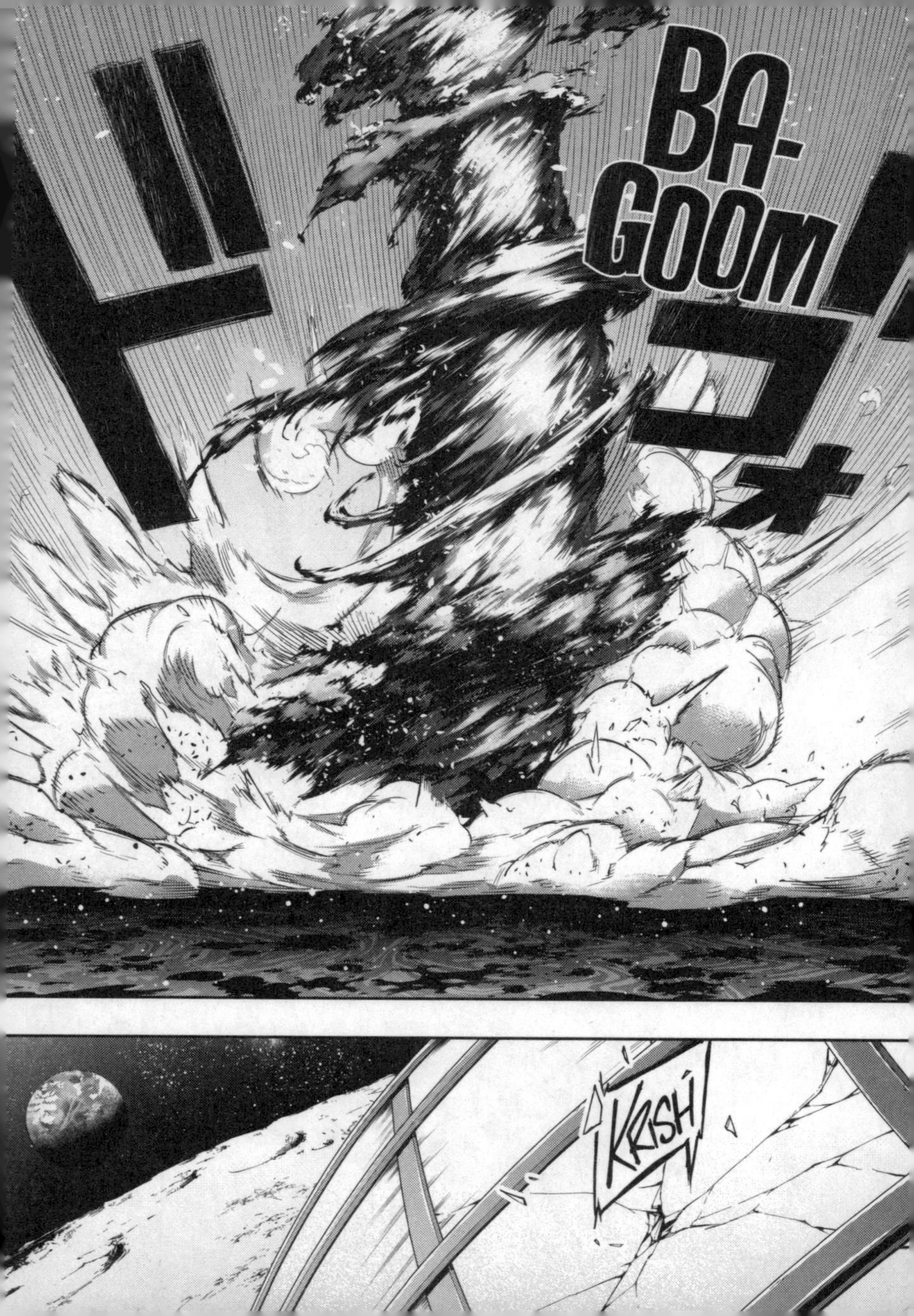
BA-GOOM
KRISH

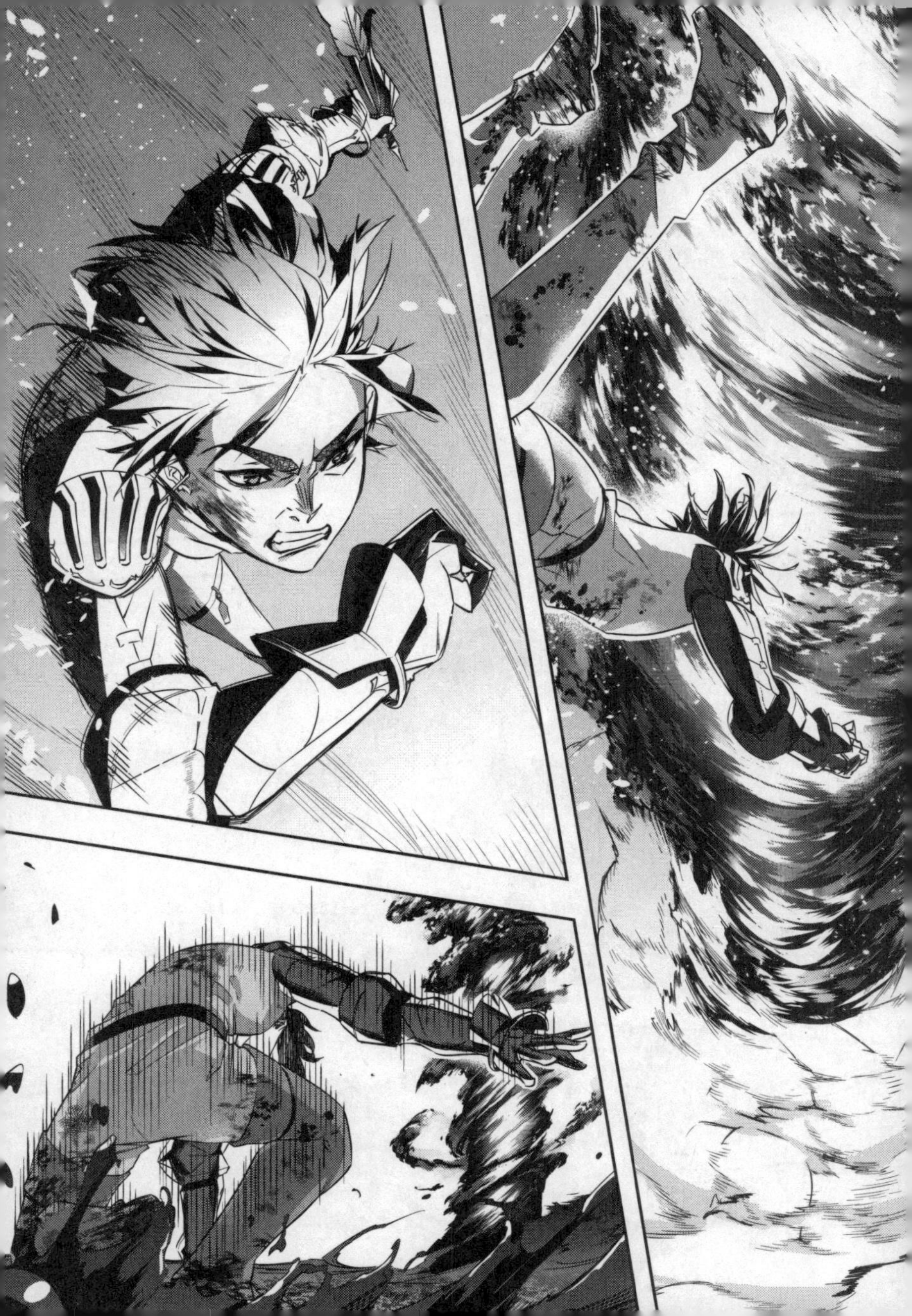

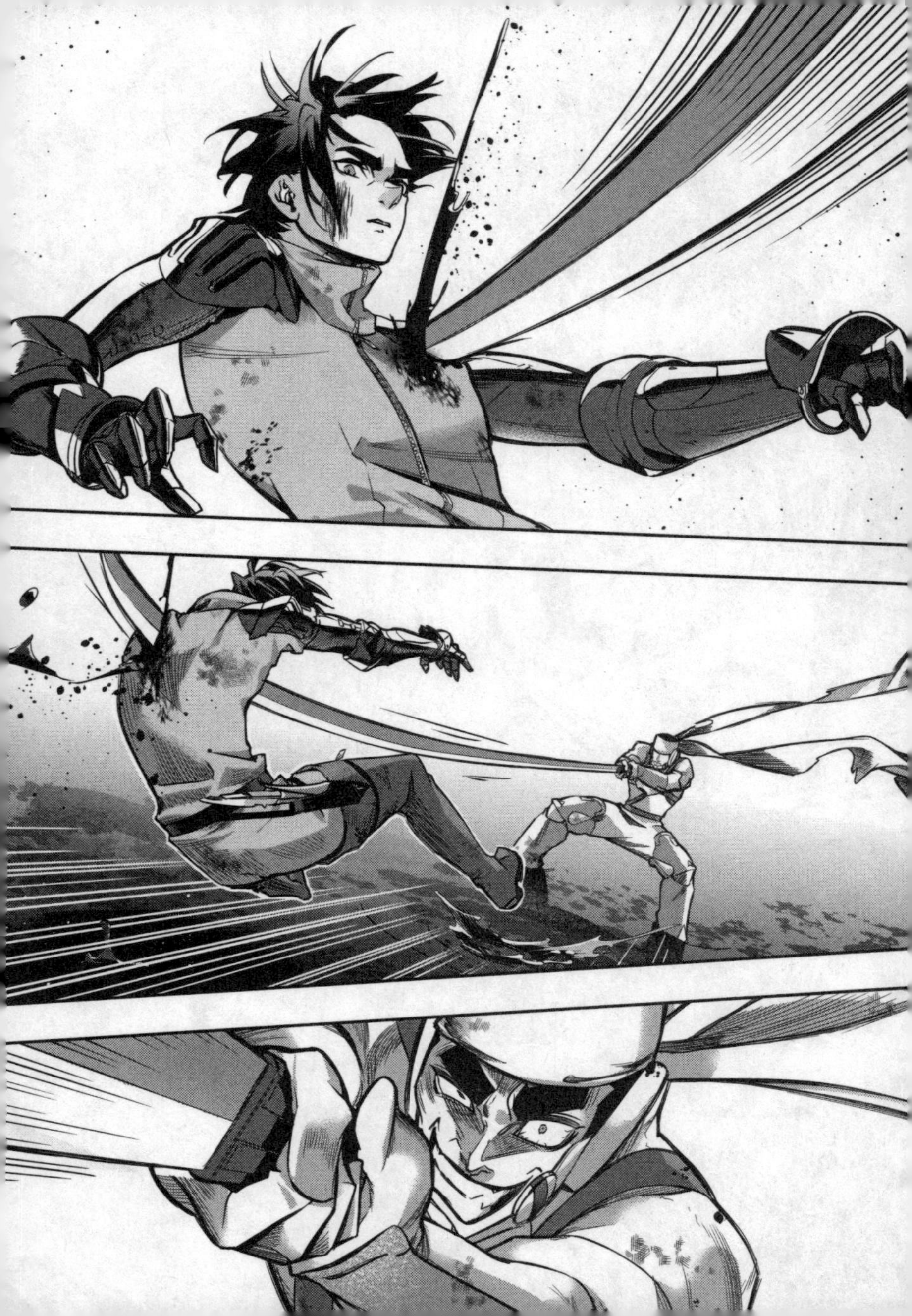

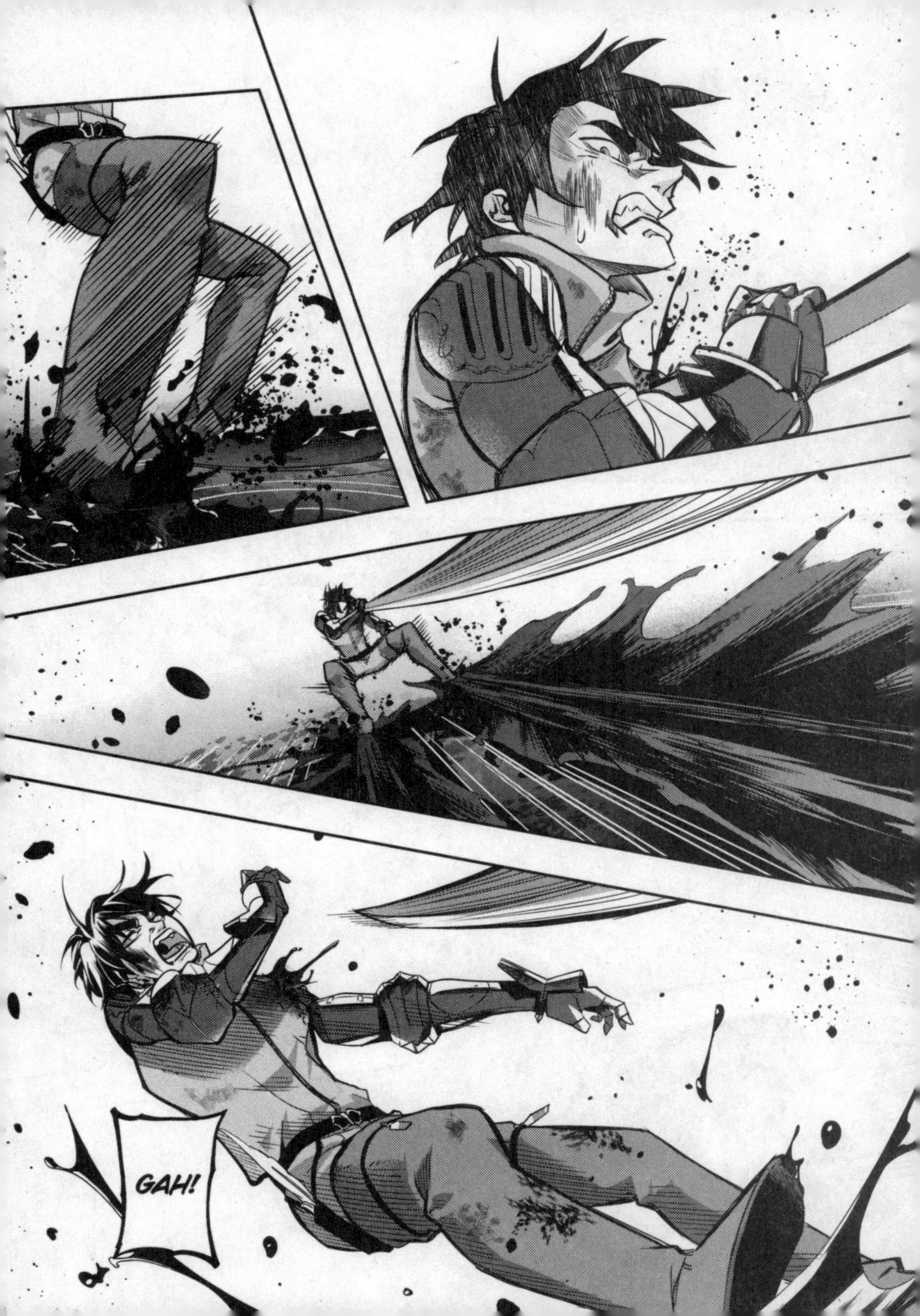
GAH!

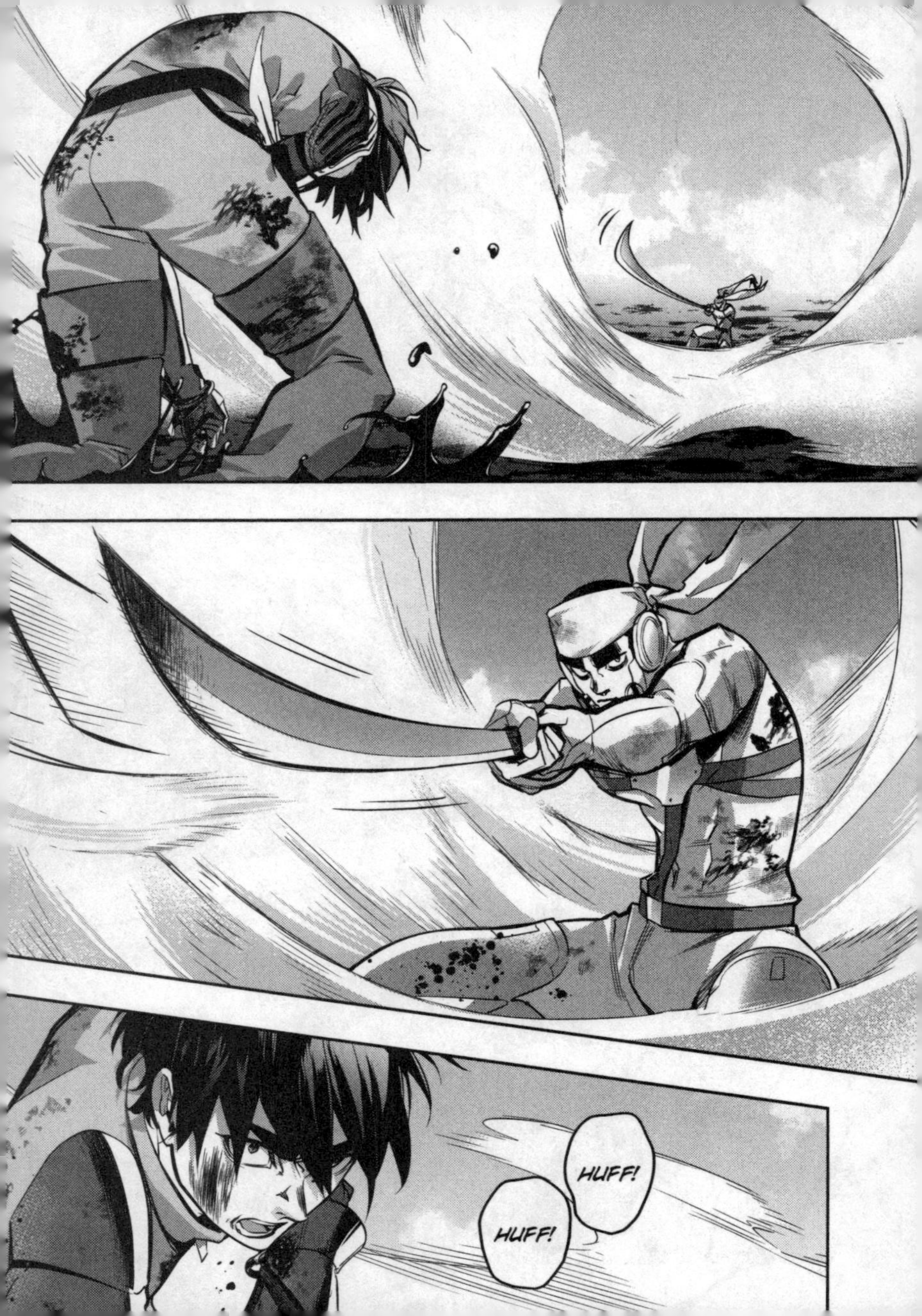
HUFF!
HUFF!

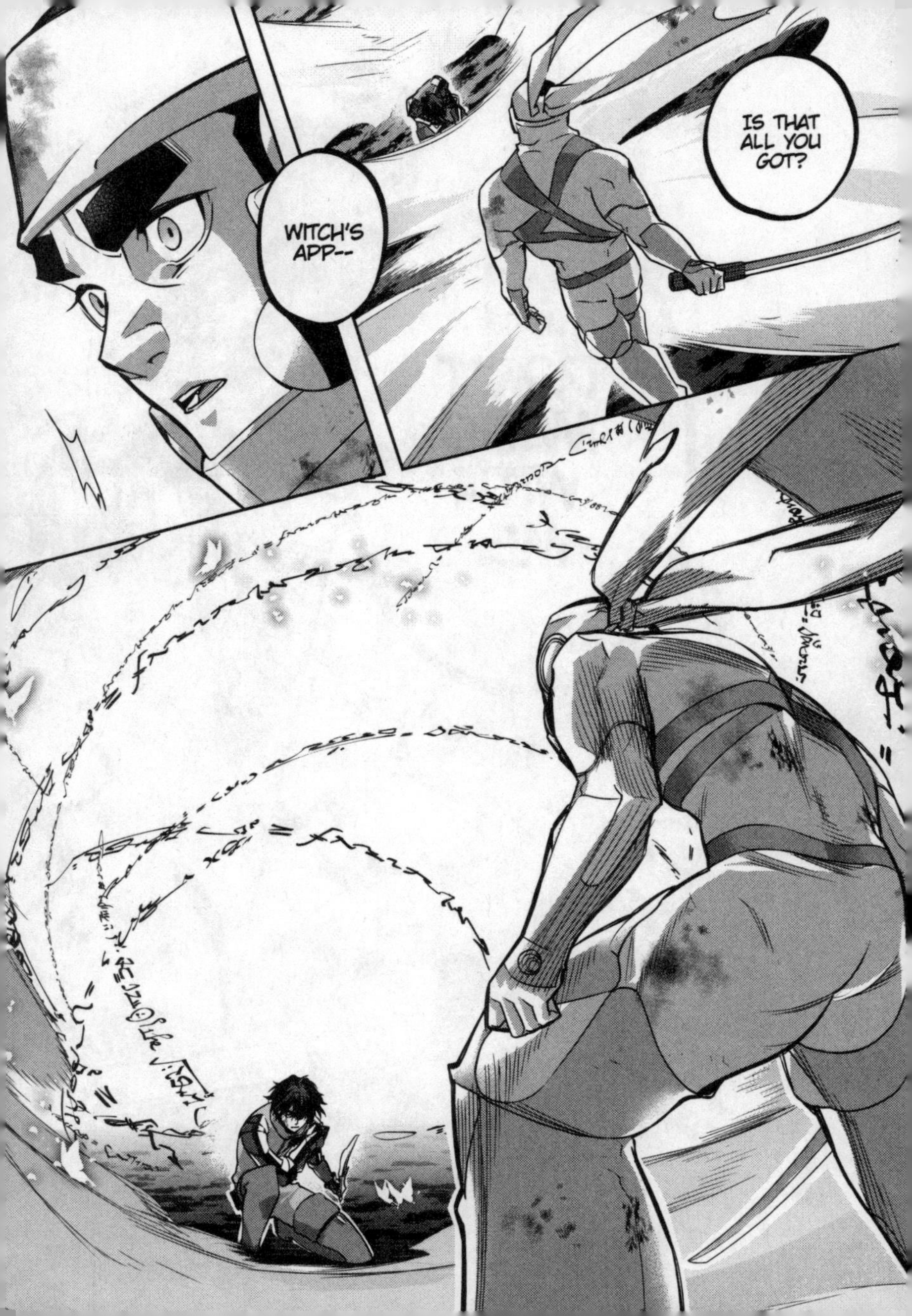
IS THAT ALL YOU GOT?
WITCH'S APP--

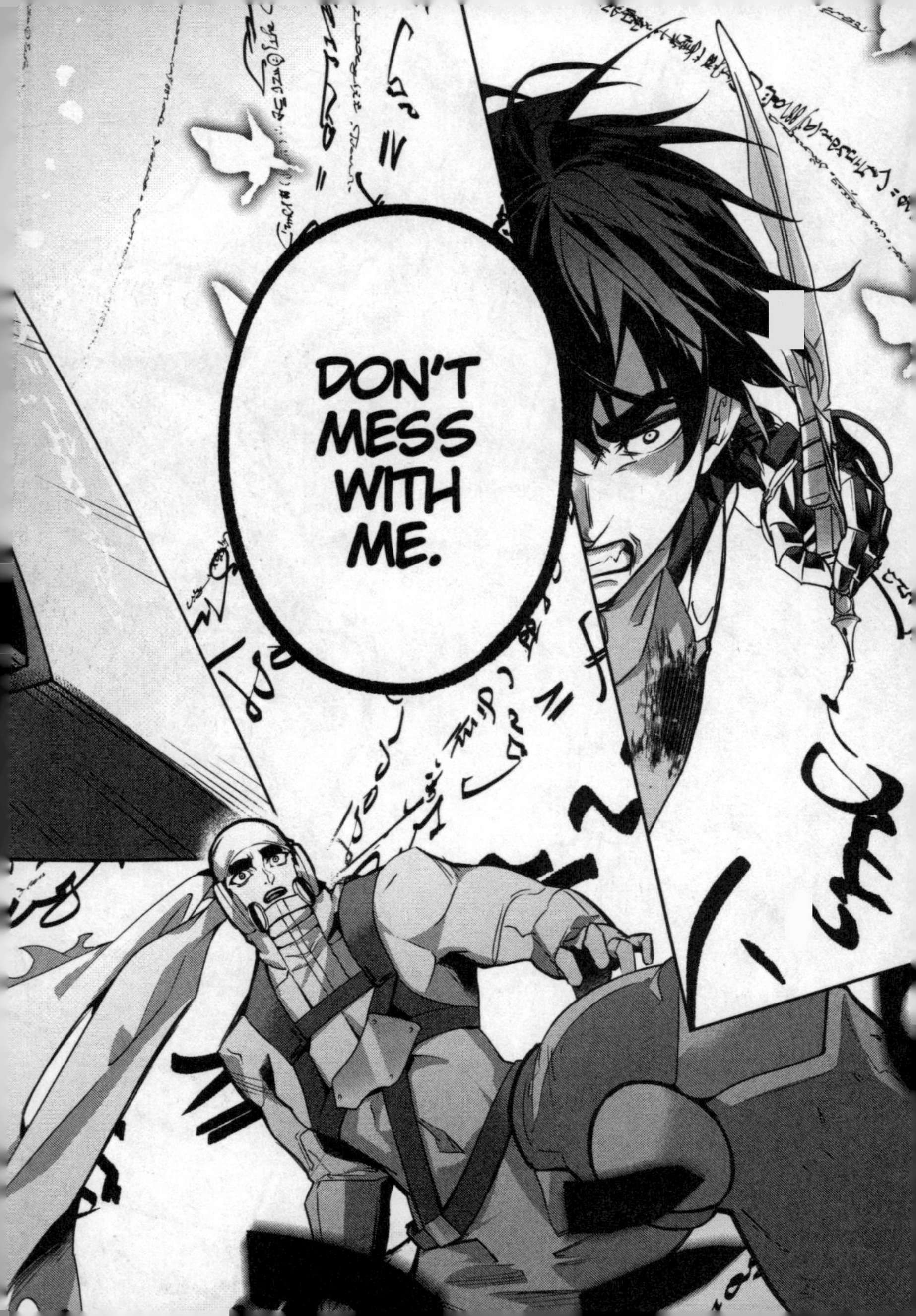
DON'T MESS WITH ME.

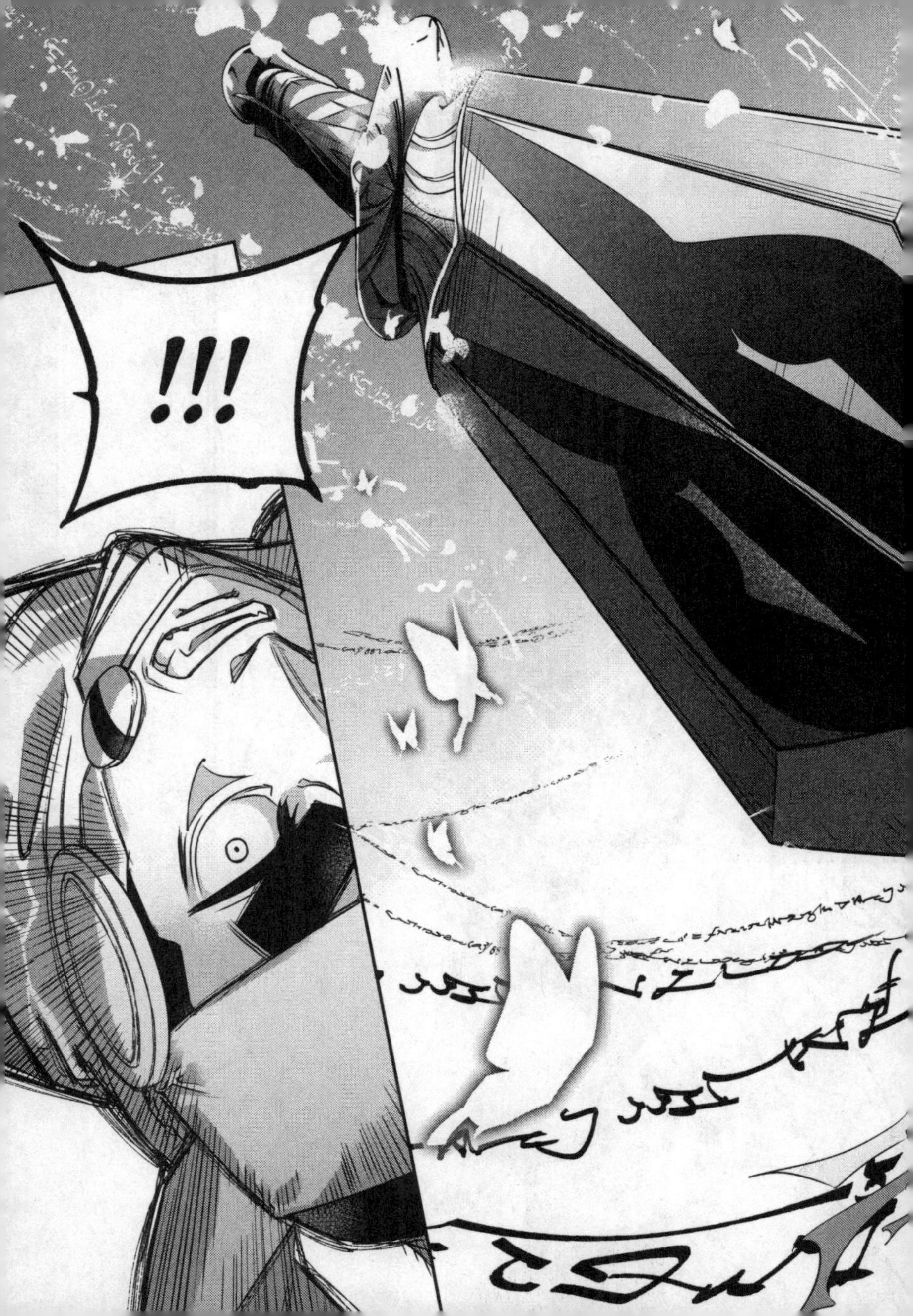
!!!

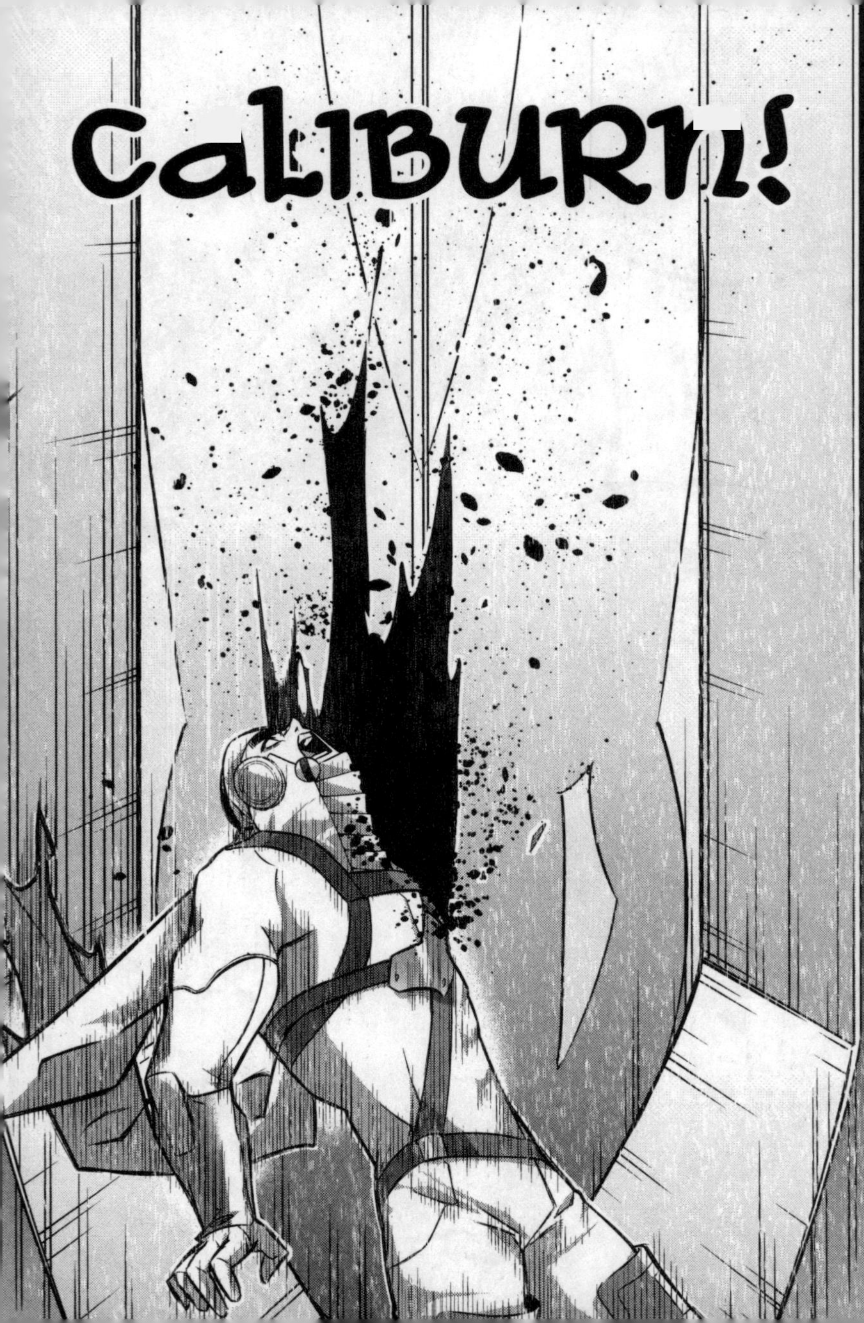
CALIBURN!

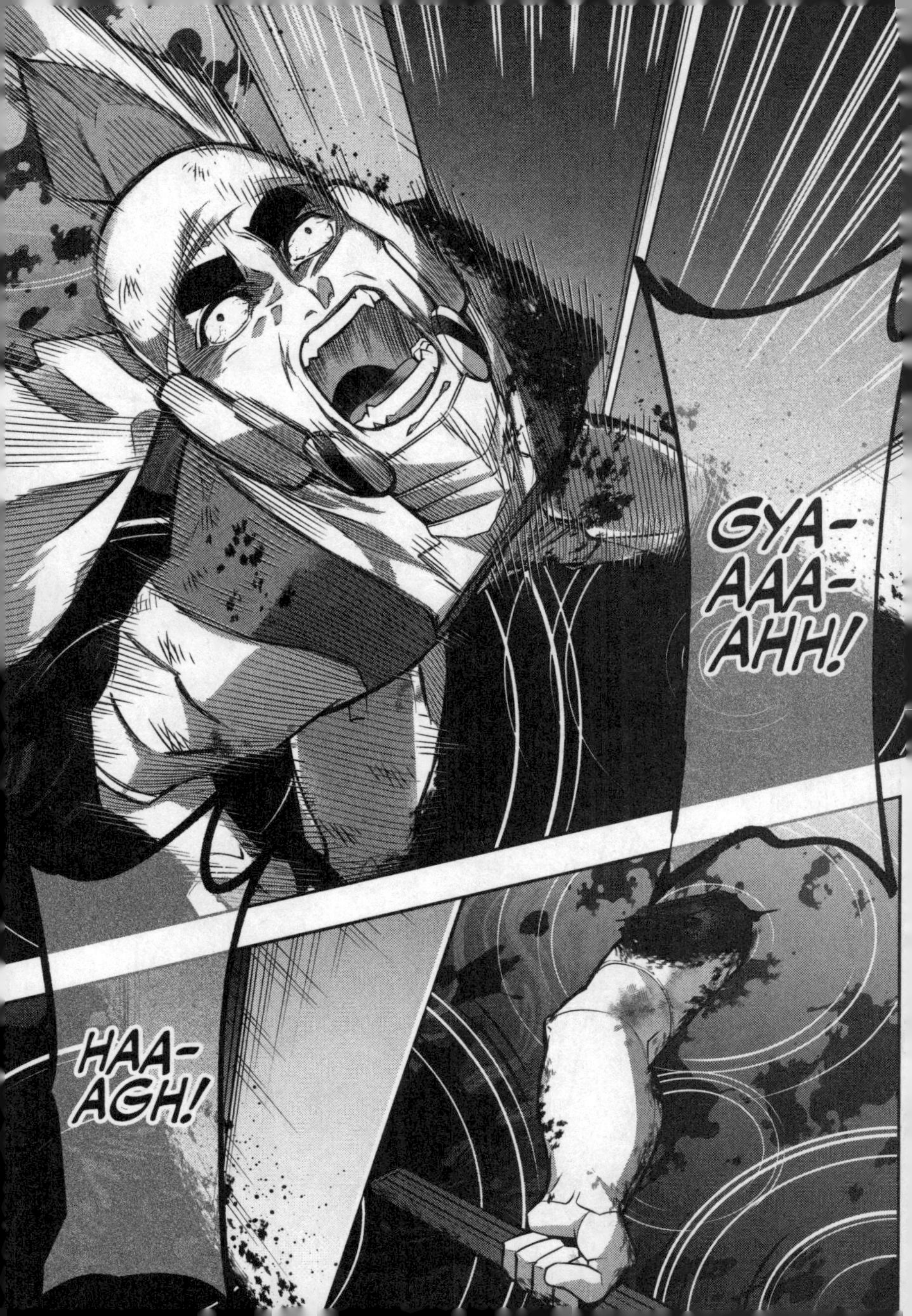
GYA-AAA-AHH!
HAA-AGH!

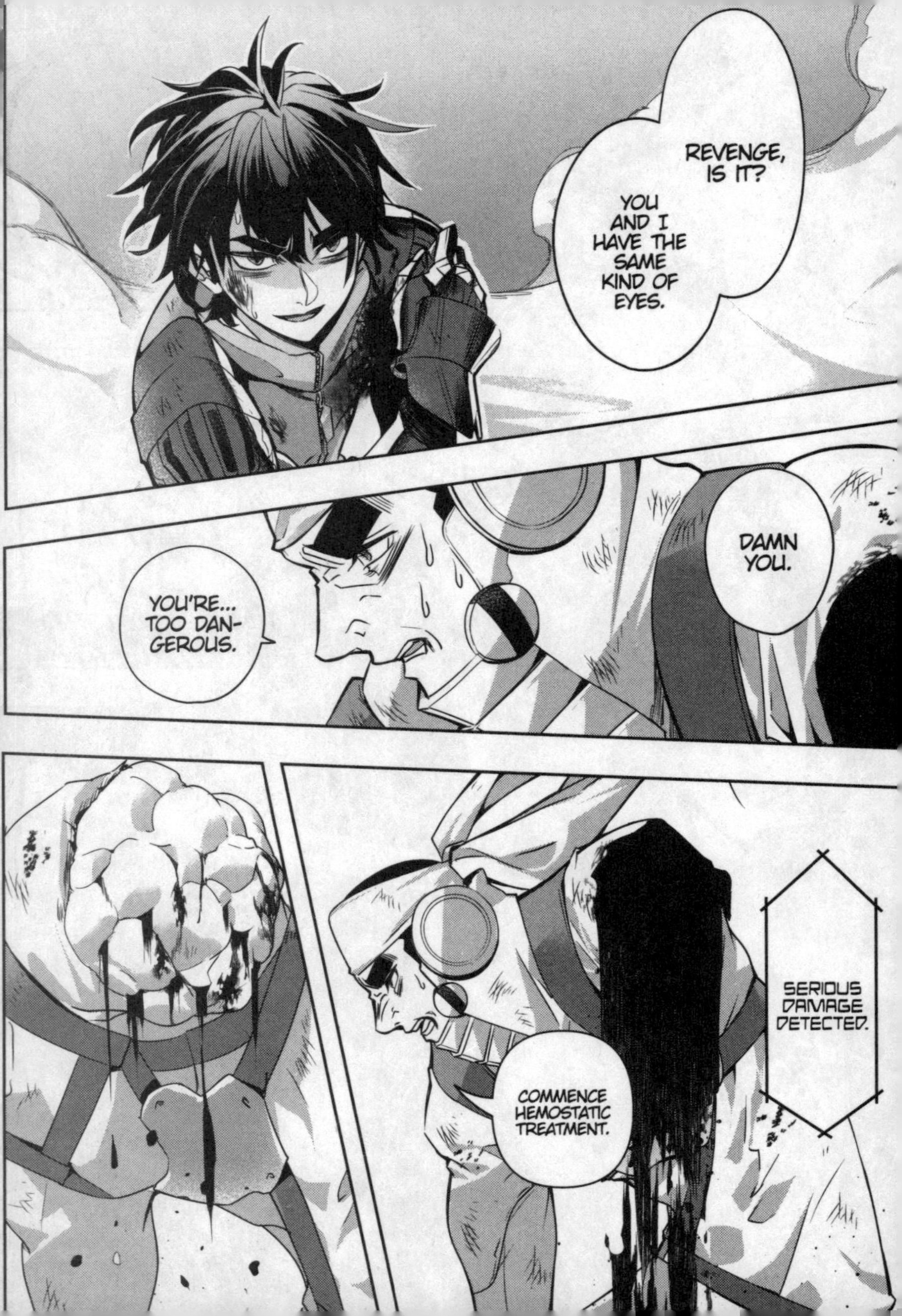
REVENGE, IS IT?
YOU AND I HAVE THE SAME KIND OF EYES.
DAMN YOU.
YOU'RE... TOO DAN-GEROUS.
SERIOUS DAMAGE DETECTED.
COMMENCE HEMOSTATIC TREATMENT.

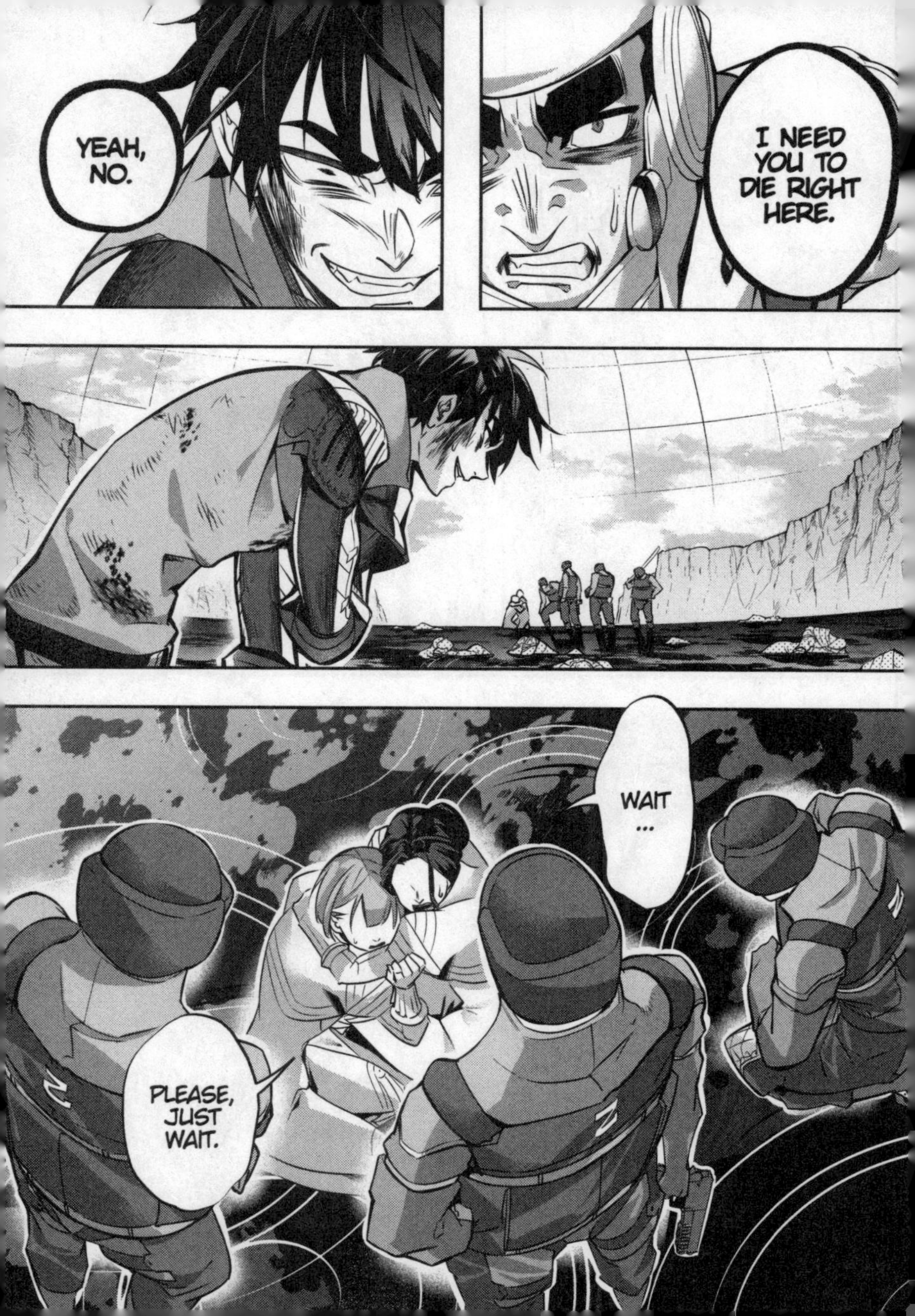
I NEED YOU TO DIE RIGHT HERE.
YEAH, NO.
WAIT ...
PLEASE, JUST WAIT.

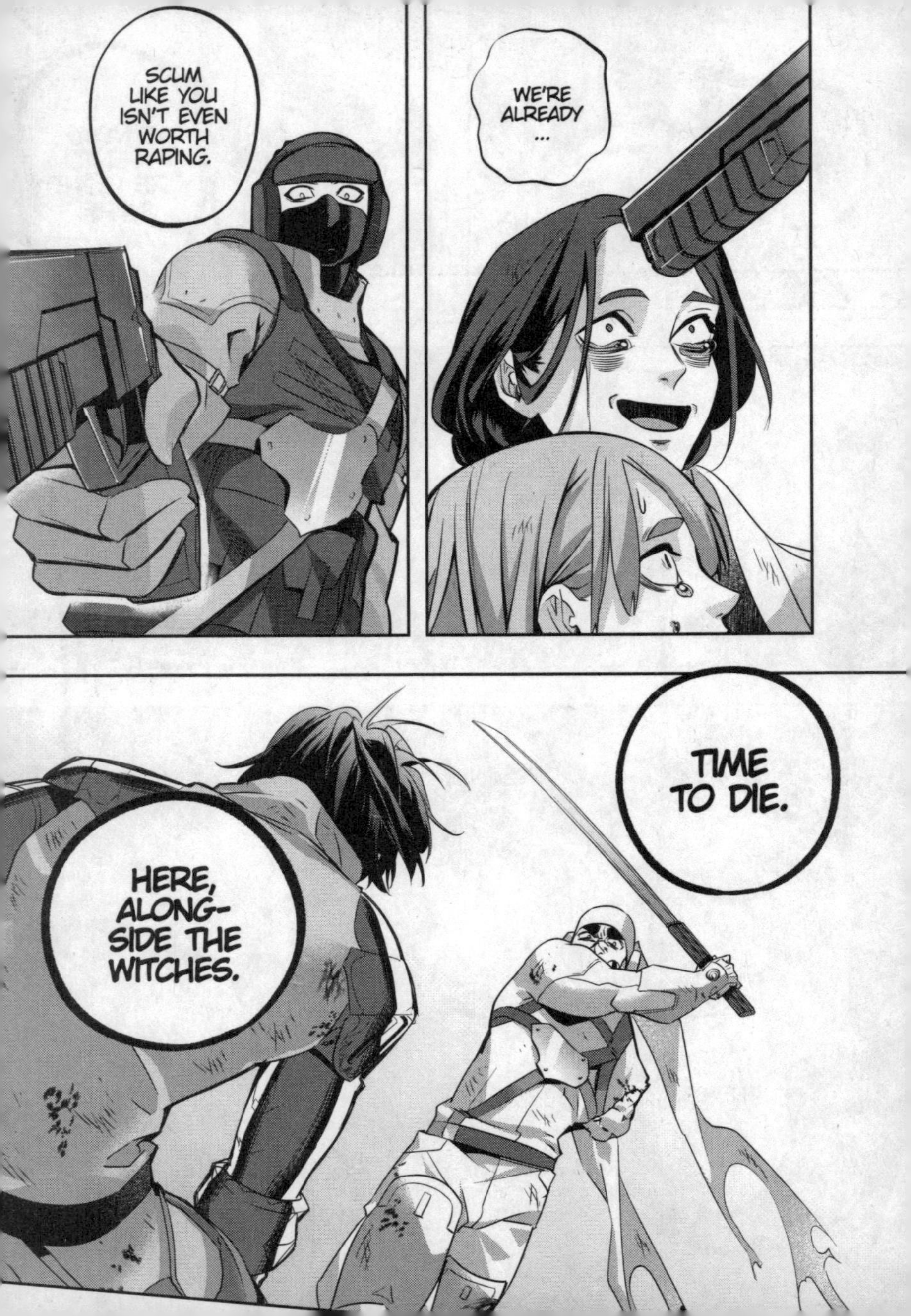
WE'RE ALREADY ...
SCUM LIKE YOU ISN'T EVEN WORTH RAPING.
TIME TO DIE.
HERE, ALONG-SIDE THE WITCHES.

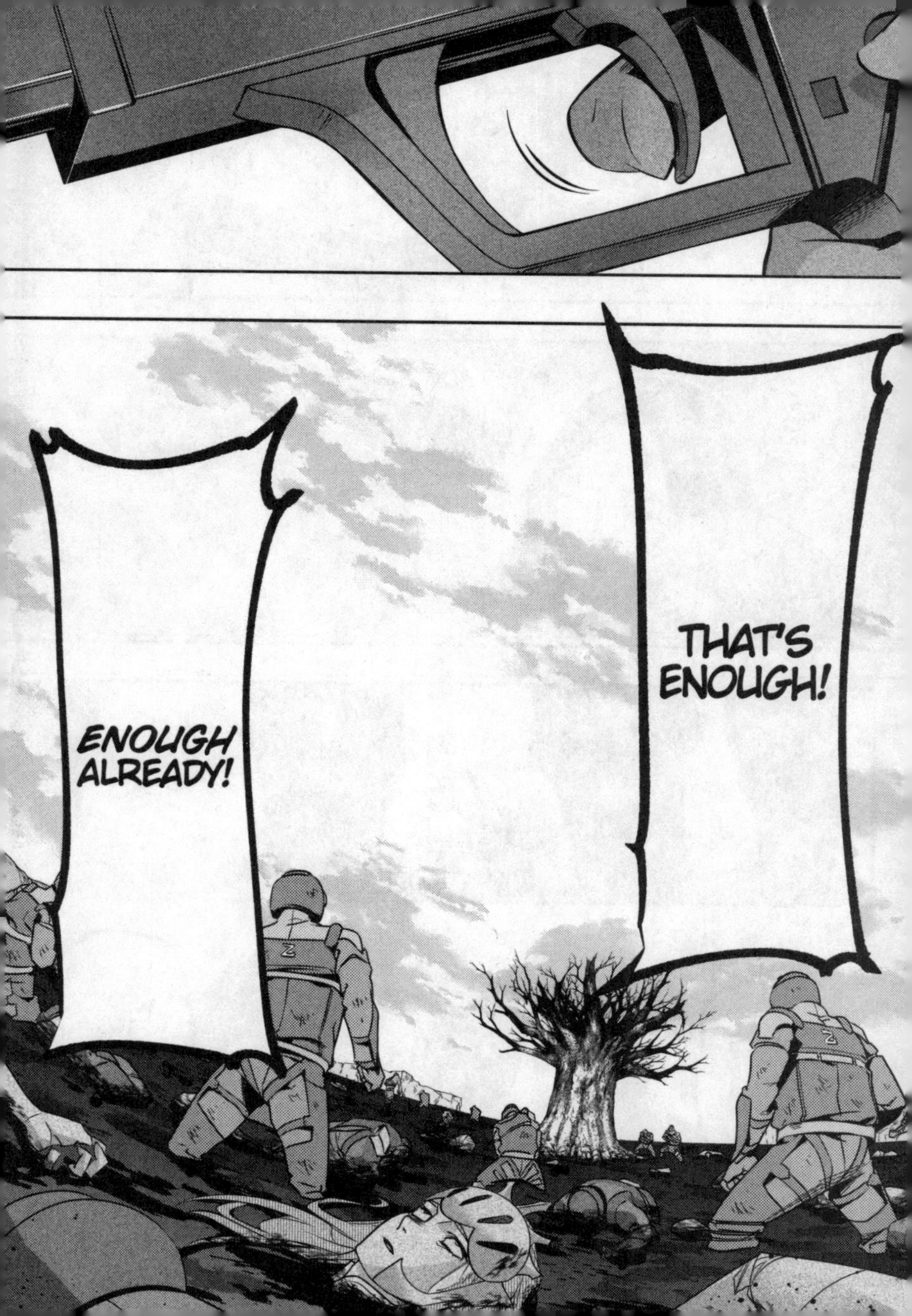
THAT'S ENOUGH!
ENOUGH ALREADY!

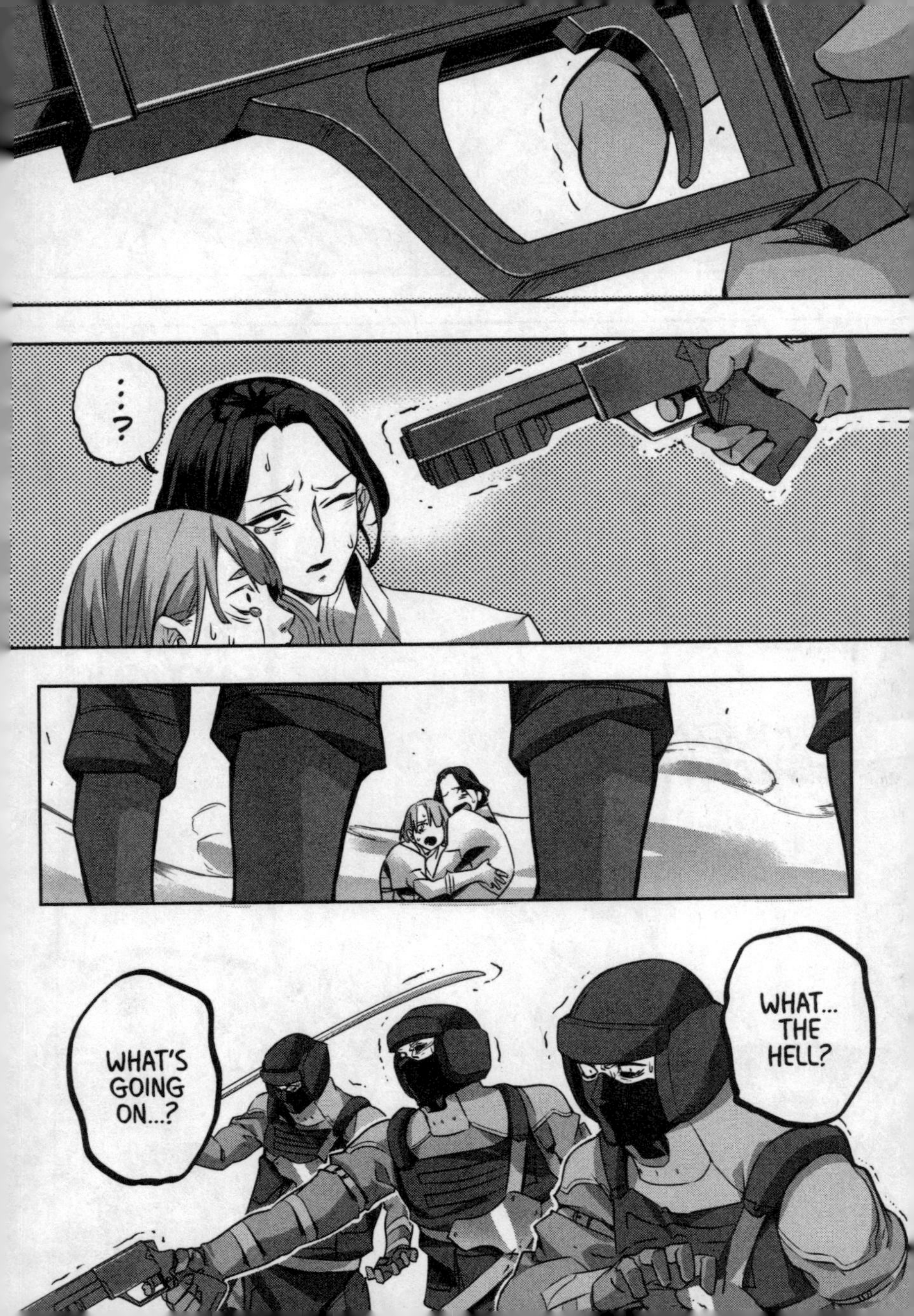

...?
WHAT... THE HELL?
WHAT'S GOING ON...?

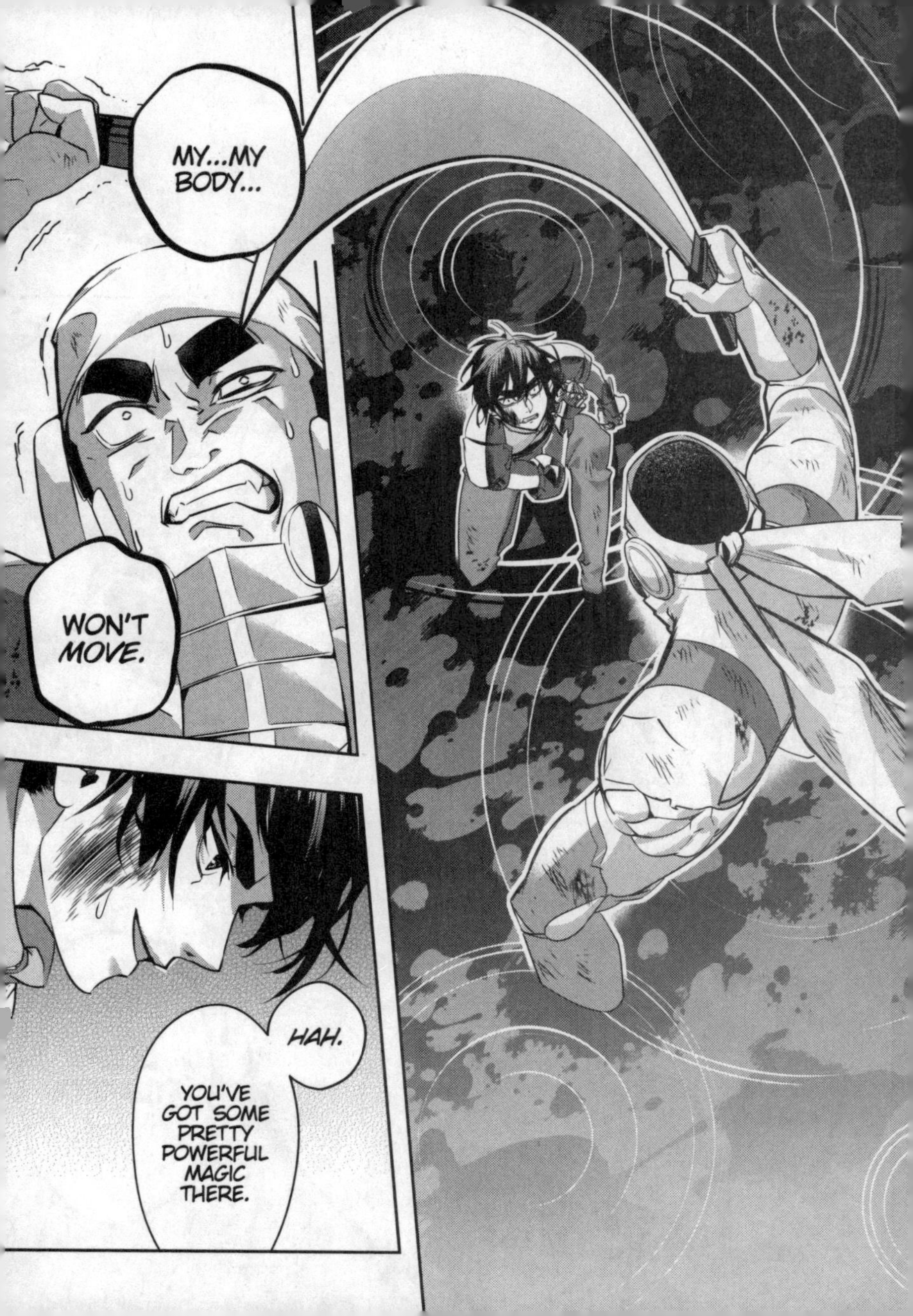
MY...MY BODY...
WON'T MOVE.
HAH.
YOU'VE GOT SOME PRETTY POWERFUL MAGIC THERE.

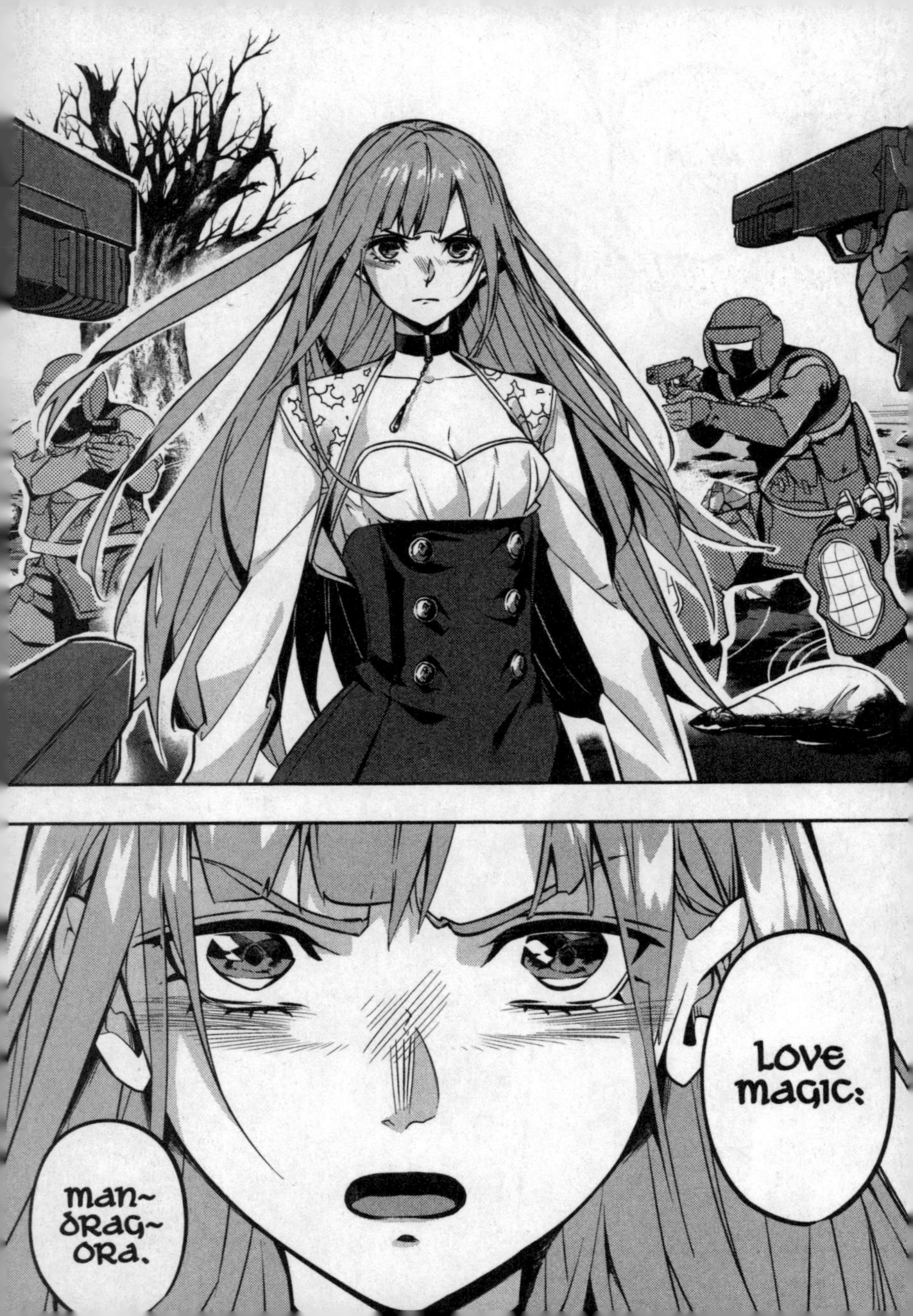
LOVE MAGIC:
MAN-DRAG-ORA.

THE
KINGDOMS
OF RUIN

THE
KINGDOMS
OF RUIN

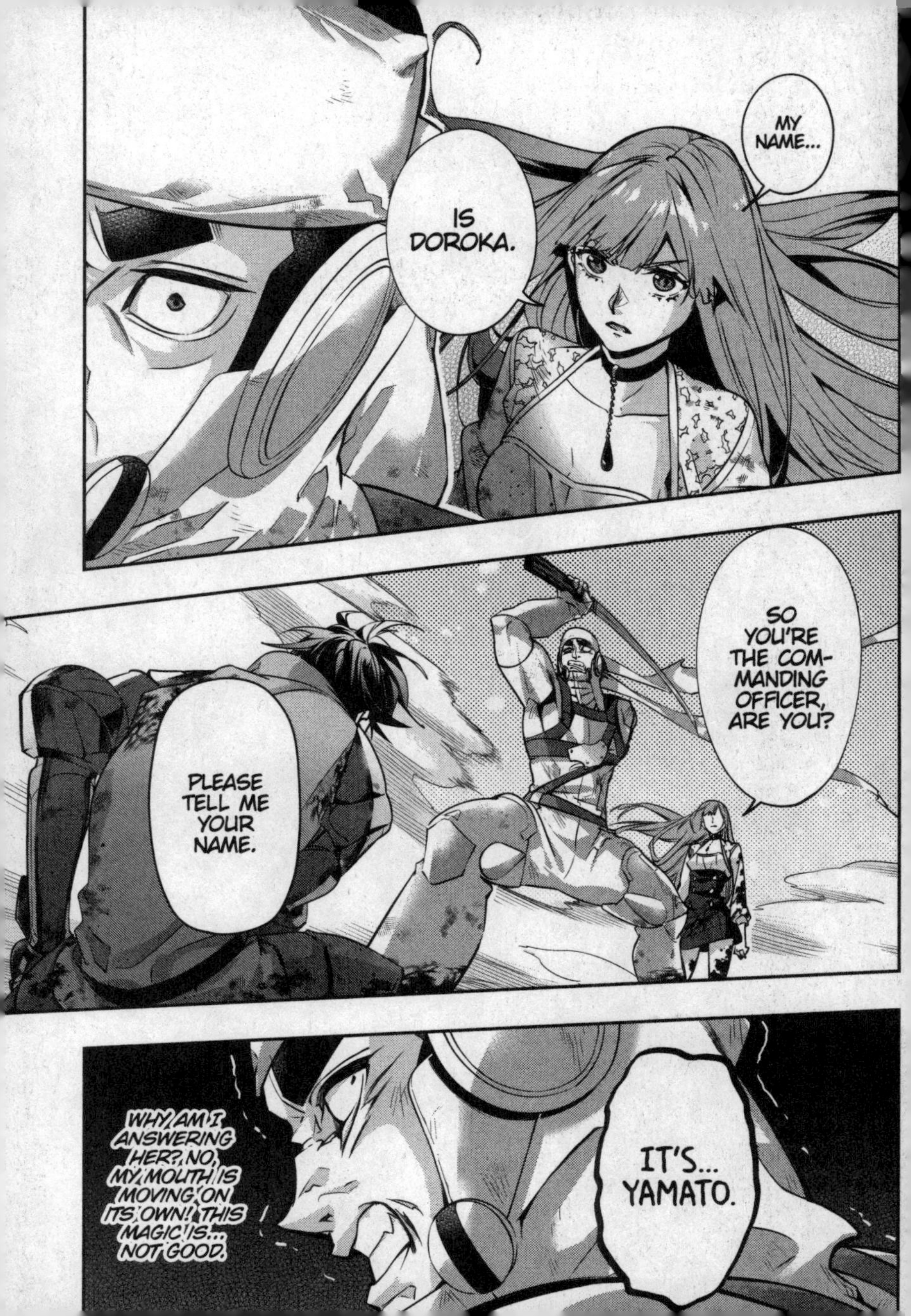
MY NAME...
IS DOROKA.
SO YOU'RE THE COMMANDING OFFICER, ARE YOU?
PLEASE TELL ME YOUR NAME.
IT'S... YAMATO.
WHY AM I ANSWERING HER? NO, MY MOUTH IS MOVING ON ITS OWN! THIS MAGIC IS... NOT GOOD.

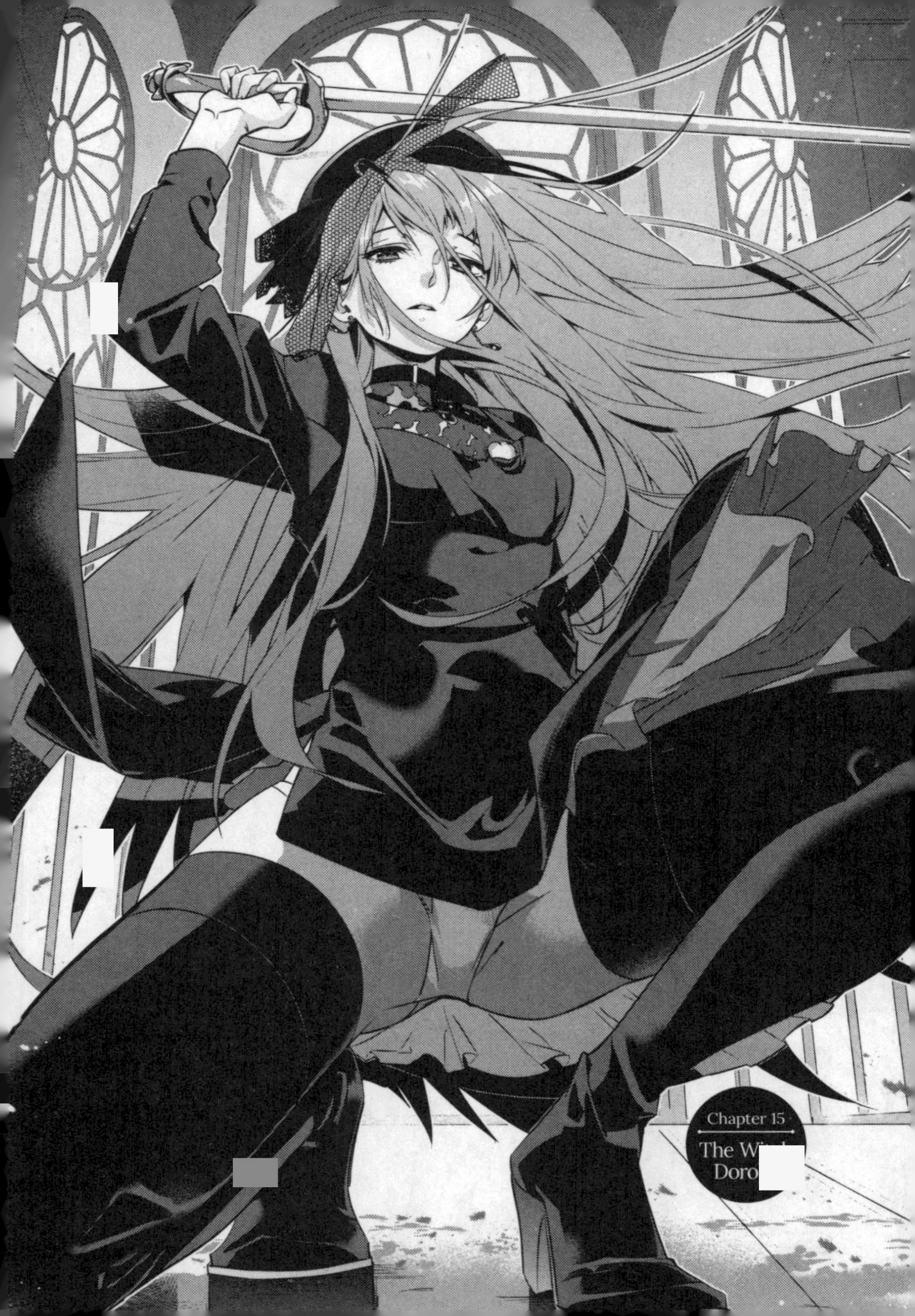
Chapter 15
The Wi
Doro

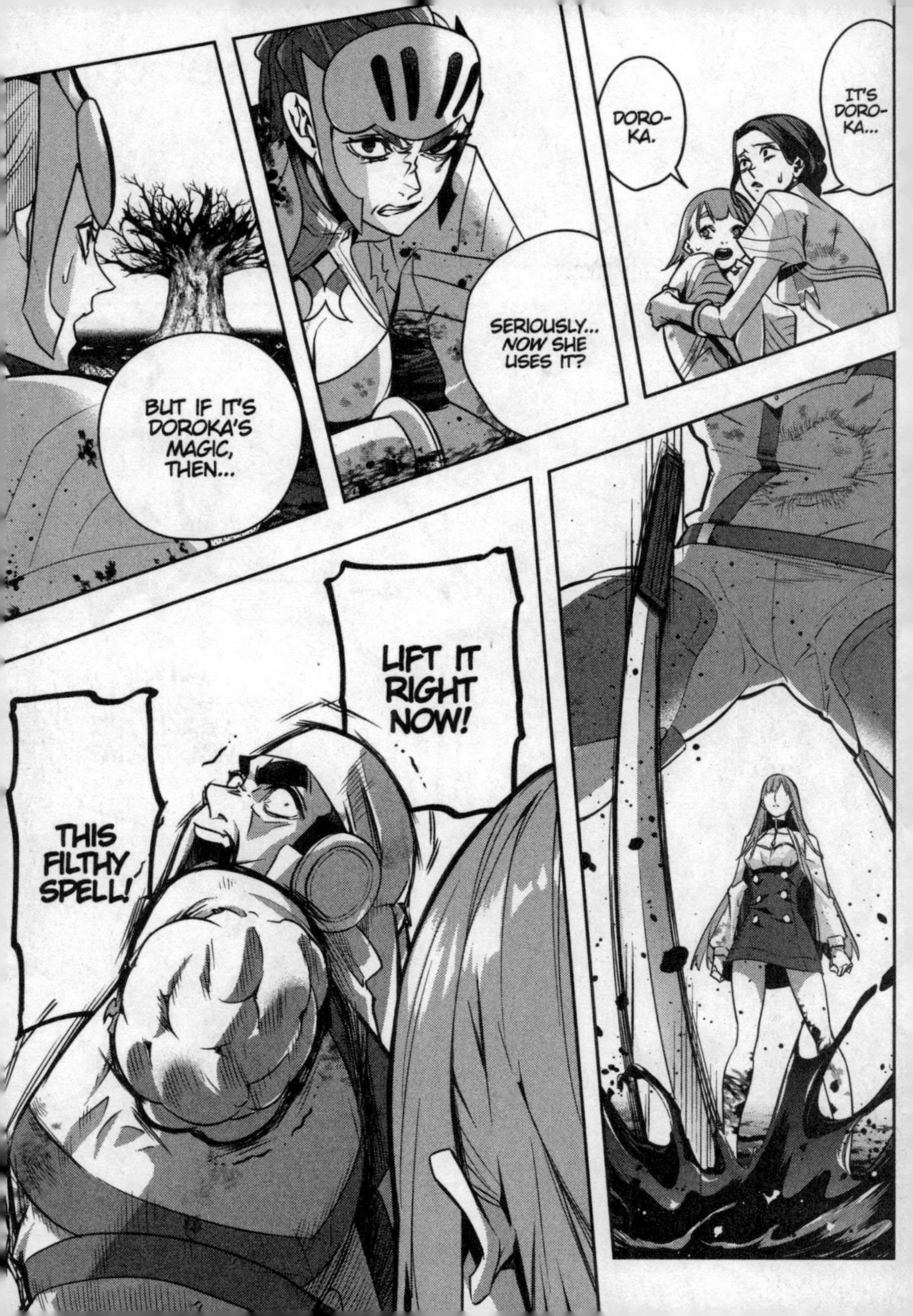
IT'S DOROKA...
DOROKA.
SERIOUSLY... *NOW* SHE USES IT?
BUT IF IT'S DOROKA'S MAGIC, THEN...
LIFT IT RIGHT NOW!
THIS FILTHY SPELL!

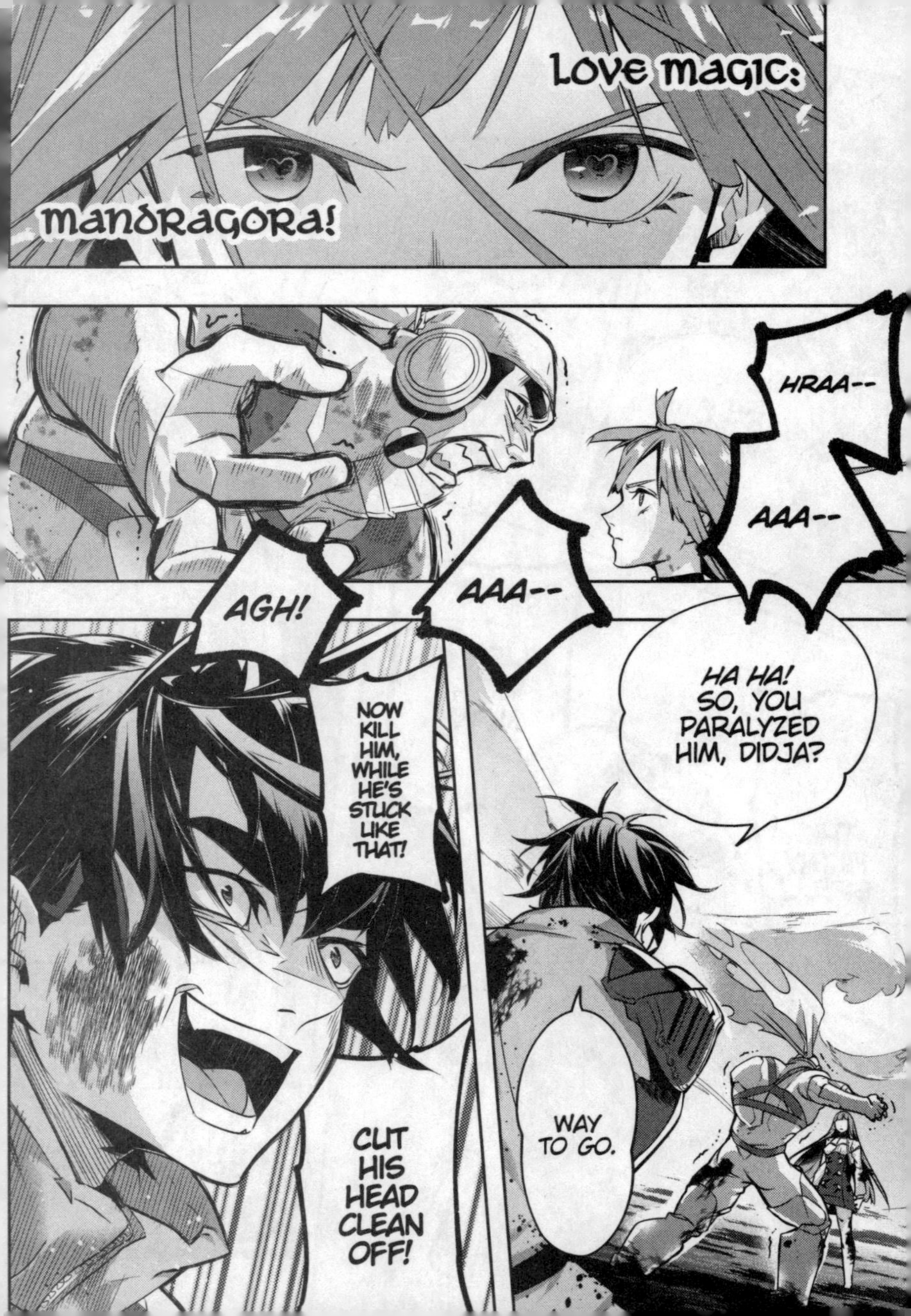
LOVE MAGIC:
MANDRAGORA!
HRAA--
AAA--
AAA--
AGH!
HA HA! SO, YOU PARALYZED HIM, DIDJA?
WAY TO GO.
NOW KILL HIM, WHILE HE'S STUCK LIKE THAT!
CUT HIS HEAD CLEAN OFF!

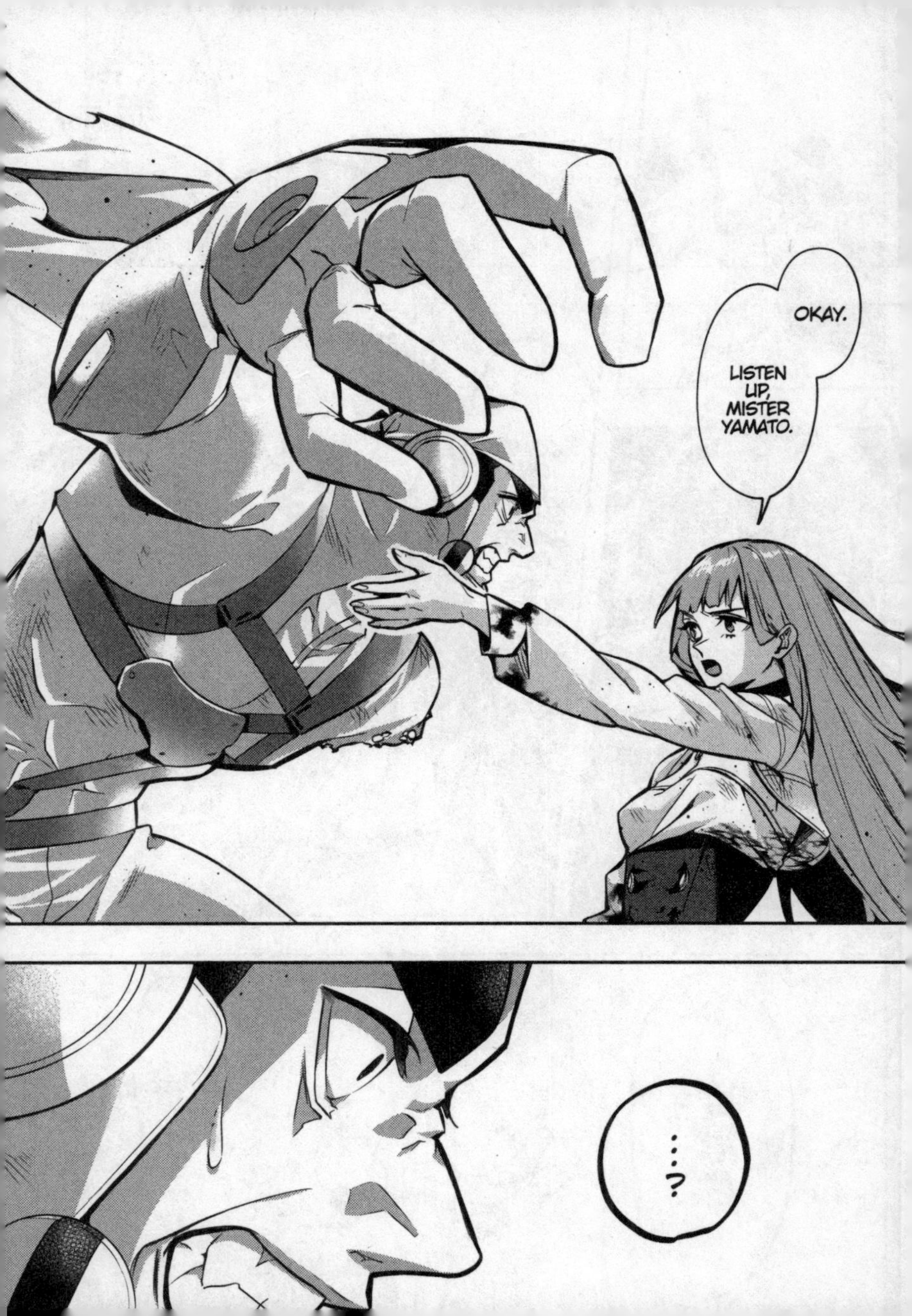
OKAY.
LISTEN UP, MISTER YAMATO.
...?

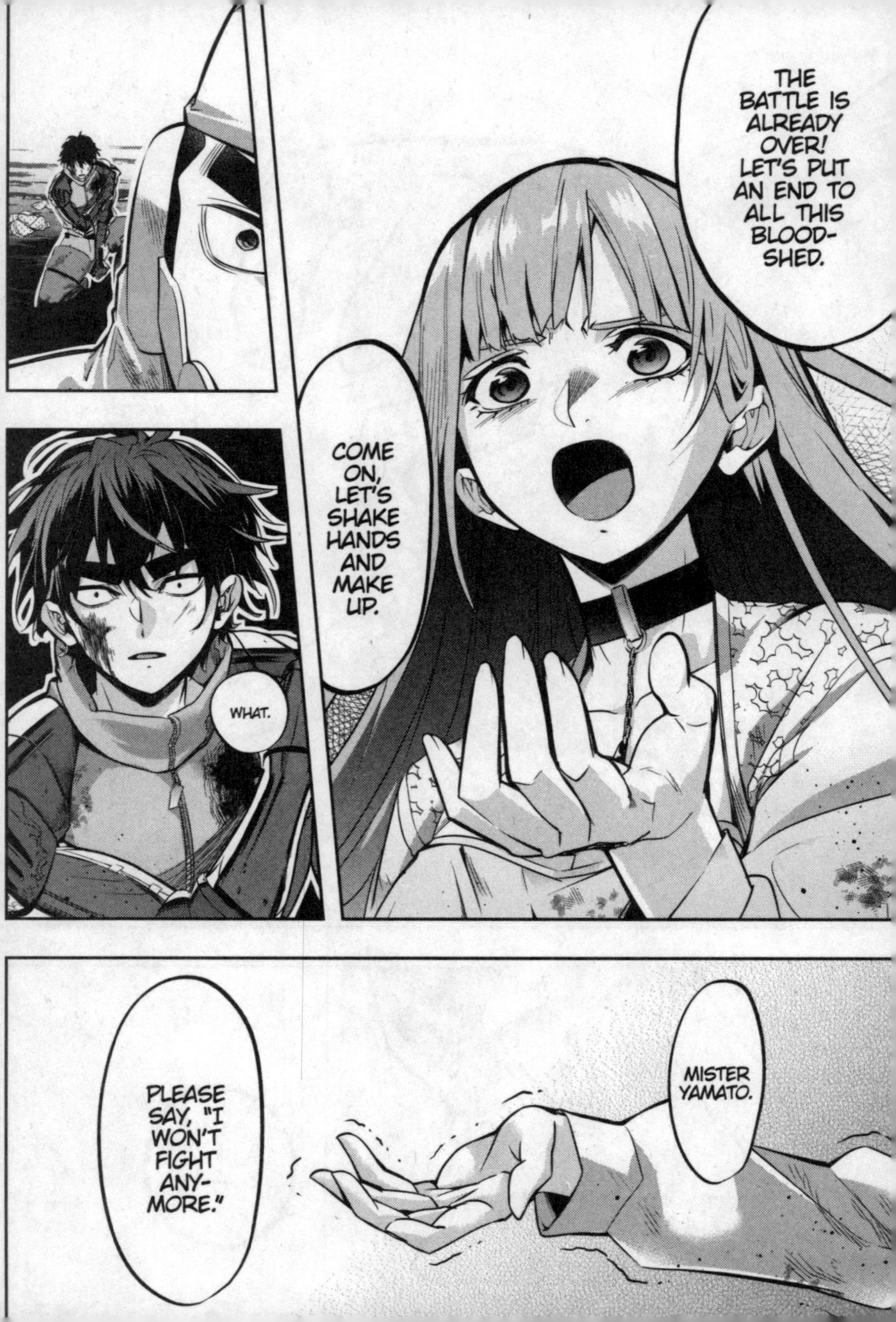
THE BATTLE IS ALREADY OVER! LET'S PUT AN END TO ALL THIS BLOOD-SHED.
COME ON, LET'S SHAKE HANDS AND MAKE UP.
WHAT.
MISTER YAMATO.
PLEASE SAY, "I WON'T FIGHT ANY-MORE."

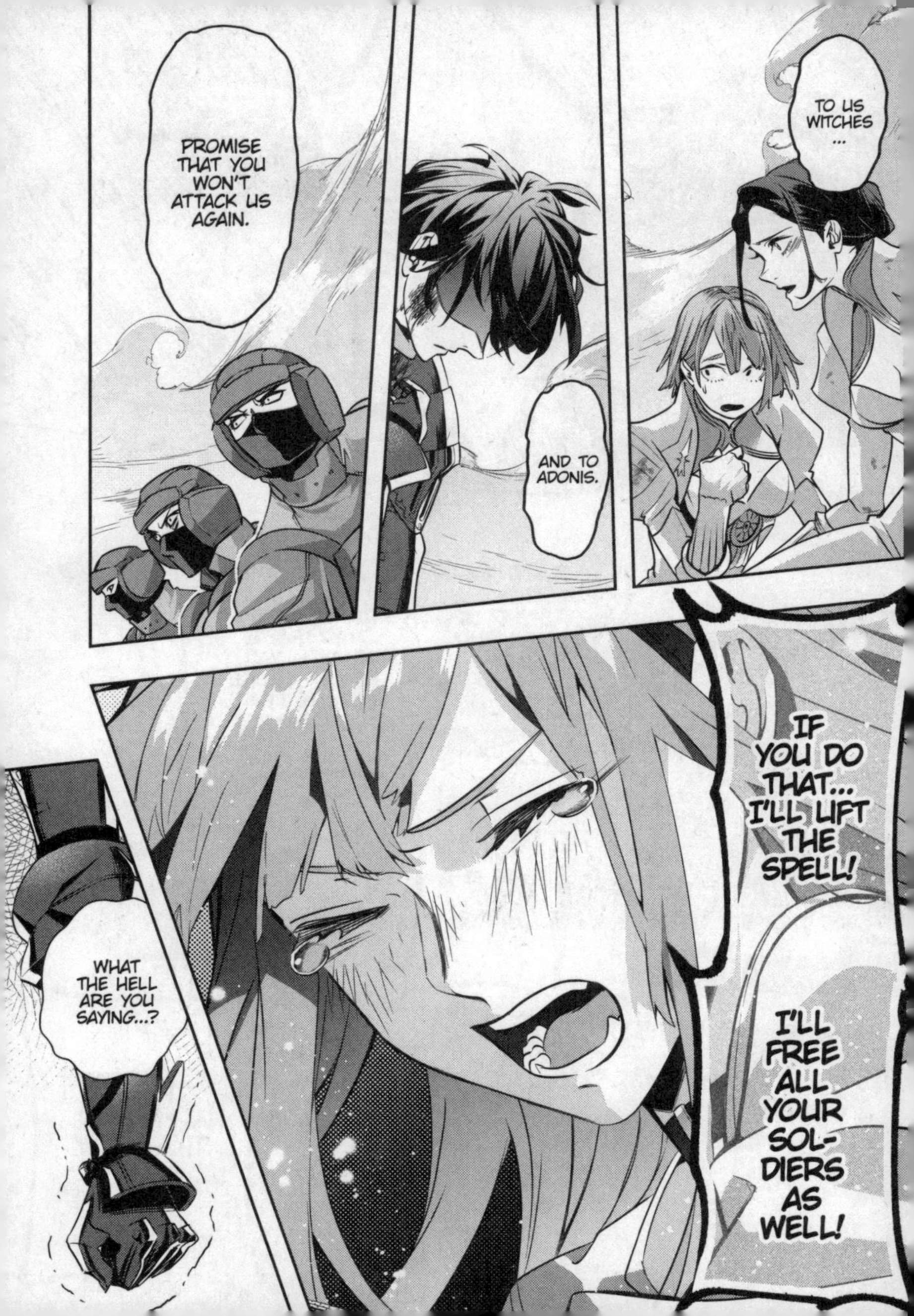
TO US WITCHES ...
AND TO ADONIS.
PROMISE THAT YOU WON'T ATTACK US AGAIN.
IF YOU DO THAT... I'LL LIFT THE SPELL!
I'LL FREE ALL YOUR SOL-DIERS AS WELL!
WHAT THE HELL ARE YOU SAYING...?

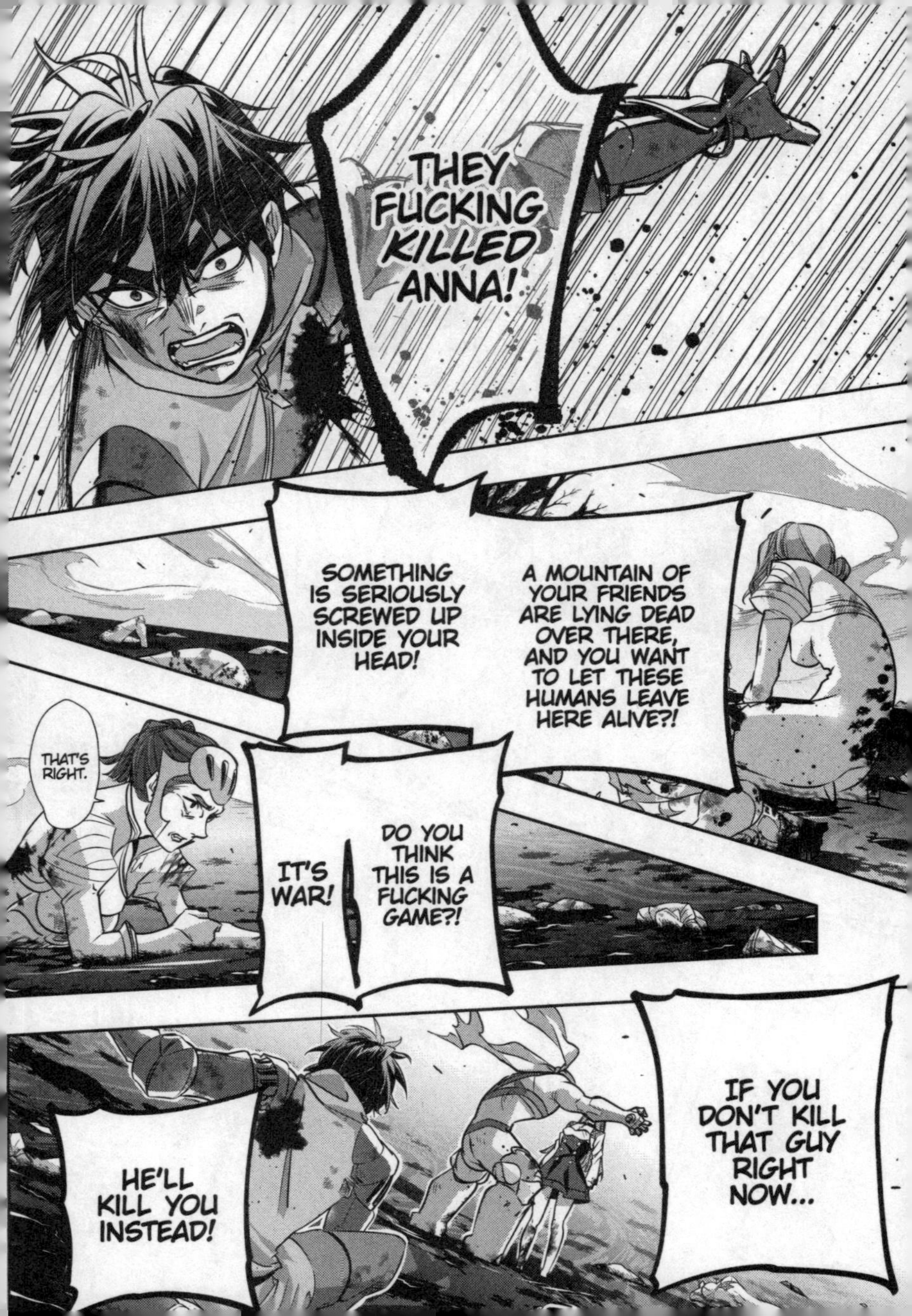
THEY FUCKING KILLED ANNA!
SOMETHING IS SERIOUSLY SCREWED UP INSIDE YOUR HEAD!
A MOUNTAIN OF YOUR FRIENDS ARE LYING DEAD OVER THERE, AND YOU WANT TO LET THESE HUMANS LEAVE HERE ALIVE?!
THAT'S RIGHT.
DO YOU THINK THIS IS A FUCKING GAME?!
IT'S WAR!
IF YOU DON'T KILL THAT GUY RIGHT NOW...
HE'LL KILL YOU INSTEAD!

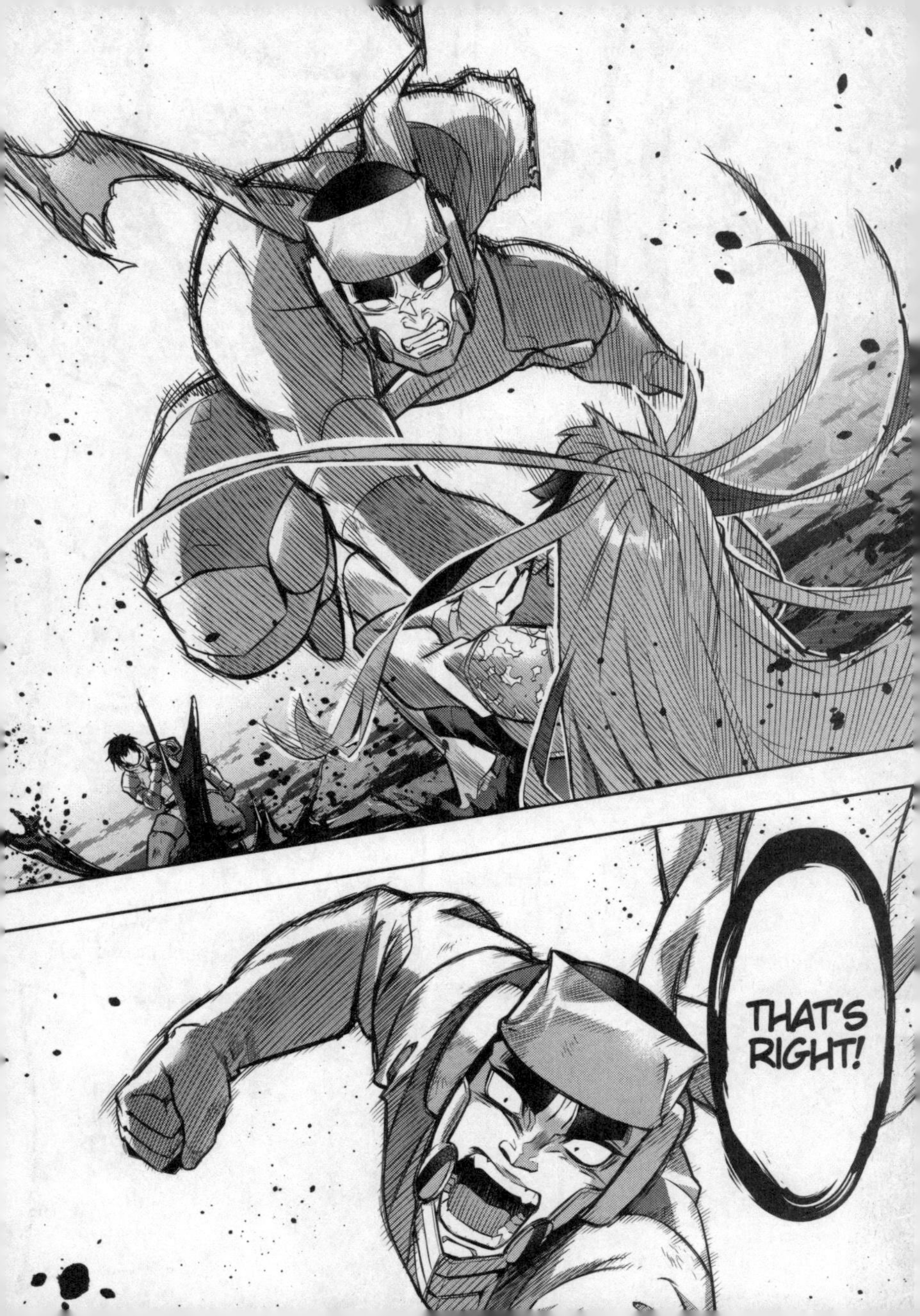
THAT'S RIGHT!

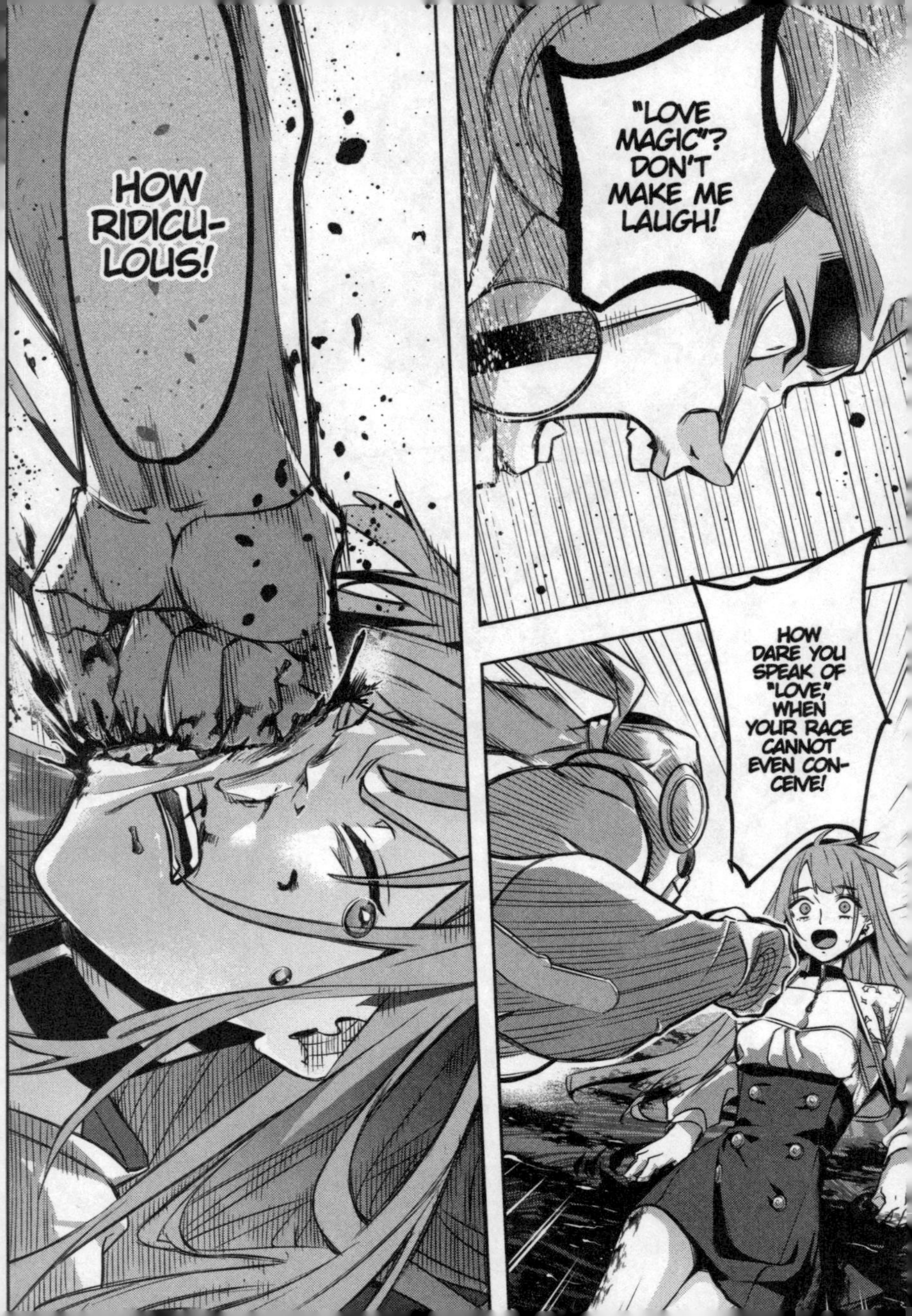
"LOVE MAGIC"? DON'T MAKE ME LAUGH!
HOW DARE YOU SPEAK OF "LOVE," WHEN YOUR RACE CANNOT EVEN CON-CEIVE!
HOW RIDICU-LOUS!

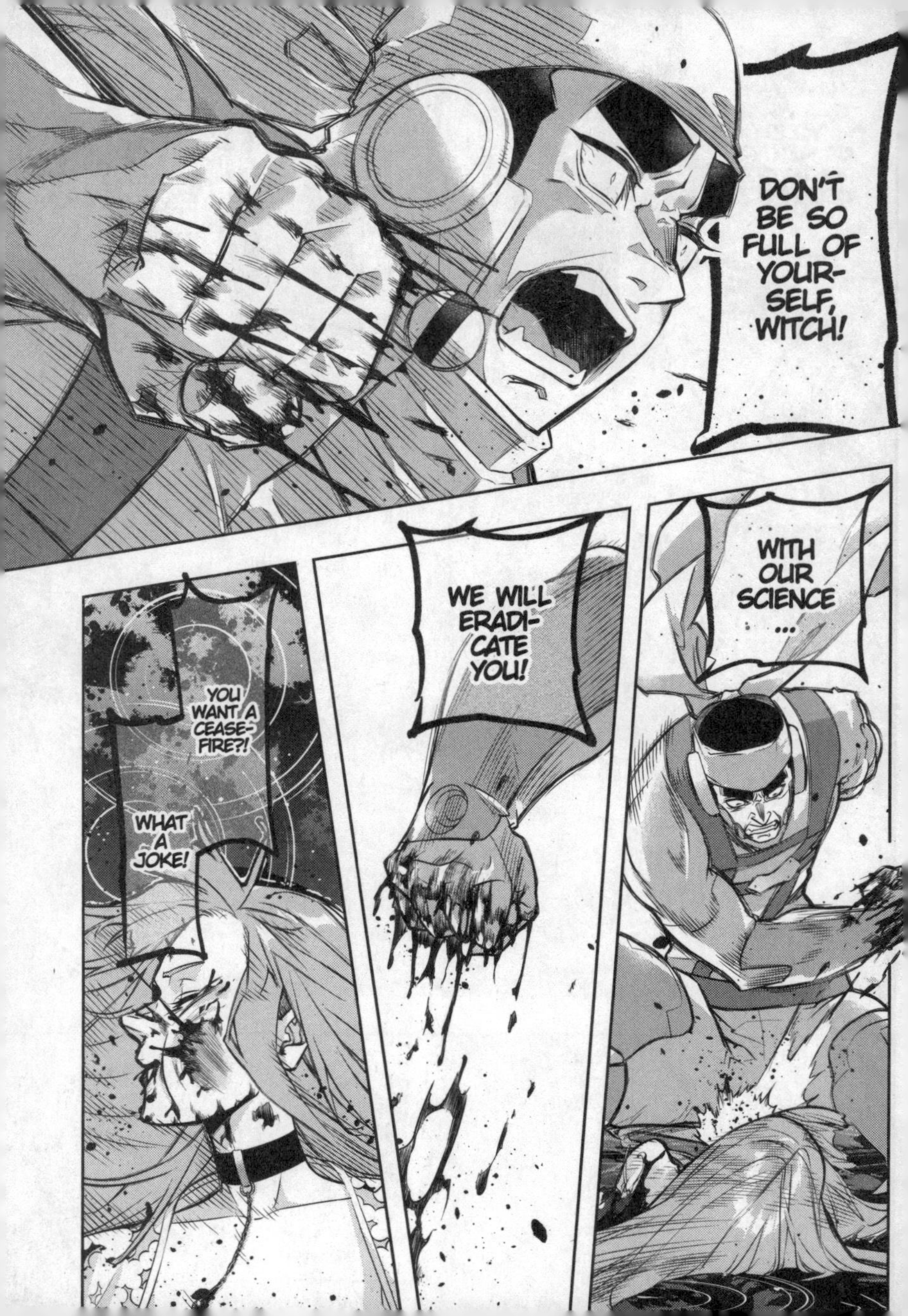
DON'T BE SO FULL OF YOURSELF, WITCH!
WITH OUR SCIENCE ...
WE WILL ERADICATE YOU!
YOU WANT A CEASE-FIRE?!
WHAT A JOKE!

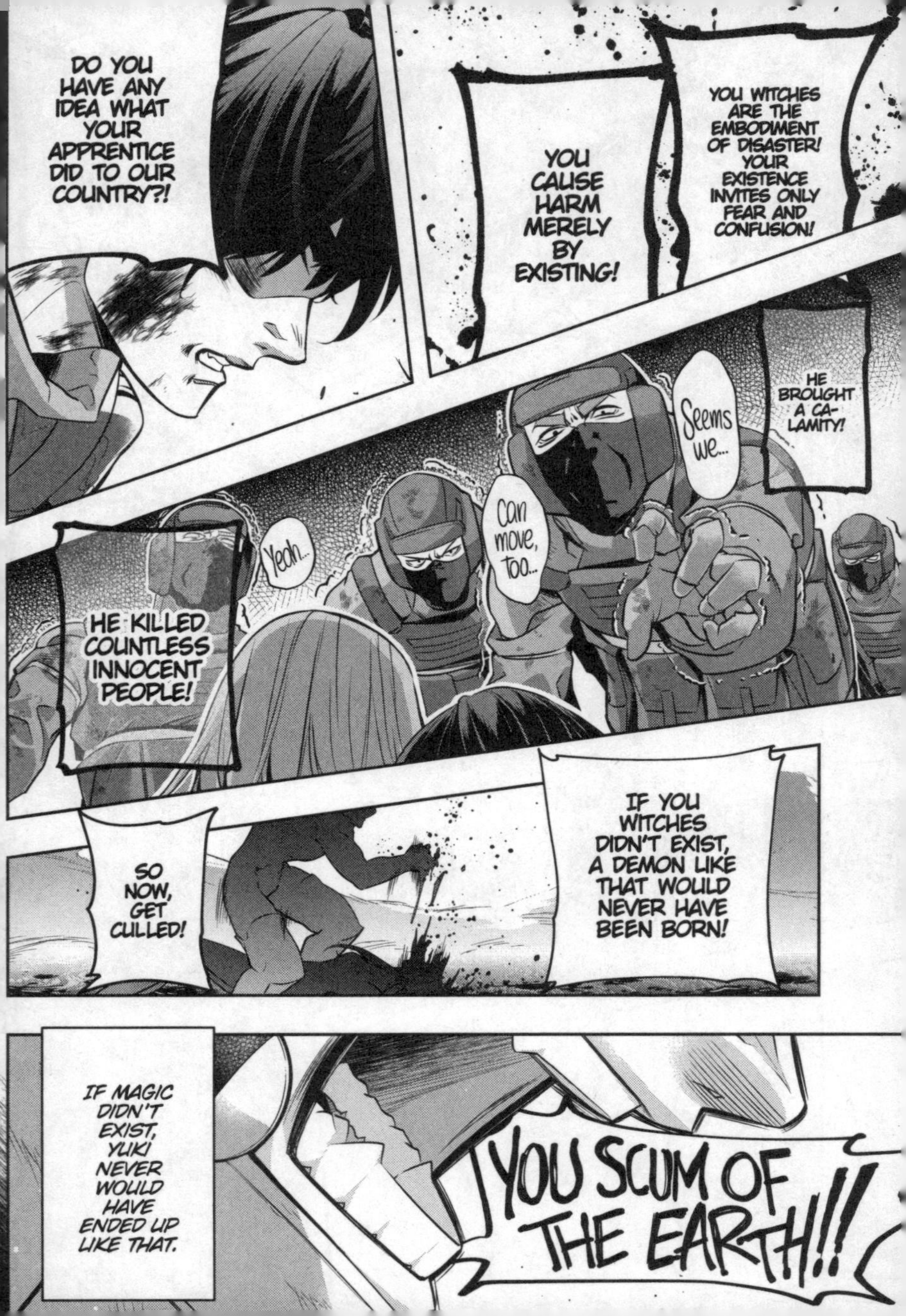
YOU WITCHES ARE THE EMBODIMENT OF DISASTER! YOUR EXISTENCE INVITES ONLY FEAR AND CONFUSION!
YOU CAUSE HARM MERELY BY EXISTING!
DO YOU HAVE ANY IDEA WHAT YOUR APPRENTICE DID TO OUR COUNTRY?!
HE BROUGHT A CA-LAMITY!
Seems we...
Can move, too...
Yeah...
HE KILLED COUNTLESS INNOCENT PEOPLE!
IF YOU WITCHES DIDN'T EXIST, A DEMON LIKE THAT WOULD NEVER HAVE BEEN BORN!
SO NOW, GET CULLED!
IF MAGIC DIDN'T EXIST, YUKI NEVER WOULD HAVE ENDED UP LIKE THAT.
YOU SCUM OF THE EARTH!!

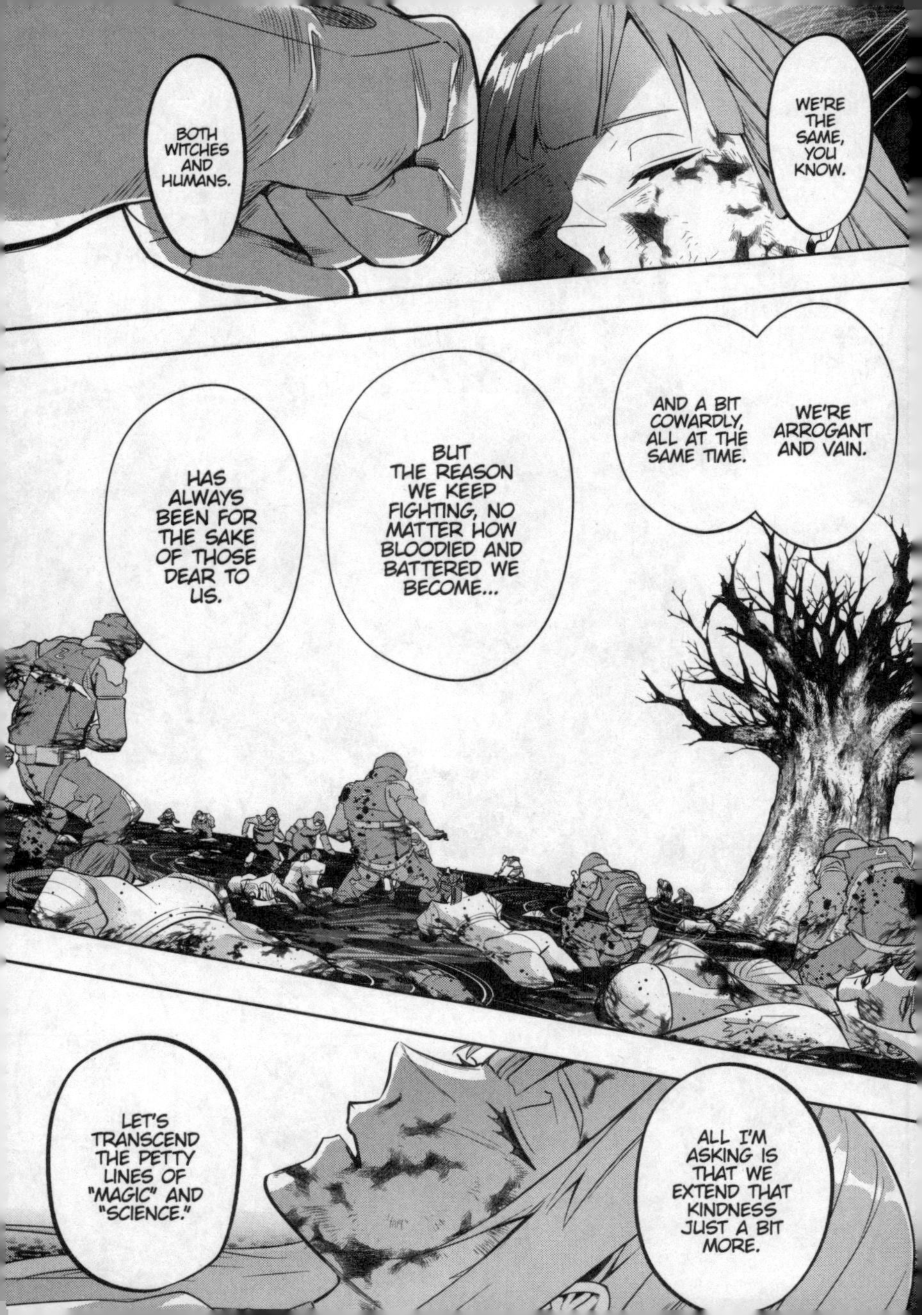
WE'RE THE SAME, YOU KNOW.
BOTH WITCHES AND HUMANS.
WE'RE ARROGANT AND VAIN.
AND A BIT COWARDLY, ALL AT THE SAME TIME.
BUT THE REASON WE KEEP FIGHTING, NO MATTER HOW BLOODIED AND BATTERED WE BECOME...
HAS ALWAYS BEEN FOR THE SAKE OF THOSE DEAR TO US.
ALL I'M ASKING IS THAT WE EXTEND THAT KINDNESS JUST A BIT MORE.
LET'S TRANSCEND THE PETTY LINES OF "MAGIC" AND "SCIENCE."

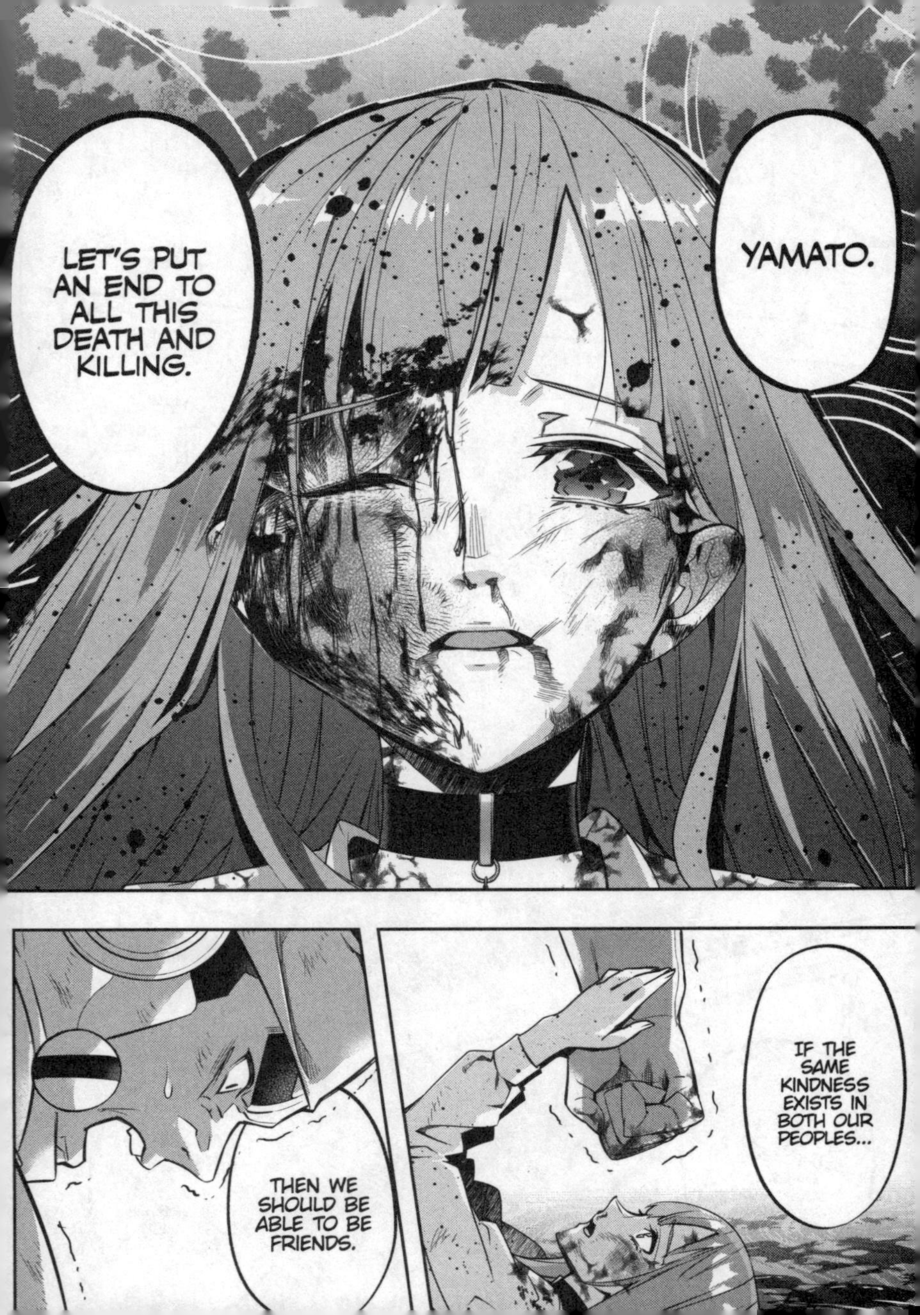
YAMATO.
LET'S PUT AN END TO ALL THIS DEATH AND KILLING.
IF THE SAME KINDNESS EXISTS IN BOTH OUR PEOPLES...
THEN WE SHOULD BE ABLE TO BE FRIENDS.

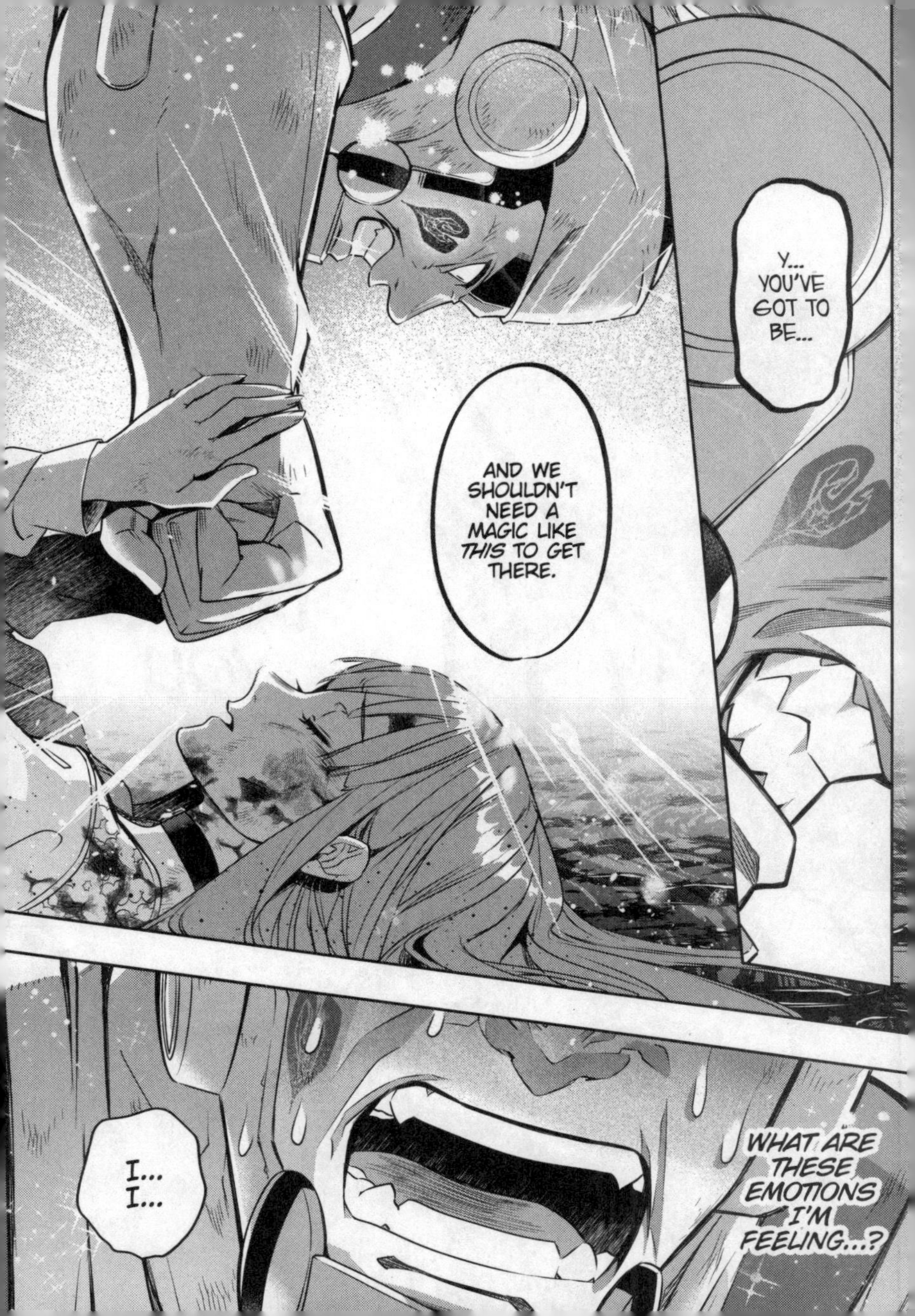
Y... YOU'VE GOT TO BE...
AND WE SHOULDN'T NEED A MAGIC LIKE *THIS* TO GET THERE.
WHAT ARE THESE EMOTIONS I'M FEELING...?
I... I...

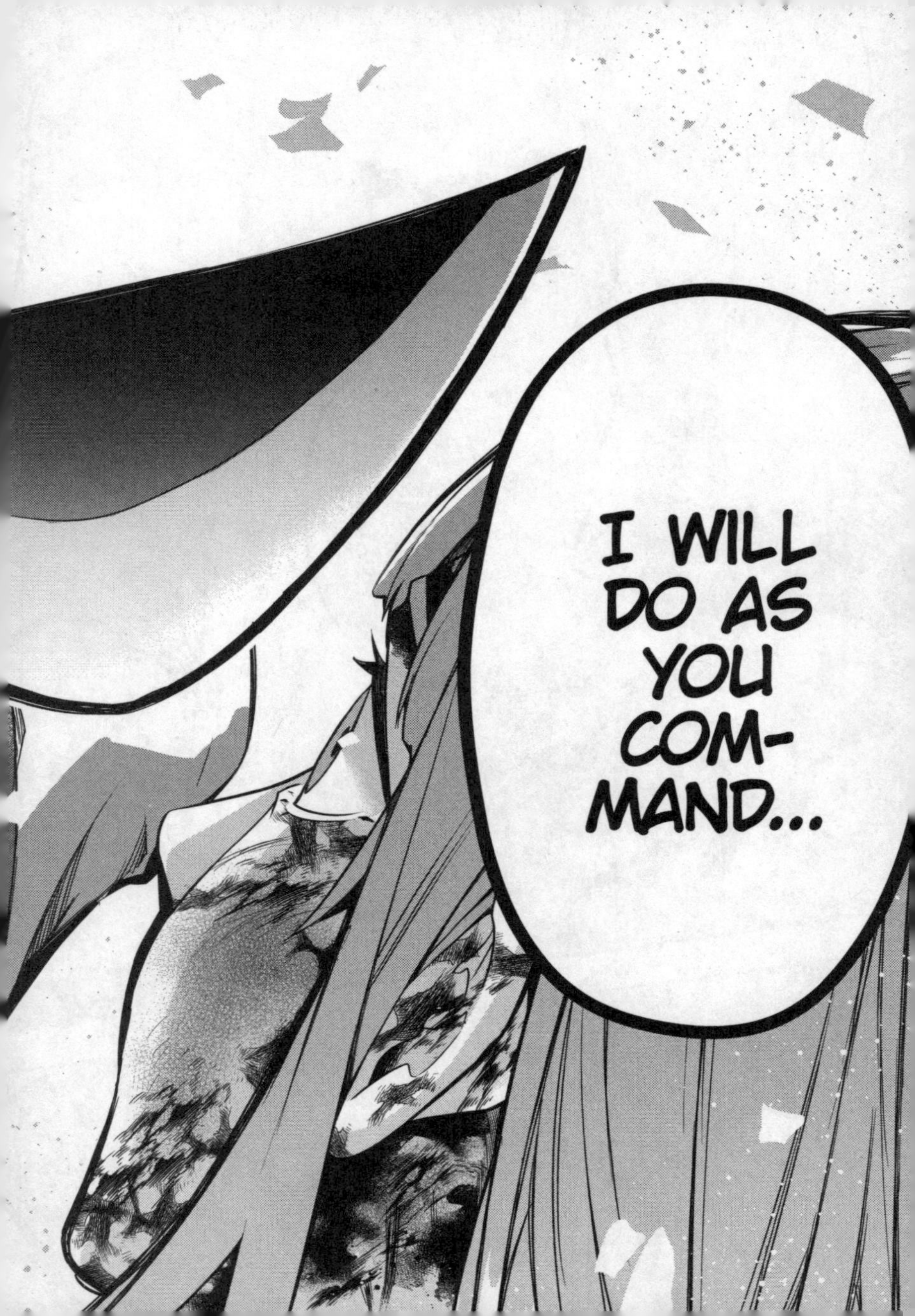
I WILL DO AS YOU COM- MAND...

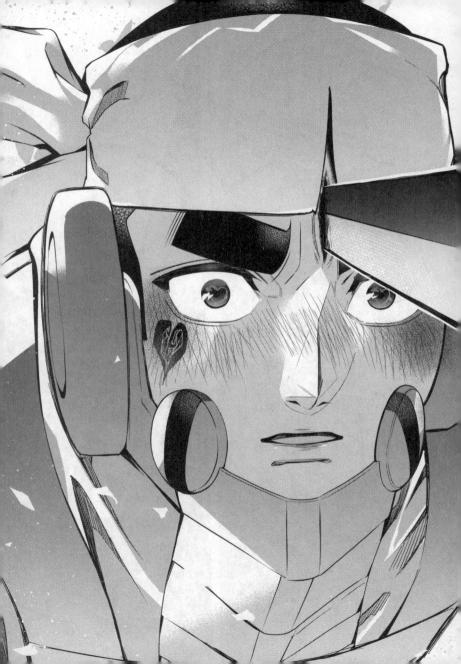

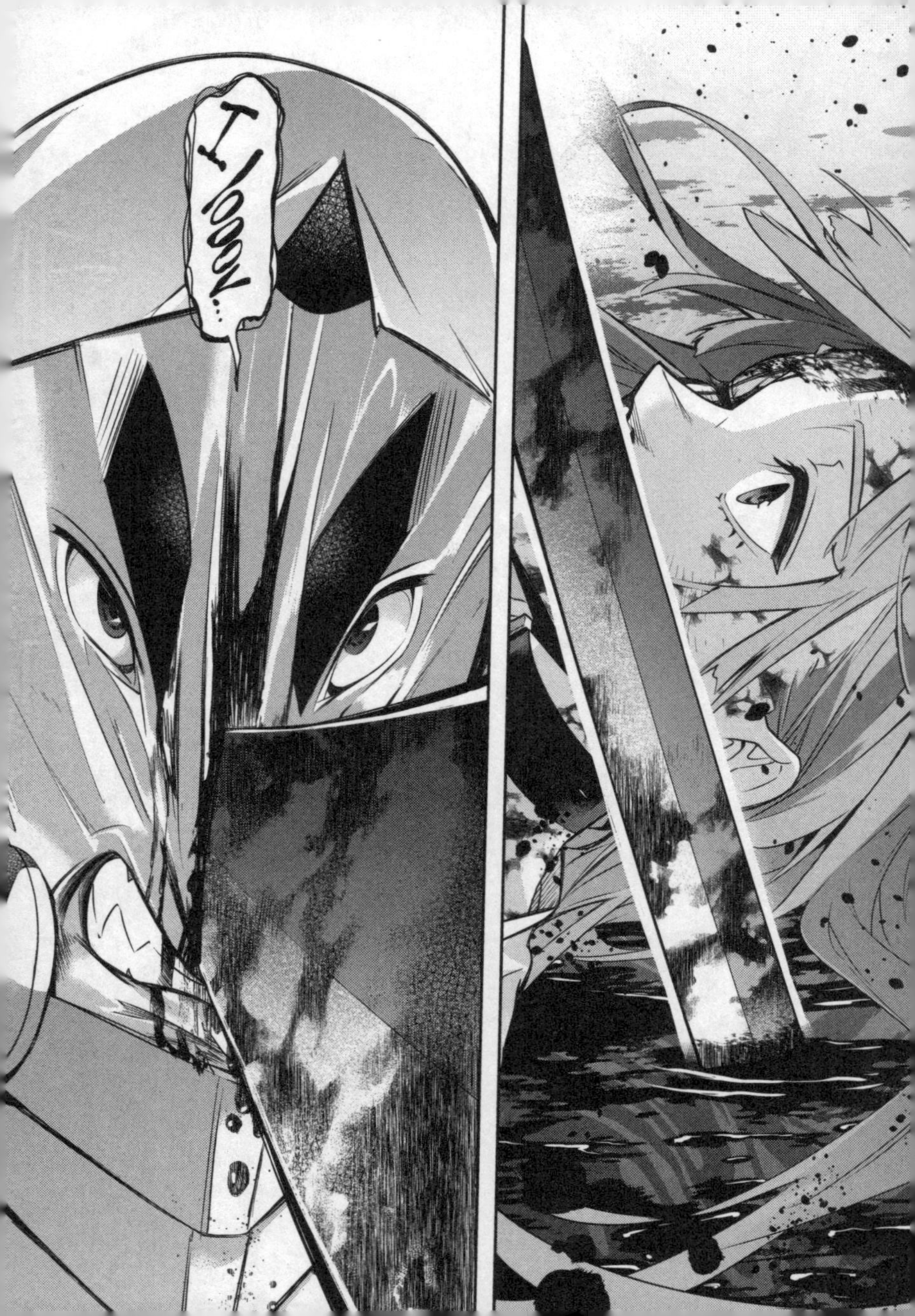
I...WON...

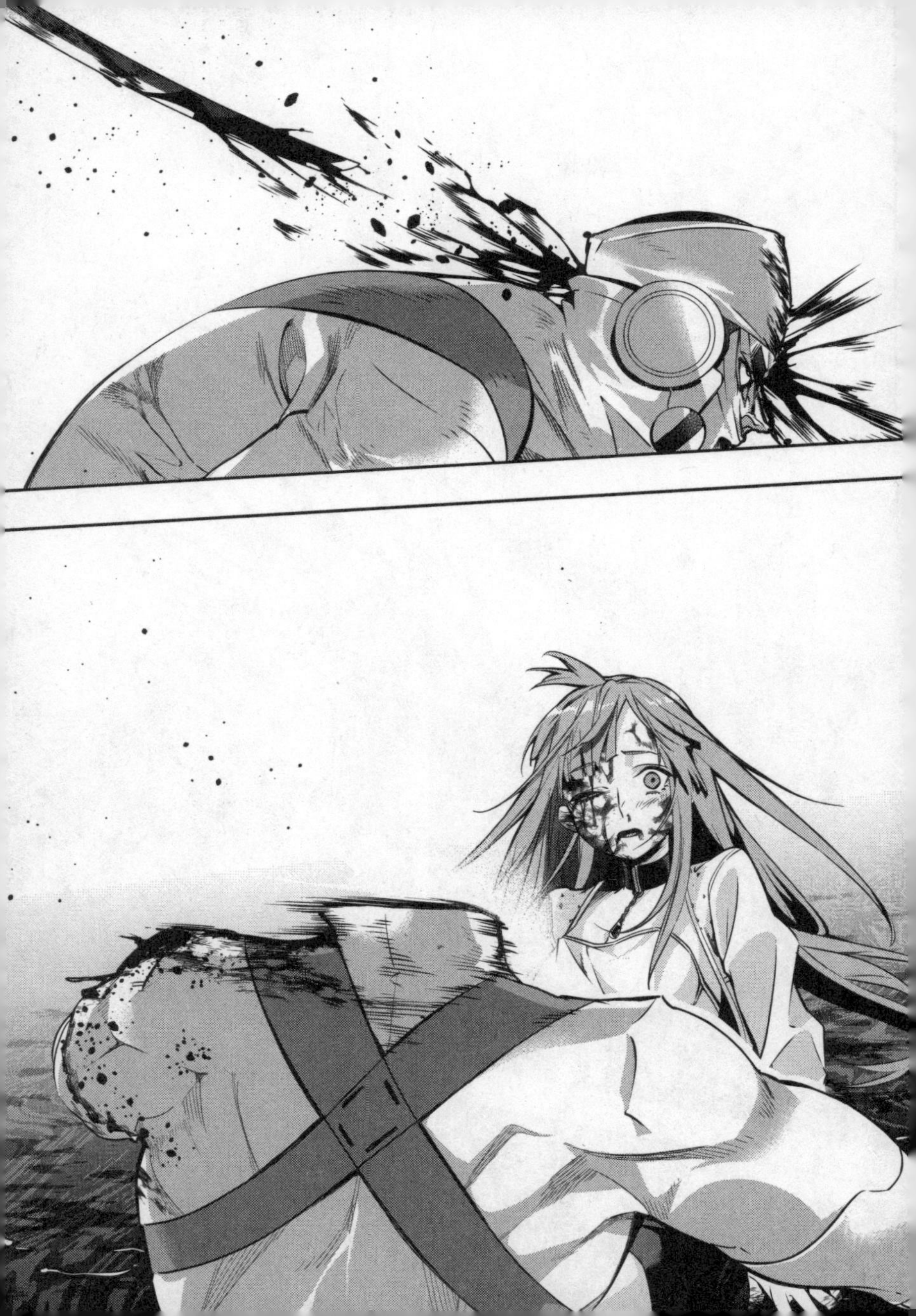

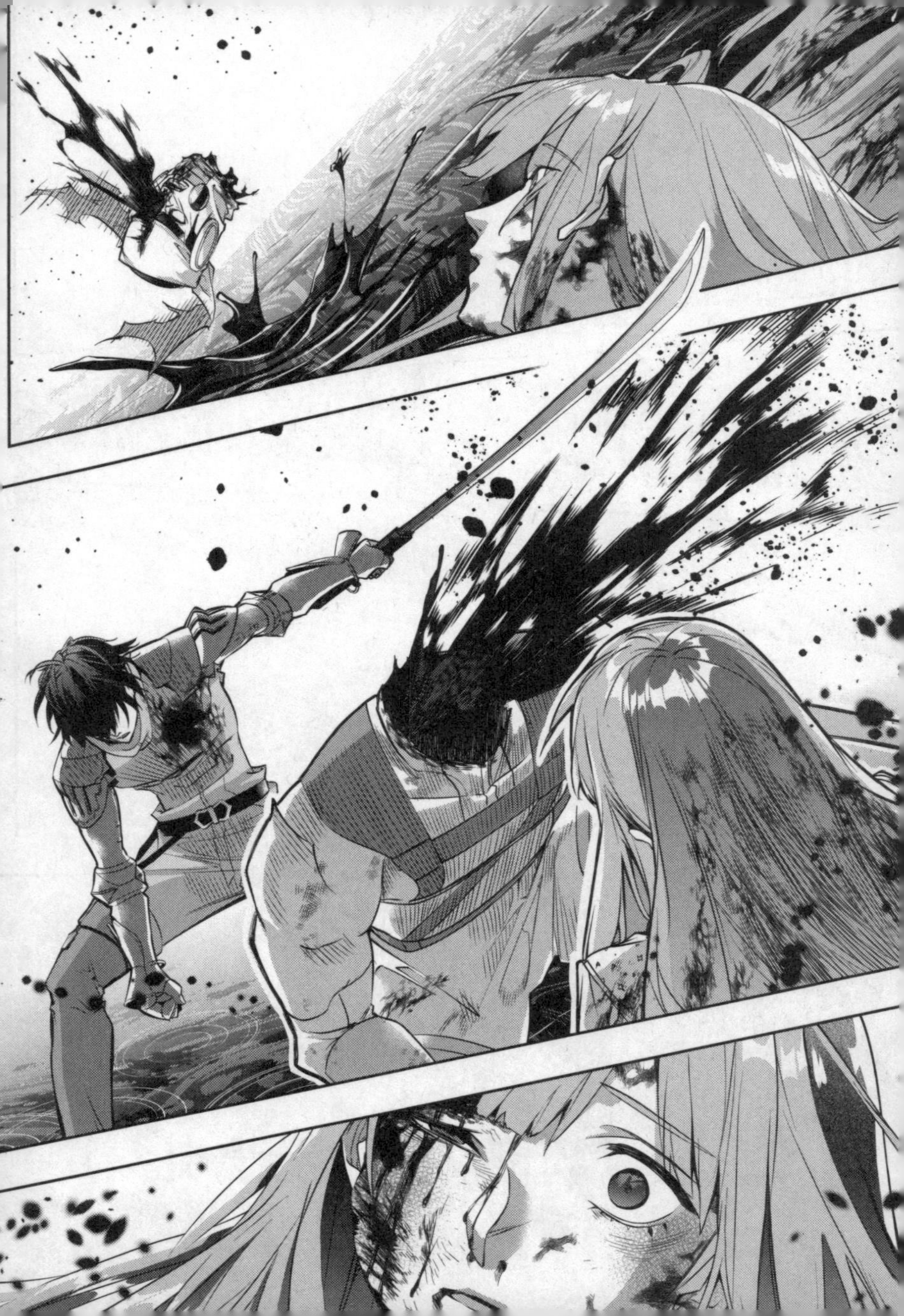

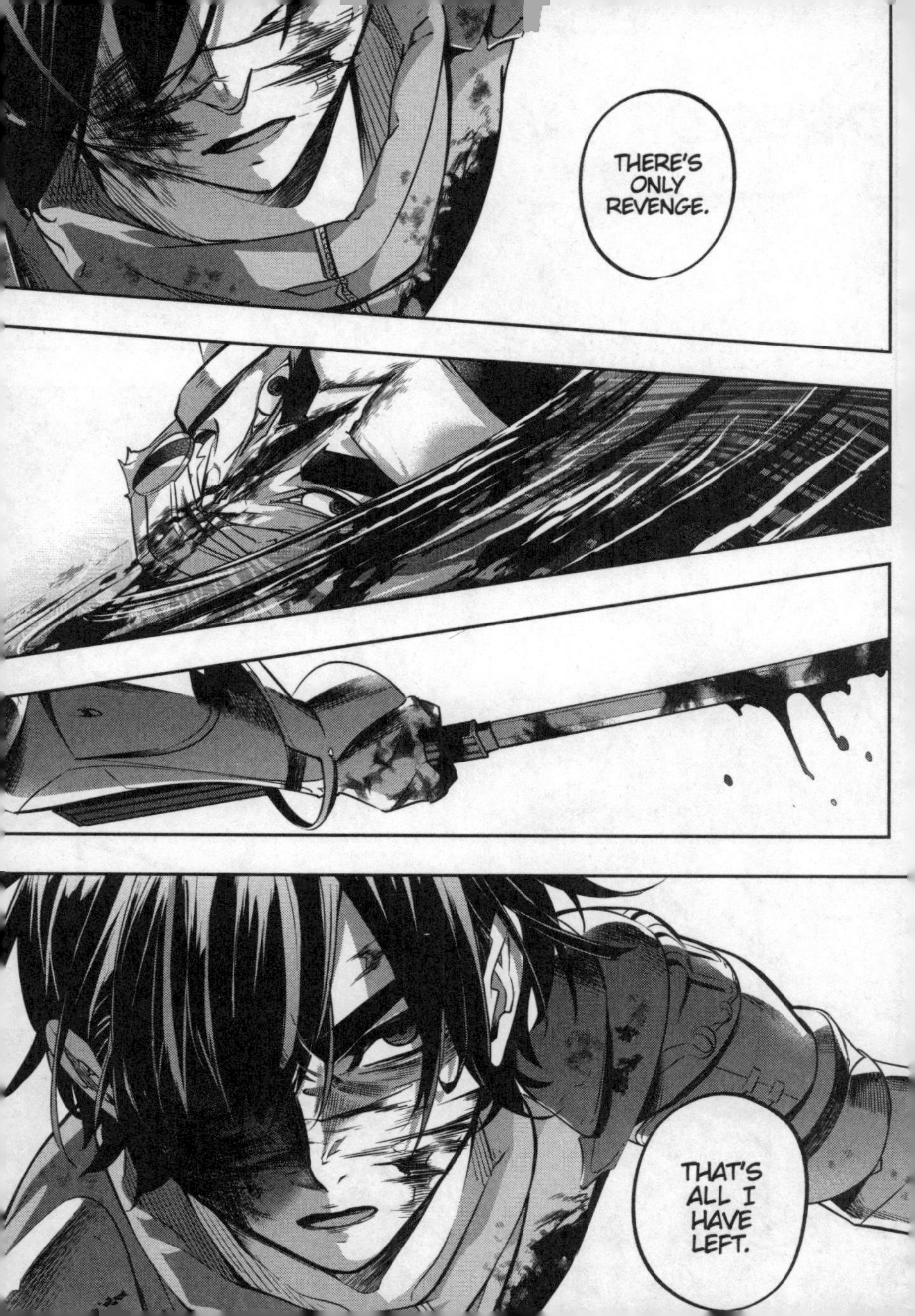
THERE'S ONLY REVENGE.
THAT'S ALL I HAVE LEFT.

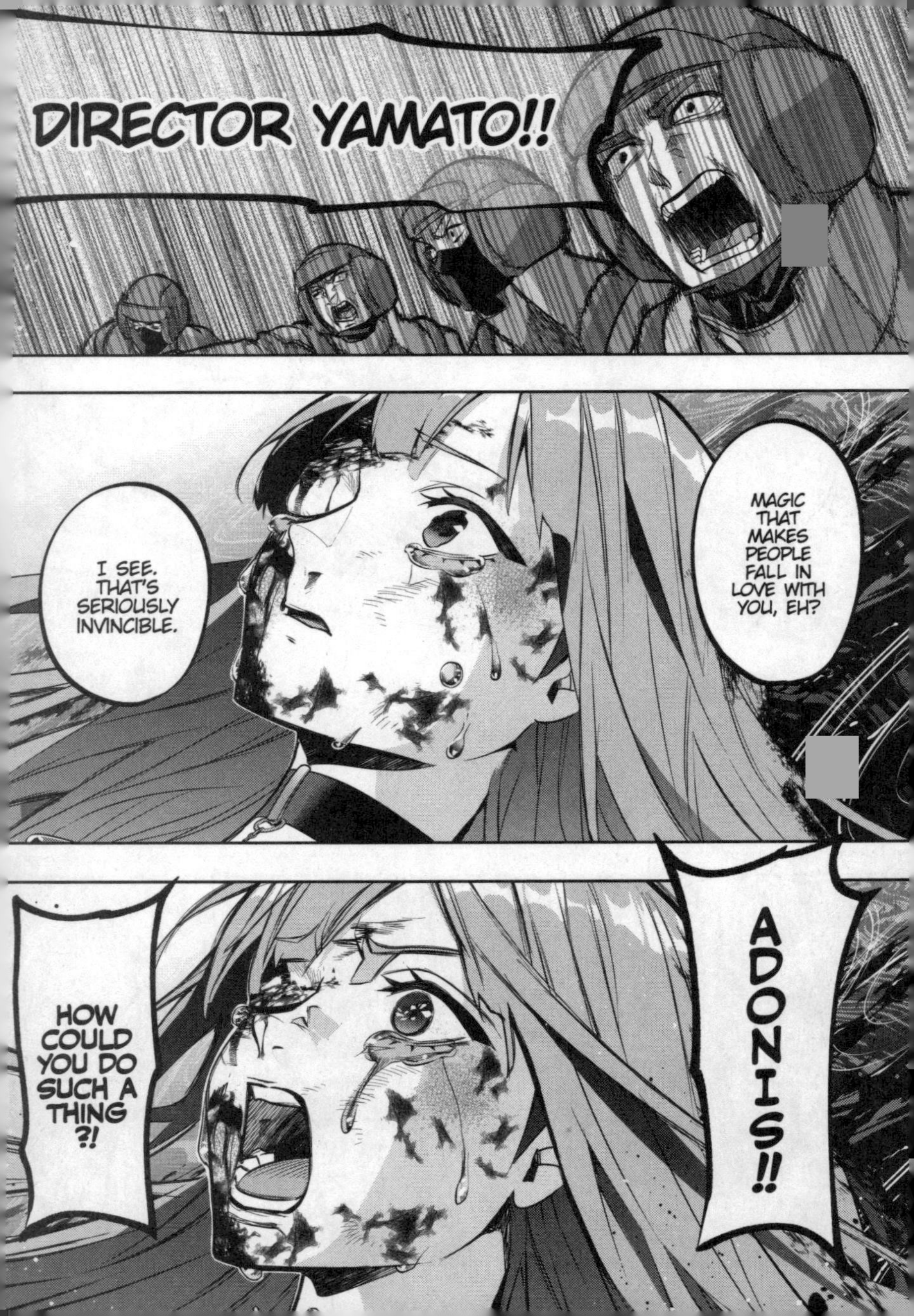
DIRECTOR YAMATO!!
MAGIC THAT MAKES PEOPLE FALL IN LOVE WITH YOU, EH?
I SEE. THAT'S SERIOUSLY INVINCIBLE.
ADONIS!!
HOW COULD YOU DO SUCH A THING?!

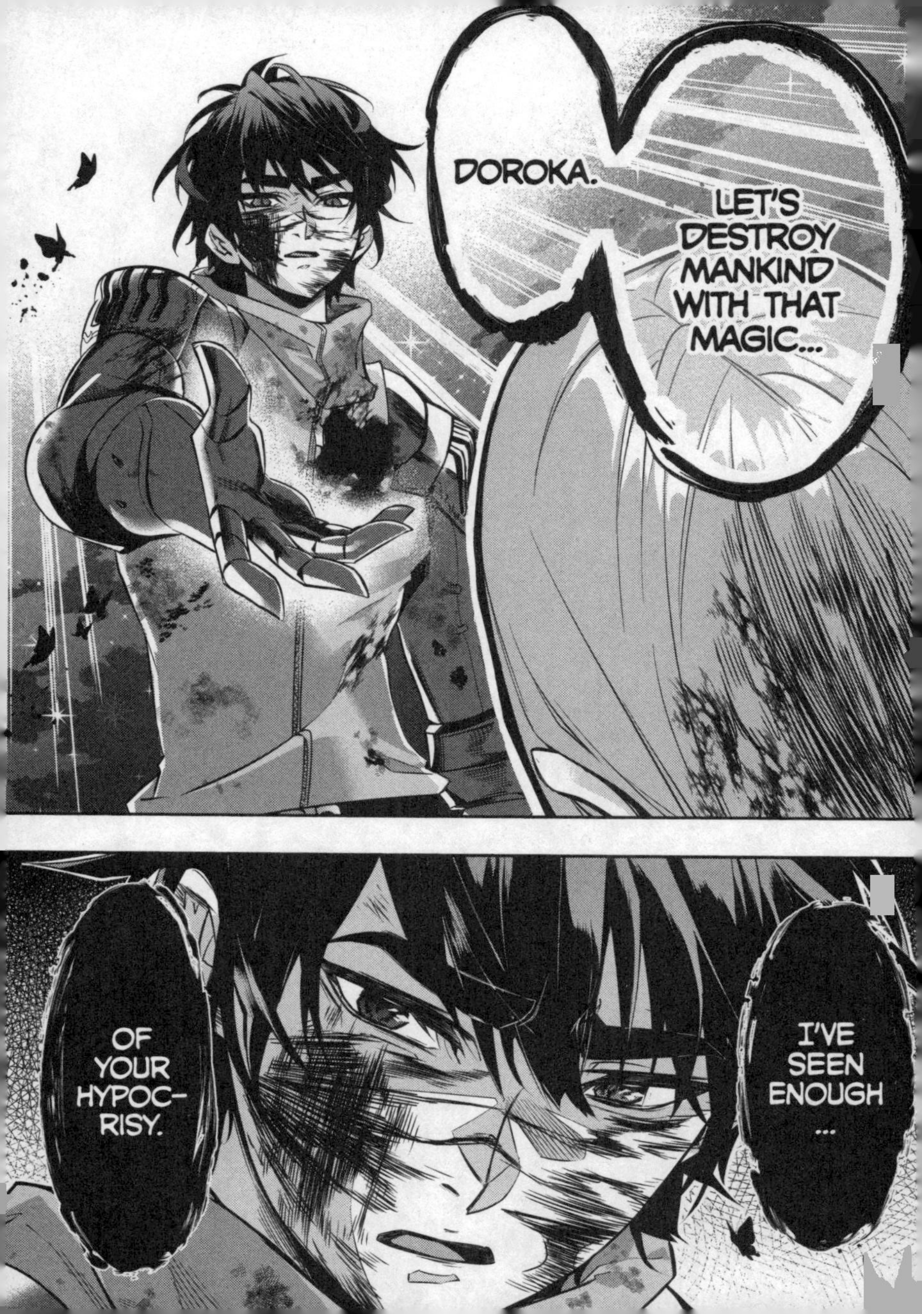
DOROKA.
LET'S DESTROY MANKIND WITH THAT MAGIC...
I'VE SEEN ENOUGH...
OF YOUR HYPOC-RISY.

THE
KINGDOMS
OF RUIN

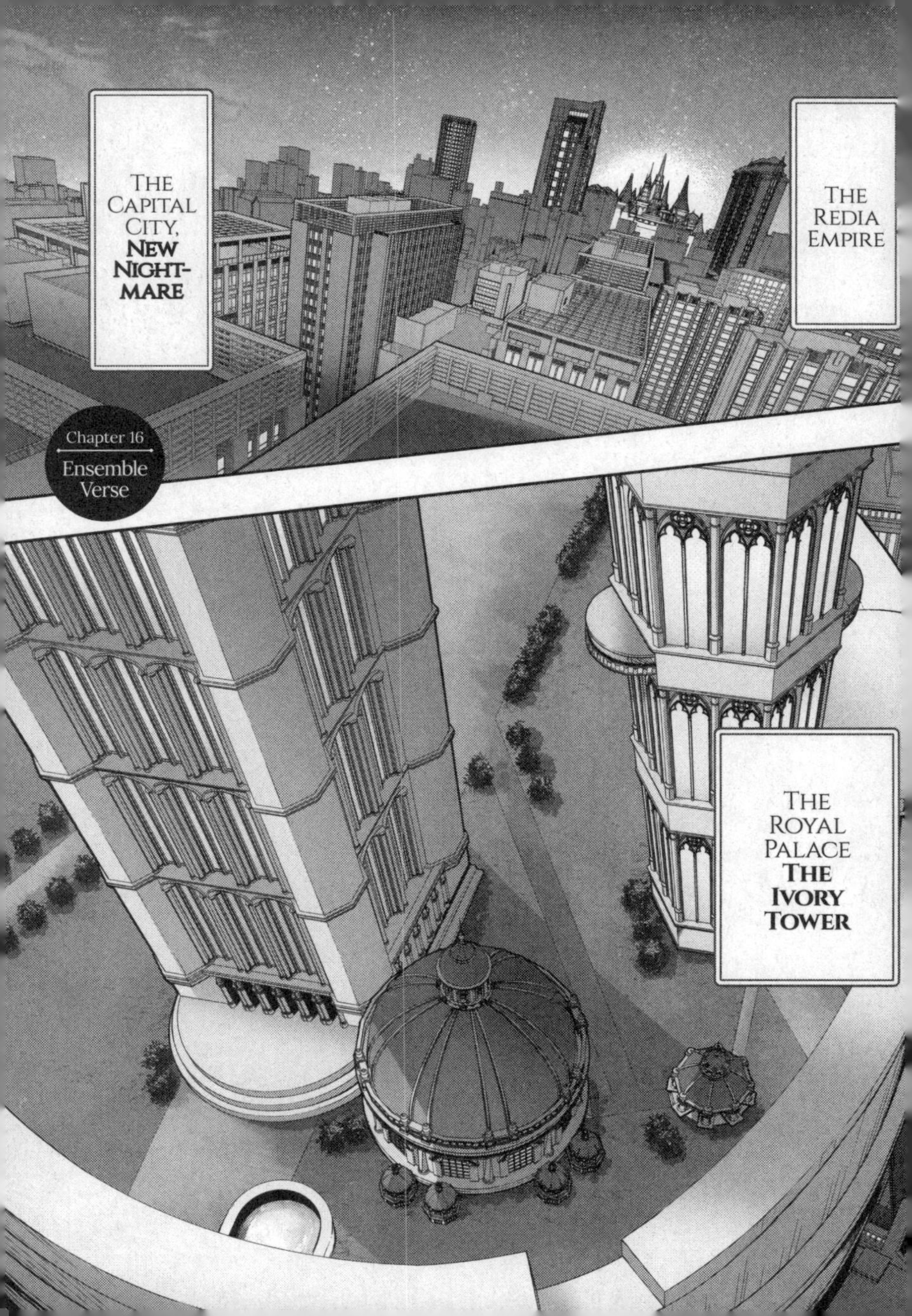
THE REDIA EMPIRE
THE CAPITAL CITY, NEW NIGHT-MARE
Chapter 16
Ensemble Verse
THE ROYAL PALACE THE IVORY TOWER

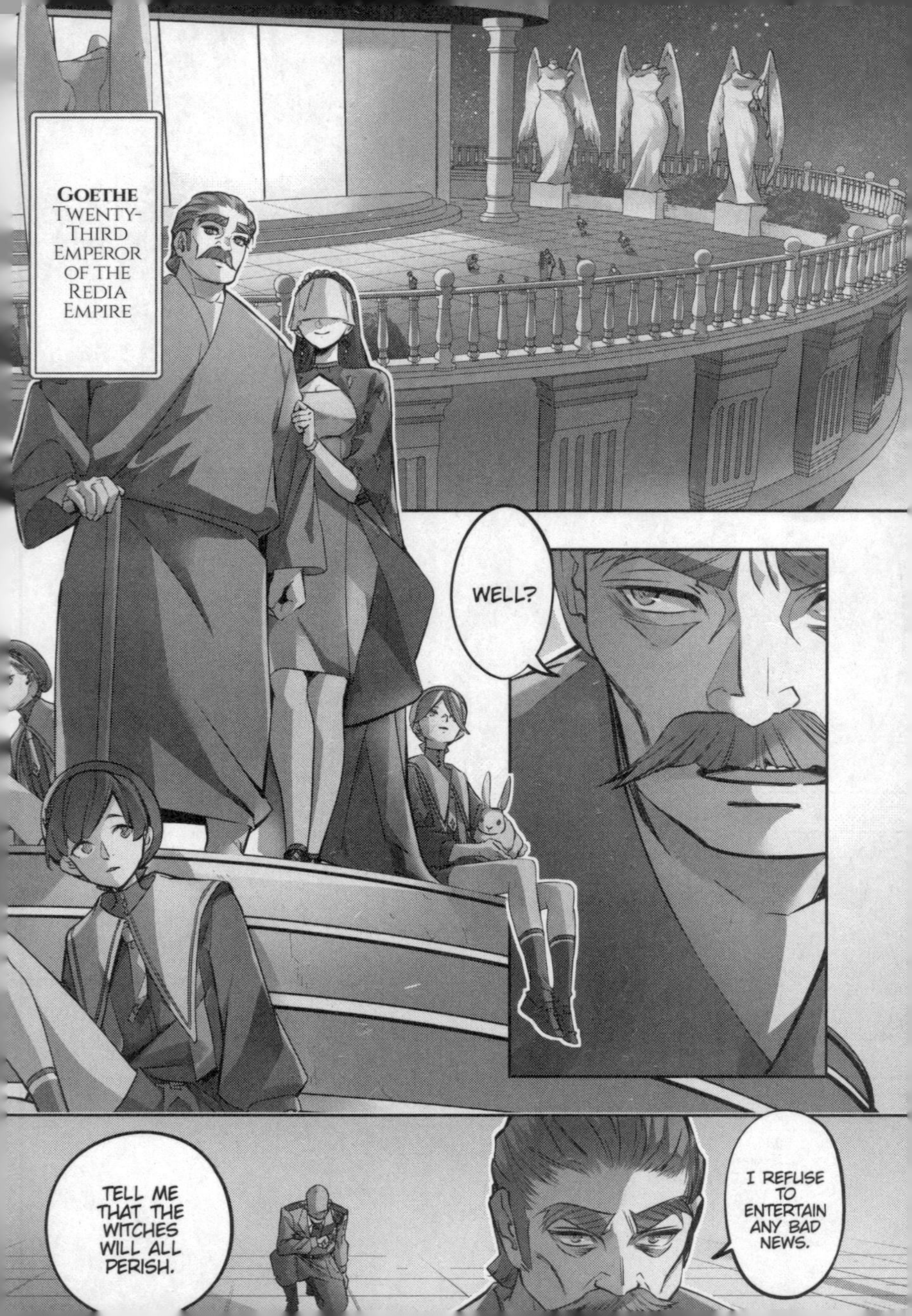
GOETHE
TWENTY-THIRD EMPEROR OF THE REDIA EMPIRE
WELL?
I REFUSE TO ENTERTAIN ANY BAD NEWS.
TELL ME THAT THE WITCHES WILL ALL PERISH.

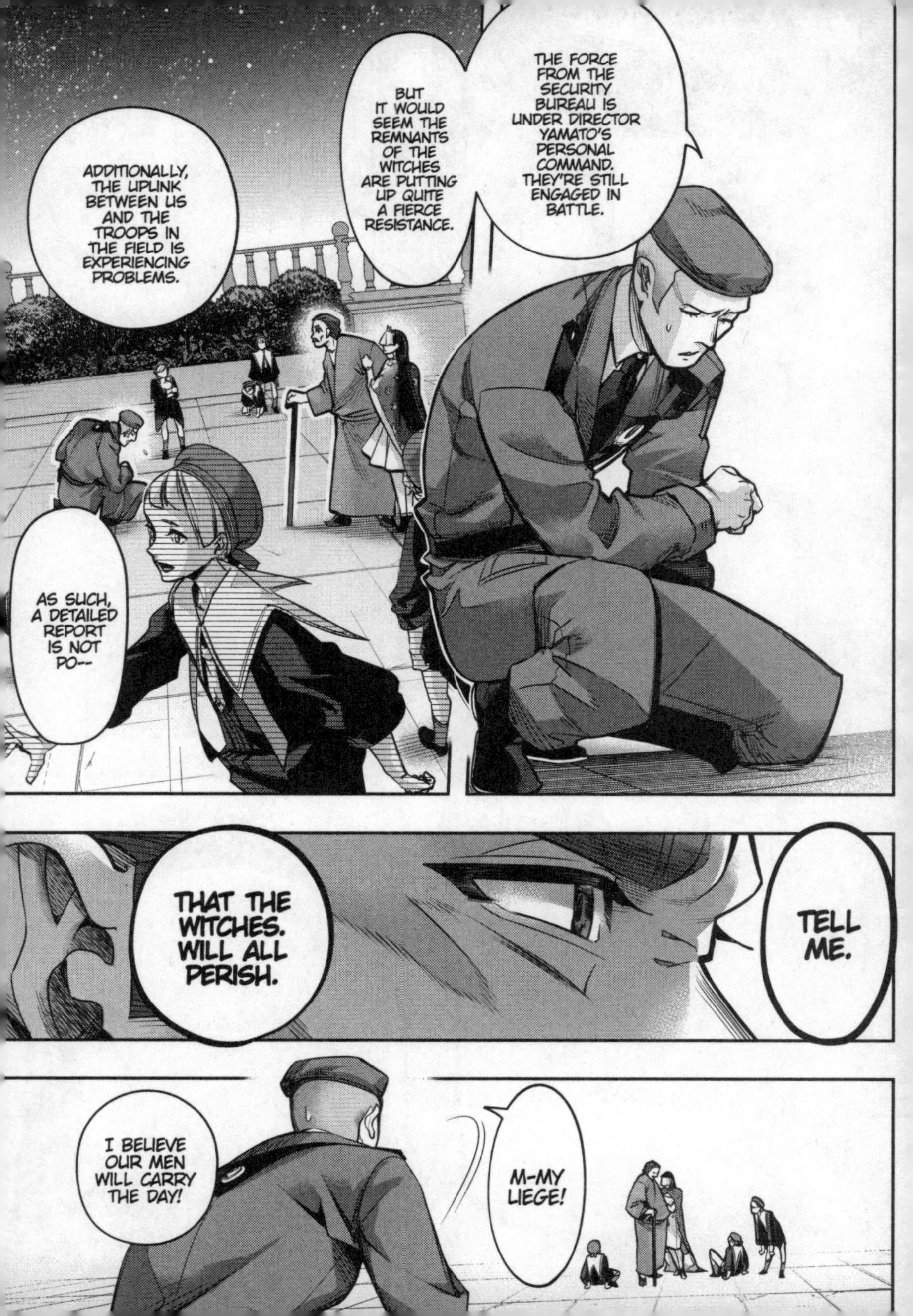
THE FORCE FROM THE SECURITY BUREAU IS UNDER DIRECTOR YAMATO'S PERSONAL COMMAND. THEY'RE STILL ENGAGED IN BATTLE.
BUT IT WOULD SEEM THE REMNANTS OF THE WITCHES ARE PUTTING UP QUITE A FIERCE RESISTANCE.
ADDITIONALLY, THE UPLINK BETWEEN US AND THE TROOPS IN THE FIELD IS EXPERIENCING PROBLEMS.
AS SUCH, A DETAILED REPORT IS NOT PO--
TELL ME.
THAT THE WITCHES. WILL ALL PERISH.
M-MY LIEGE!
I BELIEVE OUR MEN WILL CARRY THE DAY!

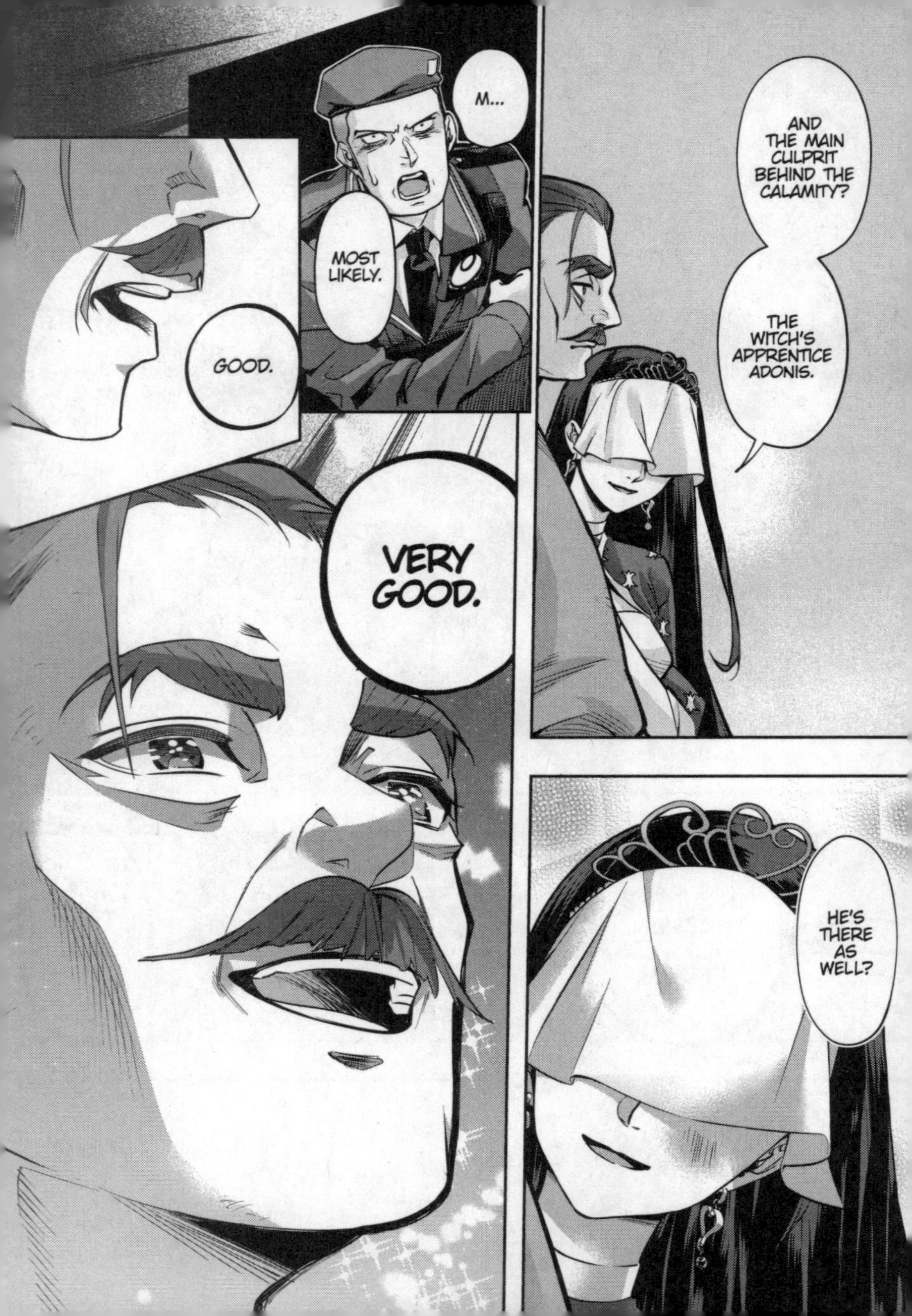
AND THE MAIN CULPRIT BEHIND THE CALAMITY?
THE WITCH'S APPRENTICE ADONIS.
HE'S THERE AS WELL?
M...
MOST LIKELY.
GOOD.
VERY GOOD.

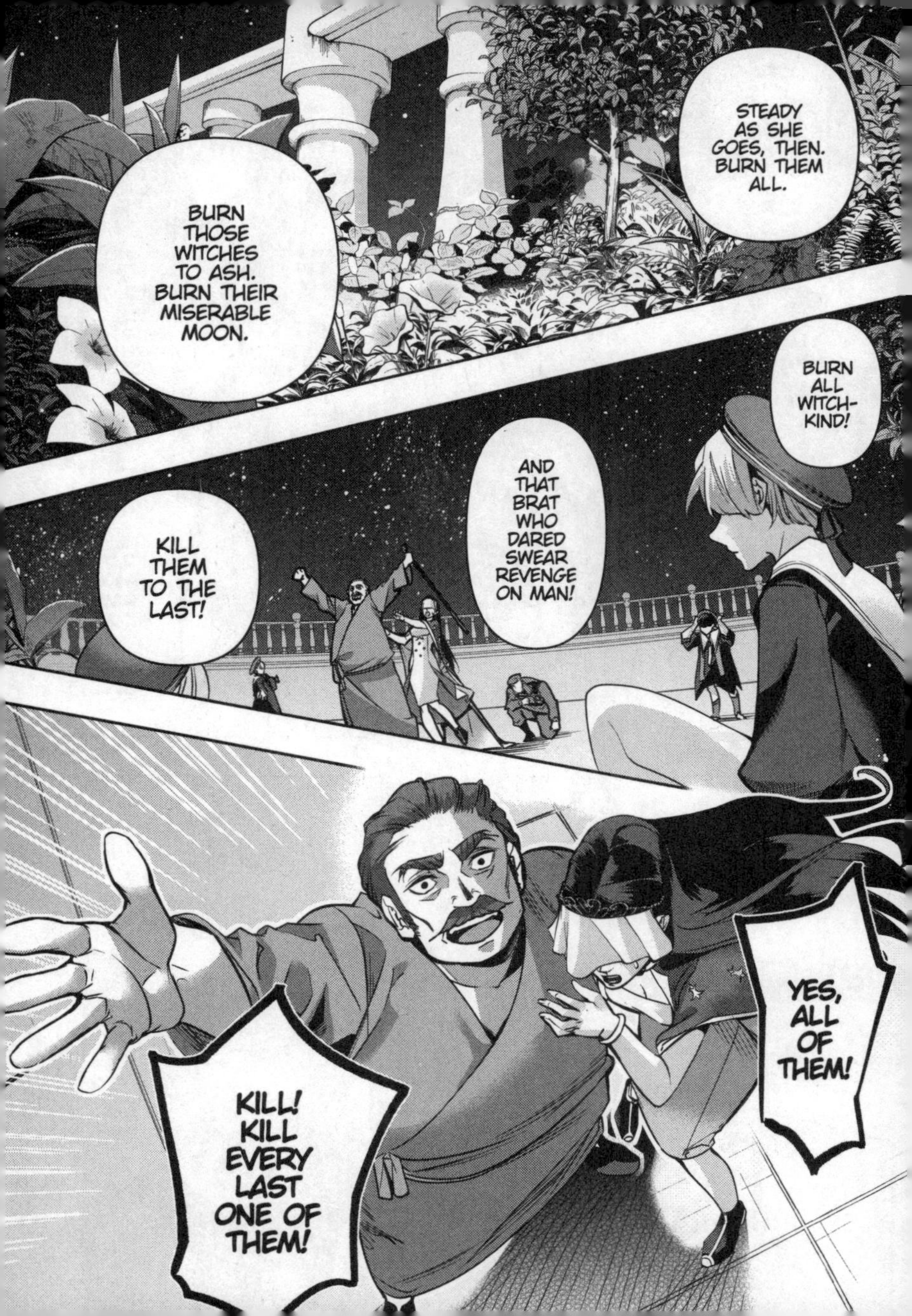
STEADY AS SHE GOES, THEN. BURN THEM ALL.
BURN THOSE WITCHES TO ASH. BURN THEIR MISERABLE MOON.
BURN ALL WITCH-KIND!
AND THAT BRAT WHO DARED SWEAR REVENGE ON MAN!
KILL THEM TO THE LAST!
YES, ALL OF THEM!
KILL! KILL EVERY LAST ONE OF THEM!

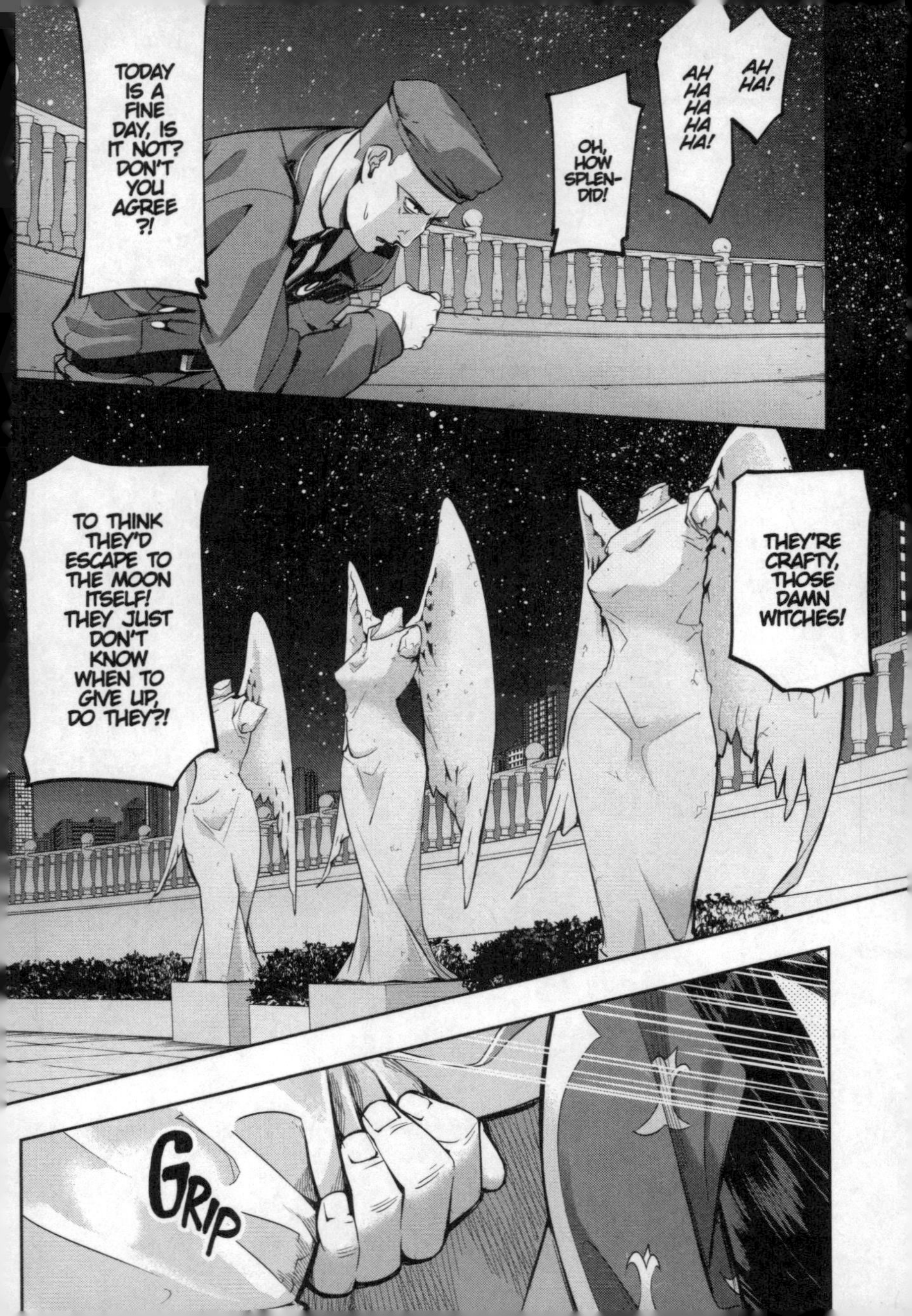
AH HA!
AH HA HA HA HA!
OH, HOW SPLEN-DID!
TODAY IS A FINE DAY, IS IT NOT? DON'T YOU AGREE ?!
THEY'RE CRAFTY, THOSE DAMN WITCHES!
TO THINK THEY'D ESCAPE TO THE MOON ITSELF! THEY JUST DON'T KNOW WHEN TO GIVE UP, DO THEY?!
GRIP

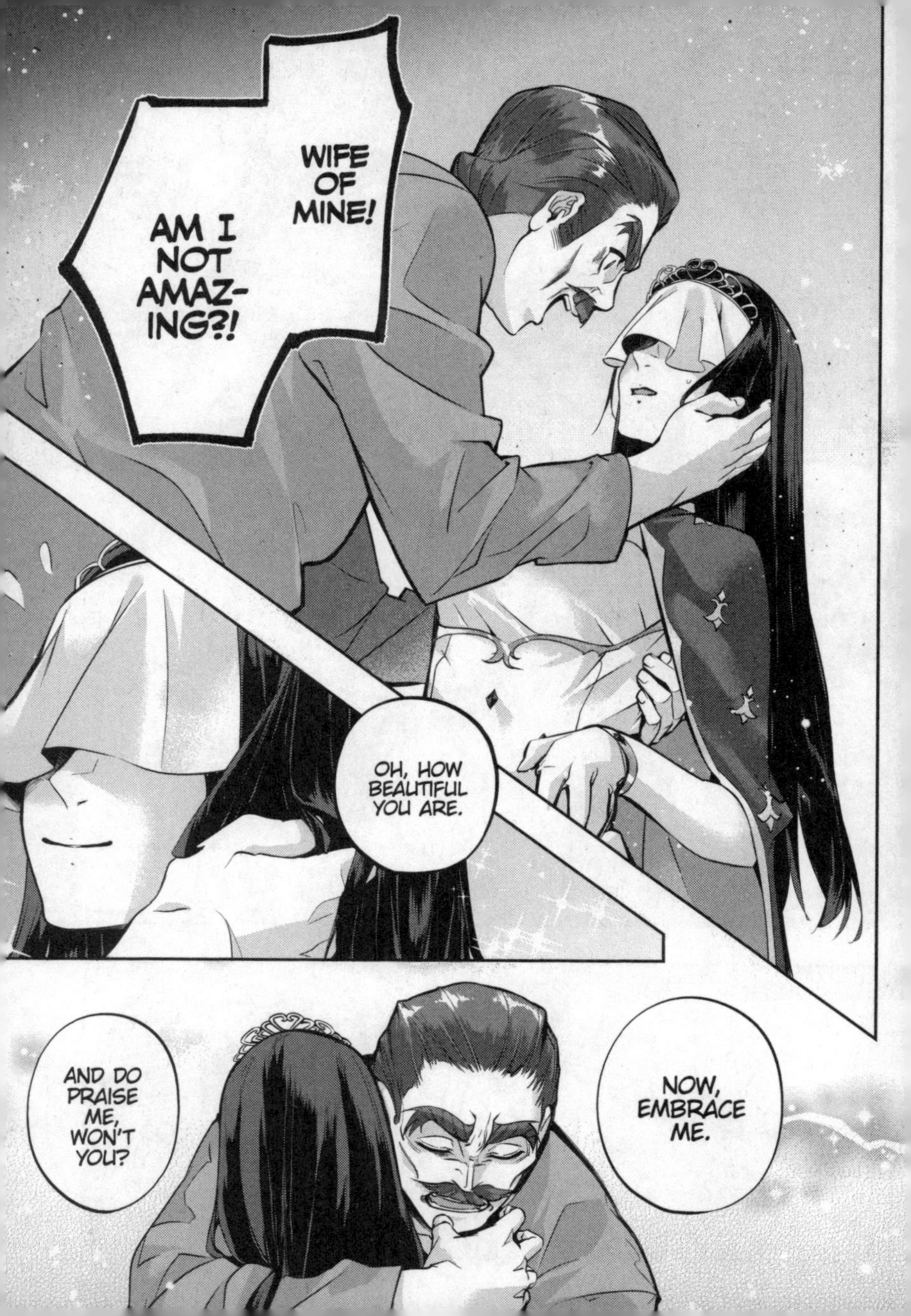
WIFE OF MINE!
AM I NOT AMAZ-ING?!
OH, HOW BEAUTIFUL YOU ARE.
NOW, EMBRACE ME.
AND DO PRAISE ME, WON'T YOU?

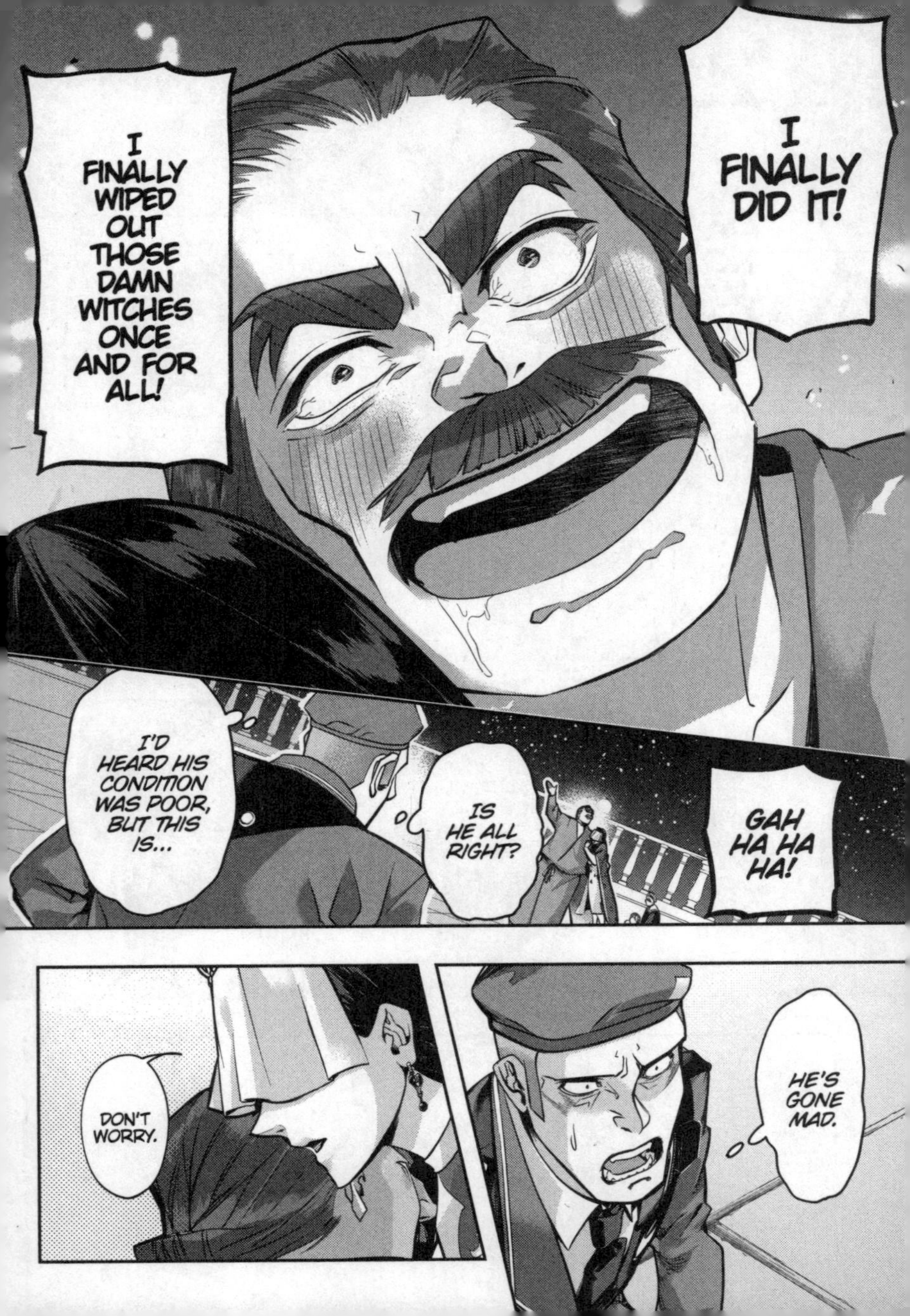
I FINALLY DID IT!
I FINALLY WIPED OUT THOSE DAMN WITCHES ONCE AND FOR ALL!
GAH HA HA HA!
IS HE ALL RIGHT?
I'D HEARD HIS CONDITION WAS POOR, BUT THIS IS...
HE'S GONE MAD.
DON'T WORRY.

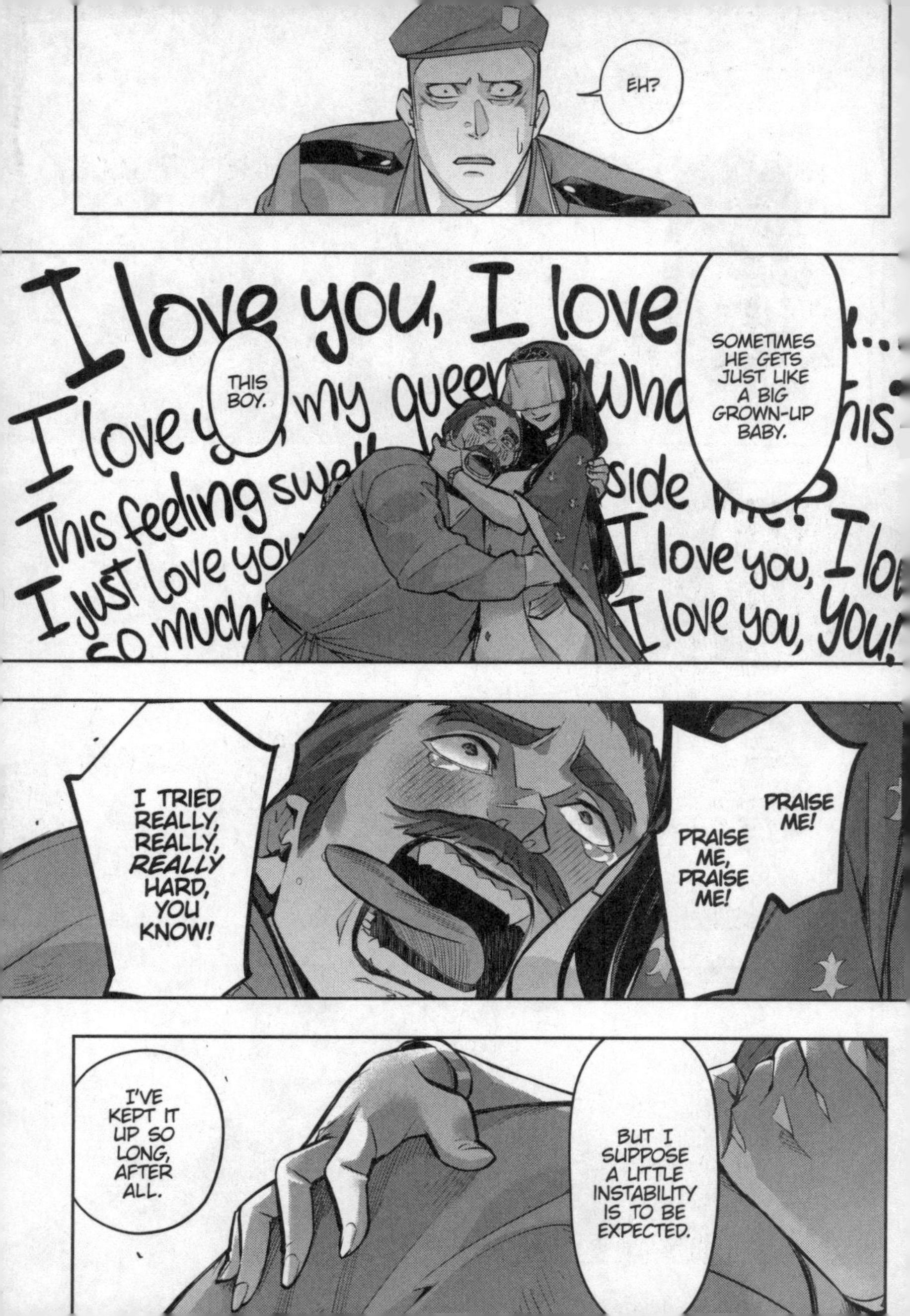
EH?
SOMETIMES HE GETS JUST LIKE A BIG GROWN-UP BABY.
THIS BOY.
I love you, I love
I love you, I lo
I love you, you!
This feeling
I just love
PRAISE ME!
PRAISE ME, PRAISE ME!
I TRIED REALLY, REALLY, REALLY HARD, YOU KNOW!
BUT I SUPPOSE A LITTLE INSTABILITY IS TO BE EXPECTED.
I'VE KEPT IT UP SO LONG, AFTER ALL.

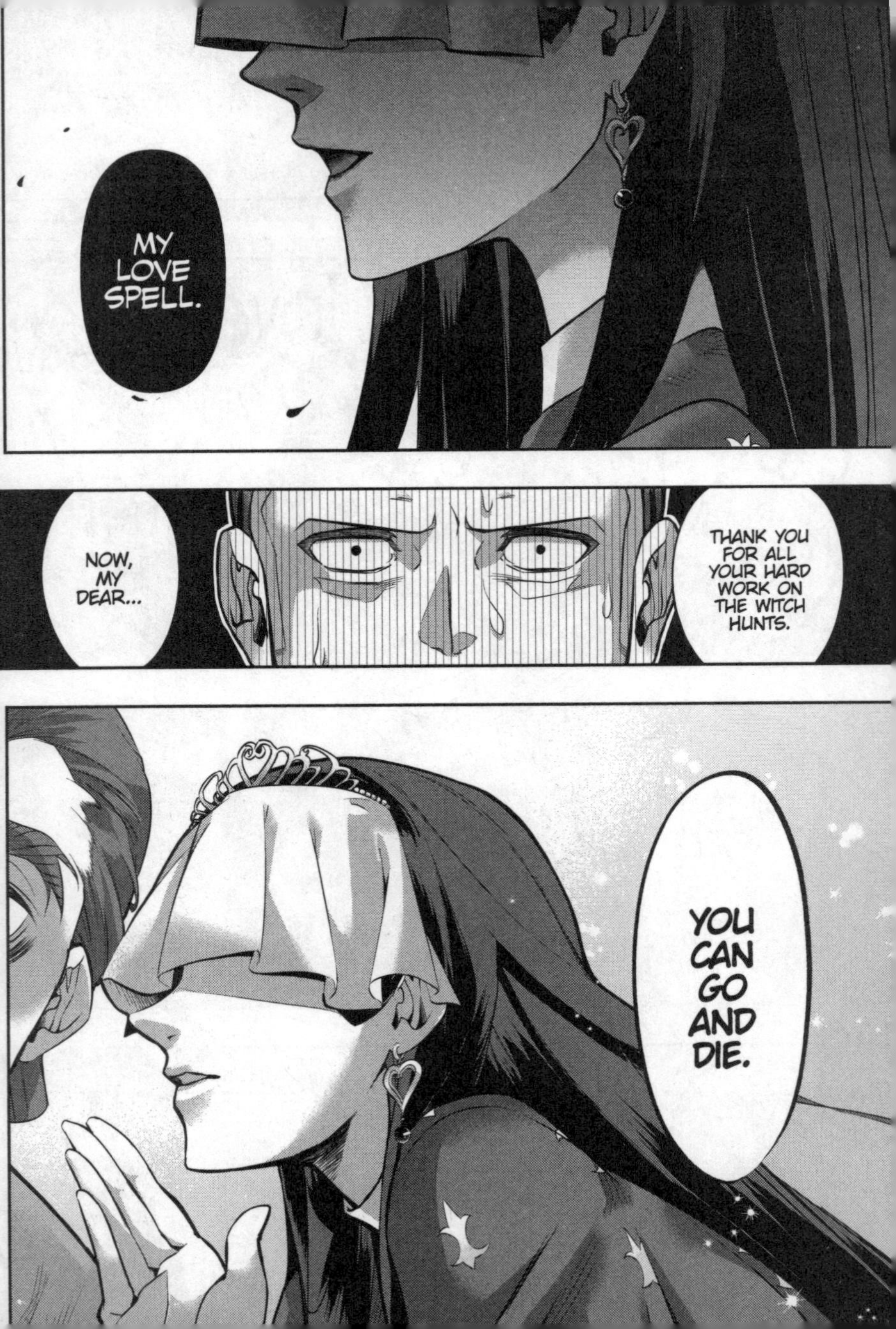
MY LOVE SPELL.
THANK YOU FOR ALL YOUR HARD WORK ON THE WITCH HUNTS.
NOW, MY DEAR...
YOU CAN GO AND DIE.

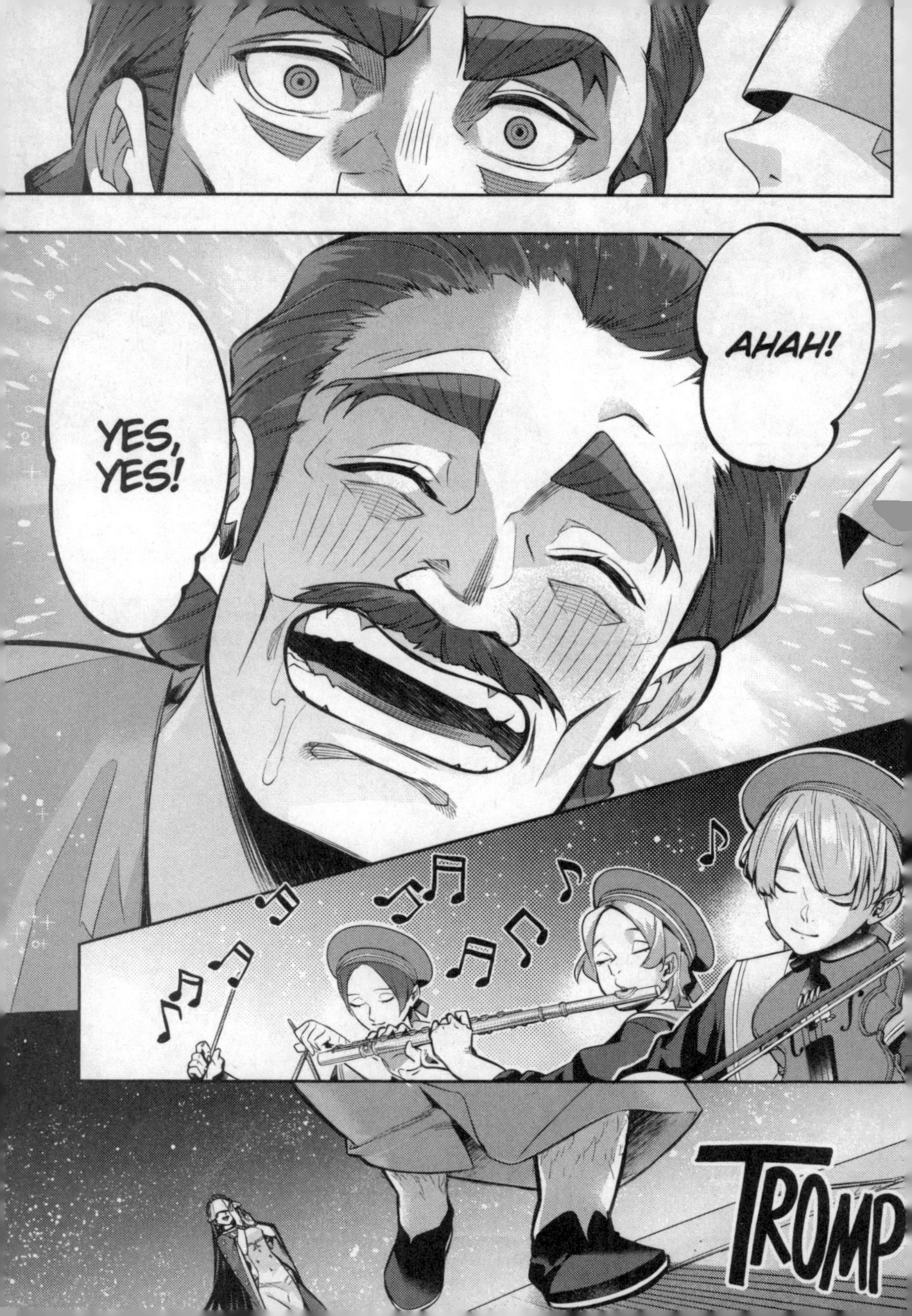
AHAH!
YES, YES!
TROMP

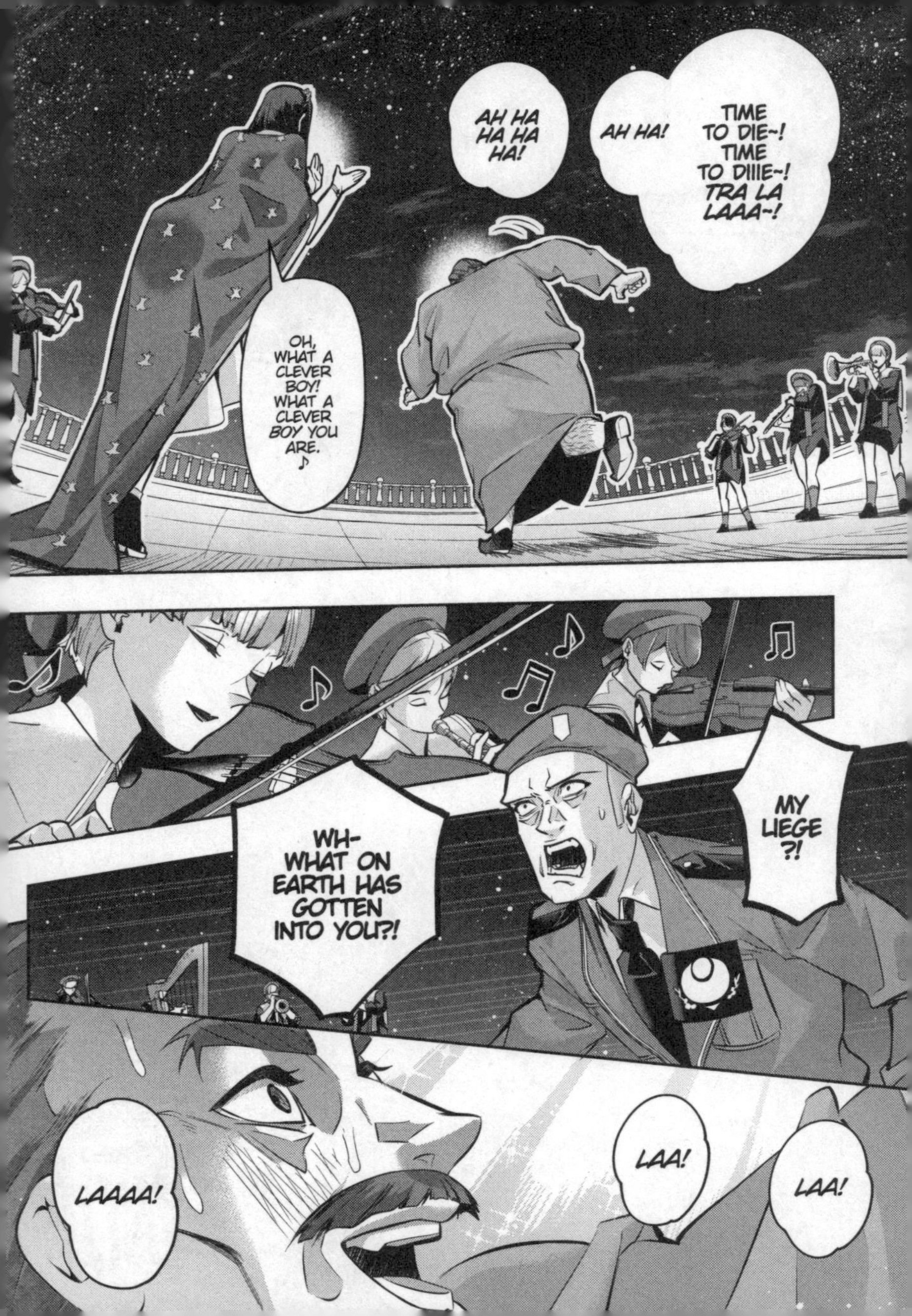
TIME TO DIE~! TIME TO DIIIE~! TRA LA LAAA~!
AH HA!
AH HA HA HA HA!
OH, WHAT A CLEVER BOY! WHAT A CLEVER BOY YOU ARE. ♪
MY LIEGE?!
WH- WHAT ON EARTH HAS GOTTEN INTO YOU?!
LAA!
LAA!
LAAAA!

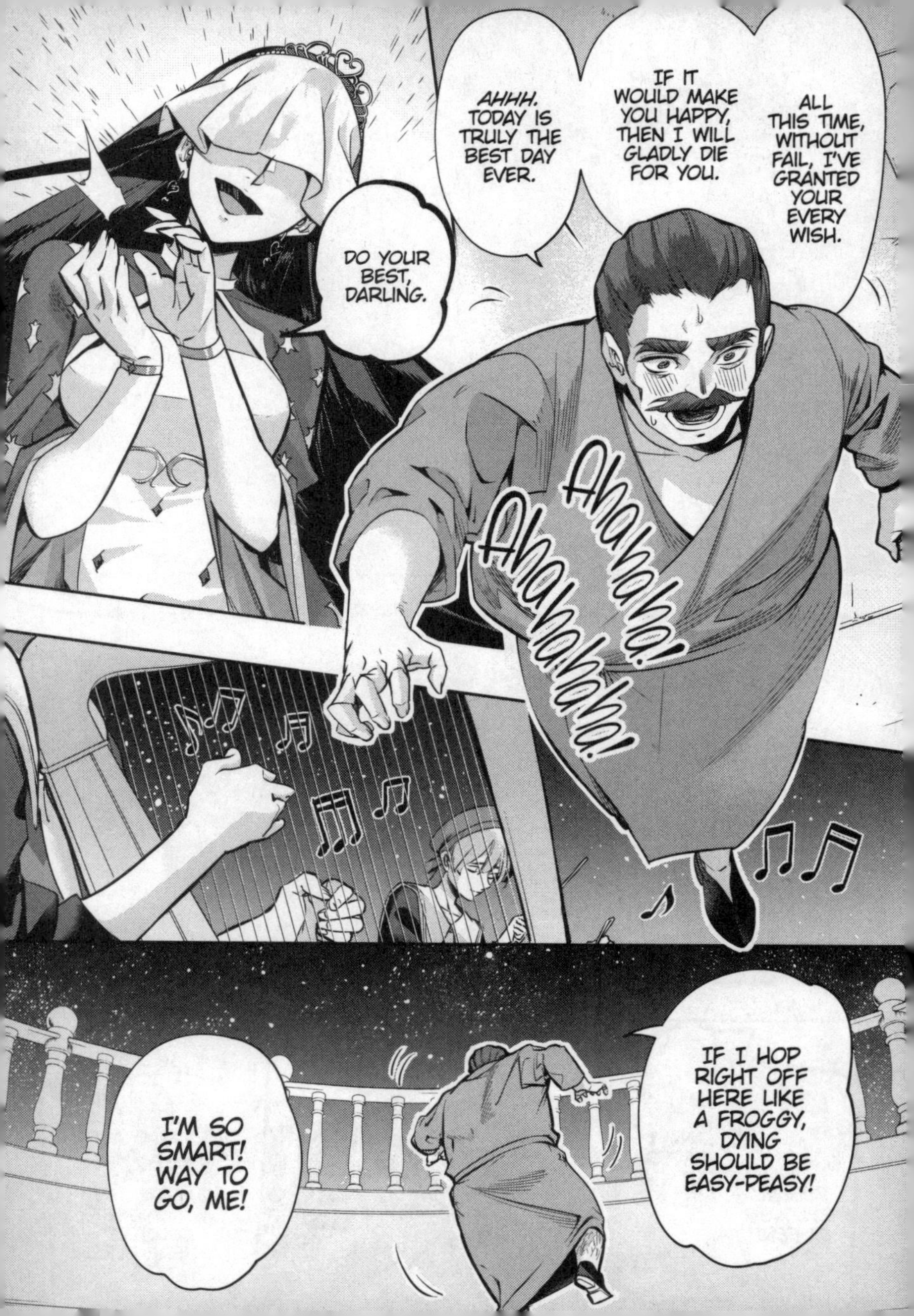
ALL THIS TIME, WITHOUT FAIL, I'VE GRANTED YOUR EVERY WISH.
IF IT WOULD MAKE YOU HAPPY, THEN I WILL GLADLY DIE FOR YOU.
AHHH. TODAY IS TRULY THE BEST DAY EVER.
DO YOUR BEST, DARLING.
Ahahaha!
Ahahahaha!
IF I HOP RIGHT OFF HERE LIKE A FROGGY, DYING SHOULD BE EASY-PEASY!
I'M SO SMART! WAY TO GO, ME!

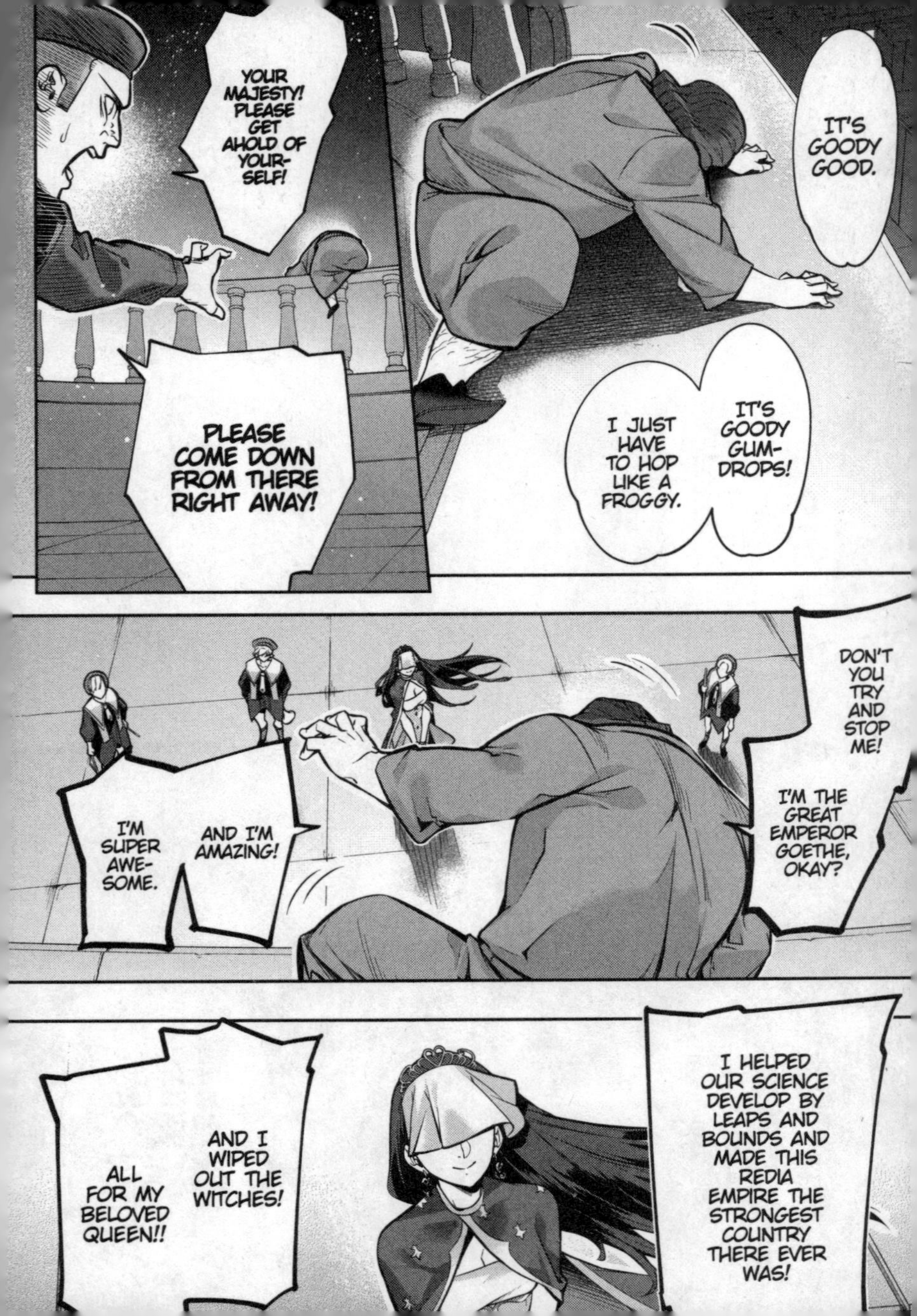
IT'S GOODY GOOD.
IT'S GOODY GUM-DROPS!
I JUST HAVE TO HOP LIKE A FROGGY.
YOUR MAJESTY! PLEASE GET AHOLD OF YOUR-SELF!
PLEASE COME DOWN FROM THERE RIGHT AWAY!
DON'T YOU TRY AND STOP ME!
I'M THE GREAT EMPEROR GOETHE, OKAY?
AND I'M AMAZING!
I'M SUPER AWE-SOME.
I HELPED OUR SCIENCE DEVELOP BY LEAPS AND BOUNDS AND MADE THIS REDIA EMPIRE THE STRONGEST COUNTRY THERE EVER WAS!
AND I WIPED OUT THE WITCHES!
ALL FOR MY BELOVED QUEEN!!

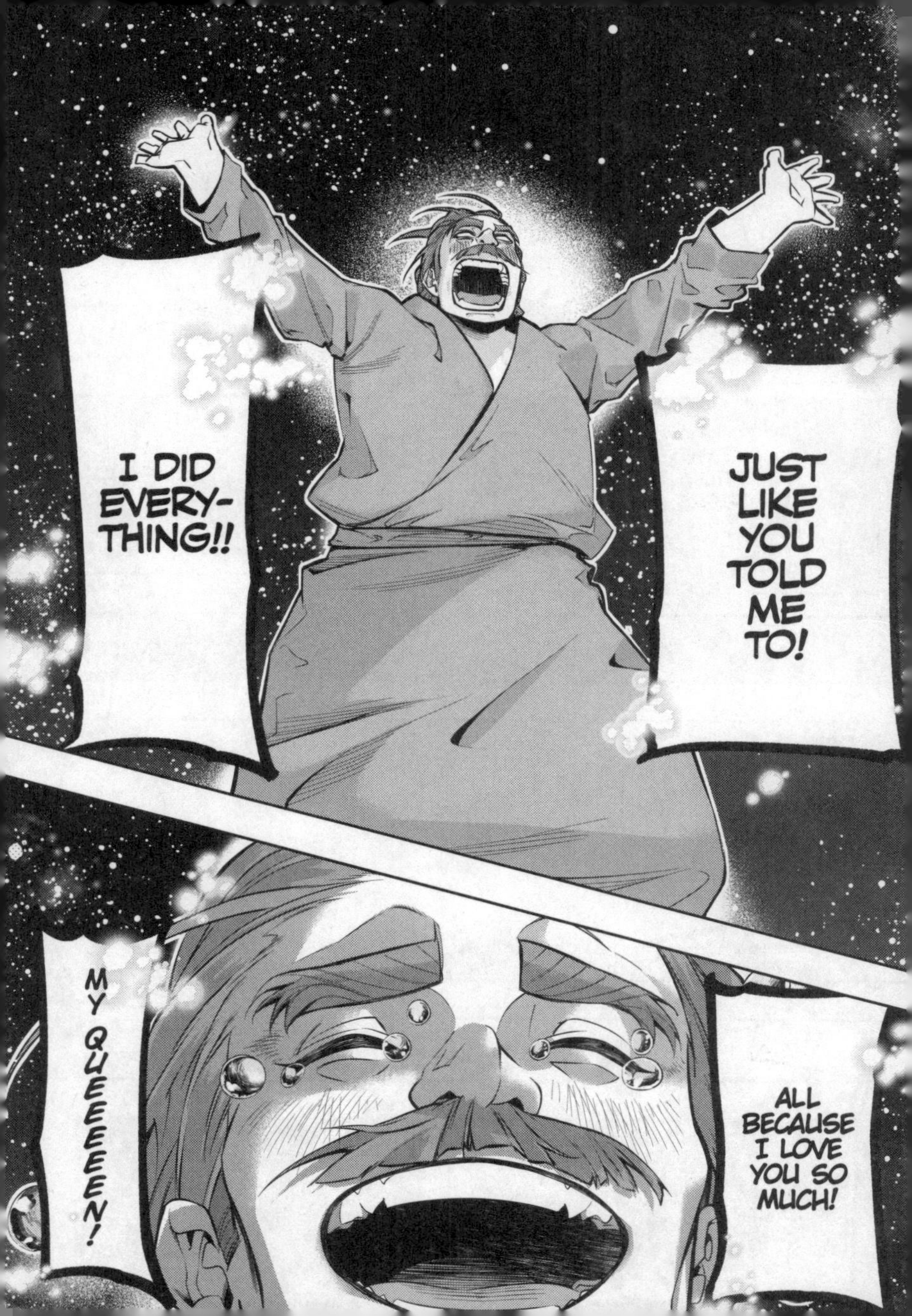
JUST LIKE YOU TOLD ME TO!
I DID EVERY-THING!!
ALL BECAUSE I LOVE YOU SO MUCH!
MY QUEEEEEEN!

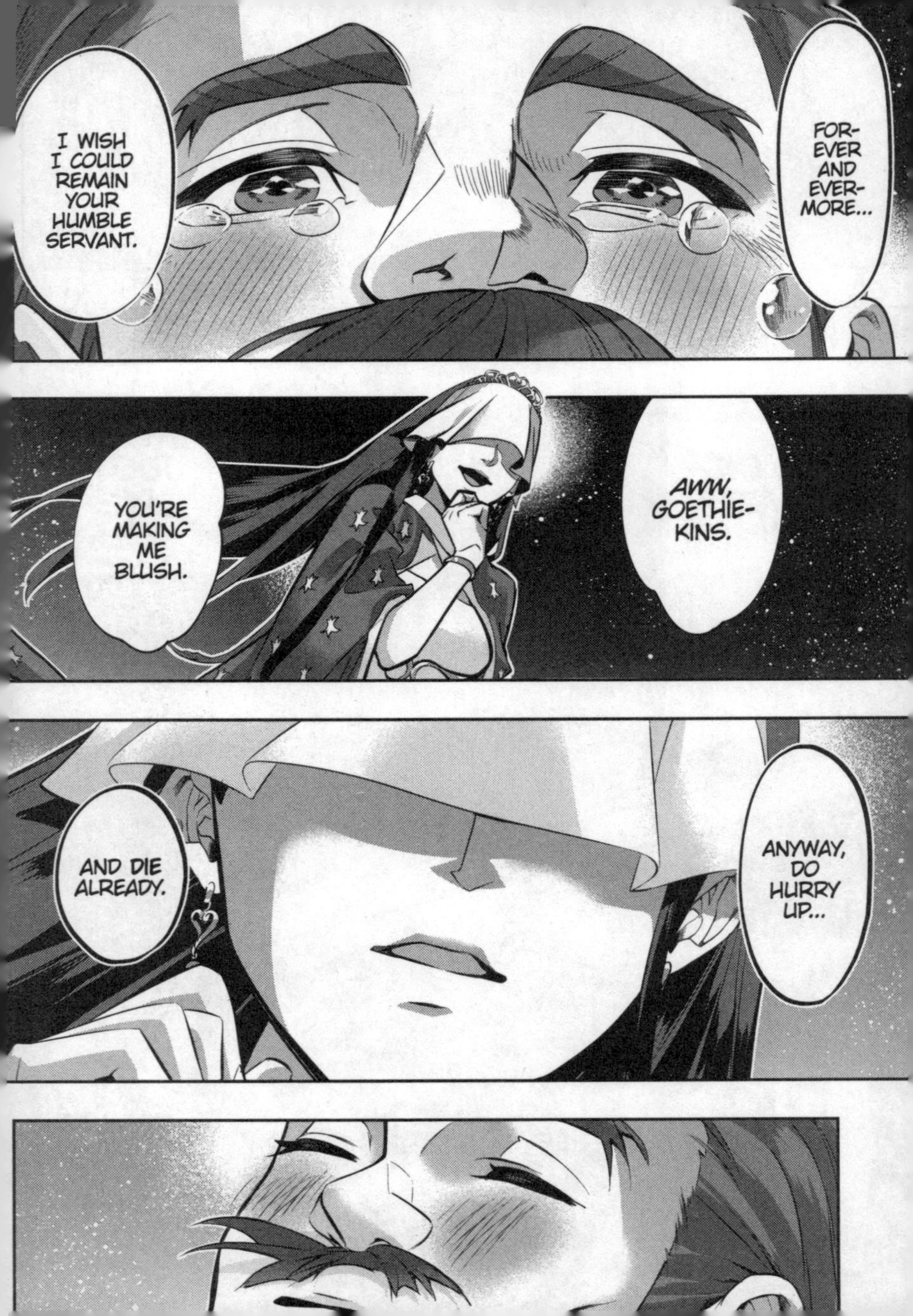
FOR-EVER AND EVER-MORE...
I WISH I COULD REMAIN YOUR HUMBLE SERVANT.
AWW, GOETHIE-KINS.
YOU'RE MAKING ME BLUSH.
ANYWAY, DO HURRY UP...
AND DIE ALREADY.

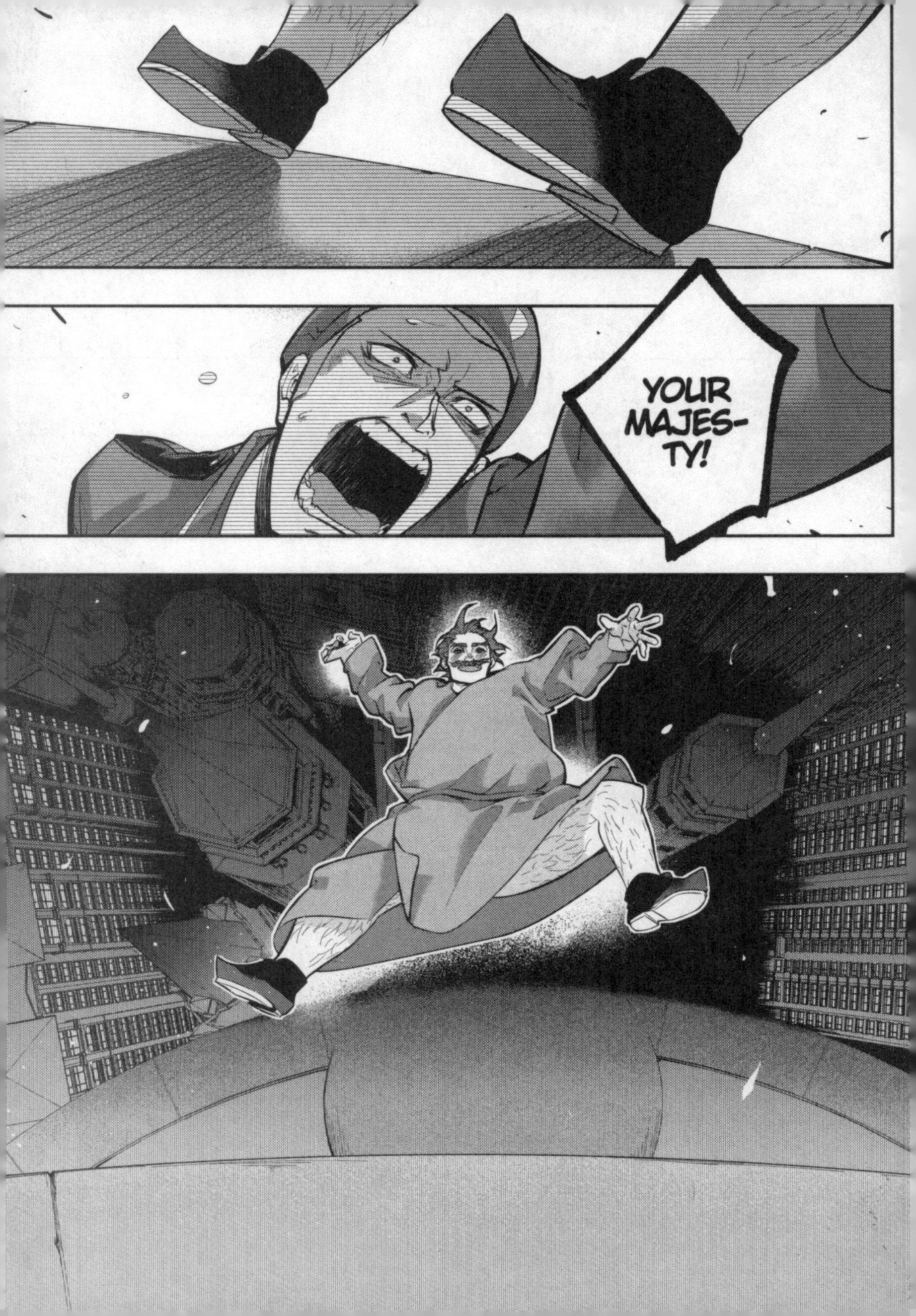
YOUR MAJES-TY!

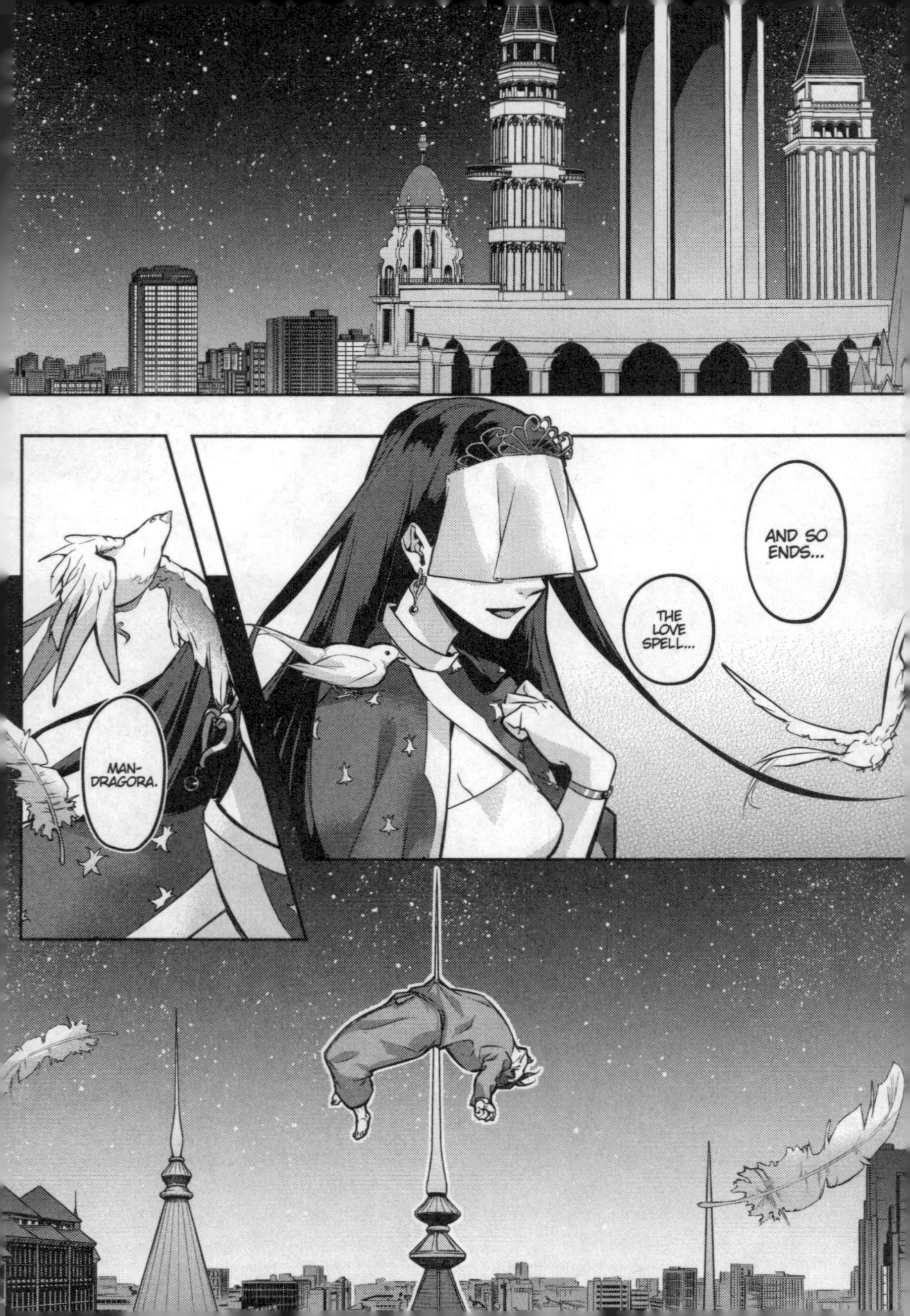
AND SO ENDS...
THE LOVE SPELL...
MAN-DRAGORA.

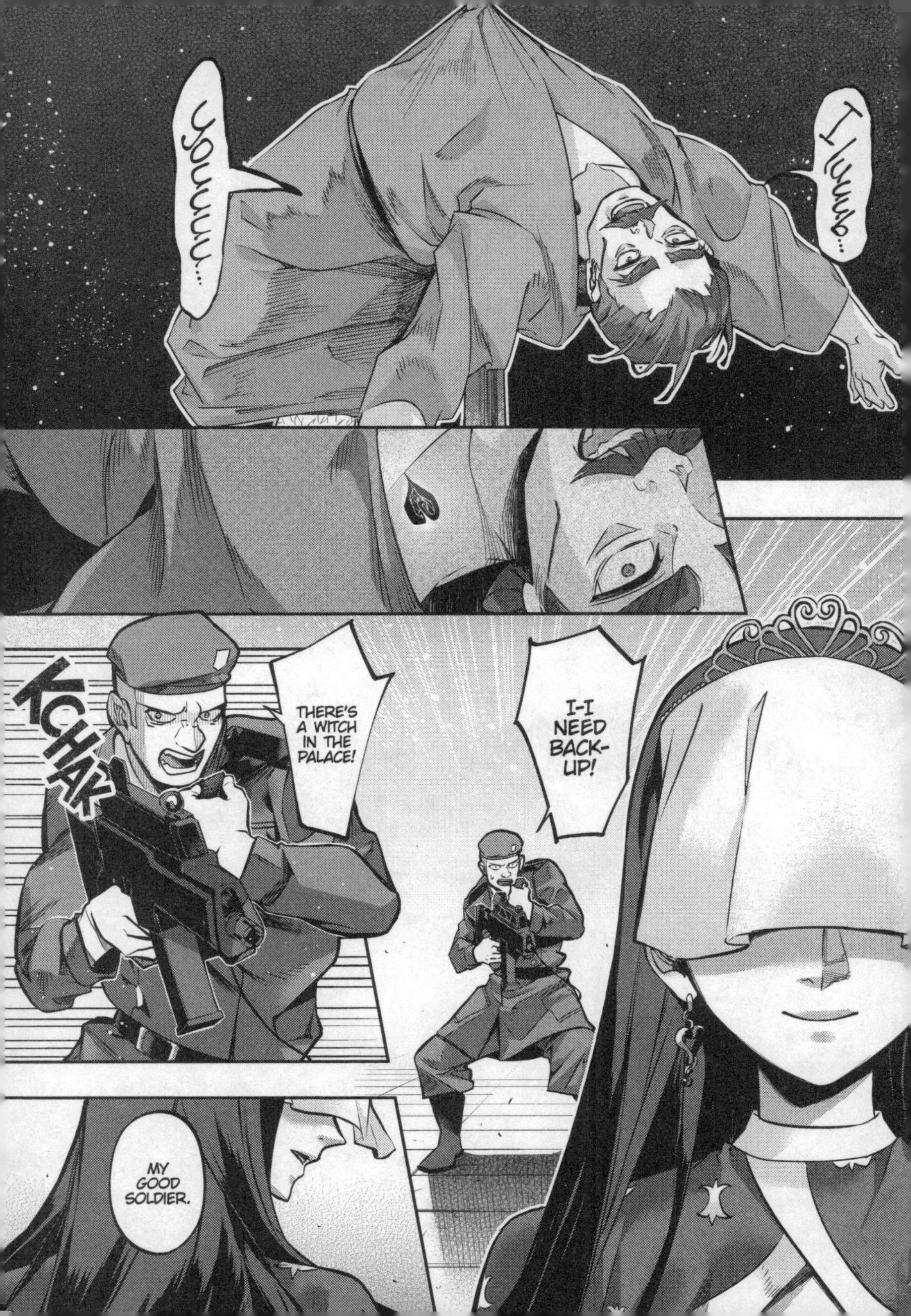
I luuuuv...
Youuuuu...
I-I NEED BACK-UP!
THERE'S A WITCH IN THE PALACE!
KCHAK
MY GOOD SOLDIER.

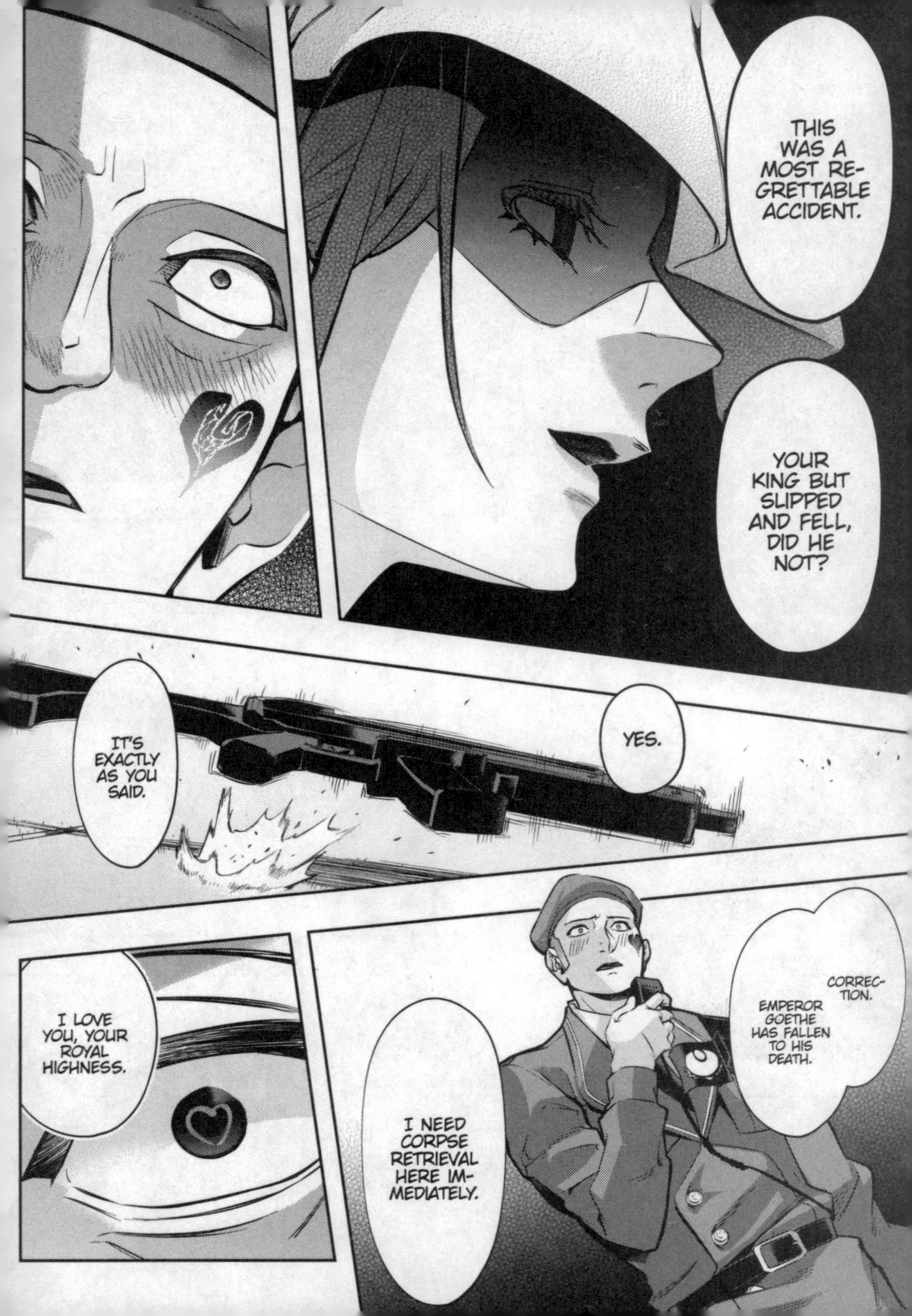
THIS WAS A MOST REGRETTABLE ACCIDENT.
YOUR KING BUT SLIPPED AND FELL, DID HE NOT?
YES.
IT'S EXACTLY AS YOU SAID.
CORRECTION.
EMPEROR GOETHE HAS FALLEN TO HIS DEATH.
I NEED CORPSE RETRIEVAL HERE IMMEDIATELY.
I LOVE YOU, YOUR ROYAL HIGHNESS.

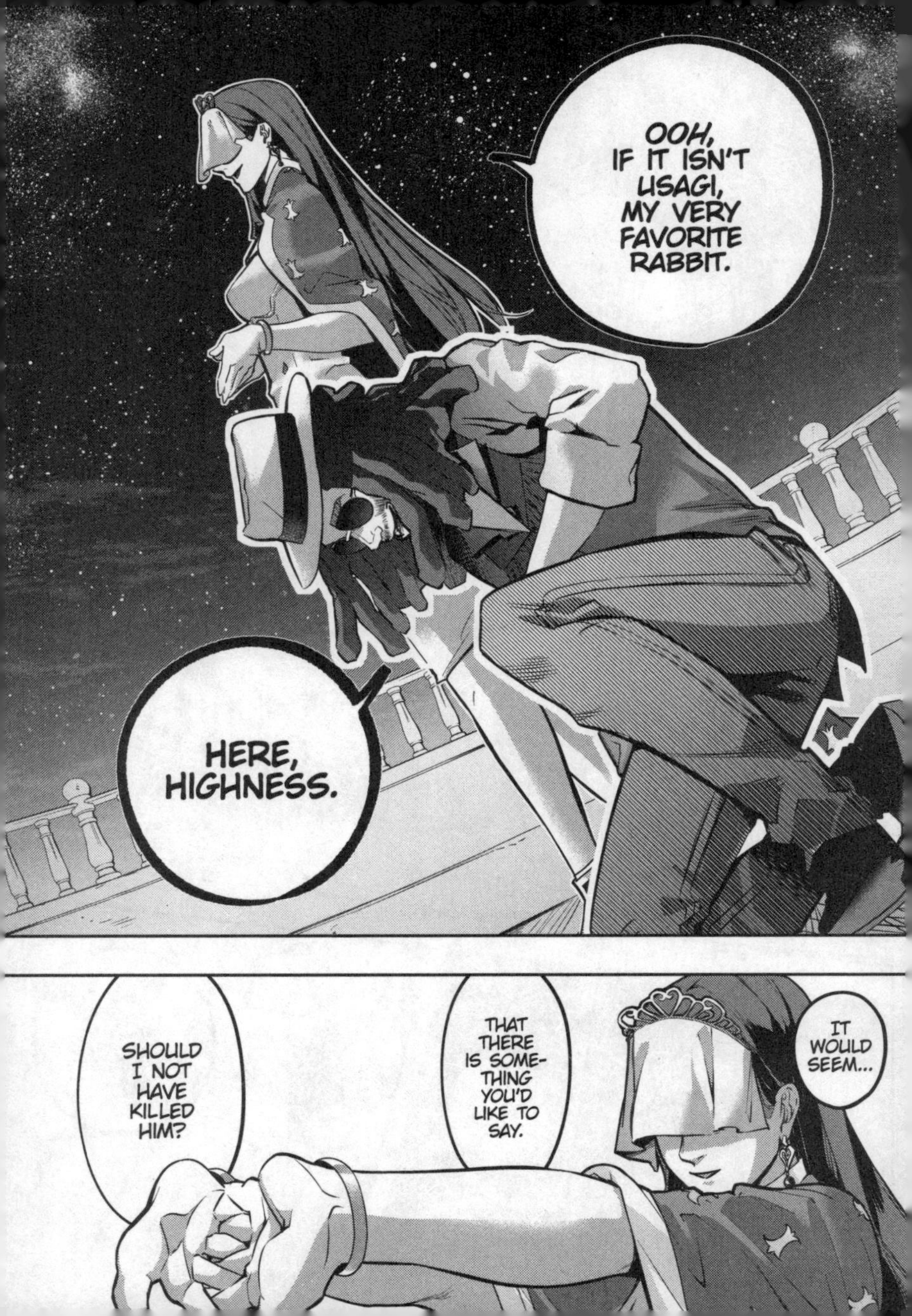
OOH, IF IT ISN'T USAGI, MY VERY FAVORITE RABBIT.
HERE, HIGHNESS.
IT WOULD SEEM...
THAT THERE IS SOME-THING YOU'D LIKE TO SAY.
SHOULD I NOT HAVE KILLED HIM?

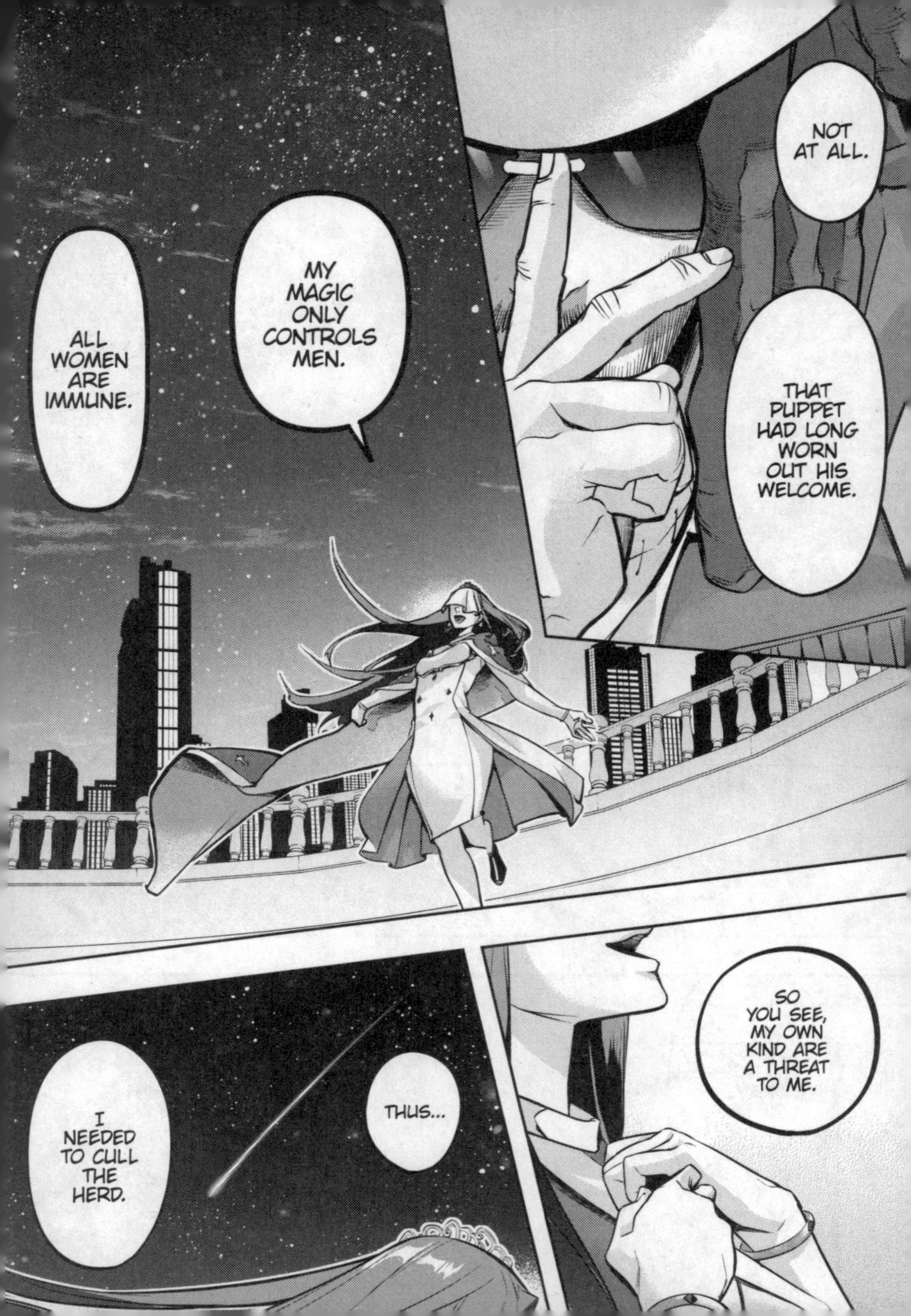
NOT AT ALL.
THAT PUPPET HAD LONG WORN OUT HIS WELCOME.
MY MAGIC ONLY CONTROLS MEN.
ALL WOMEN ARE IMMUNE.
SO YOU SEE, MY OWN KIND ARE A THREAT TO ME.
THUS...
I NEEDED TO CULL THE HERD.

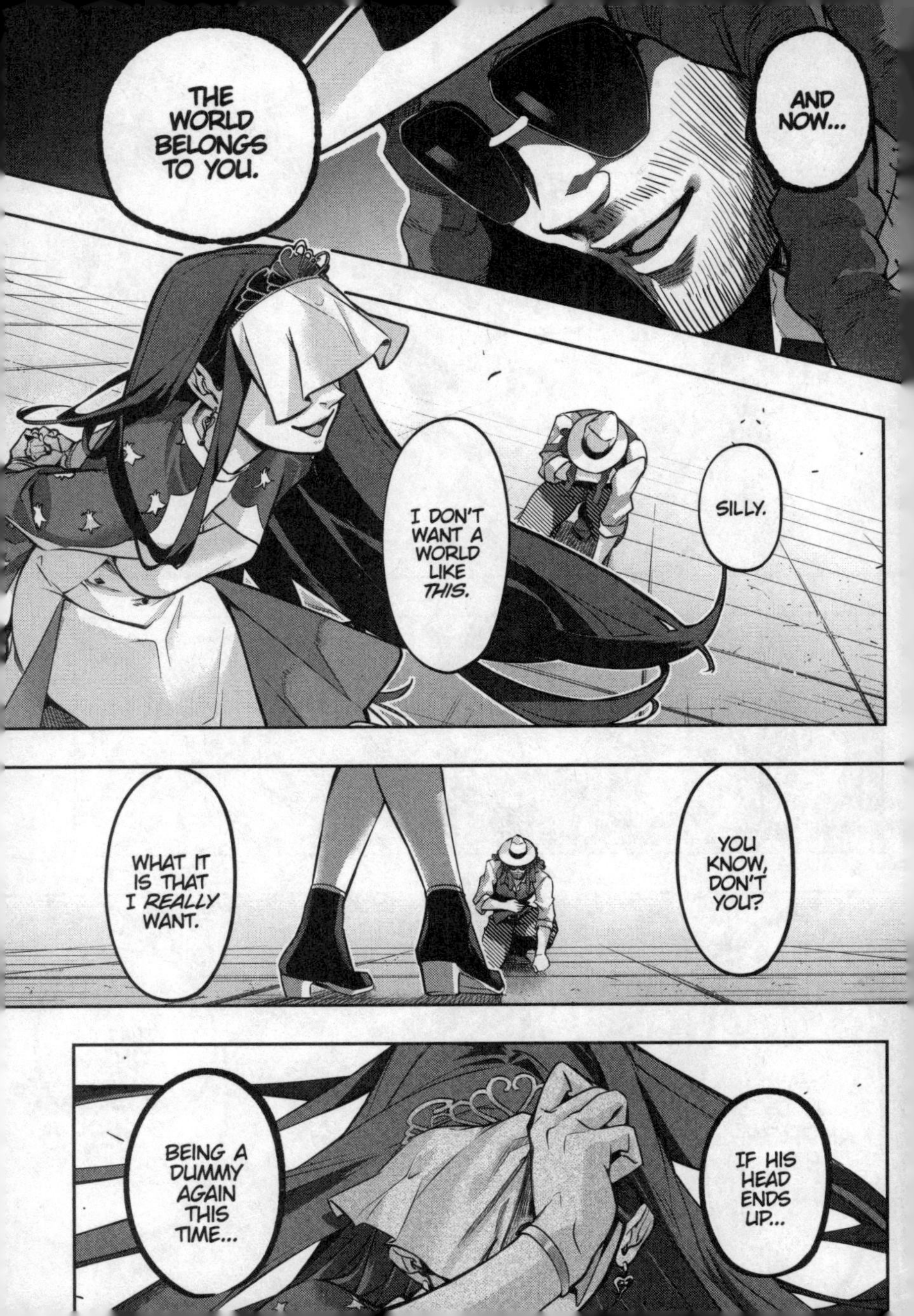
AND NOW...
THE WORLD BELONGS TO YOU.
SILLY.
I DON'T WANT A WORLD LIKE *THIS*.
YOU KNOW, DON'T YOU?
WHAT IT IS THAT I *REALLY* WANT.
IF HIS HEAD ENDS UP...
BEING A DUMMY AGAIN THIS TIME...

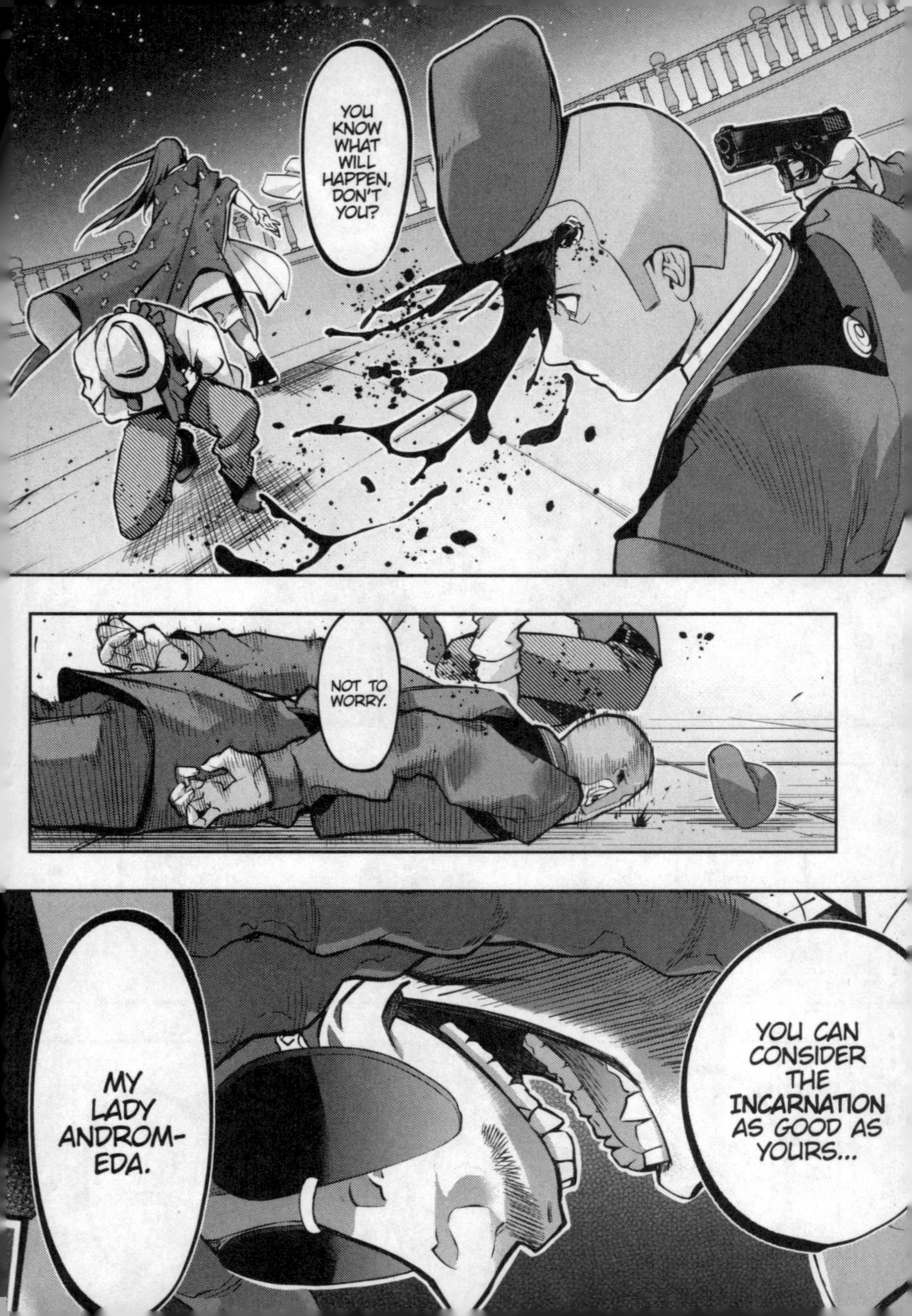
YOU KNOW WHAT WILL HAPPEN, DON'T YOU?
NOT TO WORRY.
YOU CAN CONSIDER THE INCARNATION AS GOOD AS YOURS...
MY LADY ANDROM-EDA.

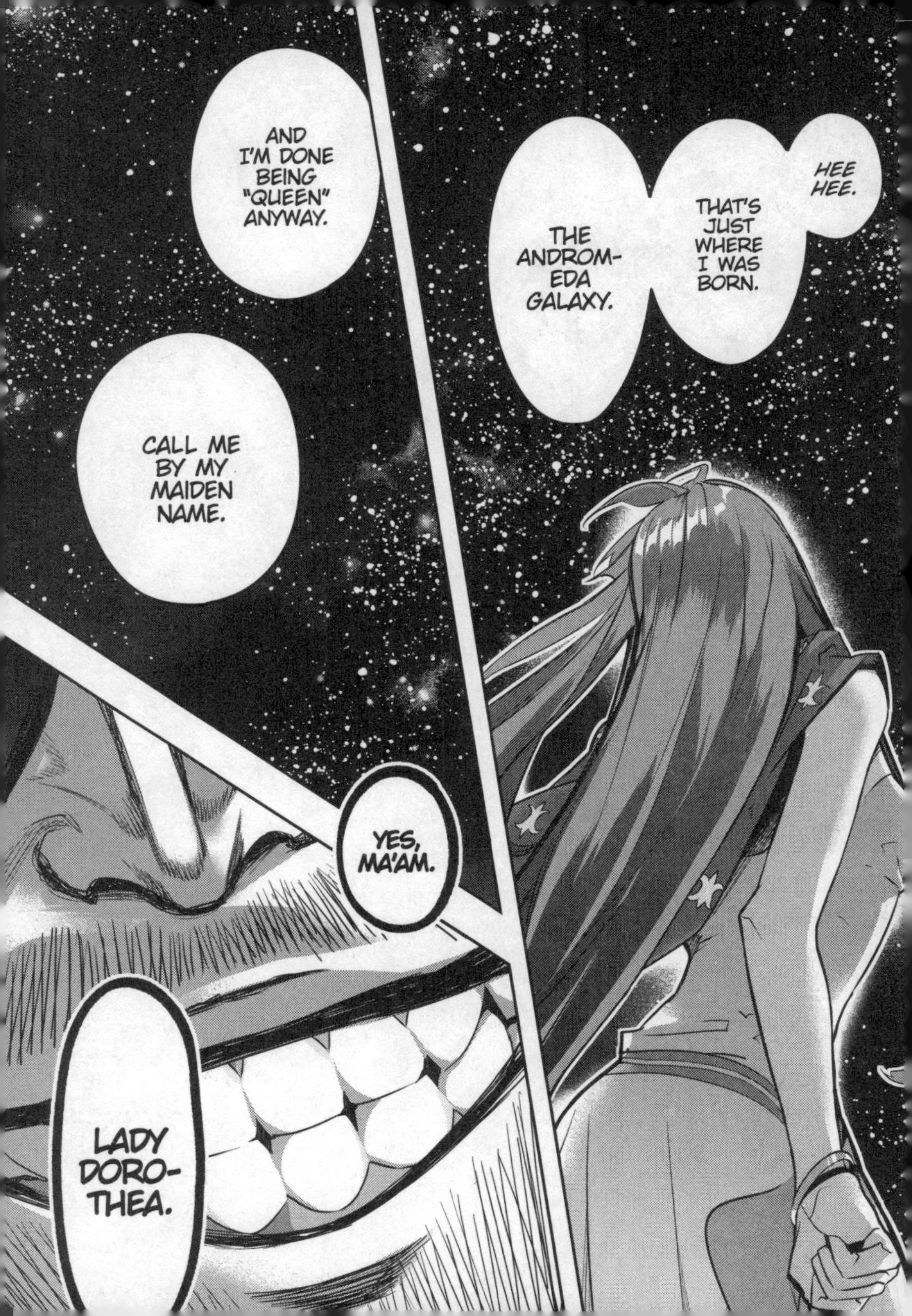
HEE HEE.
THAT'S JUST WHERE I WAS BORN.
THE ANDROM-EDA GALAXY.
AND I'M DONE BEING "QUEEN" ANYWAY.
CALL ME BY MY MAIDEN NAME.
YES, MA'AM.
LADY DORO-THEA.

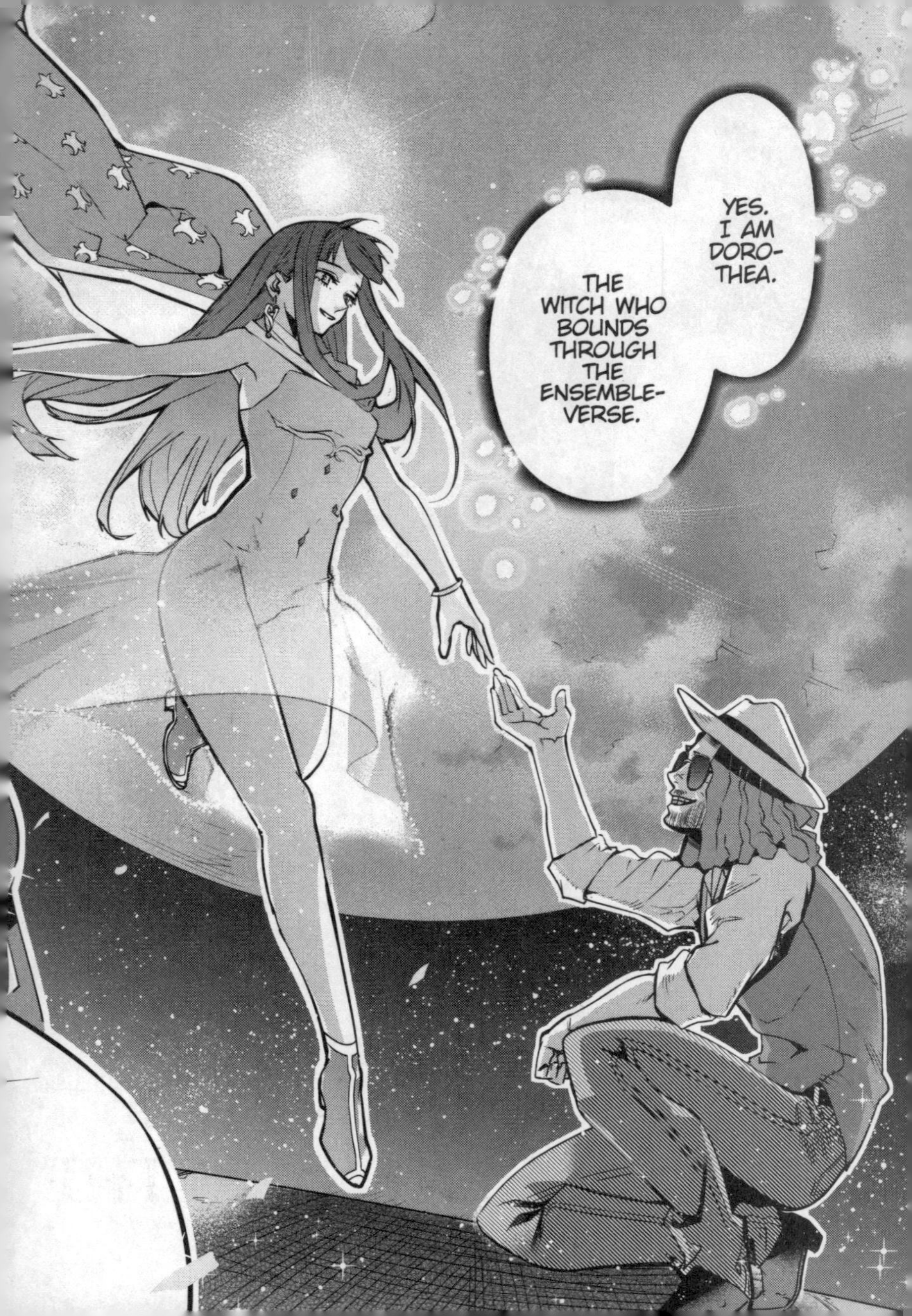

YES. I AM DORO-THEA.
THE WITCH WHO BOUNDS THROUGH THE ENSEMBLE-VERSE.

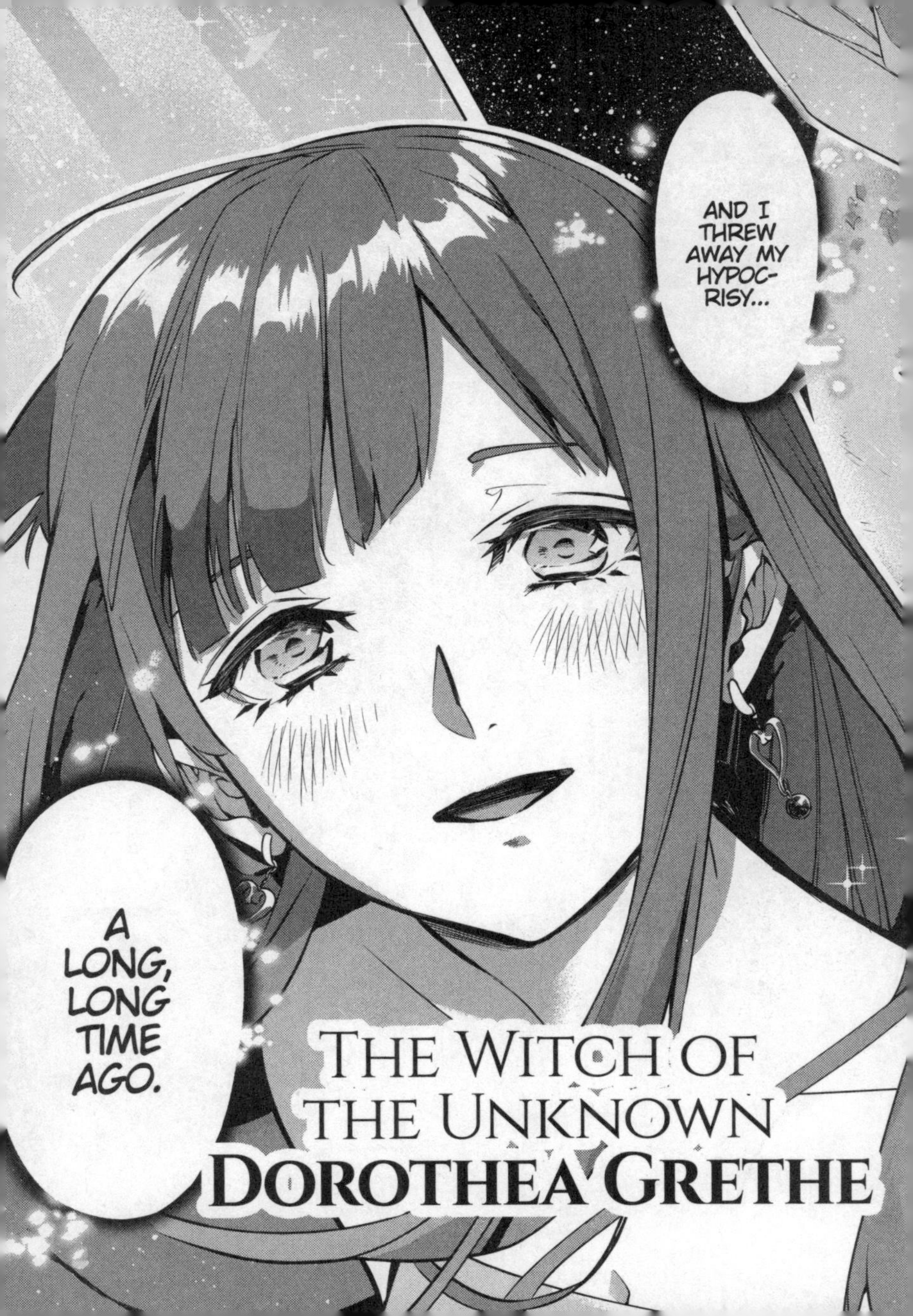
AND I THREW AWAY MY HYPOC-RISY...
A LONG, LONG TIME AGO.
THE WITCH OF THE UNKNOWN
DOROTHEA GRETHE

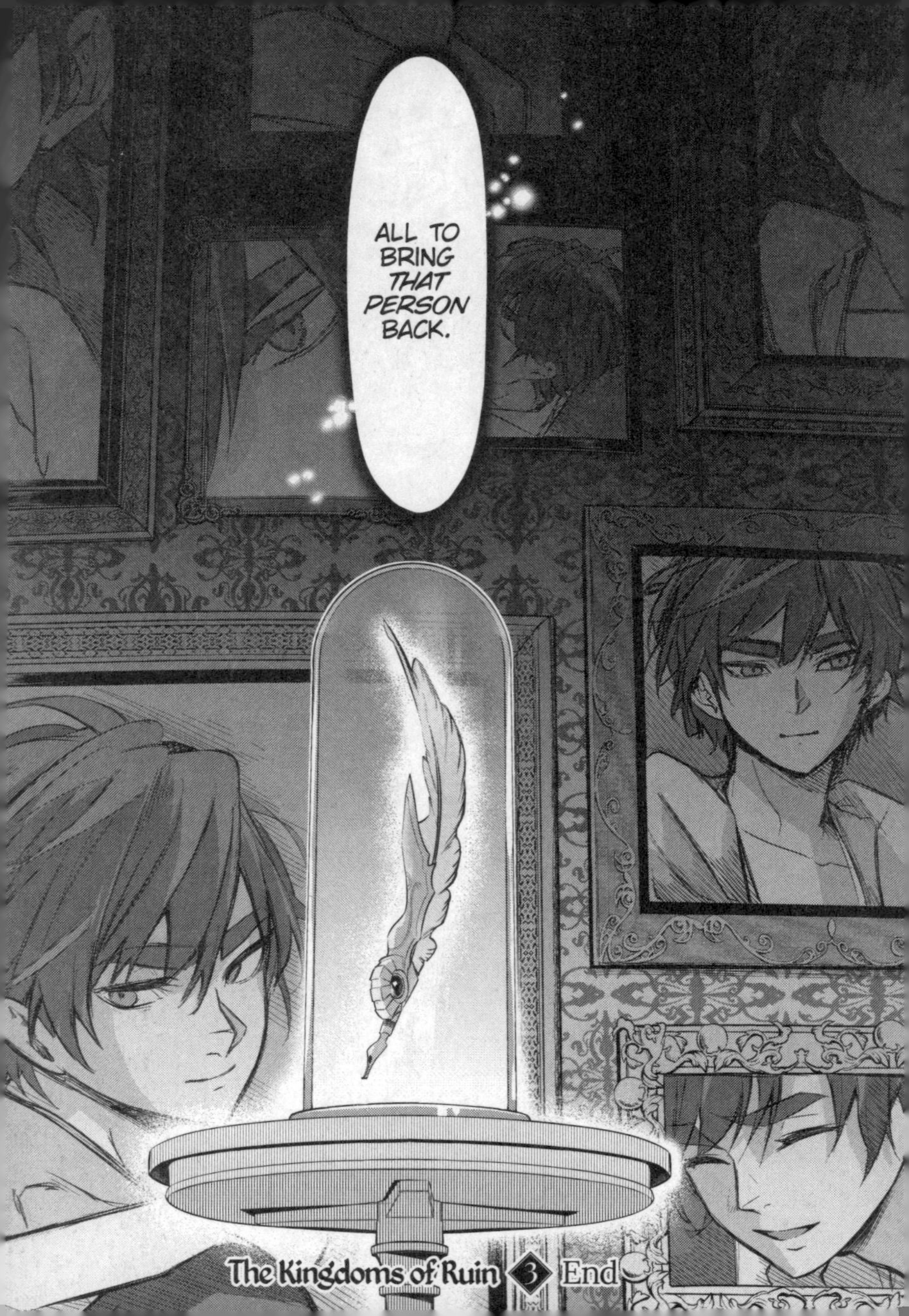
ALL TO BRING *THAT* PERSON BACK.
The Kingdoms of Ruin 3 End

THE
KINGDOMS
OF RUIN

SEVEN SEAS ENTERTAINMENT PRESENTS

THE KINGDOMS OF RUIN

story and art by YORUHASHI   VOLUME 3

TRANSLATION
Nan Rymer

LETTERING AND RETOUCH
Joseph Barr

COVER DESIGN
Hanase Qi

PROOFREADER
Dawn Davis, Brett Hallahan

EDITOR
J.P. Sullivan

PREPRESS TECHNICIAN
Rhiannon Rasmussen–Silverstein

PRODUCTION ASSOCIATE
Christa Miesner

PRODUCTION MANAGER
Lissa Pattillo

MANAGING EDITOR
Julie Davis

ASSOCIATE PUBLISHER
Adam Arnold

PUBLISHER
Jason DeAngelis

THE KINGDOMS OF RUIN VOL. 3
© yoruhashi 2020
Originally published in Japan in 2020 by MAG Garden Corporation, TOKYO.
English translation rights arranged through TOHAN CORPORATION, Tokyo.

Seven Seas press and purchase enquiries can be sent to Marketing Manager
Lianne Sentar at press@gomanga.com. Information regarding the distribution
and purchase of digital editions is available from Digital Manager CK Russell
at digital@gomanga.com.

Seven Seas and the Seven Seas logo are trademarks of
Seven Seas Entertainment. All rights reserved.

ISBN: 978-1-64827-290-5

Printed in Canada

First Printing: August 2021

10 9 8 7 6 5 4 3 2 1

FOLLOW US ONLINE: *www.sevenseasentertainment.com*

READING DIRECTIONS

This book reads from *right to left*, Japanese style.
If this is your first time reading manga, you start
reading from the top right panel on each page and
take it from there. If you get lost, just follow the
numbered diagram here. It may seem backwards at
first, but you'll get the hang of it! Have fun!!

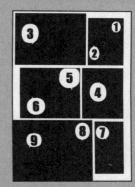